STITCH, UNSTITCH

MODERNIST LATITUDES

MODERNIST LATITUDES

Jessica Berman and Paul Saint-Amour, Editors

Modernist Latitudes aims to capture the energy and ferment of modernist studies by continuing to open up the range of forms, locations, temporalities, and theoretical approaches encompassed by the field. The series celebrates the growing latitude ("scope for freedom of action or thought") that this broadening affords scholars of modernism, whether they are investigating little-known works or revisiting canonical ones. Modernist Latitudes will pay particular attention to the texts and contexts of those latitudes (Africa, Latin America, Australia, Asia, Southern Europe, and even the rural United States) that have long been misrecognized as ancillary to the canonical modernisms of the global North.

Laura Winkiel, *Modernism and the Middle Passage*

Shir Alon, *Static Forms: Writing the Present in the Modern Middle East*

Aparna Bhargava Dharwadker, *Cosmo-Modernism and Theater in India: Writing and Staging Multilingual Modernisms*

Mat Fournier, *Dysphoric Modernism: Undoing Gender in French Literature*

Nergis Ertürk, *Writing in Red: Literature and Revolution Across Turkey and the Soviet Union*

Cate I. Reilly, *Psychic Empire: Literary Modernism and the Clinical State*

Adam McKible, *Creating Jim Crow America: George Horace Lorimer, the* Saturday Evening Post, *and the War Against Black Modernity*

Hannah Freed-Thall, *Modernism at the Beach: Queer Ecologies and the Coastal Commons*

Daniel Ryan Morse, *Radio Empire: The BBC's Eastern Service and the Emergence of the Global Anglophone Novel*

Jill Richards, *The Fury Archives: Female Citizenship, Human Rights, and the International Avant-Gardes*

Claire Seiler, *Midcentury Suspension: Literature and Feeling in the Wake of World War II*

Elizabeth Outka, *Viral Modernism: The Influenza Pandemic and Interwar Literature*

Ben Conisbee Baer, *Indigenous Vanguards: Education, National Liberation, and the Limits of Modernism*

Aarthi Vadde, *Chimeras of Form: Modernist Internationalism Beyond Europe, 1914–2014*

Eric Bulson, *Little Magazine, World Form*

For a complete list of books in this series, please see the Columbia University Press website.

Stitch, Unstitch

MODERNIST POETRY AND THE WORLD OF WORK

Kristin Grogan

Columbia University Press
New York

Columbia University Press
Publishers Since 1893
New York   Chichester, West Sussex

Copyright © 2025 Columbia University Press
All rights reserved

Library of Congress Cataloging-in-Publication Data
Names: Grogan, Kristin Alexandria, 1991– author
Title: Stitch, unstitch : modernist poetry and the
world of work / Kristin Grogan.
Description: New York : Columbia University Press, 2025. |
Series: Modernist latitudes | Includes bibliographical
references and index.
Identifiers: LCCN 2025000689 | ISBN 9780231219631 hardback |
ISBN 9780231219648 trade paperback | ISBN 9780231562829 ebook
Subjects: LCSH: Modernism (Literature) | Poetry, Modern—
20th century—History and criticism | LCGFT: Literary criticism
Classification: LCC PN56.M54 G77 2025 | DDC 809.1/9112—dc23/eng/20250527

Cover design: Elliott S. Cairns
Cover image: Lenore Tawney, *The Lilies Have Frozen and the Lake Is Dark* (1993).
Courtesy of the Lenore G. Tawney Foundation, New York, and Alison Jacques.
© Lenore G. Tawney Foundation. Photo: Michael Brzezinski.

GPSR Authorized Representative: Easy Access System Europe,
Mustamäe tee 50, 10621 Tallinn, Estonia, gpsr.requests@easproject.com

CONTENTS

LIST OF FIGURES vii

ACKNOWLEDGMENTS ix

Introduction 1

Chapter One
Ezra Pound's Work Ethic 33

Chapter Two
The Social Life of Sewing: Lola Ridge 68

Chapter Three
Langston Hughes's Constructivist Poetics 103

Chapter Four
Reproducing Gertrude Stein 139

Chapter Five
Lorine Niedecker and the Work of Restraint 172

Coda: Drafting Modernism 211

NOTES 219

BIBLIOGRAPHY 255

INDEX 279

FIGURES

FIGURE 2.1   Photograph of Lola Ridge at her desk (undated)   80
FIGURE 3.1   Vsevolod Meyerhold's students performing the étude "Shooting from the Bow" (1926)   125
FIGURE 3.2   Maquette for a trade union poster, "Trade Union Is a Defender of Female Labor," by Alexander Rodchenko (c. 1925)   130
FIGURE 3.3   Presentation of the *Letatlin* (1933)   137
FIGURE 4.1   Note from Gertrude Stein to Alice B. Toklas   163
FIGURE 5.1   Cover of *Homemade Poems*   177
FIGURE 5.2   Watercolor of Blackhawk Island in *Homemade Poems*   178
FIGURE 5.3   "Next year, or, I fly my rounds, tempestuous"   179
FIGURE 5.4   Polaroid photograph by Lorine Niedecker of her home on Blackhawk Island   183
FIGURE 5.5   "A Cooking Book"   184
FIGURE 5.6   *Moby Dick*, by Ann Wilson (1955)   189
FIGURE 5.7   "For Best Work" from *Homemade Poems*   198

ACKNOWLEDGMENTS

I had the great good fortune of finishing this book in the English department at Rutgers University. For their support and advice, I thank Meredith McGill, Rebecca Walkowitz, Evie Shockley, David Kurnick, Billy Galperin, Jonah Siegel, Ann Coiro, Carolyn Williams, Brad Evans, Andrew Goldstone, Elin Diamond, Mukti Mangharam, Imani Owens, and Jeff Lawrence.

The participants of the Commons group at the Center for Cultural Analysis provided helpful feedback on an early version of chapter 2. For teaching and administrative support that cleared time for writing, I thank Eagan Dean. Brittany Marshall helped to prepare the manuscript in its final stages. I'm grateful to all the English department staff for their Herculean labors. I thank my union, the Rutgers AAUP-AFT chapter, for fighting for the working conditions that make research like this possible. Finally, I would like to thank my brilliant Rutgers students for the many hours in the classroom spent thinking and talking about poetry.

I thank the Master and Fellows of St. Catharine's College, Cambridge, for a Junior Research Fellowship that allowed time for this book to simmer away. Hester Lees-Jeffries and Caroline Gonda brought warmth and friendship to my too-brief time in Cambridge. Discussing poetry over lunch with the late Glen Cavaliero was always a joy. The Catz staff made my life in the garret extraordinarily comfortable.

ACKNOWLEDGMENTS

This project got off the ground at Oxford under the sharp eye of Rebecca Beasley, a model of intellectual rigor, integrity, and commitment. Rebecca set an example of how to be a thinker and teacher that I can only hope to emulate. Many thanks to my examiners, Morag Shiach and Hannah Sullivan, for their attentive reading and feedback. For advice along the way, I'm grateful to Lloyd Pratt, Michèle Mendelssohn, Tara Stubbs, the late Laura Marcus, Emma Smith, and the incomparable Jeri Johnson.

For their financial generosity, I thank the Clarendon Fund, the Rector and Fellows of Exeter College, the Principal and Fellows of Hertford College, and the Rothermere American Institute. I particularly want to thank all the staff at Exeter College for keeping me fed and housed during this project's early days.

At the University of New South Wales, Sean Pryor first taught me how to read a poem.

I'm enormously grateful for the help and insight of the librarians and archivists at many institutions: the Beinecke Rare Book and Manuscript Library, the Bodleian Library, the British Library, the Cambridge University Library, the Harry Ransom Center, the New York Public Library, and the Smith College Special Collections.

Christopher Nealon and Paula Rabinowitz generously commented on an early version of this manuscript. I thank Chris for encouraging me to think more expansively about poetic material and Paula for advising me to make my debts to earlier feminist struggles clear.

At Columbia University Press, I thank Philip Leventhal, Jessica Berman, and Paul Saint-Amour for their care and stewardship of this project. My two anonymous readers provided valuable feedback that sharpened the book in its later stages. Thank you to Emily Simon and the production team for all their work getting the book into print.

To my brilliant friends: Hugh Foley, *il miglior fabbro*; Emily Dolmans, who sat opposite me every day while I wrote the very first draft; Andrew Dean, for the steady stream of Freud (and so much else); Rey Conquer; Natalya Din-Kariuki; Noreen Masud; Courtney Traub; Simon Ford; Julian Ramsay; Jinal Dadiya; Madeline Delaney; Will Ghosh; Katie Murphy; David Hobbs; Andrew Allen; Mark Steven; Dominick Knowles; Rachel Sobel; Lara Donnelly; Adam Ward; Eddie Cliff; Robbie Grogan; Noa Saunders; Cathryn Setz; Joe Brooker; Lyn Hill; David Hill; Jim Dowthwaite; Beci Carver; Johanna Winant, for poetry summer camp,

ACKNOWLEDGMENTS

and Brian Glavey, beautiful genius; Christian Gelder; Margaret Ronda; Kathy Lubey; and, especially, Katrina Zaat, wisest guide and true north.

To Vivien and Stephen Grogan, who opened the whole world for me.

To Zilka, Nicholas, and Hannah Grogan, who are the base upon which my life stands.

To Sophie, a model of antiwork politics.

And to my life, my love, Eloise Stonborough: for every day, for reading every page, for keeping my suspect edifice upright in air.

Excerpts from *The Cantos of Ezra Pound*, by Ezra Pound, copyright © 1934, 1937, 1940, 1948, 1950, 1956, 1959, 1962, 1963, 1965, 1966, 1968, 1970, and 1971 by Ezra Pound. Reprinted by permission of New Directions Publishing Corp. "Canto LXIX, typescript, no date," by Ezra Pound, from New Directions Publishing Corp. acting as agent, copyright © 2024 by Mary de Rachewiltz and the Estate of Omar S. Pound. Reprinted by permission of New Directions Publishing Corp.

Material by Langston Hughes used with permission of the Estate of Langston Hughes and International Literary Properties LLC.

Material by Gertrude Stein reprinted with permission of Mr. Stanford Gann Jr., Levin & Gann, P. A., literary executor of the Estate of Gertrude Stein.

Permission to quote from *The Collected Works* of Lorine Niedecker is given by Bob Arnold, literary executor for the Estate of Lorine Niedecker.

Permission to quote from *Drafts* granted by Rachel Blau DuPlessis © 2024, all rights reserved. This text is cited from the Wesleyan University Press book *Drafts 1–38, Toll* (2001) and the forthcoming complete *Drafts* from Coffee House Press (2025).

STITCH, UNSTITCH

INTRODUCTION

In 1962—at the tail end of what might be called "modernism"—a poet wrote the following lines:

> Grandfather
>   advised me:
>   Learn a trade
>
> I learned
>   to sit at desk
>   and condense
>
> No layoff
>   from this
>   condensery[1]

It's a slender *ars poetica*. Looming over the writer at her desk is her grandfather, delivering sound advice that the poet has traded for the bad business of writing poetry. A bad business because it is so lonely and immovable, sitting there at her desk; a bad business because its central verb, *condense*, hardly promises creative fulfillment; a bad business because there will be no release from her labor. To condense is to make something smaller, to compress or concentrate it. The writer concentrates in both senses of the verb: she focuses, and she produces a concentrate. To condense is also to intensify: the condensed substance is richer, denser, more valuable. In optics, rays of light that are focused or brought together are condensed; they become brighter. Microscopes and telescopes have condensers; to condense is also to bring something into clearer view. So, too, with condensation. When water vapor in the air hits a cold surface, such as a window, it cools enough to form droplets, small but visible. What does this small poem let us see?

Lorine Niedecker wrote this poem, titled "Poet's Work," the year before she retired from her job as a cleaner at the local hospital in Fort Atkinson, Wisconsin, the small town where she lived most of her life. No stranger to layoffs, she had lost her first paid job three decades earlier, when the Great Depression cut short her career as a librarian. For many years she sat at a desk in the offices of a local dairy journal and condensed the language of others. As a proofreader she removed errors; as a stenographer she wrote in shorthand. Living in Jefferson County, Wisconsin, Niedecker grew up surrounded by dairy farms, with their creameries and condenseries, and she knew well that *to condense* means to evaporate excess water and thereby to make condensed milk—rich, dense, sweet. This is literary production as removal. The poem's excess, like the water extracted from milk, melts into air.

Looming over the poem, or perhaps lurking behind the arras, is another, more literary, grandfather. Niedecker's "condensery" refigures one of Ezra Pound's famous definitions of poetry as "the most concentrated form of verbal expression."[2] In his *ABC of Reading*, Pound recounts a scene in which the poet Basil Bunting, "fumbling about with a German-Italian dictionary," finds in that book a surprising definition of *poetry* in which the German *dichten*—the verbal form of *Dichtung*, a poem—is translated as the Italian verb *condensare*. Thus, to write poetry is to condense; this is the definition of *poetry* produced by Pound's convoluted translingual anecdote. Poetry, Pound writes, is freighted with any given word's previous meanings; it is "charged": "The good writer chooses his words for their 'meaning,' but that meaning is not a set, cut-off thing like the move of knight or pawn on a chess-board. It comes up with roots, with associations, with how and where the word is familiarly used, or where it has been used brilliantly or memorably."[3]

Like the old German-Italian dictionary, Niedecker's poem is an act of translation. She translates Pound's cosmopolitan explanation into a local one, bringing the formal lessons of modernism back to her home soil. At

INTRODUCTION

the same time, she quietly one-ups Pound—the author of the full eight hundred pages of *The Cantos*—with her poem's extreme concision. But while any one poem can be shorn of its excess, the history of language is accretive. The "charge" of a given word gathers more meaning, but it does not displace the word's earlier usages. In "condensery," Niedecker layers two associations that should have nothing to do with each other—Pound and his European dictionaries, Wisconsin and its condensed milk—and in this layering, she reinterprets the work of poetry as simultaneously a self-conscious act of modernist invention and a locally grounded daily work.

In *Stitch, Unstitch*, I argue that modernist poetry took its specific shape in relation to ordinary labors and the people who performed them—at home, in hospitals, in factories, in fields—and that this enmeshed relationship provoked powerful political and aesthetic experiments for poetry. Today, literary production is most often assumed to be a kind of expert craft—difficult and serious labor, to be sure, but distinct from everyday work. This book rejects the terms of this comparison and turns instead to unseen and undervalued labors, shifting our gaze from Pound's library to Niedecker's condensery. At stake in this account is more than an expanded archive of representations of labor in literary form. I argue that from their deeply felt entanglement with working life, modernist poets imagined new forms of freedom from labor, proposed new patterns of sociality and ways of being together, and reshaped the value of writing poetry—that seemingly most useless of practices—in a world defined by the mandate to earn a living.

In the standard account, the modernist moment saw the emergence of a literary-professional model of writing that insisted on a dispassionate form of highly skilled work. The literary-professional figure cultivated expertise, embraced obscure knowledge, and advocated impersonality in their craft. This development took shape alongside the rise of a new professional class as the literary-professional modernized the skilled work of the expert artisan after the demise of aristocratic patrons and craft guilds.[4] In this version of the story, the "age of the professions" marked a historical break with modernism's Romantic antecedents. When A. R. Orage, the editor of *The New Age*, writes that Pound's "deliberate craftmanship" is "disliked in England, where it has for years been the habit of critics to pretend that poetry grows on bushes or in parsley-beds," we can hear a repudiation of Keats's demand that "if poetry comes not as naturally as the leaves to the tree, it had better not come at all."[5] Alongside the professionalization of literary culture came a number of other white-collar jobs: literary critics, editors, marketers, advertisers, and professional literary agents.[6] With the institutionalization of literature within university departments, the emergence of the poet-critic as a cultural administrator, and the MFA degree as a craft-based approach to credentialization, modernism's professional model remains with us today.[7]

The emergence of a new professional class might be the most frequently told account of modernism, but it is not the whole story. In this book, I read the aesthetic revolutions of poetic modernism as a series of encounters with the transformations of working conditions in the uneven landscape of early twentieth-century capitalism. I argue that these encounters shaped the political energies and utopian desires of modernist poetry. If we cast our eyes away from the professional model and toward the wider range of labors that formed poetic modernism, a more complex and robust narrative emerges. I write a history of modernist poetry as a history of labor to show not how poetry becomes absorbed into the values and hierarchies of waged work but rather how certain poets imagine the organization of life beyond the wage relation. Across the five chapters of this book, I roam widely in the history of work: I examine the ideology of craft and artisanal labor in Ezra Pound's poetry and criticism; Lola Ridge's immersion in the New York garment industry; Langston Hughes's dramatic poetry written to and for the global working class; Gertrude Stein's gendered and queer domestic labors; and Lorine Niedecker's revision of craft as an amateur practice rooted in invisible reproductive work. My readings are grounded in material histories of working life. But I also approach labor as a phenomenon that produced powerful ideas and values that modernists troubled over, values that are not only economic but also social and cultural. When poets write about working life, they are writing not only about the experience of, for example, making beds in a hospital but also about the values that labor produces and enforces: its organization of social life, its production and enforcement of gendered and racialized identities, the management of human freedom and unfreedom, and the containment of creative possibility. If the professional model claims certain cultural values for literary production—seriousness, expertise, authority—the poets in this study articulate their own values of inefficiency and unproductivity, social connectedness rather than isolation, preservation rather than production, and freedom from work.

This is often an ambivalent relationship. In "Poet's Work," the trouble comes in the final tercet: "No layoff / from this / condensery." Niedecker sets up an ambiguous line between the poet and other workers that is negotiated by "layoff." That noun registers the forcible removal from work—being laid off—but also suggests the voluntary end of an activity—to lay off, to cease doing something, to remove oneself. Does it indicate removal or respite? Perhaps Niedecker is bringing poetry closer to the laborer in the condensery plant or the stenographer at her desk, who share the fundamental condition of unfreedom. But she might equally be asserting poetry's difference—no layoff from *this* condensery, the work of poetry, not *that* other work. Perhaps the final line celebrates laboring without layoff as a freedom beyond the bounds of work. But we might also detect resignation or even mourning for the fact that the poet's condition, like Adam's after the fall, must be one of endless toil. Niedecker lands us heavily on that final word, *condensery*, on which the poem's pun and its rewriting of Poundian modernism hinges. Just as it announces that there will be "no layoff," it casts us adrift to puzzle over this strange noun. The poem draws a line in the sand around the condition of the poet's work—no layoff—then leaves us to ask what the contours of this experience, its freedom and unfreedom, might mean.

Not every poem in this study will be so ambivalent, and my chapter on Niedecker will show how her condensery becomes the basis for a new ethos of limited action and restraint, one with high stakes for the writer working in a world where production and consumption trump preservation and inaction. Art is commonly assumed to be "powerfully useless," in Leigh Clare La Berge's phrase, its value deriving from its economic valuelessness and its status as a supposedly privileged form of unalienated labor.[8] But even if the poet is not directly waged when she sits at her desk and in writing poetry she experiences "no layoff," this does not mean that to write a poem is momentarily to escape capitalism's grip. Beginning from the premise that poets define their writing in the terms of labor, I do not claim that poets seek recognition on capital's terms as difficult, efficient, and productive work. Rather, I argue that this position of enmeshment is the starting point for the intellectual project of reshaping a world governed by work and that this ambition was key to modernism. Poets begin by acknowledging that work is, as Michael Denning has written, "the fundamental *unfree* association of civil society," and their poetry invokes and imagines other forms of freedom.[9] For some of the poets I study, such as Langston Hughes, this freedom is nothing less than the liberation of the international proletariat. For Lola Ridge, such freedom crystallizes in the new solidarities that cut across religion and language. Ezra Pound turns to diverse historical moments to imagine the artist's freedom from wage labor. For Gertrude Stein, freedom is found in queer, unruly domestic spaces. Niedecker, meanwhile, embraces a stance of nonimposition that refuses the capitalist dictum of productive work. So, too, does reshaping the world of work produce new forms of sociality, from the theory of solidarity that Lola Ridge develops from within the multilingual spaces of the global movement of labor to Gertrude Stein's recasting of the lesbian domestic unit as a site of exploratory intellectual life. Finally, in working from a position of enmeshment with labor, poets claim for their writing valueless qualities—inefficiency, secrecy, failure, immobility, unproductivity—and imagine new ways of valuing the seemingly useless task of writing poetry.

As "Poet's Work" makes clear, the relationship between art and labor is also a question of form. Form in this poem is at once technique—the method of concentrating—and product, the slender, nine-line poem that results. "Form" here registers a renegotiation of a technical history internal to modernism while also constituting a politically charged gesture that situates the poem in a local economy. Throughout *Stitch, Unstitch*, I attend closely to such handlings of form as poets renovate both the shape and political meaning of their poems. I retain modernism's association with formal experiment but detach this association exclusively from a masculine poetics of difficulty to consider a range of poetic forms and associations. Labor, I show, is not just a question of representing certain activities but also a problem of *poetics* and of the language unique to poetry. At the same time, I expand this sense of form to material practices beyond the stanza and line, from the Constructivist theater to household ephemera and homemade books. This approach lets us see how poets understand their writing in relation to other forms of cultural production and lets us reexamine the patterns of thought and representation unique to poetry. It also expands our understanding of modernism's signature intermediality by extending it beyond painting, cinema, and music to devalued and domestic practices.

Braiding an attentive formal approach, historically grounded readings informed by twentieth-century labor history, and a Marxist-feminist perspective that insists on the unseen, undervalued, and naturalized aspects of work, this book provides an account of modernist poetry as both a history of work and an intellectual project of imagining life beyond labor. When I talk of literary production, then, I am talking about more than "poetry's hidden . . . agenda—its concern with itself," in John Hollander's phrase, and more than a history of modernist development as a reflection of contemporary working conditions.[10] If modernist works, as Fredric Jameson acknowledges, "can so often be seen, implicitly or explicitly, to be allegories of their own production," I insist on the too-often overlooked second part of this Marxist hermeneutic that shows that if art expresses the conditions of its production, it also represents a utopian reply to such conditions.[11] In the pages that follow, I show how modernist poets describe and reimagine a society governed by work and argue that it is on precisely this terrain that modernist poetry both reinvents itself and seeks to intervene in social life.

THE IDEA OF WORK: A MATERIALIST APPROACH

For Marx, the originary difference between human and animal activity is ideation. "A spider conducts operations which resemble those of the weaver," he writes, "and a bee would put many a human architect to shame by the construction of its honeycomb cells." But "the architect builds the cell in his mind before he constructs it in wax. At the end of the labor process, a result emerges which had already been conceived by the worker at the beginning, hence already existed ideally."[12] The "exclusively human characteristic" of labor is a dialectical process between man and nature, "a process by which man, through his own actions, mediates, regulates, and controls the metabolism between himself and nature" and "acts upon external nature and changes it, and in this way he simultaneously changes his own nature."[13] This conscious purpose and subordination are, as Jennifer Bajorek glosses, "man's original *tekhne*: the means by which he makes, in addition to the (other) things he makes, himself."[14] We imagine a thing and make it real, and in so doing, we both change the world and are ourselves changed.

Marx distinguishes labor, the act of working, from labor power, a person's mental or physical ability to work, which under capitalism is bought and sold as a commodity. In a capitalist system in which the ruling class owns the means of production, the worker has only their labor power to sell: it is "*external*" to the worker; he "does not affirm himself but denies himself"; and his labor is "not voluntary, but coerced; it is *forced labor*."[15] What is unique to capitalism is this enforced selling of one's labor power, which in turn creates modernity's connected social world. Meanwhile, Nancy Fraser offers an important corrective to the framework of the exploited worker selling their labor power when she insists on "the crucial role played in capital accumulation by unfree, dependent, and unwaged labor," that is, "labor that is expropriated, as opposed to exploited," which forms "a hidden condition of possibility for the freedom of those whom it *exploits*."[16]

Running throughout Marxist thought is the more amorphous category of living labor, "labor-power in action," the sensual activity on which the "dead labor" of capital parasitically feeds.[17] Taking up Marx's definition, Michael Hardt and Antonio Negri argue for the importance of the "savage energies of living labor," which is "always subjugated but always liberating itself": "Living labor produces life and constitutes society in a time that cuts across the division posed by the workday, inside and outside the prisons of capitalist work and its wage relation, in both the realm of work and that of nonwork. It is a seed that lies waiting under the snow, or more accurately, the life force always already active in the dynamic networks of cooperation, in the production and reproduction of society, that courses in and out of the time posed by capital."[18] Living labor "is the internal force that constantly poses not only the subversion of the capitalist process of production but also the construction of an alternative"; the subjectivities it produces "are the agents that create an alternative sociality."[19] In the Marxist tradition, labor and living labor not only encode the exploitation and alienation of human labor power by capital but also preserve the human capacity for the creation of alternatives. I begin with three ideas core to a humanist Marxism: first, that ideation is internal to the labor process; second, that the dialectical process of labor is both externally and internally transformative; and third, that while labor power is harnessed, sold, and exploited, living labor as a potential revolutionary life force has the power to transcend and exceed the conditions of labor's exploitation.

As early as *The German Ideology*, Marx acknowledged that the dialectical process of labor, wherein people act on and change the external world while also changing their own natures, must be understood materially. "As individuals express their life," he writes, "so they are. What they are, therefore, coincides with their production, both with what they produce and how they produce. The nature of individuals thus depends on the material conditions determining their production."[20] The transformations of spirit and nature that the dialectical process of labor entails must be understood as historically determined. In this book, I trace the material roots of poetry's ideas and theories of labor, following Barbara Foley's mandate that one task of Marxist criticism "is to recognize the limits of texts that express the desire for a better world in idealist terms, while understanding that this idealism is itself grounded in historical circumstances that are comprehensible in a materialist framework."[21] Indeed, as Kathi Weeks points out, "materialism as Marx and Engels conceive it is a matter not merely of the social construction of subjects but of creative activity, the capacity not only to make commodities but to remake a world."[22] This sense of materialism guides my approach to labor as both a process of creating social and cultural values and the starting point for modernist poetry's world-transforming ambitions.

Underpinning the argument of *Stitch, Unstitch* is a Marxist approach that finds in poetry historically situated expressions of utopian desire that share ground with the desires of today. In *The Political Unconscious*, Jameson reminds us that our readings of the past are "vitally dependent on our experience of the present"; that is, the call to historicize begins from our present situation. As a philosophy of history, Marxism offers a way out of the "ideological double bind" of antiquarianism and projection (seeing the past as identical to the present). It also offers a way of seeing the "claims of monuments from distant and even archaic moments of the cultural past on a culturally different present": "Only a genuine philosophy of history is capable of respecting the specificity and radical difference of the social and cultural past while disclosing the solidarity of its polemics and passions, its forms, structures, experiences, and struggles, with those of the present day. . . . Only Marxism can give us an adequate account of the essential *mystery* of the cultural past, which, like Tiresias drinking the blood, is momentarily returned to life and warmth and allowed once more to speak, and to deliver its long-forgotten message in surroundings utterly alien to it."[23]

If we begin from the premise that our conditions are the same as those that produced literary modernism, we obviate the need for the act of resurrection that is historical thinking. Historicism does not show how the past is "reflected" or "represented" in literature, but it creates the conditions that might allow us to understand something distant and so understand the claims it makes on the present. T. J. Clark argues that modernism is strange to us not because our age is divorced from the past, but because our present is the triumph of the "holocaust" of modernity that modernism senses and registers. Creating a memorable image, Clark writes, "Modernism is our antiquity, as overgrown and labyrinthine as Shelley's dream of Rome."[24] For Clark, we are modernism's uncomprehending descendants, who might yet learn from a time not our own. If the cultural past is a corpse that must be warmed to life by the critic, it is nevertheless able to make powerful demands on us. The word I find most useful in Jameson's Tiresian account is *solidarity*—a word that particularly informs my reading of the poetry of collective life in chapters 2 and 3—because it implies a common interest and common struggle without requiring identical conditions. To identify, resuscitate, and translate the solidarities of the past such that they can speak more clearly to a present that is modernism's posterity: this is the task of Marxist historicist criticism.

In his chapter on Joseph Conrad in *The Political Unconscious*, Jameson argues that art not only is the "expression" of its historical conditions but also "constitutes a Utopian compensation for everything lost in the process of the development of capitalism." He frames this utopian compensation in explicitly formal terms. The rise in popularity of abstraction in art, for example, not only expresses the fragmentation and reification of daily life under capitalism but also "compensates" for the loss of anti- or precapitalist values. In Jameson's example, abstraction insists on quality rather than quantity; it emphasizes feeling, color, and intensity within a world of measure, categorization, and routinization. The symbolic acts of literature that are "ideology and Utopia all at once" preserve, in this dialectic, an ambivalence that makes them worthy of study, an "ultimate ambiguity" that lies in an "attempt to stand beyond history." For Jameson, this recognition of the dual expressive and Utopian-compensatory character constitutes "an enlarged perspective for any Marxist analysis of culture."[25] As Carolyn Lesjak points out, recent arguments for surface reading and against the supposedly "extractive" processes of political-formalist close reading tend to forget the second half of Jameson's hermeneutic: its insistence on utopia.[26] But analyses of utopian impulses within modernist aesthetic form—rather than utopia as the thematic preoccupation of, say, genre fiction—are relatively submerged within Jameson's own work. The Jameson of *The Political Unconscious* preserves the utopian as something negatively present in the general tension between form and content. In this book, I identify modernism's utopian counterimpulses not only in this dialectical tension but also on the level of individual formal and aesthetic choices. In my historically grounded readings of poetry's radical imagination, I move toward what Ruth Jennison describes as "a turn from dour Marxism and toward a vigorously historical utopianism."[27] At the same time, I acknowledge where the writers' choices and positionalities—Stein's reliance on racialized service labor, for example, or Niedecker's limited solidarity with her fellow custodial workers—temper such utopianism, and chapter 1 shows how Pound's vision of a society governed by natural rather than market-driven laws goes hand-in-hand with authoritarian rule. The utopianisms that energize this book—the plans for life outside the unfree arrangements of wage labor, the new intimacies and solidarities that arise—are understood to be both historically determined and reaching outside of history. I embrace and expand upon the utopian impulses of Jameson's dialectic to understand literature not only as a reflection of its conditions but also as an idealist reaching toward another world.

The early twentieth century was not the first time in history that literary work was bound up with its mode of production.[28] But this entanglement takes on a new urgency under the transformations of labor, both intellectual and manual, that defined the historical moment of modernism's emergence and its maturation. Capitalist accumulation—the dynamic, uneven growth of capital—must feed the expansion of production with an ever-increasing supply of labor power. It creates this supply through certain mechanisms: encouraging population growth, creating new migrant streams, drawing "latent" labor power such as that of women and children into the workforce, and creating and implementing labor-saving technological innovations.[29] In the United States, the late nineteenth century saw rapid industrialization that drew independent artisans into factories, mills, and foundries, where their labor was swiftly degraded into simplified tasks, and "the process as a whole [was] lost."[30] The efficiency-driven principles of scientific management, with its time-and-motion studies, piecework, and division of labor, were widely adopted and refined. Taylorism did not limit itself to the shop floor: popular women's media attempted to bring the "efficiency gospel" to the "unorganized industries" of the home, where labor-saving devices were marketed to consumers and the home became a sphere in which capitalist discipline was articulated.[31] Women were brought into waged labor in large numbers, and new forms of gendered work proliferated.[32] Meanwhile, the growth of the formal workforce drew more and more people into the period's labor militancy. The Industrial Workers of the World was established in 1905 in Chicago, and its revolutionary leadership ushered in the radicalism of the 1910s before the state-sponsored backlash to leftist activity of the 1920s. Most significant of all was the revolution in Russia and the establishment of the workers' state. In an era of a new globalism, unions, workers, and artists articulated an internationalist vision that linked their struggles to those taking place abroad.

In recent years, scholars have taken up Cedric Robinson's framework of "racial capitalism" to describe capitalism's concurrent dynamics of social differentiation and capital accumulation. For Jodi Melamed, capitalism's "antinomies of accumulation require loss, disposability, and the unequal differentiation of human value, and racism enshrines the inequalities that capitalism requires."[33] While the dispossessions characteristic of capitalist accumulation create and intensify racial distinctions, "race serves as a tool for naturalizing the inequalities produced by capitalism, and this racialized process of naturalization serves to rationalize the unequal distribution of resources, social power, rights, and privileges."[34] Capitalist accumulation draws more and more people into either exploitation or expropriation and designates "particular regions for production and others for neglect, certain populations for exploitation, and still others for disposal."[35] It also tends to produce obstacles to its expansion. Periodic crises, endemic to the accumulation process, create fresh conditions for accumulation, because, as David Harvey writes, the capitalist system is "highly dynamic and inevitably expansionary; it forms a permanently revolutionary force which continuously and constantly reshapes the world we live in."[36] The modernist moment was ruptured by the global shockwaves of the Great Depression, which not only intensified the unevenness and impoverishment of global capitalism but also furnished opportunities for a newly radical "cultural front," in Michael Denning's phrase, that touched everything from literary arts to popular film.[37] In this varied, uneven world—where labor was newly rationalized, professionalized, and feminized; newly radical and newly policed; producing new gender identities and enforcing new norms, both within and outside the formal workplace; newly technologized; and riven with crisis and inequality—the old question of the relationship between writing and work was asked with a new urgency and in new forms.

Recently, Joseph North has taken Jameson to task for helping to inaugurate a "historicist/contextualist" paradigm for literary criticism that, North argues, represents a conservative triumph in its turn from cultural intervention to cultural diagnosis. For North, Jameson's call to "always historicize!" has become "the horizon beyond which the disciplines of literary study have so far been unable to see." "Very few people," North writes plainly, "start reading a novel by Virginia Woolf with the primary aim of learning more about British cultural life in the 1920s."[38] But Jameson's version of history is much more finely grained than North's picture suggests. For Jameson, history is the force that helps us make sense of texts; we do not read texts for what they tell us about their time but for a particular interaction they have with their time. The "historic" does not register an event or development so much as a relationship or entanglement. Still, I want to note two tendencies of historicist criticism within modernist studies today that are particularly relevant to the study of literature and labor. The first is a form of technological determinism in which the emergence of certain technologies and their organization—new forms of writing and recording, new media and means of mass communications, new techniques for timekeeping and time management—are seen as both new subject matter for modernism and transformative to the writing process.[39] The second and related tendency is exemplified by historical studies that confine their analysis to specific spheres of activity or emergent jobs: collections on the secretary, books on the emergence of the literary clerk, and analyses of the domestic sphere, for example, have all been written within the last two decades.[40] Taken together, they paint a rich picture of modernism as an engagement with transformations of labor and technology, and many of them are indispensable for this study. But in looking at modernist labor through the history of the typewriter or the secretary alone, such an approach risks reifying the conditions it describes. Modernism comes to look like the emergence of so many new technologies or so many new kinds of jobs, and the totality is lost. In this book I work to balance the fine-grained historical work of studies of specific kinds of labor—which is, after all, the purview of the academic monograph—with a more capacious approach that attempts to see modernism as more than a response to any one emergent technology or sphere. Structurally, each chapter of this book is located in a specific sphere, from the garment trades through the Taylorization of the domestic sphere to institutional caretaking. This structure allows me to perform the kind of historical work key to understanding the past's claims on us, and the wide scope of this book moves us closer to the horizon of seeing modernism as a totality.

Throughout this book I take a historical approach that is attentive to the coincidence of latent and emergent forms of work, or what Harry Harootunian names "uneven temporalities produced by incorporating and metabolizing pasts in the present."[41] Capitalism does not develop in a linear or uniform fashion; rather, it requires uneven development—*development* here encompassing both mal- and underdevelopment—as an essential part of the accumulation process. The Warwick Research Collective draws heavily on Jameson's ideas of modernity as both singularity and simultaneity to write a provocative account of combined and uneven development and ultimately of world literature as the literature of the modern capitalist world system.[42] Understanding that capitalism requires unequal development allows us to make sense of modernism's seeming contradictions—how white-collar bureaucracy develops alongside rural immiseration, for example. My attention to unevenness is both global, driving the choice of writers and chapters, and local, shaping specific readings. In chapter 2, for example, I use the Singer sewing machine as a node in a set of readings that map such unevenness. I show how Lola Ridge observes the machine used in the tenement factories of the New York garment trade while being watched over by the Singer tower and the center of corporate power in the metropole. In a comparative reading with Aimé Césaire's *Cahier d'un retour au pays natal*, in which the speaker's mother sews all night "for our hunger" on a Singer machine, we come to see how the gendered labor of sewing develops unevenly across factories in the American city and the colonized home. This perspective requires that we see modernism not as a series of labors or technologies to be isolated and studied in their literary appearances but rather as a continual conflict of residual and emergent forms in a highly uneven, contested, and contradictory field.

In her influential account of the tripartite structure of *vita activa*, Hannah Arendt distinguishes between labor, which reproduces natural and biological life and fights against the inevitability of decay, and work, which "fabricates the sheer unending variety of things whose sum total constitutes the human artifice."[43] The highest realization of *vita activa* is the fully political category of action, the realization of freedom through plurality and being-in-common. Arendt's distinctions loosen the relationship between the maintenance and reproduction of human life and the creation of an object world, a relationship I insist upon in the chapters that follow. In this book I locate political action and resistance within work, rather than separating the political into its own category of analysis.[44] I use both *work* and *labor* to describe activities of making that take place within and outside the formal workplace, that are waged and unwaged, that are creative and not. Collapsing these categories is an expansive gesture that allows me to explore the politically charged terrain of work and labor without reifying divisions of manual and intellectual, waged and unwaged, productive and unproductive. This interchangeability of terms provides a political perspective that aims to overturn the hierarchies interrogated by this book and to create space for the alternative structures of value, freedom, and sociality that are the horizon of this work.

A MARXIST-FEMINIST PERSPECTIVE

Stitch, Unstitch takes its title from modernism's best known labor poem. When W. B. Yeats writes "A line will take us hours maybe; / Yet if it does not seem a moment's thought, / Our stitching and unstitching has been naught," he is lamenting the double work of the poet, who must work hard to craft beautiful lines and harder again to make that effort invisible. It is better, he tells us, to "go down upon your marrow-bones / And scrub a kitchen pavement" for at least that hard labor—not as hard, he tells us, as writing poetry—is socially legible. Yeats's speaker explains this invisibility to "a beautiful mild woman, your close friend," who adds her own experience of invisible labor: "To be born woman is to know—/ Although they do not talk of it at school—/ That we must labour to be beautiful." This disclosure prompts the poet to label that labor as the postlapsarian condition of life for, Yeats tells us in a labored rhyme that underscores his point, "there is no fine thing / Since Adam's fall but needs much labouring."[45] "The masculinity of modernist canonical poetry," Rachel Blau DuPlessis reminds us, needs "to struggle against the perceived 'femininity' of poetry as a mode of practice," yet here Yeats draws an uneasy alliance between the man who writes poetry and the woman who must work to make herself beautiful.[46]

My title draws on Yeats's association between poetry and femininity to register the centrality of gendered labor to this project and to signal my attention to the invisibility shared by poetry and gendered work. The repetition of my title—the doing and undoing, the stitching and unstitching—both nods to the revisions that certain poets, like Stein and Niedecker, perform on the masculinist ideologies of other poets and signals my commitment to a feminist revision of Yeats's complaint.

This book finds a language to express how gender operates in modernist poetics in a Marxist-feminist critique developed in the 1970s that has enjoyed a recent revival among critics and activists alike. The Wages for Housework campaign, inaugurated by the International Feminist Collective at the 1972 International Feminist Conference in Padova, Italy, was a movement that had at its core a vital revision to Marx's oversight of how reproductive labor produces labor power, that same labor power harnessed and exploited in the production of surplus value. Instead of an object, the work of birthing and raising children, caring, cleaning, and cooking makes the working class itself. In *The Power of Women and the Subversion of the Community*, Mariarosa Dalla Costa and Selma James write that domestic labor "produces not merely use values, but is essential to the production of surplus value." "This is true," they continue, "of the entire female role, as a personality which is subordinated at all levels, physical, psychological, and occupational, which has had and continues to have a precise and vital place in the capitalist division of labor, *in the pursuit of productivity at the social level*."[47] Yet the centrality of domestic labor to the reproduction of the working class and the production of surplus value has been obscured. "Our isolation in the family while doing our work had hidden its social nature," Dalla Costa and James argue. "The fact that it brought no wage had hidden that it was work. Serving men and children in wageless isolation had hidden that we were serving capital."[48] Marx wrote that the concept of a productive worker—a worker whose labor produces surplus value—"implies not merely a relation between the activity of work and its useful effect, between the worker and the product of his work, but also a specifically social relation of production," a relation "which stamps the worker as capital's direct means of valorization." But Marx further acknowledged that to be a productive worker "is therefore not a piece of luck, but a misfortune."[49] From the Wages for Housework perspective, capital denies women entry into this social relation "by denying housework a wage and transforming it into an act of love," as Silvia Federici writes:

> To have a wage means to be part of a social contract, and there is no doubt concerning its meaning: you work, not because you like it, or because it comes naturally to you, but because it is the only condition under which you are allowed to live. Exploited as you might be, you are not that work. . . . Housework was transformed into a natural attribute, rather than being recognized as work, because it was destined to be unwaged. Capital had to convince us that it is a natural, unavoidable, and even fulfilling activity to make us accept working without a wage. In turn, the unwaged condition of housework has been the most powerful weapon in reinforcing the common assumption that housework is not work.[50]

Or as Dalla Costa and James put it, "*Where women are concerned, their labor appears to be a personal service outside of capital.*"[51] Housework is not "a job like other jobs" but rather "the most pervasive manipulation, and the subtlest violence that capitalism has ever perpetrated against any section of the working class" because of its naturalization as a natural attribute, "an internal need, an aspiration, supposedly coming from the depth of our female character."[52]

The demand for a wage was only ever the first step in the *refusal* of that work because to be bound by the wage is not only to be recognized as a laborer but also to gain the ability to refuse to perform that labor. The demystifying project of Wages for Housework was not "one demand among others, but a political perspective that opens a new ground of struggle."[53] More is at stake here than the refusal to cook and clean because the operations of capital have hidden the nature of women's reproductive labor under the naturalized guise of womanhood. The revolutionary significance of the campaign is no less than "*the demand by which our nature ends and our struggle begins because just to want wages for housework means to refuse that work as the expression of our nature.*"[54] To struggle for the wage is to "gain the power to break with our imposed social identity."[55] By revealing that housework and the whole sphere of reproductive labor are productive labor—that is, a value-producing activity whose product is the working class—and by insisting that this fact has been concealed, naturalized, and abstracted as love and nature, the perspective of Wages for Housework looks not just to the refusal of housework but also to the dismantling of the social form of gender.

The Wages for Housework perspective is foundational to this book's understanding of labor as a structure that produces, enforces, and naturalizes cultural values, including gendered identities. An analysis of labor as more than just as a value-producing activity in the narrow economic sense and an awareness of the work-based construction of gender allow us to move feminist critique from "airy indeterminacy," in Denise Riley's phrase, to "the more substantial realms of discursive historical formation."[56] In her wide-ranging polemic against the cultural centrality of work, Kathi Weeks deploys the category of the "work society" to ask why, as she puts it rather mournfully, "do we work so long and hard?" Weeks takes up Moishe Postone's critique of Marx in *Time, Labor, and Social Domination* to argue that work is "for the most part an abstract mode of domination," naturalized, privatized, and made, by its social role, to seem like "something that might be tinkered with but never escaped." Only when we see work as "not just an economic practice" but rather as a "social convention and disciplinary apparatus" will we be able to see it as a "fully political phenomenon."[57] By employing the category of the work society, work comes to look like a phenomenon whose hold over us is not simply the economic need, experienced by the vast majority of people on this planet, to labor for wages but rather an abstract mode that creates subjects—governable, disciplined, responsible—and enforces social and cultural values. The horizon of Weeks's polemic is, like the Wages for Housework campaign, the refusal of work, and the first step in the refusal of work is its full political visibility.

That work enforces genders, that it is a site where gendered social roles are articulated, and that, in the transformations in women's waged and unwaged labor in the twentieth century, it produces legible new subjects are phenomena that have been richly described by scholars of modernism. Feminist modernist scholars have located the shifting terrain of labor as the site of the production of new gendered, classed, and racialized identities for women, as the work of Morag Shiach, Katherine Mullin, and Juno Richards has shown.[58] In chapter 2, I spend time with the emergence of just such a "type"—the young woman garment worker who rejects monogamy, maternity, and religion in favor of radical struggles for a future—but my guiding interest in this book, especially in its last two chapters, is in how poetry becomes a site where the naturalization of gender through labor is theorized and alternative gendered ways of being are proposed. "There are no genderless subjects in any relationship structuring literary culture," writes Rachel Blau DuPlessis, "not in production, dissemination, or reception; not in objects, discourses, or practices; not in reading experiences or in interpretations."[59] There are certainly no genderless subjects in any study of labor and its cultural values. Even in chapter 1, on Ezra Pound, the abstraction I trace—the fantasy that places craft work in the hands of the director, the engineer, the duce—is nothing less than a project to rescue masculine poetry from the taint of feminized production and the "unnatural" forms of capitalist accumulation seen as corrupting natural production.

What is so radical about the Marxist-feminist analysis of Wages for Housework is, as Amy De'Ath comments, that "the method they suggest for theorizing the dialectical relationships between concrete activities and the abstraction of gender begins not with the commodity, the wage, nor the laborer, but with the 'formless' histories and structural relations obscured by these forms of appearance."[60] Marxist-feminism takes as its starting point the labor that takes place in the "hidden abode" of reproduction and its obscured status as a value-producing activity, and feminists after Wages for Housework would go on to reveal further aspects of waged and formal labor that are naturalized as gendered qualities, which thereby produce and enforce normative standards of gender. By reading the history of poetry with this demystifying perspective in mind, we can attune ourselves to the value of activities that capital designates as valueless, to how capitalism manages ordinary life through the abstraction of gender, and to how these gendered abstractions obscure histories of struggle. These are histories that the writers in this study, working from the fraught, feminized, and devalued position of "poet," examine both implicitly and explicitly. In this book, poetry emerges as a site and mode of thinking through which these obscured relations are sensed, articulated, and resisted.

In her 2011 preface to the essays collected in *Revolution at Point Zero*, Federici issues a mea culpa for her earlier stance toward domestic labor and historicizes that stance as forming part of a collective rejection of the reproduction of human life by the generation who grew up amid the devastation of the Second World War. She rearticulates the project of Wages for Housework as "the need not to measure our lives by the demands and values of the capitalist labor market" and writes that "it is through the day-to-day activities by means of which we produce our existence, that we can develop our capacity to cooperate and not only resist our dehumanization but learn to reconstruct the world as a space of nurturing, creativity, and care."[61] Certain feminists have taken issue with this later turn, arguing that it represents a move from the more fertile analytic of gender as an abstraction to a too-literal romanticization of the home, but it strikes me that Federici's later turn is simply the utopian corollary to her earlier critique.[62] This turn is not, she clarifies, "a question of identity; it is a labor question"; it is not to concede a naturalized understanding of femininity rooted in the home but rather to honor the history and practice of reproduction as a site of resistance. It means, moreover, "refusing to obliterate the collective experiences, knowledge, and struggles that women have accumulated concerning reproductive work, whose history has been an essential part of our resistance to capitalism."[63] In this book I take up both the revolutionary demystifying perspective of the earlier Wages for Housework campaign and the utopian perspective of the later Federici and her commons, which seeks in such practices of daily labor alternative forms of knowledge, experience, and social life.

LABORING MODERNIST STUDIES

The Waste Land, the exemplary modernist poem, is contoured by the temporal and spatial bounds of the working day. The first section of the poem, written when T. S. Eliot was employed as a clerk in the Colonial and Foreign Department at Lloyds Bank, closes with that most modern of daily migrations: commuters, figured as a great stream of the undead, flowing from the south bank of the Thames across London Bridge into the financial district of the City for the day's work:

> A crowd flowed over London Bridge, so many,
> I had not thought death had undone so many.
> Sighs, short and infrequent, were exhaled,
> And each man fixed his eyes before his feet.
> Flowed up the hill and down King William Street,
> To where Saint Mary Woolnoth kept the hours
> With a dead sound on the final stroke of nine.[64]

We don't see what happens in the firms of the City after the clock strikes nine, and in the poem's next section we shift to a pub, where the landlord's repeated cries of "HURRY UP PLEASE IT'S TIME" suggest the "bells and clocks" whose spread inaugurated the new time-discipline of labor that E. P. Thompson locates as a hallmark of the shift to industrial capitalism.[65] *The Waste Land* is a poem that understands the voracious appetite of the working day. Because capitalist production drives "towards the appropriation of labor throughout the whole of the twenty-four hours in the day," Marx writes, "the worker is nothing other than labor-power for the duration of his whole life," such that "all his disposable time is by nature and by right labor-time."[66] But the poem also bridles against its work-bound enclosure, eventually moving us from the nighttime to the ocean's shore and then to the desert. The poem's driving antagonism emerges not only from the divisions between high and low culture and between the bankers and the barkeepers but also from its prolonged encounter between the perfunctory time of the modern working day and the expansiveness of historical time, where a walk along the Thames in the margins not claimed by work is always an encounter with the Thames of Spenser and Chaucer. In the poem's fragments, shored against ruin, we move vertiginously in and out of the binds of the modern working day.

Since the financial crisis of 2008 and its ramifications in higher education—not least the swift degradation of academic working conditions and the rise of a new academic labor militancy—scholars of poetry have focused more and more on the history of labor across periods and its implications for our present.[67] In *Whitman, Melville, Crane, and the Labors of American Poetry: Against Vocation*, Peter Riley argues that "poetic vocation"—a cultural logic in which the day job is seen as an impediment to the "pure" work of poetry—offers a false promise of escape from lesser and contingent labors that ultimately reinforces hierarchies of labor. In the transformations of labor in the late nineteenth century, Riley finds a set of practices that challenge these hierarchies at precisely the moment of their emergence and entrenchment. Against the privileged separation from the job market, exemplified by the modernism of Eliot and Wallace Stevens, Riley locates the poetry of Whitman, Melville, and Crane as examples of an entanglement with lesser, nonvocational labors whose work sits ill at ease with "that apparently purest of callings," that is, the work of the poet.[68] In his argument against the professional model of modernism, Riley shows us how powerfully that model persists, even in its negation. Meanwhile, Jasper Bernes's *The Work of Art in the Age of Deindustrialization* argues for the historicization of the period since the "long downturn"—as the historian Robert Brenner has described the period of economic contraction, speculative bubbles, privatization, and class victories for capital that took hold in the early 1970s—as a distinct period for both political economy and literary study. In Bernes's account of poetry written since the end of the Second World War, the relationship between art and work is co-constitutive: artists draw their techniques from work, reimagining and recasting them, whereas industry "looks to art for transposable techniques, means, and materials that it can borrow and put to work."[69] In attempting to trace how poetry transforms capitalist working conditions, Bernes seeks a literary origin story for those transformations. However, a new history of capitalist transformation isn't to be found in *Stitch, Unstitch*; that is the purview of historians of capitalism. Rather, I write a history of how labor is taken up as a problem for poetry and poetics with ramifications for poetry's aesthetic possibilities and its social imagination.

Closer to this study is John Marsh's *Hog Butchers, Beggars, and Busboys: Poverty, Labor, and the Making of Modern American Poetry*, which argues that from 1909 to 1927, American poets self-consciously sought to distinguish their poetry from genteel Victorian verse by engaging the "taboo" subjects of poverty and labor, even as the poets embraced a nostalgic "romantic anticapitalism" that had little investment in the material improvement of workers' lives.[70] Marsh's revisionist history persuasively recasts modernist poetry as a site of engagement with "the labor question," but in his account modernist poets embraced a position of qualified and ultimately toothless sympathy with workers. In contrast, *Stitch, Unstitch* argues that across an expanded modernist period from 1910 to 1964, poets wrote from a position of enmeshment with labor as a general condition of life. Modernist poetry, in my account, was fundamentally entwined with the demands to earn a living, reproduce human life, and live according to the dominant values produced by work. In attending to this enmeshed position, *Stitch, Unstitch* excavates modernist poetry as a formally complex archive of thought about the meaning of work and life beyond work. Further, where Marsh sees modernist poets as looking backward toward premodern and precapitalist pasts, in my account this nostalgia was only one strand of modernism; the writers in this study are for the most part oriented toward the future.

INTRODUCTION

I also counter the long-standing scholarly oversight—shared by but by no means unique to Marsh and Riley—of gendered and reproductive labor in narratives of modernist poetic work. While I share Riley's interest in poetic entanglements with devalued labors, I enter this terrain through histories of gendered labor and through feminist challenges to labor's hierarchies and values. Riley sees modernism as a conservative ideological reaction that scuppers the emergent potential of the late nineteenth century, whereas Marsh sees engaging with labor primarily as an opportunity for modernist self-definition against antiquated Victorianism. In my account, modernism is not merely reaction; instead, it is a moment of potential. From within the crises and transformations of the early twentieth century, modernist poets set about imagining a world beyond work.

Scholars of contemporary literature and contemporary poets also trouble over labor's meanings and values. For the poets Mark Nowak, Ed Roberson, Anne Boyer, and Jill Magi and for the scholars Margaret Ronda, Jennifer Ashton, and Lindsay Turner, contemporary poetry is fertile ground for examining experiences of selfhood in alienated labor; the precarity that now defines sectors of the economy from academia to food delivery; the ongoing transformations wrought by automation and artificial intelligence; and the "recalcitrant and minimized forms of life characteristic of contemporary economic crisis," as Ronda puts it.[71] *Stitch, Unstitch* brings the lessons of this contemporary swell of interest in labor to bear on the modernist moment not because I see these periods as identical but because these recent studies have produced a wealth of insights that can enliven our historical readings. I take my coordinates from recent scholarship emphasizing the gendered nature of work, the development of subjectivities through labor, and the restructuring of care and reproduction. Temporally, *Stitch, Unstitch* is anchored in the early decades of the twentieth century, but it reaches until the early 1960s. My final chapter takes a strand of second-generation modernism—Niedecker and the objectivists came up in the political radicalism of the 1930s—and traces its revision of modernism in its maturity. At moments throughout the book, I turn to contemporary poets for whom the questions that animated modernism are particularly relevant. And in my coda, I look to Rachel Blau DuPlessis and the revision of the modernist epic in *Drafts*, her "poem of a life." Here, modernism is taken up as an unfinished project as well as an inheritance that requires feminist revision. If we are no longer precisely in the modernist moment, we are still in a moment of its institutional importance and vexed intellectual legacy.

Today, modernist scholarship tends to emphasize not a rupture between modernism's heyday and our time but a relationship of continuity, however fraught. Since Douglas Mao and Rebecca Walkowitz named the "temporal, spatial, and vertical" expansion of the "New Modernist Studies," that temporal expansion has often meant that modernism is seen to absorb the present.[72] A glance at the program of the 2022 Modernist Studies Association conference, for example, lists papers on the 2001 film *Amélie*, the filmmaker David Lynch, the poet Claudia Rankine, and the novelist Eden Robinson; the earliest of these, Lynch, was born in 1946. Against this stretching of modernism, the date that Tyrus Miller pinpoints as the beginning of "late" modernism—1926, the year of the general strike—begins to look rather early indeed. But even that lateness looks both backward and forward, and Miller writes that in the 1920s "the phosphorescence of decay had illumined the passageway to a re-emergence of innovative writing after modernism."[73] Arguments for modernism's relevance often rely on claims that modernism presaged conditions we experience today. John Attridge, for example, notes that "modernism's typists, telegraphists, clerks, bureaucrats, and insurance workers bear witness to the birth of a modern 'informatic' society, which anticipates in many ways the full-blown information economy of the late twentieth century."[74] In a recent collection on the new modernist studies, Mao writes that the anticontextualist polemics of Rita Felski and Joseph North have less relevance for modernist studies "because so many of the 'contexts' of modernism clearly persist in our own time"; for modernist scholars, Mao suggests, "the implications of their work for the here and now are fairly evident."[75] This narrative of continuity has supplanted an earlier account of modernism as a break with the past, a narrative that built problems of periodization into the DNA of modernist studies. "How long can a break persist before it becomes a continuity in its own right?" asks Michael North. "Can the break continue to happen, over and over again?"[76]

Such is the expansion of modernist studies that the designator *modernism* can no longer be instantly taken to mean literature from the very end of the nineteenth century until about the Second World War, produced predominantly in Britain, continental Europe, and certain circles in the United States. If modernism has expanded to the present, it has also reached far backward in time, a gesture made most notably by Susan Stanford Friedman, who argued that modernism can be seen in the aesthetic changes that accompany technological change and rupture in any historical moment—including, provocatively, the Tang dynasty.[77] Yet the problem with this approach, as Paul Saint-Amour points out, is that it unhooks modernism from any history of capitalism—a history that is the precondition for a study like this.[78] Meanwhile, scholars working in the arena of the global have reattached modernism to a broader, asymmetrical history of capitalist unevenness to challenge modernism's association with the Anglo-European core and scholarship that sees non-European modernisms as primarily derivative. Perhaps no project has been more extensive than Alys Moody and Stephen Ross's *Global Modernists on Modernism* anthology, which collects seventy-five texts written in nineteen languages by authors from the Caucasus to the South Pacific in a comprehensive, totalizing approach.[79]

In light of this disciplinary expansion, my own claims to expansion might seem rather modest.[80] Broadly, all the writers I study in this book are American. My use of *American*, however, is not a stable one. Pound and Stein lived much of their life in Europe. Langston Hughes spent significant time abroad, and my chapter on him focuses on his time in the USSR. Lorine Niedecker was a lifelong Midwesterner who spent little time outside her home state of Wisconsin. And Lola Ridge was born in Dublin and grew up in the South Pacific before immigrating to the East Coast of the United States. Spanning both the imperial core in Europe and the regional periphery in the United States, this project is global in its orientations and sensitive to the global transformations of labor. I attend to the spaces of labor, literal and imagined: from the evocation of Chinese agriculture in Pound's late cantos to the tenement factories of the Lower East Side in Ridge, the Russian workers' theaters that Langston Hughes attended, the bourgeois interior in Stein, and the institutional spaces of reproductive labor in Niedecker's late poetry. I intend to bring spaces that we might expect to find in a global project—non-Anglo-American nation-states such as the USSR, for example—into conversation with places that might not immediately be seen as having much to do with the expansive ambitions of a global project. The queer home of Stein and Toklas and the Wisconsin homes and hospitals where Niedecker sewed curtains and cleaned floors are equally part of this global reach. *Global* in this account, then, means both international and extremely local; it reaches inward as much as outward.

Similarly, in my choice of key poets, I balance canonical and noncanonical writers; Niedecker and Ridge in particular are only now enjoying a critical renaissance. But this book does not perform the vital archive-expanding work of recovery projects, such as those by Paula Rabinowitz, Barbara Foley, Cary Nelson, and Alan Wald.[81] The work of overturning Cold War–era cultural amnesia about leftist and proletarian cultures is not the project of this book. Moreover, while Rabinowitz's work on proletarian women writers is an important forebear for this project, the political commitments and positionalities of the writers I study in this project are more varied. As Christopher Nealon observes, it is "not only the poetries of witness and documentation, or movement poetries, that are worrying over the destiny that capitalism is forcing us toward."[82] Although leftist and working-class poets are a crucial part of this project, my aim is to show how far-reaching the concern with labor was. I gather a more politically and experientially diverse set of writers to show labor's importance as a general concern *across* categories of race, class, and gender. We may not immediately imagine Stein as a writer occupied with the transformations of domestic labor, but my chapter on Stein shows that she, too, troubled over labor's forms and values. When placing Stein's queer domesticity alongside Ridge's wayward young women garment workers, for example, a richer vision of how modernist poets understand labor emerges.

This study draws on the rich formalist traditions of reading modernist poetry. Marxist poetry critics have often found political energies encoded in specific poetic forms and techniques. In her study of objectivism, Ruth Jennison argues that modernist parataxis registers the social, cultural, and economic unevenness of Depression-era capitalism in the United States, with its "topography of vertiginously contiguous high and mass cultures, urban and rural economic landscapes, and agricultural and industrialized social relations."[83] For Mark Steven, the imprint of communism can be felt on American poetry primarily in the ambitions of the modern epic.[84] While, like these critics, I take up Jameson's method of reading for the social significance of form, my readings throughout this book are more generically and formally promiscuous. I assemble an expansive archive of modernist poetic form, from Pound's epic to Niedecker's haiku- and nursery-rhyme-informed miniature, from the poetic sequence to the script and chant. While I aim to place poetry in its historical context, many of the readings in this book are unabashedly low to the ground, attentive to the qualities of poetry that both mark it as a distinctive aesthetic experience and are the particular ways it does its thinking.

This book matches its commitment to a finely grained close reading as a method of bringing out the subtlety of modernist poetic theorizing about labor with an expansive approach to nonpoetic material.[85] I build on the work of Sarah Ehlers, who positions Depression-era poetry alongside photography and journalism, and Amy Elkins, with her expansive study of the aesthetics and feminist politics of craft, by reading the poetry under study alongside a range of other material: popular journalism, Constructivist theater and set design, homemade books, notes and household ephemera, watercolors and drawings, and recipe books.[86] *Material* here designates practices beyond the stanza and line that cut across cultural divisions, object making, and performance and that form the broader aesthetic milieu from which poetry emerges as a distinct but enmeshed participant. This material approach also extends Nealon's observation that in the poetry of the twentieth century, capital appears as "matter" that encompasses subject matter, as an object of inquiry and representation, and, in matter's more material sense, as the "material practices of making texts" that together produce a "textual imaginary" that stages "confrontations between poetry and capital."[87] By turning outward, I stage other confrontations that inform my readings of the poetry, just as they informed the poets as they wrote. For Langston Hughes, for example, the development of an explicitly political aesthetic that might express the collective dreams of the global proletariat emerged after his encounter with postrevolutionary Soviet avant-garde practitioners, especially in the realm of the theater, who were refining a revolutionary aesthetic informed by Soviet Taylorism in the years before the veil of Stalinism fell. When Niedecker turns to homemade books, she is infusing her decades-long practice of writing in the "low" and feminized genre of the nursery rhyme with its material corollary; the result is a nuanced intervention into modernist ideologies of craft. By extending my understanding of the realms of the formal and the material to this broader cultural terrain, I expand the possibilities for a political-formalist analysis of literary modernism and its intermedial experiments.

I want to illustrate this book's approach by returning to where I began, with Lorine Niedecker's figuring of poetic work as a distinctive kind of unproductive quasi freedom. Niedecker's insistence on the inactivity of poetic work—"to sit at desk / and condense"—brings poetry closer to the defining condition of women's work: that it looks like nothing is being done. But if poetry is women's work, it is also, for Niedecker, associated with a compromised womanhood and a failure to meet normative standards of femininity for working-class women. In an earlier poem, written in 1950 but set "in the great snowfall before the bomb," Niedecker dramatizes the poet's simultaneous immersion with and alienation from her fellow workers. The poem's speaker "worked the print shop / right down among em / the folk from whom all poetry flows / and dreadfully much else."[88] We are in a printshop, where industry language is proofed and printed by "the folk"; the poet is both one of them ("em") and marked as other (she goes "down" to work "among" them). "Dreadfully" much: too much or too little flows from these folk—the language of the printshop is misogynistic name-calling ("I was Blondie") and the "rehashed radio barbs" of wartime mass media in the lead-up to the atomic assault on Hiroshima and Nagasaki by the United States. Niedecker is a great poet of the sting in the tail, and in its final lines the poem turns inward:

> But what vitality! The women hold jobs—
> clean house, cook, raise children, bowl
> and go to church.
>
> What would they say if they knew
> I sit for two months on six lines
> of poetry?[89]

"But what vitality!" The exclamation breaks up the poem's reflections and plunges us into the busy lives of the women, filled with paid and unpaid labor, child-rearing, leisure, and church. Within and against this world there is poetry, slowly produced and kept close to the chest. That whittled final tercet underscores poetry's particularity. If gender is constructed and reproduced in and through labor, the poet's failure to perform the full social labors of the women and to demonstrate their vitality also makes her a failed woman, one illegible to her busy coworkers. Perhaps the poet is shamed by the social illegibility and nonproductivity of her work. Or perhaps she relishes its difference from the demands of busyness and daily labor. That question (what would these women think?) is answered by implication as soon as it is asked (the hardworking and hard-pressed women would be confounded and probably appalled by the singular slowness of poetry). In its rhetorical asking, the line constructs a charmed circle of two between Niedecker and her reader. Capitalist values in this poem are clear: price, productivity, and war. Poetry, meanwhile, is invisible, contemplative, and unproductive. Against barbarism and nuclear devastation there is poetry, small and still, illegible to the folk yet indebted to them, flowing from their habits and speech yet utterly separate. If the speaker fails to do gender on capital's terms—work, church, bowling—she also clears a protected space for alternative ways of being, unproductivity, and creation to flourish in the dark, and she names that space: poetry.

Chapter 1 begins with the dominant ideal of literary labor today: the idea that poetry constitutes a unique form of craft. Rarely was this model articulated with more force or sustained interest than in the poetry of Ezra Pound. In this chapter I argue that across his career, Pound abstracts craft from a practice into an attitude. I trace the development of craft from Pound's early encounter with the British guild socialist movement to his late cantos. In his 1913 *Contemporania* poems, Pound skewers American labor journalists and defines the craft ideal as a unity of ethics and form. I show how in the early 1920s Pound attempted to conceptualize poetic value beyond the wage relation and associated the craftsman with theories of good governance and ethical rule. This association finds practical expression in his "Bel Esprit" scheme to remove Eliot from his job at Lloyds Bank and finds aesthetic expression in the material worlds of the Venetian cantos. As craft moves from a practice of making to a practice of seeing and looking above all else, Pound's craftsmen multiply: I draw a line from Pound's Malatesta to his embrace of Henry Ford and scientific management, a line that quickly leads to Mussolini. In the chapter's final section, I turn to the cantos that Pound wrote in the 1950s and to the significance that Chinese agrarian practices held for Pound as an idealized form of work governed by natural rhythms and a protected space outside of capitalist accumulation. Considering the use of parataxis and Chinese characters, I find a formal parallel for the textual operations of the late cantos in the *Mostra*—the Fascist exhibitions—with their dehistoricized idealization of precapitalist agrarian labor. In tracing craft's gradual mystification, I show how ways of working take on abstract values, and I unpick the political work that such abstractions perform.

Chapters 2 and 3 turn to explicitly leftist poets and problems of collective life, poetic form, and the global scale of modernism's poetics of work. When Lola Ridge emigrated from Australia to New York, she turned her attention to the Yiddish-speaking Jewish inhabitants of the Lower East Side who labored in the city's needle trades. I read Ridge's sequence "The Ghetto" as occupying a fraught space between contemporary ethnographic journalism, Whitmanian universalism, and the anarcha-feminist intellectual circles in which Ridge moved. "The Ghetto" finds new social and political possibility in the figure of the young woman garment worker who rejects religion, monogamous marriage, and child-rearing in favor of a politically committed and intellectually expansive life. Ridge's poem moves between intimate, detailed portraits of young women garment workers and those of alienation from the Yiddish speakers among whom the poem's speaker lives. Not speaking Yiddish is important to "The Ghetto," I argue; it accounts for both the poem's visual knowledge and the limits of the speaker's insights. I show how in "The Ghetto" Ridge resists developing modernist ideas of sudden insight as the basis of knowledge and embraces instead a new labor for the poet, one consisting of attentive observation that nevertheless understands and values its own limitations. The literature of garment work is often treated today as a problem of knowledge and scale—of how to understand distant and convoluted global supply chains. Writing from within the global movement of labor in the early decades of the twentieth century, Ridge not only presages these problems but also provides us with a vocabulary of solidarity that embraces limited knowledge and subjective difference.

Chapter 3 turns to the revolutionary verse written by Langston Hughes in the 1930s. In this chapter I show how Hughes's project at the time was to find a political aesthetic that could agitate for the emancipation of the global working class. The basis of that aesthetic, I show, was Russian Constructivism, with its roots in postrevolutionary Soviet Taylorism. Before I turn to the USSR, I spend time with the poems of racialized service labor in Hughes's second collection, *Fine Clothes to the Jew* (1927), alongside a handful of blues poems by Sterling Brown, which I read as registering the circularity of low-waged service labor through the spatial containment, irony, and repetition of the blues form. Turning to the 1930s, I trace Hughes's contact with the Russian Constructivist theater and the Soviet workers' theatrical movement. In a series of readings of Hughes's 1938 pamphlet,

A New Song, and of uncollected poems from this era, I draw out the formal resonances between Hughes's performance poetics and the Soviet avant-garde—particularly the acting theory of the playwright Vsevolod Meyerhold, the participatory stage design of Nikolai Okhlopkov, and the graphic design of Alexander Rodchenko—in the period immediately before Stalinist repression. This chapter shows how Black writers turned to postrevolutionary Russian art to articulate the international struggles of labor. Where Hughes's theatrical work from this period is bound by the material constraints of performance, his poetry of the same era adopts the ideas of Constructivist performance to declare a utopian horizon for the working class. Like Vladimir Tatlin's flying machine, the *Letatlin*, what Hughes describes in his poems of the 1930s might be unachievable, but those poems move us closer toward that liberatory horizon.

The final two chapters of the book deal at length with the poetics of social reproduction in the work of two very different writers. Chapter 4 pushes the meta-poetics of this study to its limit by turning to the work of Gertrude Stein. Stein is, I argue, a poet deeply concerned with social reproduction. I begin by tracing how, in the context of her early rejection by publishers, Stein self-consciously aligns her writing with the devalued labor of reproduction. *The Making of Americans* is an epic of social reproduction for both its narrative tracing of the development of the American middle class and its portrayal of writing as a reproductive labor. I then read *Tender Buttons* against Christine Frederick's *The New Housekeeping*, which seeks to bring a Taylorist work discipline into the domestic sphere. Simultaneously invoking and deforming contemporary household-management guides, *Tender Buttons* redescribes the home as a site of unruly, queer experiments with language. The chapter ends with an extended reading of Stein's poetic sequence *Stanzas in Meditation*, which I approach as an effort to describe the intellectual character of queer intimacy. I read the *Stanzas* in relation to the Stein–Toklas archive and the swath of love notes that Stein wrote for Toklas, which I approach as a queer reproductive labor. Ultimately, I suggest that Stein and Lyn Hejinian after her theorize reproduction not as the replication of the world exactly as it is but as the generative, endlessly dynamic process of making and remaking a life.

What was the fate of the modernist craft ideal as the century progressed? Chapter 5 revisits artisanal labor by plumbing the relationship between thrifty, amateur, homemade crafts and reproductive labor in the later poems of Lorine Niedecker. In 1964, after retiring from her final waged job as a hospital cleaner, Niedecker sent three homemade books of poetry to friends. Focusing my analysis on archival editions of these handmade books and on Niedecker's drawings, watercolors, and a recipe book, I position Niedecker as a participant, however ambivalent, in the postwar feminist embrace of craft techniques and amateur practices. Niedecker rejects artisanal values of mastery and develops instead a new work ethic that prizes restriction, nonimposition, and restraint. The chapter ends with a reading of the poem "Laundromat" in which I argue for the possibility of eruptive social feeling within the ordinary spaces of reproductive labor. I suggest that Niedecker's invisible reproductive work of cleaning hospitals provides the ground for this insistence on the value of spareness and maintenance and that these values inform her later environmental turn and commitment to ecological preservation, an issue that would become more pressing for poets writing since Niedecker in the era of accelerating climate crisis. Niedecker, like Bernadette Mayer after her, insists that gendered reproductive struggles and environmental struggles are one and the same.

Finally, the coda considers the intellectual and institutional legacy of the modernist poetics of work in the career of a major poet working today who takes up the complex inheritance of modernist poetics: Rachel Blau DuPlessis. In DuPlessis's poetry, experimental essays, and scholarship, modernism amounts to an unfinished and unfinishable intellectual project that sits at odds with the material conditions of gendered labor and maternity. DuPlessis intervenes in modernism's legacy by rewriting the modernist epic into a nonlinear process of continual feminist becoming. In the provisionality of her long poem, *Drafts*, DuPlessis reminds us that if we are far from the conditions of modernism today, its methods and concerns continue to shape the poetry of our present.

Chapter One

EZRA POUND'S WORK ETHIC

In the sweltering northern Italian heat of July 2015, scholars from around the world flowed into Dorf Tirol, a small village perched in the Alps, to attend the Ezra Pound International Conference (E.P.I.C.). There, in Schloss Brunnenburg, a thirteenth-century fortress nestled at the base of the perilously steep Ezra Pound Straße, or Via Ezra Pound, the delegates gathered to debate the poet's life and work. They paused for meals made from produce grown in the castle's grounds and, at the end of the day, for wine from the vineyards that contour its slopes ("the vines grow in my homage").¹ We can imagine discovering a scene like this in a sketch for an unpublished canto: a group of scholars gather in a castle in the shadow of the mountains to discuss the meaning of poetry. At the conference's end, a bus arrived to transport the delegates through the Italian countryside to Tschengls, a tiny village in the Vinschgau Valley. The delegates assembled in the sunshine on a Tyrolian slope to toast the unveiling of three marble pillars, built from stone selected by Olga Rudge decades ago, that rose from the earth. The pillars form a monument to the poet and are a realization of the lines Pound gives three times in Canto XCVII: "The temple is holy 山 because it is not for sale" (XCVII, 696, 698, 699).

Few poets have pillars rising in tribute to them from Tyrolian slopes, and few conferences involve the unveiling of a marble monument, not to mention the quasi-transubstantiate experience of drinking wine from vineyards named for the object of study. Those pillars are the Chinese character *shān*, 山, mountain, executed in stone. The three pillars form a larger counterpart to another, more famous sculpture associated with Pound: the *Hieratic Head of Ezra Pound* (1914) by Henri Gaudier-Brzeska, one version of which sits in the courtyard of Brunnenburg.[2] Another is inside the castle. It seems that everywhere you go in Brunnenburg, you run into the *Hieratic Head*, whose phallic form literalizes the poet's macho poetics ("the mind is an upspurt of sperm," he once wrote).[3] The material presence of Pound—the pillars, the sculpted heads, even the wine—cannot fail to impress themselves on anyone who studies the poet. Pound's is a material presence, but a mystical one, too, and the mystical and material fold into each other. In the castle, a poster of Pound's face asks, "Ezra Pound: Poet or Prophet?"

Some eight hundred miles away from Dorf Tirol is Kettle's Yard, the beloved Cambridge gallery and former home of the art collector and curator Jim Ede and his wife, Helen. Kettle's Yard houses the Edes' collection of paintings, drawings, and sculptures in and among their furniture, wildflower bouquets, and stones from British beaches. The gallery creates a delicate interplay between the artistic and the domestic, the crafted and the ordinary, the object and the object's setting. In the light-filled rooms of Kettle's Yard, a sketch by Barbara Hepworth is just as significant as the light that changes in a bedroom throughout the course of the day. More than that, the sketch and the light come together to form a total, integrated aesthetic experience. Sculptures and maquettes by Gaudier-Brzeska are scattered throughout the house, and the attic is entirely devoted to his work. The first image that greets visitors to the Gaudier-Brzeska space is his famous 1914 ink drawing of Pound, familiar to readers as the cover image of *Literary Essays of Ezra Pound*. The attic is a distinct zone in the house, set apart from its lived-in rooms; it has no beds, flowers, or stones. It is the part of the house that is the most formal and least intimate, and Pound's sharp inky features preside over that change in function and tone.

"The temple is holy 山 because it is not for sale": in those thrice stated lines Pound asserts a principle of artistic labor, namely, that the products of the artist's making are unique and valuable because they are uncommodified. More than unique, these products are blessed and an expression of divine virtue. For Pound, artistic labor should be like that uncommodified temple for uncommodified art will lead to the spiritual improvement of a society at large, but that is possible only when artists are properly supported. "Get us an age of leisure," Pound urged the historian and critic Howard Mumford Jones in 1935, "and FEED the men who want to do a little SERIOUS work on prosody."[4] For Pound, only artistic labor counts as "serious work," and because it is uncommodified, it shares the values of virtuous toil—seriousness, expertise, commitment, and the possibility for spiritual improvement—which come together under the sign of craft. When I describe a "craft ideal" in this chapter, I am referring to a set of principles for the nature and organization of artistic work rooted in a revival of preindustrial and anti-capitalist ways of artisanal making. But I am also talking about an associated set of social values that craft invokes. Craft, for all of its promised solidity—the umbilical tie between maker and material, the sculptor working the stone—is slippery. And that slipperiness is put to work to make certain social, ethical, and political claims for poetry, claims that remain with us today.

This chapter follows the development and politics of Pound's craft model. In and through the language of craft, Pound developed ideas of artistic technique and art's social and political importance. Because craft is at once so malleable and so persistent in Pound's thinking, over the half century that this chapter traces we will travel diverse terrain: from British guild socialist magazines through a scheme for a basic income for artists to Venetian glass workshops; from factories organized into orchestras to American railway workers; and from the agrarian practices of ancient China to the fascist exhibitions of Pound's present. I show how craft ideals are harnessed to articulate protofascist (and then explicitly fascist) principles: the authoritarian individual, the idea of patrimonial heritage, and a syncretic view of a national past. Pound's theory of poetic craft emerges from guild socialism, yet we will also see how protofascist dictatorial ideals underpin even that earliest articulation of poetic labor.[5] Craft appeals because of its supposed solidity; the certainty of carved wood or cut glass and the proximity of maker to material offers an alternative to alienated work and the division of labor. The solidity of craft paradoxically lends itself to a mystification in which its real origins and practitioners are obscured, thus investing it with intangible values. Across Pound's thinking, craft becomes increasingly abstract, moving from a practice to an attitude or stance to a set of values surrounding that work: a work ethic.

Craft remains with us today as a powerful way of understanding poetic creation as a distinctive kind of making implicitly resistant to the alienation of labor under capitalism.⁶ Pound was by no means the first (nor the second, nor the tenth) exponent of the craft model for artists working in the period of industrial expansion. But a Poundian version of the craft model, which emphasizes seriousness and expertise, has come to define modernist literature as a reaction to industrial modernity. If modernist studies has—rightly—moved away from understanding its object of study predominantly in the terms defined by Pound and Eliot, it is still the case that Pound's theories of craft, especially those of his early essays and poems, are the most widely read aspects of the poet's work. To put it crudely, someone who would never consider writing about *The Fifth Decad of Cantos* or *Thrones* might begin a course on modernism with "In a Station of the Metro." In this chapter, I contend that those early poems—the Pound that remains with us—presage and rehearse ideas that are fully developed after Pound's "conversion" to fascism.⁷ Later, in Pound's committed fascist era, we find that craft ideals underpin his poems' social and historical worldview and that these ideas are gradually abstracted as those poems progress. We also cannot talk of modernism's political ideas without dealing with Pound's politics. The task of this book is to attend to the utopian impulses of modernism's poetics of labor, and here we see how Pound's fascism constitutes a "perverted utopian promise," as Alberto Toscano glosses Ernst Bloch on the promises of fascism; indeed, Pound's vision of a fascist society is perhaps the most fully realized utopia in this book, if not in modernist literature.⁸ In his comprehensive study of Pound's fascism, Tim Redman convincingly argues that "Pound's activity on behalf of Italian fascism needs to be understood historically and with a great deal of specificity."⁹ But craft's lack of specificity, or its shifting specificity, is precisely what makes it so useful—and so insidious. It is in these more nebulous zones, first of anticipation and later of mystification, that craft does its political work.

EVERY ARTIST A CRAFTSMAN

In 1908 Pound arrived in London, where he cut his teeth as a journalist on the heterogeneous pages of British periodicals. Among these was *The New Age*, a socialist weekly purchased in 1907 by the Fabian arts group and edited by A. R. Orage.¹⁰ In its first issue, the guild socialist A. J. Penty outlined the magazine's intention "to rescue art from the gallery and bring it back again into relation with life."¹¹ This would be done by returning art to its "architectonic" basis in the architecture of the Middle Ages, when "every craftsman was then to some extent an artist, while every artist a craftsman."[12] This project of reconnecting work to craft, and craft to life in general, would be pursued under the sign of guild socialism. Taking their cues from the nineteenth-century medievalism of John Ruskin, William Morris, and the Arts and Crafts movement, the guild socialists argued for state control of industry organized through a network of national guilds. In *Signs of Change*, Morris wrote that "the mediaeval craftsman was free in his work, therefore he made it as amusing to himself as he could; and it was his pleasure and not his pain that made all things beautiful that were made, and lavished treasures of human hope and thought on everything that man made, from a cathedral to a porridge-pot."[13] Guild socialists echoed Morris to argue that craft could restore pleasure, life, and time to workers. The commodification of labor power "does violence to the natural instincts of man," and wage labor "has always been repugnant to the disposition of men."[14] Unlike the syndicalist strategy of industrial sabotage and strikes undertaken by militant trade unions, the fundamentally antirevolutionary guild socialists focused their energy on shifting control over production and distribution to the guild.[15] "The real revolution," Orage claimed in August 1913, "is to be found in the destruction of wagery and not in political action; the real revolution is the transformation of the wage-system into a labor monopoly."

In his columns for *The New Age*, Pound wrote about contemporary British labor politics from the standpoint of an American observer. Pound's pieces from this time tend to echo the style and commitments of the magazine's other contributors. In his series "Through Alien Eyes," he proposes a tax on "men who make a profit on the labor of other men," a tax that would "end the vicious circle whereby all labor is turned to the loss of the laborer."[16] In the third installment of the series, Pound turns his attention to the national coal strike of 1912. In March and April of that year, British miners went on strike for thirty-seven days to secure a minimum wage. Orage saw the government's hurried passing of the Coal Mines (Minimum Wage) Act through Parliament as a failure and deemed its widely publicized success "a lie for the men's consumption."[17] Pound contrasts the miners with the "shop-keeping type" and the idle rich (as well as the "idle poor" and the "parasitic East End"), arguing that the "real strength of the nation" will be found in its "producers, the million men who struck and the rest of their sort and calibre."[18] He comments on the strikes: "If anything were calculated to give me faith in the future of England and a belief in her present strength, it was your coal strike—which your papers misrepresented. This thing will be written in the history when the future produces a Burckhardt. A million men going out of their work and keeping order. No! This thing is stupendous. . . . Believe me: *Nascitur ordo*."[19] Pound is referring to Jacob Burckhardt, the Swiss art historian and author of the influential book *The Civilization of the Renaissance in Italy*, whose German writing Pound would praise in *Gaudier-Brzeska: A Memoir* as having the "verve of the best French prose."[20] More important to Pound than the quality of Burckhardt's prose, however, was his analysis of the Renaissance as a cultural whole, which two years earlier had given Pound an early model for his theory of the "luminous detail."[21] Pound's primary interest in the strikers is an aesthetic delight in their orderliness. He describes the strike proleptically as a modern aesthetic event like the Renaissance, the significance of which will be perceived in some future time.

In these early essays, Pound articulates his method of the "luminous detail," which prizes intellectual efficiency through brevity, selection, and sudden understanding. In "I Gather the Limbs of Osiris," printed in *The New Age* in 1911 and 1912, Pound insists on the importance of the vivid apprehension of singular facts that "give one a sudden insight into circumjacent conditions, into their causes, their effects, into sequence, and law." Art then becomes a process of apprehension and neutral presentation for the artist "seeks out the luminous detail and presents it. He does not comment. His work remains the permanent basis of psychology and metaphysics."[22] In Natalia Cecire's reading, the "luminous detail" becomes incorporated into what she refers to as an "epistemic virtue," which is less a method or technique than "a set of principles by which knowledge can be secured."[23] These principles of artistic production come together under the heading of "technique." Technique, Pound writes, "is the means of conveying an exact impression of exactly what one means in such a way as to exhilarate." Technique is "seriously studied" by the serious artist, immune to fads, who acquires rare expertise for "only that man who cares and believes really in the pint of truth that is in him will work, year in and year out, to find the perfect expression." Technique "is thus the protection of the public." A sleight of hand is present in this "thus," with the serious study of technique moving quickly into an act of social responsibility.[24] When the "method" of the luminous detail becomes the social responsibility of "technique," the artist's objectivity becomes a matter of what David Kadlec terms "the crafting of poems for the truing of the world."[25]

Pound's early accounts of artistic labor emphasize "civility, consideration, and efficiency" as requirements for the socially improving work of art.[26] In the first installment of "The Serious Artist," which began serialization in Dora Marsden's *The New Freewoman* in October 1913, a year before the magazine was rechristened *The Egoist*, Pound aligns the artist's work with that of the scientist and the doctor and endows it with the same diagnostic and curative responsibilities. "The arts, literature, poesy are a science, just as chemistry is a science," he writes; the arts "begin where the science of medicine leaves off or rather they overlap that science." In the first installment of the series, Pound writes of "the immorality of bad art. Bad art is inaccurate art. It is art that makes false reports." In contrast, "good art can NOT be immoral."[27] "Good" (and moral) art is "hygiene," it is "physical wellbeing," and it is brought about by a specific kind of professional. The two methods available to the physician are diagnosis and cure:

> As there are in medicine the art of diagnosis and the art of cure, so in the arts, so in the particular arts of poetry and literature. There is the art of diagnosis and the art of cure. They call one the cult of ugliness and the other the cult of cure.
> The cult of beauty is the hygiene, it is sun, air and the sea and the rain and the lake bathing. The cult of ugliness, Villon, Baudelaire, Corbière, Beardsley are diagnosis. Flaubert is diagnosis. Satire, if we are to ride this metaphor to staggers, satire is surgery, insertions, and amputations.[28]

Form, then, is never "merely a technical discussion."[29] Rather, these early essays are striking for yoking together the aesthetic and the ethical and for drawing on the professionally validating language of the scientist and physician to do so. For Pound, poetic making and social and political world-building were always intertwined. Pound describes the artist-craftsman's qualities in protofascist terms that already frame the artist as a dictator: an individual uniquely capable of sight and selection who is responsible for the "hygienic" restructuring of the world.

In April 1913, Pound published a group of verses in *Poetry* under the title "Contemporania," his first major poetry publication since *Ripostes* in 1912.

Many of the poems were reprinted as "The Contemporania of Ezra Pound" in *The New Freewoman* in August of the same year.[30] The "Contemporania" collection bears the stamp of Pound's ambivalent relationship with American cultural production, embodied in the fraught paternity of Walt Whitman. Pound lived in New York for eight months between 1910 and 1911; he would later write about this return and the state of American architecture and design for *The New Age*. "I don't know that America is ready to be diverted by the ultra-modern, ultra-effete tenuity of Contemporania," Pound wrote to Harriet Monroe in October 1912.[31] In "A Pact" Pound makes "a truce" with Whitman, with the raw material of American poetry: "It was you that broke the new wood, / Now is a time for carving."[32] Pound begrudgingly acknowledged his formal debt to his predecessor, admitting that "when I write of certain things I find myself using his rhythms."[33] One of these things is contemporary American politics, which we see in the poem "Pax Saturni" ("Saturn's Peace"), eventually retitled "Reflection and Advice." The poet sends his songs, "O smooth flatterers," back to the United States to "Say there are no oppressions, / Say it is a time of peace, / Say that labor is pleasant." He punctuates these lines with the refrain "And you will not lack your reward."[34] Pound takes the Whitmanian techniques of the anaphoric line and the ecstatic, celebratory catalog but transforms Whitmanian sincerity into diagnostic irony.

"Pax Saturni" begins with an epigraph:

> *Once . . . the round world brimmed with hate,*
> *. . . . . and the strong*
> *Harried the weak. Long past, long past, praise God,*
> *In these fair, peaceful, happy days.*

Pound attributes the lines only to "A Contemporary." Its author was John Reed, the American communist journalist who would become famous for his account of the Russian Revolution, *Ten Days That Shook the World*, which Pound would go on to read and praise in the 1920s. The epigraph comes from Reed's poem "Sangar," published in *Poetry* in December 1912 and dedicated to Lincoln Steffens, another correspondent Pound would praise a decade later after hearing his lectures in Paris on the Russian Revolution. But the revolution was still four years away, and Pound's satirical teasing preceded his respect. Reed responded angrily to Pound's use of the quotation. He wrote a note to Pound, published in *Poetry* in June 1913, claiming that the lines had been taken out of context and were intended to be read as ironic commentary: "Mr. Aggressively Contemporary Pound, here in America very few people believe that these are 'fair, peaceful, happy days.' And of course the event which I symbolize occurred very recently—Lincoln Steffens' magnificent try for peace during the trial of the McNamaras. Perhaps I wrong you, but no one else misunderstood my lines."[35] Reed is referring to the trial of two trade unionists, J. B. and J. J. McNamara, on charges stemming from the 1910 *Los Angeles Times* dynamiting. In June 1910, Los Angeles ironworkers went on strike to organize closed shops—workplaces with mandatory union membership—and demand higher wages. The vehemently anti-union owner of the *LA Times*, Harrison Gray Otis, had used the publication to attack organized labor. On October 1, 1910, a bomb exploded in the *LA Times* building, killing twenty-one people and injuring many more. The McNamara brothers, members of the International Association of Bridge and Structural Iron Workers Union, were arrested the following year. The trial became a cause célèbre for labor activists. Steffens arrived during the trial and attempted to negotiate plea bargains for the brothers. J. B. McNamara was handed a life sentence, and J. J. was sentenced to fifteen years in prison, returning to labor organizing upon his release nine years later. In the wake of the affair, Steffens launched a campaign to ease class tensions that drew in social workers, industrialists, and politicians.[36] Reed's poem turns the McNamara trial into a battle between the hero, Sangar, "most curiously named / 'The Mad Recreant Knight of the West,'" and a Hun invasion. Its style is typical of the optimistic Christian socialism that Reed and Steffens shared in the 1910s. The poem ends with Sangar's death at the hands of his son and his entry to the afterlife: "There was joy in Heaven when Sangar came."[37]

Reed called "Pax Saturni" a philippic, believing himself and Steffens to be the targets of the poem's barbs about "the accuracy of reporters" and "the unbiased press."[38] The McNamara case was reported in *The New Age*, and it is also likely that Pound, who was in the United States at the time of the bombing, had followed it in American media.[39] Harriet Monroe dubbed Pound's poem "risqué" and objected in particular to later lines about sex workers, pimps, shop girls, and their employers: "Speak well of amateur harlots, / speak well of disguised procurers, / speak well of shop-walkers, / speak well of employers of women." Pound argued that "it would weaken it to say 'Speak well of John Wanamaker who pays his shop-girls five dollars per week, and of others who do the same.'"[40] Pound lumps the American press as a whole in with capitalists like Wanamaker and with unserious artists and unethical physicians. But "Pax Saturni" is not specifically about the McNamaras or even Reed but rather an American strain of blinkered optimism that refuses to speak about inequality or exploitation in adequate terms. In this sense it is a satire on Whitman's optimism regarding the significance and progress of American labor, an optimism that Pound sees inherited by journalists and agitators like Steffens and Reed. Pound's ironic treatment of the McNamara case also reveals a fundamental ideological difference between Pound and Whitman and underscores the younger poet's refusal of the American democracy that his forebear had celebrated. In its antidemocratic poetics, the poem presages the authoritarianism that Pound would soon embrace.

This is the poetry of diagnosis: it treats social relations directly, usually satirically. In the poetry of cure, Pound elaborates a theory of artistic labor in the form of the poem itself. In 1912, Pound had argued that Whitman was a "reflex" who "left us a human document, for you cannot call a man an artist until he shows himself capable of reticence and of restraint, until he shows himself in some degree master of the forces which beat upon him."[41] The language of "mastering forces" is uniquely Pound's; it is hard to imagine Whitman conceiving of poetry in terms of mastery. In the first version of the "Contemporania" sequence that Pound sent to Harriet Monroe, "A Pact" was the penultimate poem, the sequence ending with "Epilogue," a poem that addresses America directly: "I bring you the spoils, my nation / I, who went out in exile, / Am returned to thee with gifts."[42] Enriching Whitmanian form with the poet's transnational contact, "Epilogue" performs the synthesis that "A Pact" had promised. The sequence's final published version, however, ends not with "Epilogue" but "In A Station of the Metro." In the poem's whittled form, Pound does his promised "carving" of the raw materials offered by Whitman:

> The apparition   of these faces   in the crowd :
> Petals   on a wet, black   bough .

The poem is equally painterly—the faces and petals suggest dabs of color and light—and sculptural, with the wood of its bough and the demarcated spaces between its phrasal units. But this crafted poem is also an apparition, and, as Daniel Tiffany reminds us, "the content of the poem alludes to the Image as phantom, even as its mode of creation identifies it as an artifact."[43] Its colon and line break imply a metaphor, and in the switch from observation to description it dramatizes the "luminous detail" in action. Out of this crowd of people, a few faces "appear," as if by magic, to the mind capable of seeing them and interpreting their significance. Experience is distilled through a singular vision; the eye of the poem is set against the masses that it sees. "In a Station of the Metro" describes a crafted world not simply in its artisanal descriptions but also in the relations it draws between clear observation and description. In this sense, the turn of "In a Station of the Metro" is an instance of what Jessica Berman calls "resdescription," which she defines as "places where the text casts a new version of the world or intervenes in its unfolding in a manner that resists or revises social reality."[44] Pound's famous description of the poem's composition is relevant here. The idea came to him "not in speech, but in little blotches of color"; he writes of composing "a thirty-line poem," which he destroyed "because it was what we call work 'of second intensity.' Six months later I made a poem half that length; a year later I made the following hokku-like sentence."[45] Here, *craft labor* refers to both working with materials and, more importantly, singular intelligences acting on moments of sudden clarity. More than concerted activity, poetic labor concerns revelation, decision-making, and curation, which displace action and instead center the line of sight. Choosing to end the sequence with "In A Station of the Metro," then, signals a major turn: away from Whitman and his democratic vision and toward the singular revelations of the individual intelligence.

THE GLASSMAKERS

The first canto rewrites the *nekyia* of *The Odyssey*, in which Odysseus descends to the underworld to seek counsel from Tiresias, through its tellers and retellers, showing that the mastery of literary tradition, as T. S. Eliot wrote, is a matter not of passive inheritance but of tremendous labor.[46] Imploring Andreas Divus, the Renaissance translator of the epic into Latin, to "lie quiet," Pound assumes the place of both Divus and Odysseus. This literary labor is sublimated into the bodies of the sailors, who "set keel to breakers, forth on the godly seas, and / We set up mast and sail on that swart ship" (I, 3). This is a sea thick with gods, and the physical labors of the sailors are set against the magical work of the boat's maker, who is soon named: "Circe's this craft." This is the first time the word *craft* appears in the poem. It designates the boat but also carries the senses of the artisanal skill of boat-making and of Circe's powerful witchcraft. Triply burdened with meaning, craft always points to more than itself.

Pound's first serious effort to bring about an age of leisure for poets came in 1922 when, having recently arrived in Paris, he set about trying to extricate T. S. Eliot from his job at Lloyds Bank. In Pound's scheme, named "Bel Esprit," subscribers would pay an annual fee of ten pounds to ensure Eliot's financial security. The scheme aimed to put into practice the principles of C. H. Douglas, a former engineer whose books *Economic Democracy* and *Credit Power and Democracy* were serialized in *The New Age* in 1919 and 1920. Douglas argued that the most pressing economic and social problems could be traced to the rate of consumption and distribution of wealth.[47] For Douglas, unemployment was a sign of economic progress, not decay, because it freed people from the bonds of labor, and he frequently wrote against the social stigma attached to receiving unemployment benefits.[48] He proposed the establishment of a national dividend that would support both the unemployed and the free time of artists: "It is ... generally suggested that leisure, meaning by that, freedom from employment forced by economic necessity, is in itself detrimental; a statement which is fragrantly contradicted by all the evidence available on the subject. It is hardly an exaggeration to say that 75 percent of the ideas and inventions, to which mankind is indebted for such progress as has been so far achieved, can be directly traced to persons who by some means were freed from the necessity of regular, and in the ordinary sense, economic employment."[49] Douglas saw forced employment as a form of social control to be remedied by both monetary reform and the national dividend—a precursor to a universal basic income. In an article in *The New Age* in 1922, Pound justified his Bel Esprit scheme by citing Douglas's plans for the "release of more energy for invention and design" and writing that "the only thing one can give to an artist is leisure in which to work. To give an artist leisure is actually to take part in his creation."[50] Eliot was only to be the first liberated artist of many in a much larger program of reform, which Pound emphasized was "NOT charity" but an enactment of his "belief that the way to make a literature is to provide the few men capable of producing it with leisure."[51]

Eliot was embarrassed by the scheme and endeavored to have his name removed from Pound's plans. "Altogether the whole thing is very unsatisfactory," he wrote to Richard Aldington in June 1922. "The method proposed by Ezra is rather bordering on the precarious and slightly undignified charity."[52] When *The Liverpool Post* ran a story claiming that Eliot had accepted £800 from the scheme while maintaining his job at the bank, Eliot immediately threatened legal action and demanded (and received) a retraction from the paper.[53] He was equally perturbed by receiving an anonymous letter "enclosing 6d in stamps for the 'collection' which the writer had heard was being made for me" and complained to Pound, Woolf, Aldington, and Ottoline Morrell.[54] What would Pound's role have been if the scheme had worked? For Lawrence Rainey, Bel Esprit was part of a modernist "experiment in adopting exchange and market structures typical of the visual arts, a realm in which patronage and collecting can thrive because its artisanal mode of production is compatible with a limited submarket for luxury goods."[55] Pound wrote to Wyndham Lewis from Siena, Italy, in April 1922 that "if there aren't thirty or fifty people interested in literature, there is no civilization. & we may as well regard our work as a private luxury, having no aims but our own pleasure. You can't expect people to pay you for enjoying yourself."[56] Poetry is both a private luxury, capable of being produced and consumed by few people, but it is a luxury that creates "civilization." "It is for US who want good work, to provide means of its being done," Pound wrote to William Carlos Williams. "WE are the consumers and we demand somethg [sic] fit to consume."[57] Yet Pound's role in this scheme is not primarily as a consumer of poetry but as a patron. Pound, as Bel Esprit's director, provides the conditions under which poetry can be written.

This vision of the patron and tastemaker comes together in the figure of the quattrocento ruler and condottiero Sigismondo Malatesta. In May 1922, Pound visited the church of San Francesco in Rimini, also known as the *Tempio Malatestiano*, for the first time, a visit that would inspire a new block of cantos. Initially published as "Malatesta Cantos (Cantos IX to XII of a Long Poem)" in the July 1923 issue of *Criterion*, they were moved to the position of Cantos VIII to XI when they appeared in "A Draft of XVI Cantos" in January 1925.[58] Pound's Malatesta is a generous ruler who provides the conditions necessary for work and delights in the products of artistic labor. This Malatesta declares that "until the chapels are ready / I will arrange for him to paint something else / So that both he and I shall / Get as much enjoyment as possible from it" (VIII, 29). It is unsurprising that Pound writes this appreciation of apprenticeship into his early canto. Pound's Malatesta promises the craftsman payment of "so much per year," a pension "so that he may come to live the rest / Of his life in my lands," and freedom "so that he can work as he likes, / Or waste his time as he likes" (VIII, 29). The emphasis in these cantos is not on the artisan's labors but on Malatesta's policies—his labors. Malatesta's entry secures the idea that acts of provision and organization constitute meaningful and, in fact, superior work: "He, Sigismondo, *templum aedificavit*" (VIII, 32). Malatesta "began building the TEMPIO," Pound writes, a line that attributes the church's construction to its funder (IX, 35).[59] The line foreshadows how Pound would attribute the draining of the Pontine marshes near Rome to Mussolini, "having drained off the muck by Vada / From the marshes, by Circeo, where no one else wd. have drained it" (XLI, 202). Construction designates not labor performed by workers but an action directed by the efficient tyrant. In Canto VIII, Pound quotes from Plethon's description in *On the Events Among the Greeks After the Battle of Mantinea* of Plato's visit to Dionysius, tyrant of Syracuse, where Plato "had observed that tyrants / Were most efficient in all that they set their hands to" (VIII, 31).[60] The Malatesta cantos have commonly been read as a turning point in the poem's composition. In Hugh Kenner's description, the second canto in the sequence outlines two formal paths for the rest of the cantos: on one hand is the gathering of letters, on the other the construction of the church: "the one a clutch of documents proper to one's time, the other a deliberate concentration of pieties and traditions, the parts finely crafted."[61] The Malatesta cantos are thus a moment of two formal paths and two identifications: the poet is at once the apprentice craftsman, with freedom to create what he will, and Malatesta, the efficient tyrant.

"The parts finely crafted": Pound was often praised as a craftsman, or *fabbro*. Which of Pound's poems are "crafted"? Peter Brooker describes Pound's life in London as combining "a bardic sense of poetry's grand mission with a dedication to the craft of prosody."[62] If *craft* is a shorthand for versification, then the "crafted" line might mean the difference between "a tin flash in the sun-dazzle" (II, 7) and "on his return was recd. Gouverneur Morris and Mr Astor with a pubk. Dinner at Tammany Hall" (XXXIV, 167).

In *A Preface to Ezra Pound*, Peter Wilson writes of the "finely crafted lines" of Canto LII, by which he means lines such as "Now is cicada's time / the sparrow hawk offers birds to the spirits," not the violent antisemitism that dominates the canto's opening ("a further diatribe against usury among other things," as Wilson would have it) (LII, 260).[63] When Pound is anthologized, his lyric poems unsurprisingly tend to be overly represented; when Pound created his own anthologies, as Sean Pryor points out, he tended to include the less popular cantos.[64] Pound designated the paradisal cantos his "beauty spots": beautiful, yes, and perhaps defining, in the way that a beauty spot can distinguish an otherwise plain face, but aberrant. It is not only their prosody and their description of a paradise; the "finely crafted" label designates the poet's intention. This distinction allows readers to see the "uncrafted" lines as unintended or aberrant. But the Malatesta cantos make clear that the grab-bag selection of material is equally the product of a craft intelligence. For Pound, crafted poetry was the poetry of cure; for his readers, it is equally so. But when, as readers, we take on the role of physician and apply the principles of craft, what we are curing is not the social world but the poet.

I have suggested that Pound's theory of craft is a theory of looking—of the powerful eye of the dictator, expressed subtly in "In A Station of the Metro" and explicitly in the Malatesta cantos. That eye is embedded in, not incidental to, his "finely crafted" cantos, rather than being a metastatic growth of his later antisemitism. Take, for example, Canto XVII, undoubtedly one of the loveliest and most frequently anthologized. It was the only canto Yeats selected for inclusion in *The Oxford Book of Modern Verse*; in the Faber and Faber edition of Pound's *Selected Poems 1908–1969*, it is the only canto between XIV and XX, and it has the distinction of being reprinted in full rather than in excerpts. After navigating the stony, prosaic blocks of Malatesta's *tempio* and postbag and having fought our way through the waste and decrepitude of the hell cantos, Canto XVI gives us a glimpse into a paradise. We are walked through the "quiet air / the new sky" that surrounds the calm scene in which we find "the heroes / Sigismundo, and Malatesta Novello, / and founders, gazing at the mounts of their cities" (XVI, 69). But this is only a taster amid a *purgatorio*; we quickly move back to the First World War, where we will stay until the canto's end. The next canto begins "So that," returning us to the beginning that concludes the first canto and draws Odysseus out of the underworld.

"So that the vines burst from my fingers": the "So that" (meaning "thus" or "in this way") combined with the temporally unmarked "burst," both present and past tense, locate us in an immanent paradise. This poem has all the markers—the nymphs and goddesses, the shells and vines, the colored waves—that we come to associate with Pound's perfect worlds. This canto locates us in Venice, although it does not make that clear yet; it is "the good place," Donald Davie tells us, "a sort of heaven of cut and squared masonry."[65] The early lines of the canto guide us through a series of sensory and material encounters:

> So that the vines burst from my fingers
>   And the bees weighted with pollen
>   Move heavily in the vine shoots:
>   chirr——chirr—chirr-rikk—a purring sound,
>
> . . . .
> Flat water before me,
>   and the trees growing in water,
>
> . . . .
> And the water green clear, and blue clear;
> On, to the great cliffs of amber.
> (XVII, 76)

We touch, and our touch is so forceful that the vines burst; we hear bees; we see the flat and colored sea:

> Cave of Nerea,
>   she like a great shell curved,
> And the boat drawn without sound,
> Without odour of ship-work,
> Nor bird-cry, nor any noise of wave moving,
> Nor splash of porpoise, nor any noise of wave moving,
> Within her cave, Nerea,
>   she like a great shell curved
>
> (XVII, 76)

The poem's theophany is sculptural, the goddess "like a great shell curved" registers sculptural form as "curved" which collapses into "carved." There is no blank space in paradise; even when we are told that sound, odor, and noise are absent, the poem registers them anyway as "bird-cry," "splash," and returning waves. This canto works by forcing an encounter between contrary things: sound against silence, water against stone, waves against malachite and amber. Our senses are always running into one another.

Even the light—"the light not of the sun"—confounds. It might be internal, celestial, or simply reflected off another source, but the poem never tells. Even less certain is the withheld noun in "first pale-clear of the heaven." We may well assume that light is the agent most likely to be both pale and clear, which might clarify the mysterious providence of the "light not of the sun." But the floating "first pale-clear" might be something else, a cloud, perhaps, or something less material—a thought, an idea. These shifts and uncertainties of meaning extend to the materials that make up this paradise. We find "sand as of malachite" (is it fine and dry, or the glossy veined sand ridges of a low tide?) and the "trees growing in water, / Marble trunks out of stillness." The trees are the timber piles driven deep into the alluvial mud on which all of Venice is built. It is not the trees that are growing, then, but the city that grows on top of them. Donald Davie puts it this way, taking us back to the light not of the sun:

> Pound compresses into a single perception the whole process of the composition of marble from the incrustation of sunken timber by algae, through shell-encrusted cliff and cave, to the hewn stone of the palazzo with its feet in water. Thus "Marble trunks out of stillness" are balks of timber encrusted by limestone deposits, but they are no less ("On past the palazzi") the hewn columns of some Venetian portico, which is "the rock sea-worn" as well as the wood stone-encrusted. The light is said to be "not of the sun," and this for all sorts of reasons: because it is light as reflected off water in the open air or inside a cave or inside a Venetian portico, because it is light refracted through water when we imagine ourselves submerged along with the just-forming limestone.[66]

In Davie's reading, the "marble trunks out of stillness" are both limestone-encrusted timber foundations and marble columns, at once foundation and facade. They are both above and below the water, at once present and carrying the evidence of their past selves. Another reading is that there are two types of pillars: the "trees growing in water," which are the timber pillars, and the "marble trunks out of stillness," which are the porticos we see when, in the next line, we are carried above ground. In this reading, Pound moves us from material and foundation to finished craft. Davie's reading draws on the British art critic Adrian Stokes's 1934 book, *The Stones of Rimini*, about the Istrian marble used by Venetian builders and carvers. "Istrian stone," Stokes writes, "seems compact of salt's bright yet shaggy crystals. Air eats into it, the brightness remains. Amid the sea Venice is built from the essence of the sea."[67] We have just-forming limestone and a city that is made in and from seawater. Canto XVII does not so much present us with a formed paradise as show us its formation, just as it shows us the goddess Nerea being curved and carved from shell. Sean Pryor describes this as a lack, writing that there is "something absent about this shifting otherworld, something not yet achieved."[68] For Kenner, it is less a question of incompleteness than of something partially withheld from view; he writes that the canto gives us "a congeries of gleaming and glancing effects which we are never allowed to see except in mist or by night."[69] However, I see this canto not as registering lack or incompleteness but as insisting on process. As we are taken calmly through Venetian waters, we are submerged in the gradual, material, and mystical creation of this world.

If this is a world being made, then who are its makers? Late in the canto we encounter two fifteenth-century men, "Borso, Carmagnola, the men of craft, *i vitrei*." The "men of craft" are also men of statecraft, and we hear an echo of the obsolete use of *craft* as strength, might, or force, still extant in the modern German *Kraft*. To be a "man of craft" is less to work individually with any of the poem's materials, its malachite or marble, than to bring a world, Venice, into being through state power and force. Borso and Carmagnola are not just men of craft, they are *i vitrei*, the glassmakers. It is a powerful designation, a particular kind of *fabbro* that sits heavily and authoritatively at the end of the line and identifies the men with Murano glass, central to the Venetian economy. It also repeats the elision between the powerful man and the worker: the men did not make glass; they made an economy built on the production and sale of glass. We have shifted here from Istrian stone to Murano glasswork, which, as Stokes (and Davie) remind us, is also from and of the sea; as Stokes writes, "Venetian glass, compost of Venetian sand and water, expresses the taut curvature of the cold undersea, the slow, oppressed, yet brittle curves of dimly translucent water."[70] We are in a world where made things resemble the material from which they are made. *I vitrei* designates a unity of the social and the natural orders.

Thus, *i vitrei* has a more powerful meaning: the men are social visionaries. Peter Liebregts writes that the term designates "those who translate and transpose the divine, crystal vision into earthly reality through art," and he cites a typescript draft of the poem that insists on this fact more clearly:

> the light with the eye's light
> in one moment,
> as the glass blower puts forth his sphere
> light as air in the glass
> but as glass fixed, so is memory perfect
> hic sapienza, hic amor,
> so set in the record / a sphere, bright and translucent[71]

The glass sphere is gorgeously evocative: the glassblower-craftsman is not just a maker of objects but a crafter of globes, of entire worlds in miniature. In much later cantos, glass and crystal mean visionary sight: "Light & the flowing crystal / never gin in cut glass had such clarity / That Drake saw the splendour and wreckage / in that clarity / Gods moving in crystal" (XCI, 631); "the crystal, / a green yellow flash after sunset" (C, 738). In the Pisans, the crystal sphere offers talismanic protection: "the sphere moving crystal, fluid, / none therein carrying rancour / Death, insanity / suicide degeneration" (LXXVI, 477). The associations between crystal, glass, sudden clarity, and warding off mental degeneration are soldered to the principles of clear design and insight that Pound admires in Malatesta, "as the sculptor sees the form in air . . . / as glass seen under water" (XXV, 119).

Canto XXVII is a *paradiso*, so it must also be a tomb. Borso is attacked with arrows by the Serenissima, and Carmagnola is publicly executed. The canto ends with an elegiac image: "sunset like the grasshopper flying" (XVII, 79). We will encounter Venice and its "masters of wool cloth / Glass makers in scarlet" again in Canto XXVI, when the city succumbs to "the vice of luxuria" (XXVI, 122), and the world of *i vitrei* collapses. Pound's crafted worlds—his paradises—should be perfect. But they never quite arrive at what Louis Zukofsky termed the "perfect rest" that the lyric poem can attain, even though they seem to offer it.[72] Pound offers us images for clarity beyond the glass seen underwater. Chrysoprase, a kind of gemstone chalcedony that appears early in the canto, is rendered as "Chrysophrase," perhaps to underscore writing: "Chrysophrase, / And the water green clear, and blue clear" (XVII, 76). But just as the process of glassmaking—heating sand until it melts, then reshaping the molten material into its new form—reshapes the elemental foundations on which our world rests, so, too, do the crossed sensory wires of this canto unsettle sound, liquid, and solid matter. Trying to make a resolved object of this canto will fail for the poem is not, after all, primarily interested in crafted objects. What it is interested in is crafted worlds. It doesn't describe glass objects; rather, it uses the language of artisanal making to write a crafted Venice. If craft has always brought poetics and world-making together, here we see it become more fully social. We have moved from the momentary sight of imagism, the sudden flash, to the articulated social world. Craft, too, attaches itself to a lost unity of social organization and natural order, which has since been displaced by the degeneracy of the present. We are beginning to see a fuller articulation of craft as a return to a mythical past, and as the dream of a new world made under a tyrannical eye.

WORKSHOP ORCHESTRATION

Working our way through Pound's series of dictatorial figures can feel like unpacking a set of nested dolls: inside Malatesta is Confucius; inside Confucius is John Adams; and the central doll, of course, is always Mussolini. In the mid-1920s, Pound turned his attention to the organization of factory labor under scientific management, which briefly added another doll to the collection. In the December 1926 issue of *New Masses*, the major cultural organ of the Communist Party USA, a small feature was printed under the optimistic title "Pound Joins the Revolution!" The piece reprinted a letter Pound wrote to one of the magazine's founding editors, Mike Gold, expressing Pound's interest in the journal and asking for a copy of John Reed's *Ten Days That Shook the World*, Scott Nearing's *Dollar Diplomacy*, "or whatever you think most necessary for my education."[73] Pound's next piece for *New Masses*, "Workshop Orchestration," speculated about the aesthetic possibilities of bringing music into the factory, an idea that

Pound modeled on George Antheil's score for Fernand Léger's film *Ballet Mécanique*. In "Workshop Orchestration," Pound envisages the noise of a modern factory arranged into work songs and sea chanteys: "Say there are forty small stamping presses in a room, let them start not one at a time, raggedly, but kk! on the snap of the baton; and stop, and then the periods of sound grow gradually longer, and the rests ever so slightly longer in proportion, but so graduated that the difference of ten seconds in the rest is a sensible, appreciable division."[74] The article is distinctly Pound's in that factory labor becomes an occasion for the forging of new aesthetic forms. For Pound, the factory provides an opportunity for artists to experiment with the medium of sound and with aesthetic arrangement, which is framed as a process of social betterment. He goes on to argue that "the men at the machines shall be demechanized, and work not like robots, but like the members of an orchestra."[75] The piece was received coolly, and Pound's relationship with Gold declined thereafter.

In the same year that he published "Workshop Orchestration," Pound wrote the first draft of "Machine Art," a longer essay that makes a techno-optimistic argument about the ability of machines "to eliminate work and produce leisure."[76] "Machine Art" outlines two lessons that can be learned from machines. The first is separation and delineation into ever more particular and precise parts. Certain machines, like the machine press built by the E. W. Bliss Company, offer lessons in clear and efficient organization "because each press seems intent on its one particular job" (*MA*, 69). "The necessity," Pound writes, "is to keep one's different ideas from barging into one another" (*MA*, 69). The second is the arrangement of these separate elements into a harmonious whole. These are the lessons of scientific management's division of labor, which breaks the labor process into concise operations that together form a rationalized total process, applied to art. "When I consider the disagreeable noises I have heard in factories," Pound writes, "it seems to me that they are mainly disagreeable for one sole reason, namely that they are not organized" (*MA*, 73).[77] The hero of this essay is not the individual member of the factory-orchestra, but the arranger or conductor, embodied in the figure of Henry Ford. "I have no reason to disguise my interest in either his theories or his practice," Pound writes. "*He has already experimented in tempo*" (*MA*, 81, emphasis in the original). Scientific management's organization of time grants industrial labor the rhythm of music. What matters is that factory labor can be perfected if properly organized under the hand of the conductor-engineer. The "engineering mind" is praised as "the most satisfactory mind of our time" (*MA*, 78), a living version of the dynamic and active parts of the machine with which the essay began, who is also simultaneously the craftsman. The engineer also becomes a modern craftsman.[78] But he quickly moves to tyranny. Declared "biologically preferable to the bureaucrat," with his "rust and fungus," in an image that draws on earlier language of "hygiene" and channels the fascist insistence on the decay of the present, the tyrant "has in him some principle of life and action" (*MA*, 78). That emphasis on action chimes with a fascist anti-intellectualism and recasts the industrial engineer as a figure of exemplary masculinity against the emasculation of the bureaucrat. Soon after, Pound will begin describing Mussolini as an engineer, builder, or craftsman. "I don't believe any estimate of Mussolini will be valid unless it starts from his passion for construction," he declares in *Jefferson and/or Mussolini*. "Treat him as *artifex* and all the details fall into place. Take him as anything save the artist and you will get muddled with contradictions."[79] Later in the book Pound quotes Mussolini in their meeting: "The secret of the Duce is possibly the capacity to pick out the element of immediate and minor importance in any tangle; or, in the case of a man, to go straight to the centre. . . . 'Why do you want to put your ideas in order?'"[80] Mussolini appears as the human embodiment of the Bliss press, artist and machine in one.

Throughout the period that Pound wrote with admiration of Ford and scientific management, he had been reading Marx, but by the mid-1930s his flirtation with Marxism had come to an end. In *Jefferson and/or Mussolini*, Pound wrote that "Marxian economics were invented in a time when labor was necessary, when a great deal of labor was still necessary and his, Marx's, values are based on labor."[81] Convinced that technological advancement had greatly reduced the physical work involved in production—he took this idea from Douglas and found its "proof" in scientific management—Pound rejected Marx's version of the labor theory of value and his account of capitalist accumulation in favor of Douglas's idea of "cultural heritage": "that is, the great aggregate of mechanical inventions, improved seed and agricultural methods AND even civilised habits."[82] In Douglas's idea he found a model for a paternalistic and nationalist theory of cultural inheritance that displaced socially necessarily labor time and eclipsed the social relations of labor. Pound describes this using a craft analogy, writing in *ABC of Economics* that "Marxian economics deals with goods for sale, goods in the shop. The minute I cook my own dinner or nail four boards together into a chair, I escape the whole cycle of Marxian economics."[83] Peter Nicholls suggests that the main problem with this shift in Pound's thought is his failure to understand the social relations of production or the conversion of concrete into abstract labor.[84] The systemic thinking of Marxism forecloses on the idea of the individual who, by virtue of their intelligence and resourcefulness, can "escape the whole cycle." Pound relegates socially necessary labor to a historical, pretechnological past; at the same time, "cultural heritage" affirms a fascist ideal of civilizational progress. Pound's rejection of Marxism on the grounds of rejecting the social relations of labor is a significant moment in his turn to authoritarian individualism.

One persistent problem with Pound's economic thought, in Nicholls's view, is his "explicit recasting of fiscal problems as ethical ones."[85] This was an old problem, and Pound's declaration in 1935 that "you cannot make good economics out of bad ethics" mirrors his statement from two decades before in "The Serious Artist" that good art is ethical art.[86] It is frequently observed that Marx's main influence on Pound was as a historian, but Pound was just as attracted to Marx as an ethicist.[87] Take Canto XXXIII, which excerpts and modifies material from chapters 13 and 15 of *Capital*. Pound compresses a passage concerned with a parliamentary report from 1842 on the uses of child labor in English industry: "limits of his individuality (cancels) and develops his power as a specie. (Das Kapital) denounced in 1842 still continue (today 1864) report of '42 was merely chucked into the archives and remained there while these boys were ruined and became fathers of this generation" (XXXIII, 162). Child labor was a moral fixation for Pound. In 1913, when he was quarreling with Harriet Monroe about the "Contemporania" poems, Pound threatened to expand his lines about exploitation for "child labor requires a villanelle all of its own."[88] But this is the Pound of the 1930s, so instead of a villanelle we have a column of prose. Pound includes several more extracts from *Capital* on the abusive labor of children in factories and the legislation surrounding it, especially the law of 1848 which "limited" the work of "young persons" to ten hours a day (XXXIII, 163).[89] Why this passage, and why child labor (of all the industrial abuses detailed in *Capital*)? The answer, I think, is the sentence "These boys were ruined and became fathers of this generation." Child labor interrupts generational progress—it disrupts historical transmission and taints patrimony and thus constitutes for Pound a form of usury, which "slayeth the child in the womb" (XLV, 230). *Capital* enters the text not as history but as ethics to shore up the healthy lineage and patrimony of the good society.

One of Pound's ciphers for the worker-artisan and an exemplary "man of action" draws these ideas of lineage together: Thaddeus Coleman Pound, the poet's grandfather and a lumberman, railroad builder, and politician who represented Wisconsin's Eighth Congressional District in the U.S. House of Representatives. In an installment of "Patria Mia" (1912), Pound compares nineteenth-century railway workers with "the present type," a comparison he frames as a degradation of masculinity: "The type of man who built railways, cleared the forest, planned irrigation, is different from the type of man who can hold on to the profits of subsequent industry. Whereas this first man was a man of dreams, in a time when dreams paid, a man of adventure, careless—this latter is a close person, acquisitive, rapacious, tenacious. The first man had personality, and was, 'god damn you,' himself. . . . The present type is primarily a mask, his ideal is the nickel-plated cash register."[90] In an article in *The New Age* from 1920, Pound identifies Thaddeus as one of the "particularly-efficient super-laborers" who are "the trump cards in Capital's hand," and, moreover, in a distinctly Poundian conflation, artists: "A man may enjoy creating a railroad or a factory exactly as he may enjoy creating a poem or a picture."[91] In 1924 Pound requested information about the U.S. presidents from his father, Homer Pound, who responded by sending him material from his grandfather's scrapbook. For Pound, the tragedy of Thaddeus is that he was gazumped by more adept capitalists who thwarted his railway ambitions. That railway misadventure opens Canto XXII: "An' that man sweat blood / to put through that railway / And what he ever got out of it?" before "the other type, Warenhauser," the American "Lumber King" "beat him, and broke up his business" (XXII, 101).[92] In a 1942 radio speech, Pound returns to his grandfather: "I said last time that my grandad had been in it before me. Said this was MY war, and that my granddad had been in it before me. And we were and ARE BOTH on the same side. Last time I saw the old man, I must have been about twelve years of age. I can still see him settin' in our so called library in Wyncote in a big spring rockin' chair, facin' a funny patent iron coal grate that was under my greatgrandma's picture."[93] Pound recasts capitalist accumulation as an antifamilial, nongenetic form of growth, similar to his fixation on "usura, sin against nature," which "slayeth the child in the womb" and "lyeth / between the young bride and her bridegroom" (XLV, 229, 230). In the folksy hearthside scene of the radio speech, Pound positions himself as the natural heir to Thaddeus's "war." In the figure of Thaddeus, Pound's radical anticapitalism becomes a matter of patrilineal inheritance. Pound's fantasy of paternal inheritance calls back to the "biologically preferable" engineering mind and so leads us back to the "hygiene" practiced by the serious artist. Thaddeus, another of Pound's nesting dolls, crystallizes a fantasy of untrammeled masculine and white heritage. This emphasis on natural lineage and familial inheritance also signals what I will describe for the remainder of this chapter: Pound's abstraction of his anticapitalism poetics of craft into a vision of an integrated natural world.

CONFUCIANS OBSERVE THE WEATHER

Reading Pound means encountering innumerable inconsistencies and contradictions. One part of his thinking, however, was consistent: his wholesale commitment to Italian fascism. That commitment cannot be written off as a "stupid suburban prejudice," as Pound famously described his antisemitism in a weak mea culpa to Allen Ginsberg; it was, after all, nurtured for decades in the heart of Mussolini's dictatorship. Nor can it be forgiven as one of the "errors and wrecks" of *Drafts & Fragments* (CXVI, 816). I have suggested that the seeds of Pound's fascism were sown in the craft poetics of his early poetry, well before his explicit support for Mussolini. Many in his early intellectual milieu followed a similar path. Several of Pound's fellow contributors to *The New Age* drew a straight line from guild socialism to Italian fascism, and Tim Redman has shown that the magazine provided Pound with an early education in antisemitism.[94] In 1923, Odon Por described Mussolini's corporate state as "a formidable Labor Movement with numerous Trade Unions, Co-operatives and Guilds."[95] A. J. Penty similarly argued that "the Corporate State is only another name for the Regulative Guild State."[96] Like Por and Penty, Pound, in 1939, would advocate "state-controlled pools of raw products and the restoration of guild organization in industry."[97] By the late 1930s, Pound saw Italian fascism as a successful version of Britain's failed guilds.[98]

I want to end this chapter by looking at a central feature of Pound's late thinking about labor: the natural world and its cultivation through agriculture. The mythic figure of the farmer was an important one for the Italian fascists. For the 1937 and 1938 *Battle for Grain* series of propaganda images, Mussolini was filmed and photographed bare-chested and wearing a flat cap, standing among farmers or threshing grain.[99] For Pound, agriculture came to signify more than the means of sustaining life; it meant the natural economic order. Pound's campaign against the "unnatural" effects of usury ("wool comes not to market / sheep bringeth no gain with usura" [XLV, 229]) was part of a broader attraction to ostensibly "natural" monetary forms. Significant in this regard was Pound's reading of the German economist Silvio Gesell's book *The Natural Economic Order*, in which Gesell developed his idea of *Schwundgeld*, or stamp scrip. The holder of *Schwundgeld* notes was obliged to attach small stamps to the notes at regular intervals that would force the money to depreciate regularly. Stamp scrip was supposed to turn currency into any other degradable natural form to disincentivize accumulation. As a direct tax on money, the plan was intended to encourage free spending and consumption because to amass the notes would mean that they would decrease in value. In his late poems, Pound turns to examples of cyclical repetition and ritualistic rejuvenation as economic models that preserve natural rhythms and forestall accumulation. In Canto CVIII, he cites the English Renaissance jurist Edward Coke's proposal for taxation: "That grosbois is oak, ash, elm, / beech, horsbeche & hornbeam / but of acorns tithe shall be paid" (CVIII, 789). The great timber trees Pound cites cannot be used as a tithe because they grow so slowly; acorns, in contrast, "renue yearly" and so can be used as a tithe without doing violence against nature.[100] As with taxation, so, too, does Pound look to work that is "informed by task rather than clock," as Ian F. A. Bell observes in an insightful essay that puts the middle cantos into conversation with E. P. Thompson's classic essay on time and work discipline.[101] For Pound, a day governed by sun and land, not by clock and factory, at once provides the time-release necessary for making art and constitutes an integrated, living artwork.

We see this in the middle of *The Fifth Decad of Cantos*, published in 1937, when we enter an idyllic world where labor and leisure are harmoniously balanced. Known as the "Seven Lakes Canto," Canto LXIX adapts the contents of a "screen book" owned by Pound's parents and given to the poet in 1928. The album contained eight ink paintings of the Xiao and Xiang Rivers in central South China, each flanked by a Chinese poem on the left and a Japanese translation on the right.[102] Of the cantos, the "Seven Lakes

Canto" is the closest descendant of *Cathay*, with its painterly landscape descriptions. A typescript draft of the poem insists on this inheritance more clearly than the final version:

> Wild   geese   on   the   sand   bar
>   as   it   were   more   snow   at   their
> Bullrushes ,   have burst into snow-tops   on their heads
> ~~Milky jade~~ film covers ~~it all~~
> All thus covered with jade , a film of
>   whitish film ,
>   The water congeals   ,   Sai Yin ,
>   men or sain yin,
> are unhurried.
>
> as   if   a   jade   film
> all   as if all inside a jade ~~bar~~ block
>
>   water as if congealed
> As if the water congeals ,
>   the men of Sai Yin
>   are unhurried.[103]

This world is encased in a "jade film," a "whitish film"; precious white jade is the binding agent of this world, where we exist "as if inside a jade ~~bar~~ block." The repetition of "congeals" builds on the "whitish" and "milky" jade. But this is "water as if congealed," that is, water that is turning solid or becoming ice; thus, the film of whitish jade comes to mean a layer of ice or snow. Pound has frozen his idyll in time, and through it men move slowly, "unhurried." In another typescript, that line would become "at San Yin / they are a people for leisure," and in the final published poem it was modified to just "a people of leisure" (XLIX, 244).[104] The slowness with which these lines move, always repeating and turning back on themselves, traces the slow movement of the men down the river. This is the "age of leisure" that Pound envisioned, where work and leisure are organized according to natural rhythms and equally balanced: "Sun up; work / sundown; to rest" (XLIX, 245). Covering all of this is the film of milky white jade, encasing the world in beauty but also partially obscuring it.

In the "Seven Lakes Canto," Pound joined a number of other white writers who saw China as an agrarian paradise that preserved an unbroken connection between people and land. In his 1942 preface to Tsui Chi's *A Short History of Chinese Civilisation*, Laurence Binyon writes that "at the core of [the Chinese] civilization is a great love of nature," which is "expressed in the peasant's intimate trust in the 'good earth.'"[105] In the opening lines of the China cantos, published in 1940, Pound writes an origin myth of Chinese agrarianism:

> Fou Hi taught men to grow barley
> 2837 ante Christum
> and they know still where his tomb is
> by the high cypress between the strong walls.
> the FIVE grains, said Chin Nong, that are
> wheat, rice, millet, *gros blé* and chick peas
> and made a plough that is used five thousand years
> (LIII, 262)

Agriculture is figured as the original form of labor taught by the legendary emperors. The men that Fou Hi instruct in the first line become the men of today who "still know where his tomb is," and this is less a tomb than a living lineage for the plough has been "used five thousand years." Later in Canto LIII, we are brought forward to the twentieth century: "black earth is fertile, wild silk still is from Shantung / Ammassi, to the provinces / let his men pay tithes in kind," Pound writes, making reference to the fascist Charter of Labor (LII, 262–63). Here, Pound compares the fascist policy of *ammassi*, the mandatory requisitioning and stockpiling of cereals, to the fixed 10 percent tax rate of the nine-fields system used in China in 500 and 400 BCE. Both are forms of early economic intervention to manage production and distribution, which appealed to Pound as measures to thwart capitalist accumulation. Pound extends this rhyme on ancient China and fascist Italian agrarian policy into his description of Confucius as a model of ethical efficiency. In *Guide to Kulchur*, Pound praises Confucius for being "interested in increasing agricultural production" but also "against . . . sweating and speeding-up systems."[106] For Pound, China appears as both a mirror of Mussolini's corporate state and a kind of precapitalist agrarian idyll, before the wheels of accumulation were really set in motion. When

Pound moves from the eighteenth-century China of the China cantos to the revolutionary America of the Adams cantos, he implicitly compares the two countries. Pound believed that in contrast with the burgeoning capitalism taking place in America and already well underway in Europe, that economic system in China would be thwarted and not grow to maturity. Pound's use for China ends in the eighteenth century; the Chinese history cantos stop with the reign of Yong Tching and an idyllic vision of a precapitalist mode of production.[107] This China is a paradise but one with the benefit of being both historical and contemporary: at once preserved in amber and still functioning, untouched.

In his introduction to *The Oxford Book of Modern Verse*, W. B. Yeats wrote of Pound's method of history that there "is no transmission through time, we pass without comment from ancient Greece to modern England, from modern England to medieval China; the symphony, the pattern, is timeless, flux eternal and therefore without movement."[108] This method of history as eternal and frozen rhymes with the fascist theory of history on display at the *Mostra della rivoluzione fascista*, the first Exhibition of the Fascist Revolution, which opened in Rome in October 1932. In December 1932, Pound became one of the 3.8 million visitors to the *Mostra*, an experience he recorded in Canto LXVI.[109] The *Mostra* contained exhibits on farming and industry that smoothed over their specific moment of historical development. Modern machinery was linked to the past and compared to ancient Roman weapons, arranged in machinelike forms.[110] With the aim of showcasing the achievements of the first decade of Italian fascism, the *Mostra* "confused past and present as history became an explosion of images, relics and symbols. Chronology fell prey to the trajectory of national fulfillment. Nationhood, declared the *Mostra*, would be forged from the swirling images of the past."[111] Pound's syncretic view of history and the paratactic movements of *The Cantos* reflects a fascist politics that, as Harry Harootunian puts it in an essay about the fascisms of our present, is "free to imagine a fictional or fantasy temporality" that invokes "an archaic and anachronistic present."[112]

Pound's turn to agriculture marks a turn away from the present and from modern labor processes—we are far from the Pound who attentively read the industrial engineer Dexter S. Kimball. As Richard Sieburth observes, "*The Cantos* deals so predominantly with agrarian societies because these preindustrial economies allow Pound to subsume labor and production under natural process."¹¹³ Agrarian societies and the natural world are important touchstones for 1956's *Section: Rock-Drill* and 1959's *Thrones*. In the late cantos, the natural world becomes a model for work that takes place over time, as if Pound is justifying the lateness of these poems:

> in pochi,
> > causa motuum,
> > > pine seed splitting cliff's edge.
>
> Only sequoias are slow enough.
> > BinBin "is beauty".
>
> "Slowness is beauty."

(LXXXVII, 592)

BinBin is Binyon, whose lectures on East Asian art Pound attended in London in 1909. Donald Davie suggests that these lines designate "the few who are 'causa motuum', by processes as gradual as those by which a pine splits the edge of a cliff or by which the sequoia grows, are men who originate ideas as well as men who create art."¹¹⁴ *Thrones* regularly refers back to the need to "build pen yeh," which Pound glosses as "a developed skill from persistence," and it allows itself the time and space to develop that skill. It also reminds us that even as late as the 1950s, it is necessary to continue cultivating that skill, to keep building upward from the root. Like the annual harvests and repeated rituals described by the poem, so, too, do Pound's cantos and his *pen yeh* build gradually, year after year. The late cantos turn to ritual and repetition, such as the *Sheng Yu* ("Sacred Edict"), which is read aloud "each year in the Elder Spring," as we are told in Cantos XCVIII and XCIX. Temporally, at least, the late poems land us in the congealed world of ritual of the "Seven Lakes Canto."

Images of slowness and persistence recur in *Thrones*. In Canto CVI:

> So slow is the rose to open.
> (CVI, 772)

> So late did queens rise into heaven.
> (CVI, 775)

We are far from sudden flashes of insight and clarity; we have traded swiftness for patience. The rose opens slowly; the queens—in this case, Arsinoe II of Egypt—rise late into heaven. Canto CVI is a late canto that knows its own lateness, and lateness and slowness go hand in hand.[115] The sound patterning of the canto's opening, far from the heroic rhythms of the early cantos, is part of what Massimo Bacigalupo has called the late poems' "microscopic feasts."[116] The four repeated long vowels in "So slow is the rose to open" (so/slow/rose/open) knit the line together and make the opening of Canto CVI a self-contained world. This is the line about the slow opening rose in situ:

> AND was her daughter like that;
> Black as Demeter's gown,
>   eyes, hair?
> Dis' bride, Queen over Phlegethon,
>   girls faint as mist about her?
>
> The strength of men is in grain.   管   Kuan
> NINE decrees, 8th essay, the Kuan   子   Tzu
>
> So slow is the rose to open.
> (CVI, 772)

The canto's two main sources are the Eleusinian mystery rites and the *Kuan-Tzu*, a major work of pre-Han economic theory that strongly influenced Confucius and was introduced to Pound through his correspondence with the Chinese poet and scholar Tze-chiang Chao.[117] From Demeter, Persephone, and the misty girls of the underworld of the opening lines, we move to the strength of men contained within grain and, by implication, within these ancient economic books. These opening lines return us to the ongoing motif of *Thrones* of the "black shawls for Demeter," which harks back to the time Pound spent in Venice in 1908, years before the rise of Mussolini when the black shawls of ritual were replaced with the Blackshirts of fascism. The two modes—the faint, feminine, and mythical versus the strong, masculine, and concrete—are weighed against each other. Where one, "faint as mist," is uncertain, a series of questions with indeterminate pronouns (who is the "her" of the first line? What is "like that"?), the other has all the authority and precision of an essay and decree. "The strength of men is in grain," we are told in a heavy, monosyllabic line that provides the firm authority lacking in the opening lines. It contrasts against a differently gendered line from Canto LIV ("earth is the nurse of all men") while simultaneously echoing a line from Canto XCIX ("ability as grain in the wheat-ear") and reformulating and concretizing a metaphor from Canto CII ("barley is the marrow of men"). But the ultimate effect is one of integration. The *Kuan-Tzu* shores up the misty girls, while the girls of the underworld turn cultivation into a ritual.

The canto incorporates contemporary time into this world of myth and ritual. "This is grain rite," we are told twice:

> That the goddess turn crystal within her
> This is grain rite
> Luigi in the hill path
> this is grain rite
>
> (CVI, 773)

Carroll Terrell identifies Luigi as the "hunchbacked peddler" Pound saw performing the mystery rites in Rapallo.[118] Luigi is a living anachronism, emblematic of the "non-contemporaneity" that, Ernst Bloch argues, fascism synthesizes in its visions of an unrealized past and hopes for the future.[119] But Luigi does not wrench us out of the past and into the present, or out of myth and into the real, so much as reaffirm that the world as it currently is is also the world of myth. Peter Nicholls suggests that in its later stages, Pound's long poem "begins to turn in on itself, spinning around its own axis to create a purely self-reflecting world."[120] The natural world becomes one of the late poems' mirrors, reflecting the poem's values rather than offering it new material. What is so striking about the late cantos is not that representations of laboring bodies and models for poetic work are absent but that they are present while still elided, disappearing into myth. Despite frequent references to gathering or harvesting and despite the poet's pleas to the goddess of agriculture, labor in the late poems has a less firm presence than in the earlier cantos. Agrarian labor becomes for Pound a kind of idyll: not really work at all but a cultural and religious inheritance, a lineage from the *Kuan-Tzu* through the mystery rites to the present, which is figured in Luigi's atavistic appearance.

The mythic agrarian leads naturally into another favored image of composition and form in the late cantos: the "veined phyllotaxis" of Canto CVI, the mathematically precise arrangement of leaves around a stem to maximize their energy and sunlight intake, which results in extraordinary patterns and fractals in certain plants (CVI, 774). In Pound's late cantos, Hugh Kenner writes, "the precision of natural renewal has replaced the cut stone of the early cantos."[121] The attraction of phyllotactic precision is that its perfection is not worked at but innate, that it is not conscious labor at all but pure formal precision. This is an extreme development of Pound's earlier ideas of spontaneous insight. The "luminous detail" needed a mind to see it; phyllotaxis is a natural law. If removal from the hand to the eye was the first step in craft's mystification, the move from the eye to nature is its climax. And as an operation in nature, phyllotaxis claims an unimpeachable authority.

Knowing Pound's desire for overarching poetic models, we might be tempted to read phyllotaxis as just such a model for the late poems' form. But we would be forgiven for finding mathematical precision difficult to square with the jagged, paratactic textures of *Rock-Drill* and *Thrones*. The late cantos have attracted few fans; Nicholls observes that they are "the part of the poem that even dedicated readers like least."[122] For Pound's more hostile readers, this is in part because the late poems feel insufficiently worked or crafted (Pound's single redeeming feature, after all, was always the fineness of his ear and eye). In an early review of *Rock-Drill*, Dudley Fitts described not only the visual forms of the late cantos, their Chinese characters and musical notations, but also the spatial arrangement of the poems as consisting of "romantic doodles—like the compulsions of a man so fascinated by the contours of a Greek word that he is constantly jotting it down on envelopes and tablecloths."[123] Randall Jarrell suggested that the volume was made up of "indiscriminate notes," and in a 1960 review of *Thrones* John Wain suggested that "to call the Cantos a long poem is perhaps stretching the word 'poem'" for "a good deal of the Cantos, as one leafs through them page by page, consists of notebook jottings and other material which bears no relationship to verse."[124] Wain describes the late cantos as having "fewer lyrical passages and more doodling" and argues that the experience of reading them "is like listening through the keyhole to some grand old scholar, working on a vast theory of history, muttering to himself as he moves about his study, trying to put his hand on the right book, repeating dates and quotations to himself, suddenly bursting into oratory."[125] It is a remarkable image of a poetic life. The note-like quality of the late poems derives in part from their adoption of the principle of collecting on a larger scale, with each line functioning as a thing chosen and put on display. The labor that has gone into them is primarily the labor of reading and research, but the intermediary process of crafting them into objects of beauty has seemingly thinned. Part of the complaint is that the primary unit of meaning in the late poems is the individual line phrase, beyond which the poems are no longer as closely woven together as they once were. We cannot "resolve these different measures in one transcendent and all-unifying prosody," as Nicholls writes of *Thrones*.[126] But the principle of continual and seemingly undifferentiated paratactic fragmentation creates its own logic and subsumes the artifice of worked poetic form into the natural.

In its turn toward a mythologized agrarian world, Pound's late poetry represents a shift in his understanding of work: from the crafting of objects to gathering, harvesting, and collecting. This is less a way of working on the world around us than of following its lead: "Confucians," he writes in Canto XCIX, "observe the weather" (XCIX, 722). Earlier I compared Pound's later cantos with the operations of the Fascist exhibitions. In the fragmented forms of the late cantos, labor is mythologized; it becomes not an act or process but almost a religious rite, as in the *Mostra*, where the "simultaneity and timelessness of most of the displays spiritualized the history depicted."[127] The late cantos integrate the suddenness of a historical shift, a movement from the fascist present to ancient China, by freezing it in the time of ritual. This dynamic of suddenness and stability also explains why, in Pound's later poems, the Chinese character becomes so important, being incorporated as not just a structural principle but also a medium of representation. Critics have frequently noted the visual appeal of the ideograms, suggesting that they bring the late cantos closer to the condition of visual art than of poetry.[128] While Pound devoted more energy while in St. Elizabeths to studying the vocal qualities of Chinese, the ideogram remained for him a more directly painterly means of representation than the Latin alphabet ever could be. Within the tonal fluctuations and uneven texture of the late poems, the Chinese character becomes the equivalent of the still life of Pound's earlier-crafted lines, puncturing the surface of the poem with a self-sufficient and stable form. But the character is also a natural form for Pound; each individual character "is based upon a vivid shorthand picture of the operations of nature," which offers its own kind of efficiency of representation.[129] The Chinese character appeals to Pound as a timeless or unchanging medium in the same way that China comes to represent a precapitalist agrarian society in which the land was central to all aspects of society and agricultural labor was part of an organic whole. The cultivation and observation of the natural world comes to signify for Pound a kind of pure, thoroughly abstracted labor, barely labor at all.

At the end of this chapter, we are far from where we began; a reader handed "Contemporania" and *Thrones* might assume they were the work of an altogether different poet. Yet the late poems operate on the same principles that Pound articulated in the early 1910s. The theory of the image as a "complex" guides the constellated fragments of the late poems; the artist who selects and presents details without commentary is working here. Pound's emphasis on insight and selection is precisely what underpins the fragmented selections of the late poems, and his early emphasis on "hygiene" is woven into his emphasis on natural forms and rhythms. Craft's abstraction, then, is the result of its extreme development, and we have traced less a change in Pound's thought than we have observed its calcification. Writing about Pound's relationship with visual culture, Rebecca Beasley observes that in some scholarly discussions, "Pound's engagement with the visual arts has become evacuated of its history, existing only as a repository of analogies to be manipulated at will."[130] Something similar has happened to Pound's engagement with labor, but if as readers we find a series of elastic analogies, then the blame is equally to be laid at Pound's feet. Nor should we see that elasticity as accidental or incidental. Indeed, the elasticity of craft and its willingness to appear under so many guises are precisely the point. Mystification is useful; mystification justifies and naturalizes a position of authoritarianism by reassigning it to the operations of nature. By following Pound's line of thinking around craft, we can see how what emerged in the late nineteenth century as an alternative to the alienation and exploitation of labor under capitalism—and is still widely understood as such—becomes, perversely, one of the major aesthetic modes of dictatorial fascism in the twentieth century. "Go in fear of abstractions," Pound told us in 1913.[131] In that case, at least, he was right.

Chapter Two

THE SOCIAL LIFE OF SEWING
Lola Ridge

> Every morning I wake up with a renewed commitment
> to learning to be what I am not.
> —ANNE BOYER, *GARMENTS AGAINST WOMEN*

In the early spring of 1908, a poet arrived on Ellis Island, one of the half million people who passed through that year.[1] Her journey was convoluted. She traveled from Brisbane to Melbourne with her young son before setting sail across the Pacific. She paused briefly in Fiji and then in Honolulu, journeyed on to Vancouver, and then sailed south to San Francisco. Soon afterward she traveled to Los Angeles, where she deposited her eight-year-old child in an orphanage before sailing to the East Coast via the Panama Canal, a cheaper route than traveling over the American continent. She was not even Australian, although she listed herself as such when she left Melbourne. She grew up in Hokitika in the South Island of New Zealand, married a Kanieri gold mine manager, and then, in her first act of self-invention, ran away to study painting in Sydney, the closest thing the antipodes had to a bohemian capital. Nor was she a pure product of the South Pacific, having entered the world in Dublin. Christened Rose Emily Ridge, in childhood she was called Rosa MacFarlane after her stepfather. Her married name was Emily Webster before she took up the alias Sybill Robson when she boarded the ship in Brisbane. When she arrived in New York, she claimed to be an American citizen, adopted a new age—ten years younger than her actual age—and gave herself a poet's name: Lola Ridge.

It is an extraordinary life story. Unsurprisingly, when Ridge published her first book of poetry in the United States, she chose for her subject the lives of immigrants, the dispossessed, and young working women who rejected motherhood and monogamy in favor of sexual and intellectual freedom. But the subject she chose was not herself. Instead, Ridge wrote her first major poem about a group to which she did not belong, whose religion she did not share, and whose language she did not speak. The titular long poem at the center of *The Ghetto and Other Poems* describes the lives of the Jewish inhabitants of New York's Lower East Side who labored in the city's garment industry and swelled the ranks of the Jewish labor movement in the early twentieth century. As the poem's speaker moves through the tenement bedrooms and hallways, lingers among the market stalls, attends socialist committee meetings, and watches garment workers on the shop floor, she negotiates the challenges of knowledge, collectivity, and difference raised by the conditions of immigrant life and by her own positionality. For Ridge, writing from the Lower East Side in the 1910s, the modern poetic sequence of city life and labor is an epistemic project that examines the limits of knowledge for an attentive yet separate observer.

This chapter's reading of "The Ghetto" speaks to an ongoing scholarly debate over the nature of the lyric poem and its social situation. In Virginia Jackson's account, critical reading practices have reduced all poetry to lyric in a process she terms "lyricization," which suppresses poetry's many other genres, such as ballads, eclogues, songs, *Lieder*, riddles, dialogues, and chants. For Jackson, the task of the critic who takes up the methods of historical poetics is a strenuous historicization of poetic reception and circulation and a rediscovery of these occluded genres.[2] There is a sense that the dominance of the lyric has obscured something—not only the full range of historical genres but also the audiences and collectives that accompany traditions not freighted with an association between the lyric speaker and the solitary individual. As such, the stakes of lyricization are not just generic; they are also *political*. Writing in *Poetry*, Matthew Bevis reminds us that *lyric* gained currency in the third century BCE as a term used by scholars working to preserve the textual versions of songs whose musical arrangements were lost when the library of Alexandria burned. Bevis quotes Jackson's entry on lyric (although he does not identify her as the author) in the fourth edition of *The Princeton Encyclopedia of Poetry and Poetics*: "*Lyric* was from its inception a term used to describe a music that could no longer be heard, an idea of poetry characterized by a lost collective experience."³ Bevis glosses Jackson's entry: "The lyric was, from the very start, a reminder that you were missing something."⁴

In this chapter and the next, I turn to two poets—Ridge in the 1910s, and Langston Hughes in the 1930s—whose poetry turns over problems of collective life. For Ridge, writing about immigrant labor in the New York garment trades, and for Hughes in his commitment to international working-class solidarity, poetry becomes a way of addressing and articulating collective experience in all its complicated and mutable forms. My interest is in what Silvia Federici invokes when she describes "commoning" not as a collective space or system of shared goods and materials but as "the production of ourselves as a common subject," which constitutes "a quality of relations, a principle of cooperation, and of responsibility to each other."⁵ In a recent intervention, Andrea Brady argues that the development of the lyric as the privileged genre of individual expression was bound up with the historical development of the carceral state, the demise of which would "be an opportunity for *poeisis*" and for the invention of new ideas of lyric solidarity. Brady sees an opportunity to recuperate the lyric here for "rediscovering lyric as a form that is based on collective solidarities rather than solitary subjects would be only one benefit of [the abolition of the carceral state]."⁶ But there is a limit to the political imagination at work here. If we take seriously the logic of the carceral state and the possibility of its dissolution, would there be a need for collective solidarities in its aftermath? Put another way, if we can imagine something as transformative as an end to the carceral state, why can we not imagine a collective subject of poetry now?

Ridge's exploration of collective life in "The Ghetto" puts the association between the lyric and the solitary individual under pressure. The titular long poem at the center of *The Ghetto and Other Poems* is not straightforwardly or uncomplicatedly *lyric*. The flexibility of the sequence form allows for moments that are conventionally lyric—quatrains of rich and musical description, lines of rhythmic regularity—alongside looser, more prosaic, less formally wrought passages. Meanwhile, the poem's first-person speaker comes in and out of focus, and it is through this flickering speaker that the poem reaches for a collective consciousness. Ridge was not alone in these innovations. Twentieth-century American leftist poetry is, among other things, an archive of attempts to create a formally expansive lyric poetry that can articulate shared experiences. This poetry did not wait for the end of the carceral state to come into being; rather, such poetry is a product of the shared conditions of struggle that make relations of solidarity necessary in the first place, as critics working in the history of leftist poetry have shown. In *Left of Poetry*, Sarah Ehlers makes a richly formalist case for Depression-era American poets as key actors in literary history for they "altered the ideation of poetry in the early twentieth century by soldering it to ideals of collectivity and of collective political action."[7] In that era, such political action was internationalist in its commitments. Ehlers examines the lyric internationalism of the Haitian poet Jacques Roumain, and, as Amelia Glaser documents, Yiddish poets in the 1930s transfigured the historical memory of the pogroms into a poetics of international solidarity with the struggles of African Americans, ethnic Ukrainians, and Palestinians.[8]

Ridge has something to offer this discussion because the articulation of shared experience is so fraught and partial in her poetry, even though it was a project to which she was enduringly committed. Ridge's work, only just beginning to enjoy its day in the sun, can teach us something about how poetry turns to collective life and sometimes finds itself baffled. In this sense, I use Ridge's poetry to extend Oren Izenberg's claim that reading poetry can "have a transformative effect on one's felt capacities for relationship, and reorient the person toward a shared world."[9] What can we know about people who are not entirely like us but whose struggles are also our struggles? This is the problem at the center of Ridge's poetry. It is also, crucially, a problem of the labor poem and of the historical story that this book tells. Ridge's writing is rooted in her observations of the New York City garment trade and the Jewish communities that surround it. The conditions of the Lower East Side in the 1910s—the thousands of new arrivals in a new land, the cramped conditions and sweated labor, the uneven landscape of radical politics—all are central to "The Ghetto," not only as the subjects of poetic description but also for the problems of knowledge and solidarity that these conditions provoke.

"She is unknown," writes Rachel Blau DuPlessis of Lorine Niedecker, but the sentiment could easily be applied to Ridge. "She is therefore erased. Every time she is mentioned, she must be re-introduced. Proposed as a value. Re-explained."[10] Ridge sits at a rare triple intersection: she was an immigrant to the United States, which made her a keen observer of the mass migrations from Eastern Europe; she moved in the anarchist-intellectual circles of Emma Goldman, Alexander Berkman, and the Ferrer Center; and she was enmeshed in the modernist poetry world through her work editing the magazines *Broom* and *Others*. From this position, Ridge brings together the formal innovations of the modernists, the political commitments of the anarchist left, and the outsider status of the immigrant. She is ripe for the kind of recovery that has expanded the canon of modernist poetry to include hitherto suppressed leftist and women poets, but thus far her literary reputation has rested on her "compassionate attention" to Jewish life and her poem describing the Lower East Side with a "gritty" realism.[11] This seems a low bar—although perhaps less so if we consider the general climate of antisemitism and the acute prejudice of many of her fellow modernists. But "The Ghetto" is also a modernist poem that intervenes in modernist ideas of knowledge. In her descriptive practice, Ridge troubles the ideal of immediate knowledge essential to the Poundian craft model that I traced in chapter 1. She articulates instead a theory of lyric difference that acknowledges the limits and discomforts of the outsider's knowledge, even as she insists on its value.

Central to the poem's vision for a new sociality are the scenes of immigrant life and labor that Ridge describes. In "The Ghetto," the lives of young women who work in the city's sweatshops become the basis of a new struggle and a new social world that emphasize, as Juno Richards writes of the submerged diverse struggles of the feminist first wave, "daily forms of world making as an ongoing process, set apart from any stated demand" that often "took up the more diffuse terms of waiting, refusal, survival, practice, cooperation, and care."[12] Ridge's poem moves between intimate, detailed portraits of young women garment workers as they practice these everyday forms of resistance and alienation from the Yiddish-speaking inhabitants among whom the poem's speaker moves. Not speaking Yiddish is important to "The Ghetto"; it accounts for both the poem's visual knowledge and the limits of the speaker's conclusions. Rejecting modernist ideals of knowledge that privilege ignorance as the basis of sudden insight, Ridge insists on the difficulty of understanding people who both are and are not similar to you, and on the value of such a project. At stake here is a reassessment of poetic collectivity, not as a project of erasing difference but one of approaching and articulating the heterogeneous, unruly forms of collective social life.

WRITING THE GHETTO

Between 1880 and the immigration reforms of 1924, approximately two million Eastern European Jews arrived in the United States, half of whom settled in New York City.[13] Their arrival coincided with the declining manufacture of customized, made-to-measure clothing and the rise of ready-to-wear garment production. Excluded from most skilled occupations by the racist craft unions of the American Federation of Labor, and with one in three immigrants claiming previous experience in garment-making, Eastern European Jewish immigrants worked largely in the needle trades.[14] By 1900, nearly 40 percent of garment workers in New York City were Jews born overseas, mainly in Russia.[15] The New York City garment trade was part of a transnational garment economy in which migrant employers and workers produced goods for domestic consumers. The tenements of New York were often the last stop on a global network of garment work, and many Jewish arrivals had worked in the garment trades of their hometowns in Kovno or Kraków, then in London, Paris, or Manchester, before reaching America.[16]

Sweatshops—at first in tenement apartments, then in factory lofts—emerged in large numbers in Brooklyn and Manhattan. Large firms outsourced the labor of sewing precut material into finished garments to independent contractors who underbid one another to win jobs. Space limitations in New York City and the low cost of starting a factory meant that while heavy industry tended toward centralization and consolidation, the needle trades developed unevenly into a "highly decentralized crazy quilt" of small and medium firms.[17] Within the sweatshops, technological change combined with an ever-refining division of labor meant that a job that required a skilled tailor in the 1880s could by 1905 be completed by a semiskilled machine operator.[18] So, too, did a gendered division of labor dominate, and while in the early decades of the garment industry women worked as cutters, by the 1880s men predominated. When a task like buttonhole-making or pressing was worked by all genders, women were inevitably paid less. Marie Ganz, a garment worker and organizer, describes the sweatshop conditions and speed-up:

> It was in this dress and kimono shop that I learned the meaning of the speed-up system. It was a means of getting larger quantities of work out of the already hard-driven girls.... No one girl made an entire garment. Each was

a specialist, making either a sleeve, a collar or some other portion. As she completed her part the garment was passed on to the next girl by Levinson, who was always walking back and forth urging us on. Should a girl lag behind he would prod her, sometimes pulling on the garment to hurry it on to another worker.

"Hurry! Don't you see that the sleevemaker soon will have no work?" he would shout.

This sort of thing created a spirit of competition for self-preservation which ended only when the worker, too weak to compete longer with a stronger sister, broke down.[19]

While many immigrants arrived with family, the thousands who came to the United States alone found a room as a boarder in a (no doubt already overcrowded) family home. The tenements themselves were cramped and overheated, and many new arrivals to New York "sensed the discrepancy between the excitement of the streets and the depressing living conditions."[20]

Working conditions in the garment trades provided fertile soil for labor militancy, and it was in the tenements and factories of New York that Jewish radicalism took hold. The International Ladies' Garment Workers' Union (ILGWU) was chartered on June 23, 1900, and during the labor unrest of 1909 and 1910, two-thirds of the thirty thousand workers who went on strike were Jewish women.[21] The experimental, diverse character of the Lower East Side served, as Tony Michels has pointed out, as "a laboratory of political and cultural innovation" that influenced not only the United States but also Eastern Europe.[22] The shop floor was also such a laboratory, forming a space where village Jews from the *shtetl* worked alongside secular intellectuals, who might find themselves working next to agitators, organizers, and revolutionaries. A multilingual anarchist movement flourished, and by the First World War, Yiddish-language anarchism comprised the movement's largest subsection.[23] In the years preceding the war, anarchist newspaper circulation was at its highest, and anarchists did everything from distributing birth control aids to teaching art and literature to factory workers and lecturing to rooms of thousands of people. Anarchists organized meetings, lectures, and educational groups, as well as mutual-benefit societies and social events—picnics, trips to the park or countryside, and parties, including *arestatnbeler*, or "arrested balls," to raise money for political prisoners. In 1908, Alexander Berkman founded the Anarchist Federation of America, which encompassed English-, Yiddish-, and German-language branches. While there were some fleeting collaborations with Italian- and Spanish-speaking radicals, these tended to be temporary or informal. Yiddish- and English-speaking radicals cultivated a closer relationship, in no small part because of Emma Goldman's influence, the readership of her magazine, *Mother Earth*, and the popularity of her lectures.

Like many immigrants, Ridge brought little of her previous life with her to New York. One object she did bring was an autograph book given to her by her mother. Inside are quotes from friends in Sydney and sketches by Australian artists: a nude by Julian Ashton, the founder of the eponymous art school in Sydney where Ridge studied; a small painted beach scene by his son, Howard Ashton; and sketches by Mick Paul and Henry George Julius, Sydney bohemians.[24] When she undertook this enormous act of self-definition and departure from her early life, Ridge brought along a sense of herself as an artist. In 1919, she claimed to have lodged in a "five by seven room in an East Side tenement" when she arrived in New York, and she took up work as an artist's model, factory hand, copywriter, and illustrator.[25] Eventually she moved to Greenwich Village where she hosted her famous parties. Within months of her arrival she was good friends with Emma Goldman; by October 1908, she was described in *Mother Earth* as "Miss Lola Ridge, an Australian Comrade," after designing the cover for Goldman's pamphlet "Patriotism."[26] Through her friendship with Emma Goldman, Ridge encountered an anarcha-feminism that emphasized free love and sexual autonomy, organized for birth control, advocated for women's economic independence from men, and refused the political horizon of suffrage and the compromises of mainstream middle-class feminism. Ridge worked as the first manager of the Ferrer Center on St. Mark's Place (named for the Spanish founder of the "Modern Schools," Francisco Ferrer), a community center that gathered anarchists, writers, and artists from various countries and languages. After an abridged version of "The Ghetto" was printed in *The New Republic* in 1918, Ridge published four more books of verse before dying of pulmonary tuberculosis in 1941. In her obituary, the *New York Times* called her "one of the leading contemporary American poets" who had "created one of the most extraordinary poems written by an American."[27]

In the late nineteenth century and into the early twentieth, popular writing about the Lower East Side proliferated, encompassing slum tourism, sensational journalism, ethnography, and reformist exposés. Sweatshop commentary oscillated between fascination and revulsion as many writers expounded nativist concerns about the preservation of whiteness and the necessity to Americanize Jewish arrivals. Commentators wrote with concern that sweatshop conditions weakened women's bodies and their childbearing capacity, noting simultaneously that the heat in the sweatshops meant that women worked half undressed alongside men.[28] With the invention of flash photography in the late nineteenth century, readers were promised an immediate insight into life in the slums. Jacob Riis's 1890 book of journalism, photography, and illustration, *How the Other Half Lives: Studies Among the Tenements of New York*, is credited with both giving impetus to Progressive Era housing reforms, and, along with the writing of Stephen Crane, furthering the developing practice of slumming, wherein visits to the Lower East Side were seen as offering a glimpse into a culture enticingly free from white, middle-class social norms.[29] "It is quite unnecessary to go to Europe to see a genuine Jewish ghetto," wrote the *New York Times* in November 1897 in an illustrated article. "No expensive steamship fares need be paid."[30] Articles appealed to both the social reformer and the curious self-styled bohemian.[31] In 1903, Bernard G. Richards, who wrote in both English and Yiddish, published an account of the Lower East Side in the *Boston Evening Transcript*. Richards narrates the experience of a fictional friend named Keidansky who leaves Boston to spend a week on the Lower East Side "to break away for a while from the sameness and solemness, the routine and respectability of this town," finding in New York people who "feel freely, act independently, speak as they think and are not at all ashamed of their feelings."[32] For Richards, the city holds a vision of an American future: "The sun of new ideas rises on the East Side."

Ridge opens *The Ghetto and Other Poems* with a Whitmanian salutation "to the American people": "Will you feast with me, American people? But what have I that shall seem good to you?" She then offers the apples and honey eaten on Rosh Hashanah:

> On my board are bitter apples
> And honey served on thorns,
> And in my flagons fluid iron,
> Hot from the crucibles.
>
> How should such fare entice you![33]

Beginning the poem in the context of the Jewish New Year, the holiest time of the year, is an evocative gesture that may situate the poems that follow as the playing out of the Days of Awe. The lines bring in New Testament imagery—the crown of thorns, the crucible—while at the same time matching ancient ritual with the modern and industrial in the "fluid irons." Here, specific religious practices, brought together in the crucible of modern industry, become the basis of a common sociality.

In "Women and the Creative Will," her 1919 lecture on women's writing and their place in the canon, Ridge writes that the description of masses and crowds is a problem of both form and gender: "But it is easy to see why woman's work should be lacking in form. For centuries men have had the organizing of the world. They have handled large undertakings and seen things in masses and people in crowds. They have always been shaping things on a large scale and drawing parts into a whole, so perfecting their sense of unity and form. With them mental order—the easy and natural correlation of ideas—has become instinctive."[34] "The Ghetto" doesn't seek to draw its parts into a seamless whole. The poem begins by panning over Hester Street on a hot summer day, where, in an image that evokes sweated labor on the factory floor, we find the heat "nosing in the body's overflow, / Like a beast pressing its great steaming belly close, / Covering all avenues of air . . ." (*TG*, 5). Its next section narrows its focus to the Sodos family apartment where the speaker lodges. The movement of the poem is defined by such expansions and contractions, from the speaker's hemmed-in position in the opening lines of part 5, "As I sit in my little fifth-floor room - / Bare, / Save for bed and chair" (*TG*, 19) to the expansive opening of part 7, "Lights go out / And the stark trunks of the factories / Melt into the drawn darkness" (*TG*, 26). The poem's loose form moves from contained, even stanzaic structures to long, Whitmanian lines that catalog the speaker's observations. So, too, does the poem flit between modes, from its documentary opening to the parodic skewering of the Stirnerian young men in part 7 to the rhapsodic ode of its conclusion. "The Ghetto" is a sequence, diverse and uneven, displaying the constitutive feature of its form, namely, a tension between the part and the whole, between the local observation and the poem as an interrelated, organic totality.[35]

Ridge foregrounds this part–whole relation as both the formal condition of the sequence and the defining social structure of tenement living. In part 5, we watch an "old stooped mother" lighting the Shabbat candles:

> On Friday nights
> Her candles signal
> Infinite fine rays
> To other windows,
> Coupling other lights,
> Linking the tenements
> Like an endless prayer.
> (*TG*, 21)

The candles figure the poem's social vision of individuals who are coupled, linked, and drawn into a greater whole. Ridge's conceit also maps onto an anarchist social ideal in which individuals exist with full autonomy but in relations of solidarity with one another. The Shabbat candles radiating out to the tenements limn the poem's tensions and unities: between the sacred and the secular, the ritual and the mundane, the ancient and the modern, the individual and the mass, the part and the whole. The lit candles are also an apt figure for the disparate but connected form of the poetic sequence. In their classic account of the modern poetic sequence, M. L. Rosenthal and Sally Gall write that the form is distinguished by its "need for encompassment of disparate and often powerfully opposed tonalities and energies." The sequence retains the "highly subjective impulse of lyrical energy," but this new form goes "many-sidedly into who and where we are *subjectively*."[36] Braiding Whitmanian universalism, anarchist individualism, and certain tropes from ethnographic journalism together, "The Ghetto" dramatizes the pressure of forging modern subjectivity from within the crucible of the global movement of labor power and its restructuring of human life.

FIERY ATOMS: THE GHETTO'S GARMENT WORKERS

Babette Deutsch was less than impressed when she reviewed *The Ghetto and Other Poems*. Ridge's poems were too long, Deutsch complained in *The Little Review*, unfocused and diffuse in their insights. Comparing the book unfavorably to Maxwell Bodenheim's *Minna and Myself*, Deutsch writes, "There are flashes of insight as clear as his, but [Ridge] cannot sustain her attack. She works on a larger canvas, but her colors are all dull crimsons, orange and sullen black."[37] She argued that this was because of Ridge's focus on the crowd rather than the individual. "An angry mob is terrible," Deutsch wrote, "but its anger is a thing diffused and obscure compared with the deep intensity of an individual." In "The Ghetto," the crowd is figured not as an angry mob but as a violent parturition, the "cramped ova / Tearing and rending asunder its living cells" (*TG*, 26). Where the poem tropes the spectacle of the overcrowded tenements as exhausted maternity, it pays patient attention to the individual lives of the young women who live in the tenements and work in the garment industry. These women—contra Deutsch—are treated as intimately known individuals.

Deutsch's trope of Ridge's poetry as a canvas is an apt one. Ridge studied art at the Julian Ashton Art School in Sydney, where she trained particularly in representing bodies and faces. Even today, the school is known for its emphasis on portraiture and realist skills. Ridge's archive shows traces of her skill as a portraitist of women. A pen drawing of her friend the novelist and poet Evelyn Scott shows Scott seated, draped in quasi-classical style, looking into the distance. Scattered sketches of women appear throughout her archive, as well as a self-portrait in which Ridge looks directly out from the page, her gaze clear and focused. Ridge also worked as an artist's model both at the Ashton school and in New York. While there are no photos of Ridge at work modeling in her archive, there are many photographic portraits of her, often dramatically posed, the lines of her face emphasized. One photograph stands out: it shows Ridge at a desk, a typewriter in front of her (figure 2.1).[38] She is staring out the window, her profile visible but the features of her face obscured by the light outside the room. A woman has paused, perhaps in thought, perhaps in temporary distraction, from her labors. In "The Ghetto," Ridge brings the eye of the artist, and the model who knows what it is to pose, to the lives of garment workers at their labors and in the resistant daily practices—having sex with gentiles, donating to strike funds, reading, organizing, and dancing—that contour their lives.[39]

Regardless of whether Ridge did board in a tenement, she had more in common with the garment workers than possibly living below Houston Street for a brief period. As noted by Joshua Logan Walls, this is a similarity that enfolded her, even if she did not court it: the force of Ridge's identification with Jewish immigration as the condition of American modernity implicitly rewrote the Irish Catholic who grew up in the South Pacific as a Jewish immigrant from Eastern Europe.[40] At the center of this fascination, and at the center of "The Ghetto," are women not unlike

FIGURE 2.1. Photograph of Lola Ridge at her desk (undated).
Source: Permission is given by Elaine Sproat. Smith College Special Collections.

Ridge herself: newly arrived, impoverished women who worked hard for a wage and rejected religion, monogamy, marriage, and child-rearing, and who were the architects of their own intellectual and creative lives. The poem's second section begins inside the tenement apartment where the speaker lives as a boarder. Part 2 begins with "I room at the Sodos," and its subsequent descriptions are voiced by the first-person speaker who sees and hears the family at home (*TG*, 7). The elderly father is no longer a saddle maker; he "has forgotten most things" but not his practice of "lifted praise" (*TG*, 8), while his wife "is not so old and wears her own hair" (*TG*, 7). We hear about the Sodos' son, Bennie, who "stays away / and sends wine of holidays" (*TG*, 8) and who has partnered with a Christian woman. And we meet the Sodos' daughter, Sadie, a pieceworker in a factory where "all day the power machines / Drone in her ears" (*TG*, 9). At night, Sadie Sodos reads, speaks at political meetings, goes to parties, or is visited by a gentile lover whom her mother hears enter and leave the apartment (with telling hushes in between). Later we meet two garment workers who live on the floor above the Sodos family: the intellectual Sarah, "swarthy and ill-dressed," and the beautiful, comradely Anna. In a poem in which there are few named "characters," the garment workers stand out for their detailed individuation.

Sadie's section is the only time the poem takes us inside a garment factory. When the poem turns to the women at work, the first-person speaker fades to the background, and the emphasis lands on Sadie at the sewing machine, where "the fine dust flies / Till throats are parched and itch," and the heat is "like a kept corpse," suggesting a body kept unburied longer than the twenty-four-hour window mandated by Jewish law (*TG*, 9):

> Then—when needles move more slowly on the cloth
> And sweaty fingers slacken
> And hair falls in damp wisps over the eyes—
> Sped by some power within,
> Sadie quivers like a rod . . .
> A thin black piston flying,
> One with her machine.
> (*TG*, 9)

While the heat causes others to "move more slowly" and to "slacken," Sadie is "sped" and "flying":

> She—fiery static atom,
> Held in place by the fierce pressure all about—
> Speeds up the driven wheels
> And biting steel—that twice
> Has nipped her to the bone.
> (*TG*, 9–10)

Ridge refigures familiar tropes about the dehumanization of modern labor prevalent among, but by no means unique to, the Yiddish sweatshop poets. The famous concluding lines of Morris Rosenfeld's "The Sweatshop" ("*Die Werkstatt*") are exemplary: "I forget who I am in this deafening scene—/ I'm losing my reason, I'm losing my self—/ I don't know, I don't mind, for I am a machine. . . ."[41] Like the speaker of Rosenfeld's poem, Sadie is likened to her machine, but the young woman is driven by "some power within," all potential energy, quivering "like a rod" who becomes a "thin black piston flying / One with her machine." Ridge's prepositional phrase insists on Sadie's equality with, rather than subordination to, the tools of her labor.

Sadie is the most individuated figure in the poem, but she also stands in for a nascent class of radical young women garment workers. In November 1909, a mass meeting of the ILGWU was held at the Cooper Union to discuss the possibility of a strike. For two hours, union leaders and Lower East Side socialists debated. Eventually the male leadership agreed to hear from a twenty-three-year-old garment worker named Claire Lemlich, born in Gorodok (in today's Ukraine). Her brief message, delivered in Yiddish and published in English in the *New York World*, was clear: "What we are here for is to decide whether we shall or shall not strike. I offer a resolution that a general strike be declared now."[42] The "Uprising of the Twenty Thousand" lasted until February 1910 and resulted in better pay and shorter working hours, though demands for safer working conditions were not met. Ridge's readers would have been familiar with images of young women's resistance after the Triangle Shirtwaist Factory fire on March 25, 1911, which claimed the lives of 146 workers, sparking public outcry and swelling union ranks.

Factories were important centers of education, and garment workers, mostly Russian Jews, made up the majority of working girls attending public evening schools in New York.[43] "Most of us young immigrant waistmakers attend night school to learn English," remembered Rose Pesotta, "and supplement our education with the union classes in subjects of social significance. Thus we gain knowledge and poise and confidence."[44] Women who worked in factories tended to be less religiously observant than those who found work through *landsleit* relations in local shops.[45] In the factories, the workers also received an education in class consciousness. Pesotta remembered her first job after arriving in America from Ukraine:

> The making of another American begins. . . . Esther gets me a job in a shirtwaist factory and I learn the trade. I have barely missed the time when the men working in New York's garment industry had to provide their own sewing machines, needles, and thread, and when girls like myself were apprenticed to a "masterworker," who paid them a meager few cents for a day's work, out of his own wages.

> I join a virile and growing labor organization, Waistmakers' Local 25 of the International Ladies' Garment Workers' Union. At its meetings I learn about the "Uprising of the 20,000" women and girls in 1909, my sister Esther among them, who walked out of the waist factories in protest against intolerable sweatshop conditions ... imbued with their spirit, others now carry on.[46]

Upon Pesotta's arrival in Manhattan, "the making of another American begins." That making is, of course, the education in sweated labor, but it also affirms the emergence of the new class of radical women.

After the scene in the factory, the poem takes us to Sadie's life outside the working day:

> Nights, she reads
> Those books that have most unset thought,
> New-poured and malleable,
> To which her thought
> Leaps fusing at white heat,
> Or spits her fire out in some dim manger of a hall,
> Or at a protest meeting on the Square,
> Her lit eyes kindling the mob ...
> Or dances madly at a festival.
> Each dawn finds her a little whiter,
> Though up and keyed to the long day,
> Alert, yet weary ... like a bird
> That all night long has beat about a light.
> (*TG*, 10)

Note the way Sadie is described as fire: her thought fuses "at white heat"; she "spits her fire out" at a meeting or protest; her "lit" eyes kindle the mob. Like the factory speed-up that is refigured as a property unique to Sadie's character, here the threat of fire is integrated into Sadie's being. Just as Ridge counters the factory speed-up with Sadie's own furious speed, Ridge translates this major threat to safe working conditions—quickly recognizable in the aftermath of the Triangle Shirtwaist tragedy—into a characteristic internal to Sadie, who is "lit" and "kindling."

Ridge's attention to radical young women is rooted in the anarcha-feminist political scene in which she moved at the time. Anarchist feminism was a movement born largely in the sweatshops. Goldman worked in factories in Rochester and New York, and, later, Pesotta married anarchism to labor organizing with the ILGWU. Ridge's friendship with Goldman and her involvement with the Ferrer Center introduced her to the movement's rejection of suffrage based on the argument that suffrage would lead not to women's liberation but to their further incorporation into the state. She was also introduced to the beliefs that marriage, monogamy, and the structure of the family amounted to "sex slavery" and that birth control was key to women's sexual liberation. Ridge edited Margaret Sanger's magazine on birth control in 1918 and would have heard Sanger speak at the Ferrer Center. While Ridge was personally associated with Goldman, in spirit and style she shares more with another writer, Voltairine de Cleyre. De Cleyre was an American anarchist named after the French philosopher by her free-thinking father who later recanted his beliefs and sent his daughter to be raised in a convent in Ontario, from which she ran away several times. She lived an ascetic life among Jewish immigrants in Philadelphia, where she learned to speak Yiddish.[47] Raised on American-grown anarchism influenced by Thoreau and Whitman, de Cleyre shares stylistic similarities with Ridge. In her essay "Anarchism," published in *Free Society* in 1901, de Cleyre wrote that anarchism is

> once and forever to realize that one is not a bundle of well-regulated little reasons bound up in the front room of the brain to be sermonized and held in order with copy-book maxims or moved and stopped by a syllogism, but a bottomless, bottomless depth of all strange sensations, a rocking sea of feeling wherever sweep strong storms of unaccountable hate and rage, invisible contortions of disappointment, low ebbs of meanness, quakings and shudderings of love that drives to madness and will not be controlled, hungerings and moanings and sobbing that smite upon the inner ear, now first bent to listen, as if in all the sadness of the sea and the wailing of the great pine forests of the North had met to weep together there in that silence audible to you alone.[48]

"This is what Anarchism may mean to you," de Cleyre wrote. "It means that to me."[49] In "The Political Equality of Women," published in the Philadelphia *Conservator* in 1894 under the name "M. W." (for Mary Wollstonecraft), de Cleyre wrote, "*Capitalism*, with its iron-shod feet, tramps the blood from the heart of the woman, who is no more than the household goddess, but the tool which fashions profits." She continued that "women must work or starve. Let it be so. She is no more the protected animal; she becomes an individual."[50]

The anarcha-feminist insistence on women *becoming* individuals might help explain why, in a poem whose focus is the urban multitude, the second section spends so much time with Sadie and the other garment workers. Ridge matches a union politics of work-based resistance with an anarcha-feminist individualism. This self-becoming takes place outside the factory in the garment workers' nighttime activities; Sadie "reads / Those books that have most unset thought, / New-poured and malleable." The verbal choice is odd: perhaps the books "have" or contain radical thought; perhaps "have" indicates that the book has "unset"—disturbed, reformed, or dislodged—Sadie's thought. Likely it registers both the contents of the book and its impact on Sadie's "malleable" mind. After Sadie we encounter Sarah, whose mind is "hard and brilliant and cutting like an acetylene torch. / If any impurities drift there, they must be burnt up as in a clear flame" (*TG*, 11). Sarah is all intellect, at odds with her life sewing garments: "It is droll," the speaker comments, "that she should work in a pants factory" (*TG*, 11). Sarah "reads without bias—/ Doubting clamorously—/ Psychology, plays, science, philosophies—" (*TG*, 11). *Bias* is a sewing term designating the diagonal line of woven fabric where the warp and weft intersect. That Sarah thinks in terms of bias suggests that the workday has bled into her consciousness. But to read "without bias" promises both that Sarah is a voracious reader and that she is working hard to shrug off the strictures of the working day in her nocturnal intellectual life. Sarah's reading modernizes the Torah study of older men and insists on the mind-expanding curiosity of the younger generation of women. Finally, there is the beautiful Anna: "The young men turn their heads to look at her. / She has the appeal of a folk-song / And her cheap clothes are always in rhythm" (*TG*, 11). Anna "gave half her pay" during the strike and "would give anything" while "Sarah's desire covets nothing apart. / She would share all things... / Even her lover" (*TG*, 11). The poem considers Anna's comradely donation of her pay and Sarah's rejection of monogamy in the same breath, turning outward to the collective ways of living practiced by the garment workers.

Ridge's vision of a new political life arising from the garment workers departs from more familiar descriptions of the garment industry as the center of the trauma, dislocation, and loss of selfhood associated with mass immigration and sweated labor. One poet associated with this trope of generational rupture—although not without challenge—is Charles Reznikoff, whose "family-oriented poetry and prose," in Joshua Logan Wall's phrase, describes the conflicted loss and partial inheritance of writing poetry in the wake of the hard labor endured by his parents' generation.[51] Each section of Reznikoff's triptych family memoir, *Family Chronicle*, first published in 1963, is ostensibly written by a different member of the Reznikoff family and narrates their passage from Russia to the United States and their work in the textile industry. The first section, "Early History of a Seamstress," is told by Reznikoff's mother, Sarah Yetta, who recounts her entry into the garment industry, her arrival in New York, and her desire for education: "How I wanted to go to school like my friends, books under my arm. I asked Father again and again, When am I going to go to school?"[52] Sarah Yetta sublimates her desire for education into purchasing and studying dressmaking books like Glazhdinsky's *System of Cutting for Dressmakers and Tailors*, which she brings to America. In its final paragraph, "Early History of a Seamstress" returns to the struggle for learning. As the children leave school at 3 p.m., Sarah Yetta remembers "how I, too, had longed for an education" and maps this longing onto a generational failure. "We are a lost generation," she announces to her cousin in an axiomatic scene of immigrant dispossession, grief, and desire displaced onto the next generation. "It is for our children to do what they can."[53] In Ridge's poem, the garment workers are not a lost generation, nor do they embrace narratives of assimilation. Rather, they articulate a new vision for a shared social future.

In *Wayward Lives, Beautiful Experiments*, Saidiya Hartman writes a fabulated scene of missed encounter. Esther Brown, one of the book's riotous young Black women, walks through the same streets of New York as Emma Goldman, where the two women "crossed paths but failed to recognize each other."[54] Goldman here stands for a more formalized and public version of radical politics to which Brown had no connection and to whom she was illegible. Esther Brown did not write political tracts, draft plans for mutual aid, pen manifestos, or read anarchist texts. Instead, living according to her own desires was itself "to be ungovernable" for her "way of living was nothing short of anarchy."[55] With their future-oriented practices of daily living, Ridge's garment workers share more in common with these daily feminist practices than with formalized anarchism. Only Sadie "spits her fire out" at meetings, and this is one part of her fully wayward and rebellious life, as much an act of refusal as sleeping with a gentile. Later in the poem, Ridge will ridicule the organized politics of the young men in the "committee," the "lank boy," the red-bearded man with his "welter of maimed face" whose "words knock each other like little wooden blocks" (*TG*, 24). The garment workers come early in the poem, laying the groundwork for the rest of "The Ghetto" by proposing new forms of sociality, everyday resistance, and struggles for freedom. At the end of the poem, Ridge turns outward to her ecstatic consideration of life, and we hear echoes of Sadie and Sarah:

> Electric currents of life,
> Throwing off thoughts like sparks,
> Glittering, disappearing,
> Making unknown circuits,
> Or out of spent particles stirring
> Feeble contortions in old faiths
> Passing before the new.
> (*TG*, 29)

Like Sadie the fiery atom and Sarah's mind like an acetylene torch, life is sparking, electric, and in the process of creation. This version of women's rights resonates with Juno Richards's description of international radical feminist resistance in the early twentieth century in *The Fury Archives*. Richards excavates an archive of first-wave feminist thought that dislodged shared suffering and trauma as the basis of feminist political belonging and emphasized instead the daily life of feminist action, wherein "female citizenship is constituted through ongoing practice and process, rather than a prior history of woundedness."[56] Ridge's garment workers, with their diverse practices of daily resistance, would be at home in such a version of history. The poem's primary interest is not the representation of collective trauma, whether that of religious persecution or sweated labor. Rather, Ridge's focus is the radical everyday life embraced by the garment workers. These women are where the poem, which turns so definitively away from reproductive futurity, locates future-oriented social practices and a model for social life. Sarah's habit of "reading without bias" thus takes on a greater significance: as the model for the collectivity toward which the rest of the poem will struggle.

ON NOT SPEAKING YIDDISH

One thing sets the poem's speaker apart from her subjects: she does not speak Yiddish. This revelation is dramatized through an encounter with one of the "sturdy Ghetto children." Unlike the other infants, who are "lusty, unafraid," this small girl "cowers apart":

> She stammers in Yiddish,
> But I do not understand,
> And there flits across her face
> A shadow
> As of a drawn blind.
> I give her an orange,
> Large and golden,
> And she looks at it blankly.
> I take her little cold hand and try to draw her to me,
> But she is stiff . . .
> Like a doll . . .
> (*TG*, 12–13)

The encounter fails: the child "darts through the crowd / Like a little white panic" (*TG*, 13) as the offerings—the child's stammered speech, the speaker's golden orange—are met with mutual incomprehension. Such moments of contact in "The Ghetto" are rare. The encounter with the child maps a moment of failed, maybe lethal, maternity as the speaker touches the infant, who stiffens "like a doll," then bursts into frightened movement and darts away. Linguistic difference becomes freighted with the poem's rejection of reproduction and normative gender roles. The child flees from the speaker in a "white panic," an image that resurfaces soon after in the figure with the "white frock / And eyes like hooded lights / Out of the shadow of pogroms / Watching" (*TG*, 14). The jangly rhymes of this section disintegrate in the final four lines about the hooded figure, where the threat of antisemitic violence looms. Is the speaker's own observational habit included in that "watching"? Does she acknowledge that her own difference might register as a threat? Or is she differentiating this threatening observation—observation with intent—from her own practice?

THE SOCIAL LIFE OF SEWING

As Ridge was a gentile raised in New Zealand and a new arrival to New York, there was no reason for her to have any knowledge of Yiddish. But she was not alone in her ignorance. Some Jewish intellectuals who had rejected Yiddish in Europe during the Haskalah, associating the language with cultural backwardness, learned only the *zhargon* in New York.[57] Only one non-English word is spoken in Ridge's poem, and it is not spoken by a person. The fifth section describes what she sees and hears from her fifth-floor bedroom:

> I hear bells pealing,
> Out of the gray church at Rutgers Street,
> Holding its high-flung cross above the Ghetto,
> And, one floor down across the court,
> The parrot screaming:
> Vorwärts... Vorwärts...
>
> The parrot frowsy-white,
> Everlastingly swinging
> On its iron bar.
> (*TG*, 20)

Later, the parrot is compared to the woman lighting the Shabbat candles, who "seems less lonely than the bird," who "day by day about the dismal house / Screams out his frenzied word," "Vorwärts... Vorwärts..." (*TG*, 21). The parrot's cry is linguistically indeterminate: פֿאָרווערטס is the name of the Yiddish daily newspaper *The Forward* (*Forverts*) and, cognate to it, the German socialist newspaper *Vorwärts*, after which the Yiddish organ was named. Here Ridge is likely referring to the *Forverts*, the most widely circulated foreign-language newspaper in the United States at the time and a fixture of the world described in "The Ghetto." But using the standard German alphabet, not the Yiddish, highlights the speaker's—and perhaps Ridge's own—lack of knowledge. The word signifies a culture that surrounds but excludes the speaker. We can read in the parrot's sole repeated word an image of both the speaker's isolation (the parrot is "lonely") and her frustrations with her inarticulacy. "*Vorwärts*" conjures both the insufficiency of speech and a terrible imperative to go on speaking.

"*Vorwärts*" punctures the poem, carrying a sense of threat and shock. Jacob Riis described a reversal of this situation in which, amid the "shouting in foreign tongues, a veritable Babel of confusion," the shocking word is English, not Yiddish. "An English word falls upon the ear almost with a sense of shock, as something unexpected and strange."[58] Riis's scene, and the intrusion of the parrot's "*Vorwärts*," resonates with Raymond Williams's classic account of the wrenching linguistic estrangement of the multilingual metropolis that shaped modernist form. For these immigrants, "liberated or breaking from their national or provincial cultures," Williams writes, language was no longer merely a social custom but had become "a medium that could be shaped and reshaped."[59] Formal experimentation became a "common language" distinct from the social uses of language (*TG*, 45–46). Ridge's speaker hears a repeated Yiddish word and is reminded anew of her own strangeness. In the poem's seventh section, Ridge takes us to the anarchist café where the young men's egos are "cawing," setting up an association between their ineffective, competitive speech and the parrot's repeated phrase. Here, sound is divorced from sense: the men shout "words, words, words," their speech "pattering like hail" and building to "baffling minors / Half heard like rain over pools" and "majestic discordances / Greater than harmonies" (*TG*, 24–25). They scream, caw, and garble, but unlike the parrot's cry, no individual words are isolated from the discordance. Like Williams's immigrant modernists, Ridge is skeptical about the social efficacy of language, as her description of the young men's cacophony demonstrates. But she finds something shared and pure in the "majestic discordances," "gleaning out of it all / Passion, bewilderment, pain" (*TG*, 25). Her "common language" moves beyond the inefficacy of speech and into the shared terrain of political emotion.

For Ridge's early reviewers, her outsider's ignorance was the grounds of the poem's achievement. A review in the *New Republic*, in which the poem was originally published, praised Ridge for her "vision":

> ["The Ghetto"] is beyond doubt the most vivid and sensitive and lovely embodiment that exists in American literature of that many-sided transplantation of Jewish city-dwellers which vulgarity dismisses with a laugh or a jeer. The fact that Miss Ridge is not a Jewess, is herself alien and transplanted, does not disqualify her vision. On the contrary, she is disengaged so that she can move from reality to reality with a pure sense of the flood that immerses her. Could anyone less free see the "skinny hands that hover like

two hawks," or "newsboys with battling eyes," or a small girl's "braided head, shiny as a black-birds"? The outsider alone, perhaps, could observe the "raw young seed of Israel" and that insulted elder who, unperturbed, "keeps his bitter peace."[60]

Alfred Kreymborg came to a similar conclusion in *Poetry*, in which he praised Ridge's "uncanny range of knowledge" and "her realistic presentation" and suggested that "she sees the future of the race more clearly than the Jews themselves. She prognosticates the Jew as one of the leaders in the new world, and her vision is borne out by even a casual perusal of the present-day names of men who are re-moulding Europe."[61] Kreymborg aligns Ridge's status as an outsider with an insight into the association between Jewishness and modernity. This is a judgment that some of Ridge's recent readers, such as Cristanne Miller, agree with. Miller writes that Ridge's "inability to speak Yiddish may indeed have allowed the also impoverished Ridge to see her neighbors' experience with some objectivity."[62]

The judgments by Kreymborg, and more recently by Miller, come close to a modernist idea of spontaneous knowledge and intellectual clarity built out of a visual insight developed in the same decade as the composition and publication of "The Ghetto." As I traced in chapter 1, Pound's theory of the "luminous detail" went beyond merely formal ideas of technique and became the grounds of the craft work ethic, which transformed craft labor into a powerful abstraction. After he acquired the papers of Ernest Fenollosa, Pound expanded his theory from the sudden insight and the selection of details to untrained interpretation. Pound's principle of artistic insight became a racialized one, exemplified by his statements about Henri Gaudier-Brzeska's observations of Chinese characters: "He was so accustomed to observe the dominant line in objects that after he had spent, what could not have been more than a few days studying the subject at the museum, he could understand the primitive Chinese ideographs (not the later more sophisticated forms), and he was very much disgusted with the lexicographers who 'hadn't sense enough to see that *that* was a horse,' or a cow or a tree or whatever it might be, 'what the . . . else could it be! The . . . fools!' "[63]

Pound valorizes this insight precisely for its grounds in ignorance against the expertise of the "lexicographers." Expertise obscures, rather than provokes, knowledge. But the idea that being an outsider can make someone a better observer of other languages or minority groups is not entirely borne out by Ridge's poem itself. Not knowing Yiddish is important to the poem not because it grants the poet and her speaker a privileged form of knowledge but because it accounts for what the poem cannot know and what it must surmise or think harder about. Is the position of the rigorous observer possible? This is an active question in the poem. Aside from that provided by the parrot, there is little reported speech. In "The Ghetto," information is not verbal but visual; it is not sudden and untrained but patient and attentive. Ridge's lack of knowledge of Yiddish accounts for the poem's attention to surface, object, and detail: the razor strops and green and brown pickles for sale in the market, the gewgaws, the small bare room in the tenement apartment where light filters through the transom, the lights turning off in the factories and the garment workers flowing out. The poem's characters are looking attentively: the eyes of the young men are "staring as through a choked glass" (*TG*, 26), Ridge writes, "the moon like a skull, / Staring out of eyeless sockets at the old men trundling home the pushcarts" (*TG*, 28). Both are images of sight that is frustrated or partial—the choked glass, the "eyeless sockets" of the moon.

Sight is also where the speaker encounters the limits of her knowledge. Ridge often pays attention to the eyes and sight of the inhabitants. "Her eyes have the glow / of darkened lights," Ridge writes about the young girl whose Yiddish she does not understand, registering something inaccessible in the child: "A shadow / as of a drawn blind" (*TG*, 12–13). This limit also provokes other forms of attention—not observing and recording but speculating. "Did they vision—with those eyes darkly clear" (*TG*, 7), she asks, and elsewhere she encounters "eyes of mystery," resistant to probing (*TG*, 16). Eyes are where the speaker detects motive and emotion. At work, Sadie has a "bitter eye" (*TG*, 9), whereas later, at the protest, her eyes are "lit" (*TG*, 10); her mother, suspicious of Sadie's non-Jewish lover, has "narrowed eyes" (*TG*, 10). The speaker sometimes speculates in more detail, such as when she turns to a trader in the market. The trader, "born to trade as to a caul," is seen "appraising / All who come and go" with his "nimble thought" (*TG*, 18):

> Looks Westward where the trade-lights glow,
> And sees his vision rise —
> A tape-ruled vision,
> Circumscribed in stone —
> Some fifty stories to the skies.
> (*TG*, 18–19)

These lines describe the economic ambitions of new arrivals to the United States and rely on an association between Jewishness and capitalism. Ridge follows the trader's line of sight "westward" to the commercial centers just to the west of the Lower East Side. Working in the *schmatta* trades, the trader's vision is "tape-ruled" but also "circumscribed," perhaps met with hostility and antisemitism, or perhaps Ridge is registering a limitation of his desires, which can be described only in economic terms. It is conventional in Jewish thought that prayers ascend to heaven via the Temple Mount and that Jews in the diaspora west of Jerusalem face east during prayer. By trading the east for the west, and so turning his back on Europe and Jerusalem, the trader signals a commitment to American capitalist modernity. These lines, however, are a fantasy that moves away from observing this trader at his work toward imagining his ambitions and desires. Observation, no matter how rigorous, is partial. It cannot access thought or desire. Ridge trades what she sees for what the trader *might* see. Observation is necessarily limited, and Ridge must supplement its gaps.

At the same time, running through "The Ghetto" are suggestions of incomprehension and misunderstanding *between* the tenement populations. The poem describes generational divides and differences in religious observance, such as those demonstrated by the Sodos father's distance from his wife, who does not wear the sheitel, and his two children, who take gentile lovers. In part 4, there is the "old grey scholar," who is mocked by "the raw young seed of Israel" (*TG*, 17), and the mutual incomprehension of the young men of the committee and the old men, who are flung only a "waste glance" (*TG*, 23), seen as negligible and irrelevant by the politically militant. In her attention to these dynamics, Ridge challenges an anthropological view that assumes that the observed subjects are cohesive and self-knowing, insisting instead that incomprehension is a shared condition both across and within languages and groups.

Finally, "The Ghetto" opens outward in its ecstatic final section:

> LIFE!
> Startling, vigorous life,
> That squirms under my touch,
> And baffles me when I try to examine it,
> Or hurls me back without apology.
> Leaving my ego ruffled and preening itself.
> (*TG*, 29)

This is a squirmy, too-alive life, which baffles and repels:

> Life,
> Articulate, shrill,
> Screaming in provocative assertion
> (*TG*, 29)

Ridge does not dismiss her project as a failure but, contra her reviewers, insists on its difficulty and her subject's refusal to be closely examined. But her subject here is not the ghetto specifically but "LIFE!": *all* of life. In this rapid expansion, the poem calls back to the dedication's association between the rituals of Rosh Hashanah and the new American public. It also moves away from the specificity of the world that Ridge had just described and discards specificity as a horizon and measure of success. How would knowing Yiddish help her here? In broadening the project to life itself, Ridge turns away from the particular details, and differences, of her subject. But she also opens the poem up to a state of greater ambition and optimism. The poem ends in a state of ecstatic frustration of not being able to know completely, of confronting the thing that refuses to be known but trying to understand it anyway.

THE SOFT BLARNEY OF THE WIND

The Ghetto and Other Poems is a book in four parts. After "The Ghetto" comes "Manhattan Lights," a series of short lyrics about the city. This is followed by "Labor," a portrait of the American labor movement whose centerpiece poem, "Frank Little at Calvary," describes the 1917 murder of the Industrial Workers of the World organizer in Butte, Montana. The final section is "Accidentals," a more miscellaneous collection. In "The Ghetto," Sadie Sodos the garment worker appears only once more, at the end of the poem, when the speaker returns home at dawn to find that "Sadie's light is still burning" (*TG*, 28). But the needle trades, and synecdochically the garment workers, are threaded throughout the whole volume. From the long poem's first lines that conjure the sweated labor and fabric of the garment trade—"cool inaccessible air / Is floating in velvety blackness"—the garment industry is troped as being constitutive of the city itself. Later, Ridge tropes the city through textile:

> Lights go out
> And the stark trunks of the factories
> Melt into the drawn darkness,
> Sheathing like a seamless garment.
> (*TG*, 26)

The line break makes it hard to tell whether it is the factories or the darkness that is doing the "sheathing." It suggests that the factories are "sheathed" in the garment-like night, signaling the end of the working day. Such a textile description is even more pronounced in the short poems that follow "The Ghetto." Everywhere Ridge moves in the city, there is the color and texture of fabric. "Promenade" opens with "Undulant rustlings, / Of oncoming silk / Rhythmic, incessant" (*TG*, 46); bodies in the city pass "in warm velvety surges" (*TG*, 46). In "Manhattan," the poem immediately following "The Ghetto," Ridge conjures a city spun out of thread: "Out of the night you burn, Manhattan, / In a vesture of gold - / Spun of innumerable arcs" (*TG*, 36). That poem maps a city contoured by the garment industry:

> Diaphanous gold,
> Veiling the Woolworth, argently
> Rising slender and stark
> Mellifluous-shrill as a vender's cry,
> And towers squatting graven and cold
> On the velvet bales of the dark,
> And the Singer's appraising
> Indolent idol's eye,
> And night like a purple cloth unrolled—
> (*TG*, 35–36)

Two skyscrapers dominate Broadway: the Woolworth Building, at the time of the poem's composition the tallest building in the world and the home of the Irving National Bank and the five-and-dime corporation for which the building was named, and the Singer Tower, the headquarters of the Singer Manufacturing Company, whose sewing machines filled the city's factories. The Singer building looms over the city like a supervisor observing a shop floor, with its "appraising / Indolent idol's eyes," as the poet puns on both capitalist idleness and the false worship of corporate power. This image also extends workplace discipline and surveillance beyond the shop floor.⁶⁴ Against this we have the textiles—veils and velvet, purple cloth "unrolled" as the workers are released from the factory at the end of the working day. The poem ends by addressing the worker directly: "You of unknown voltage / Whirling on your axis . . . / Scrawling vermillion signatures / Over the night's velvet hoarding." This material troping is a cartographic technique that remaps the city in terms of the labor and profit extraction of the garment industry. Those workers scrawl their "vermillion signatures" over the "velvet hoarding" in an act of defiant self-expression that is also a reminder that profit is extracted from the bodies of workers.

Standing in Lower Manhattan, Ridge could see the Singer company's headquarters; walking around the city, she could watch workers enter and exit factories at the day's beginning and end. What she could not see was the extent of the Singer machine's global circulation. The Singer sewing machine was one of the first complex mass-marketed consumer goods to be sold on a large scale internationally. By 1912, Singer was the seventh-largest firm in the world, and by the First World War the machines were common in Eastern Europe, Southeast Asia, the Middle East, and Southern Africa and had a market share of 90 percent in non-American markets.⁶⁵ If a sewing machine was purchased outside the United States, it was likely a Singer. The firm borrowed its slogan from the British Empire: "The sun never sets on a Singer Sewing Machine at work." The Haitian poet René Depestre described this global market dominance in his poem "*La machine Singer*": "*Une machine Singer dans un foyer nègre / Arabe, indien, malais, chinois, annamite / Ou dans n'importe quelle maison sans boussole du tiers-monde.*"⁶⁶ We find a vivid illustration of this global presence in "*n'importe quelle maison*" in Aimé Césaire's 1939 prose-poetic masterpiece *Cahier d'un retour au pays natal*. The speaker describes the family home in Martinique, where all night long his mother sews on a Singer machine:

> At the close of foreday morning, another little house with an unpleasant odor in a very narrow street, a minuscule house that shelters dozens of rats within its rotten wooden entrails, and the turmoil caused by my six brothers and sisters; a cruel little house that relentlessly confounds the last days of every month . . . and my mother whose legs pedal for our unflagging hunger, pedal by day, by night—I have even been awakened at night by those unflagging

legs pedaling at night—and the harsh bite into the soft flesh of night taken by a Singer sewing machine that my mother pedals and pedals for our hunger, by day and by night.[67]

Children and rats proliferate in this "cruel little house," where a mercurial father might move from tenderness to rage at any point, and the mother labors, day and night, at the Singer "for our hunger." The mother "pedals and pedals"; because the children's hunger is "unflagging," so too must her laboring body never rest. At home, the poet's mother is subject to the same speed-up and intensification of work that predominates in the formal workplace. The governing mode here is gothic horror: the dozens of rats, the "cruel" house, the magic spell that breaks into rage, the "harsh bite into the soft flesh of night" (and into the maternal body) taken by the sewing machine itself, which resembles Marx's famous image of the ravenous appetites of the dead labor of capital, which, "vampire-like, lives by sucking living labor, and lives the more, the more labor it sucks."[68] Césaire's image of his mother pedaling "by day, by night" as her time and body are "bitten" by the sewing machine echoes Marx's point that there is no limit to the working day, that the capitalist tries "to make the working-day as long as possible, and to make, whenever possible, two working-days out of one."[69] The demands of profit extraction expand into the night and perhaps beyond: the line about being "awakened at night" suggests both the immediate experience of the child Césaire in the home and the haunting aftermath of his mother's labor. Meanwhile, bodies, both animal and human, multiply: the dozens of rats, the many children, the hysterically pedaling legs. From within the space of the colonized Martinican home, Césaire's image registers the scale of this labor exploitation. *Cahier* locates the home as a site of gendered labor where global capitalism is articulated and the worker's labor power is devoured.

In this chapter, I have traced how mass migration, the character of the early twentieth-century garment industry, and life within the tenements raise epistemic and representative problems for poetry. For Ridge, these problems produce new forms of solidarity, connection, and subjectivity. These questions are still live for writers working today, even though the conditions of Ridge's time are different from our own. In the "global assembly line" that predominates today, any garment might be designed in Lower Manhattan, made of textiles produced in Turkey, cut in Bangkok, sewn in Vietnam, and purchased on an iPhone made in Shenzhen via an app pitched and sold in California and engineered in India, before the garment is taken from a fulfillment center in Sunset Park to the door of an apartment in Sunnyside. Bruce Robbins coined the term "the sweatshop sublime" to describe the sudden, giddy awareness that one's everyday life is linked to this enormous, labyrinthine, global network of exploited labor. If the sweatshop sublime does not necessarily lead to understanding or action, Robbins writes, it "rightly forces on us the knowledge of social interdependence."[70]

For certain poets writing today, the recognition that the "operations of patriarchy and accumulation on a world scale constitute the structural and ideological framework within which women's reality today has to be understood," as Maria Mies writes in her foundational book on the international division of labor, forms the condition and subject of their writing.[71] In Juliana Spahr's 2011 book, *Well Then There Now*, the poet spins out meditations on her working-class childhood in Appalachia and women working globally under different but shared conditions. To do so, Spahr uses the refrain "I was trying to think." "I was trying to think about women sewing garments in Liberia," she writes in "The Incinerator." "I was trying to think about women panning the tailings of diamond gravel for gold in Sierra Leone." Spahr describes these suspended efforts of thinking as a kind of split sight that devolves into an impossible third eye: "I was trying to think about what sort of vision one needed to have in order to keep one eye on the neighborhood and then one eye on the nation and then yet one more eye on the world."[72]

That split attention is pursued in Anne Boyer's 2015 book of prose poetry, *Garments Against Women*, which feels around the edges of this global network of labor processes through the voice of a single mother living in Kansas City in the twenty-first century whose life is contoured by poverty, insecurity, and unwaged care work. When the speaker is not working—or "not writing"—she learns to sew, buying cheap notions and remaking garments from thrift stores and yard sales. The work of sewing is figured in the broader context of the speaker's waged labor and the "infinite laboratory" of capital. "I make anywhere from 10 to 15 dollars an hour at any of my three jobs," the speaker writes. "A garment from Target or Forever 21 costs 10 to 30 dollars. A garment from a thrift store costs somewhere between 4 and 10 dollars. A garment at a garage sale costs 1 to 5 dollars. A garment from a department store costs 30 to 500 dollars."[73] With each garment she works and reworks, the speaker thinks about the labor of others; the fabric that she sews contains "the hours of the lives, those of the farmers and shepherds and chemists and factory workers and truckers and salespeople and the first purchasers, the givers-away, who were probably women who sewed" (*Garments*, 29). As she sews, she reaches into a history contoured by gendered labor. "Always when I sew I think of Emma Goldman with her sewing machine, or Emma Goldman during her first night in jail 'at least bring me some sewing,'" the speaker thinks (*Garments*, 29). From Goldman, the speaker moves to the Wikipedia entry on the sewing machine and then to a sewing blog, where she reads that "each garment holds in it hours of a garment worker's life" (*Garments*, 29). As she sews, the "historical of sewing" becomes a "feeling," which begins "tendrilling" out of the speaker, connecting Boyer not only to Goldman but also to the lives of all the women who sew and have sewed. That "feeling" is also a kind of political knowledge that articulates the conditions that Boyer and these women share, without ever representing them directly.[74]

As the speaker struggles to cut fabric precisely, sew straight seams, or follow the directions of the pattern maker, she imagines that her congealed labor will reveal itself as a character flaw. "I think of some future for the garment," she imagines, "inspected in the thrift store where it will someday rest: *this was not an attentive sewist*, the future shopper thinks, and wrinkles her nose or whatever, shrugs" (*Garments*, 27). If her garments have futures, they also have histories as demonstrated when the speaker encounters the character and bodies of other sewists through the garments she reworks: "At the Salvation Army I bought a gray silk polka-dotted wrap dress made a very long time ago by a woman named Louise Jones. She sewed a 'fashioned by Louise Jones' label inside the neck of it. She gave it fine French seams. I bought that dress for four dollars along with a wide gold belt to wear with it for one dollar. The dress smells like lotion, or rather like old lotion and the smell of a body which must be the odor of the extraordinary seamstress Louise Jones" (*Garments*, 28). Christopher Oakey calls the relationship that Boyer has with other sewists "sororal" and sees it as a matter of "attempting to produce a self already formed from the lives of others that were themselves, the poem argues, coercively formed under similar conditions of production."[75] Sewing and resewing literalizes relations that are usually obscured. Silvia Federici writes that history itself is a commons, that history forms "our collective memory, our extended body connecting us to a vast expanse of struggles that give meaning and power to our political practice."[76] In Boyer's poetry, it is the labor of sewing, the repetitive motion of the body at work and the congealed labor of the previous sewer in the garment, that allows her to access this vast historical archive of women's work. It is in the force of this subjective feeling that poetry's political effects reside.

The question of how to understand the lives of others that are felt and sensed but not immediately seen animates Ridge's later poetry. Ridge wrote many solidarity poems after "The Ghetto." Her finest come in 1927's *Red Flag*, which includes a suite of four poems about the victims of legal and extralegal executions: the anarchist Albert Parsons, executed in the aftermath of the Haymarket affair; the IRA soldier Kevin Barry (misspelled "Kelvin"), executed by the British government in 1920; and an unnamed victim of state electrocution. The third poem in this suite, "Morning Ride," turns to the death of Leo Frank, a Jewish factory superintendent wrongly convicted for the murder of a thirteen-year-old employee and lynched by the Ku Klux Klan in Georgia in 1915.[77] As the speaker moves through the city, the "headlines chanting" remind her of Frank's death:

> leo frank
> lynched ten
>   say it with flowers
> wrigley's spearmint gum
>   carter's little liver—
> lean
> to the soft blarney of the wind
> fooling with your hair,
> look
> milk-clouds oozing over the blue
>   Step Lively Please
>   Let 'em Out First, Let 'em Out
> did he too feel it on his forehead,
> the gentle raillery of the wind,
> as the rope pulled taut over the tree
> in the cool dawn?[78]

It is a signature modernist moment of immersion in the ambient material of the city: the whirling, almost alive, threateningly "fanged" skyscrapers that house the city's corporations; the ads and headlines; the conductor's voice snapping us to attention; the poem's paratactic form; then the contained question of the last lines, which winnow down to an enclosed quatrain. Where the attentions of "The Ghetto" are careful and deliberate, the montage of "Morning Ride" works with what is incidentally encountered over the course of a morning. The poet doesn't set out to think about Frank; they are going about their day as his death whirs in the background. If parataxis "puts things together," as Anahid Nersessian suggests, but "does not explain why they should be so organized, nor tell some tale to justify their contiguity," the final four lines wrench out a meaning from the poem's collisions.[79] But there is a lightness of touch to this meaning, from when we are invited to "lean / to the soft blarney of the wind" and then to look at the "milk-clouds oozing," an absorption interrupted by the conductor's ushering voice. The final lines bring the day's experiences back to bear on Frank, and to the speaker's understanding of their life in the city and the social body. To exist as a body in the world, to have felt the wind on your forehead, to breathe the air common to us all, is to understand something of the last breaths of a murdered man. At the very least, it is to be capable of imagining it.

But this is ultimately a smaller ambition than that of "The Ghetto." "The Ghetto" makes a harder claim on us. It demands deliberateness and attention while testing the limits of the insight that such attention can produce. There is no place in Ridge's imagination for poetry as solitary experience; she begins from the premise that poetry is unique in its ability to express the common experiences of people who live and labor under similar conditions even if separated by generation, language, religion, or, as in "Morning Ride," death. It would be easy to dismiss Ridge's optimistic embrace of "life / pent, overflowing" as naïveté. Optimism is a difficult thing to historicize, not least because history constantly threatens to prove it misjudged or foolish. But it is also perhaps the sine qua non for any art that hopes to form new collectives out of shared struggles. As Jacques Rancière writes, literature "makes new forms of political subjectivization thinkable" by breaking through "the surface of political forms of equality to reach true equality or rather to dismiss equality in favor of the sympathy or fraternity of the subterranean drives or impersonal rhythms and intensities of collective life." It is through this process that writing "weaves . . . the fabric of the political."[80] "The Ghetto" weaves into its very fabric the epistemic problems necessary to the collective work of poetry. Rather than conceal the gaps in her understanding, Ridge embraces her poem's uncertainty and limitations and insists on the value of that uncertainty all the same. More radically, "The Ghetto" asserts that such lacunae are crucial for the project of political solidarity, and it is precisely in the poem's imperfections that we can see Ridge's utopian vision.

Chapter Three

LANGSTON HUGHES'S CONSTRUCTIVIST POETICS

> All of these poems make reference to the injustice of the wage earner's lot and in most of them there is also a reference to the workers taking over . . . Park Avenue.
>
> —LANGSTON HUGHES'S FBI FILE

On March 1, 1933, Langston Hughes wrote to Carl Van Vechten from Moscow, sending with his letter a selection of the poems he had been writing for the preceding two years. He expressed his hope that "they're good poems" and his confidence that the packet "represents pretty well the younger Negro mind today, and will be quite as timely as was my WEARY BLUES six years ago—since everything seems to be moving left at home."[1] Van Vechten, however, was less than enthusiastic. "I am going to be frank with you and tell you that I don't like 'Good Morning Revolution' (except in spots) at all," he wrote. "The revolutionary poems seem very weak to me; I mean very weak on the lyric side. I think in ten years, whatever the social outcome, you will be ashamed of these." Van Vechten declared Hughes's new poems to be "very revolutionary" but "so little poetic in tone." He continued, "I think it is possible (though difficult) to be a good revolutionist and a good artist, too, but I think you'll have to ask yourself more questions (more searchingly) in case you decide to carry on this program. Ask yourself for instance: Have I written a poem? Has it got a new idea? Has it got a new feeling into it? Will it make other people feel? Will it make other people think? Have I written a poem or a revolutionary tract?"[2] Hughes conceded that many of the poems he had sent were "not as lyrical as they might be—but even at that I like some of them as well as anything I ever did." In response to Van Vechten's prophecy, he embraced the possibility of delayed humiliation for "it would be amusing to publish a volume of such poems just now, risking the shame of the future (as you predict) for the impulse of the moment."[3]

Some of Hughes's later critics have agreed with Van Vechten's initial assessment that the poems Hughes wrote during and after his visit to the Soviet Union lack the supple artistry and aesthetic achievement of his earlier work and that this was because his energy and attention were taken up by revolutionary politics. In marked contrast to his enthusiastic reclamation of Hughes's sophomore collection, *Fine Clothes to the Jew*, Arnold Rampersad has little praise for the formal accomplishment of Hughes's 1930s verse. "Was it merely a coincidence that Hughes's art seemed to decline in his most radical years?" Rampersad asks. "Probably not. Radical socialist literary theory, as exhibited in his collection 'A New Song', tended to short-circuit the full process of Hughes's artistic genius."[4] Anthony Dawahare acknowledges that the neglect of the 1930s poems is "unfortunate," but he concedes that Hughes's project of dreaming into being an international collective of workers "may not have produced what some of us would deem formally or tonally 'beautiful' works."[5] James Smethurst observes that critics have tended to dismiss Hughes's 1930s poems as "beyond form"; for these critics, he writes, "such poetry is sloganeering, and a slogan, as everyone knows, is inherently uninteresting except perhaps sociologically."[6] In this chapter, I work to unite the sociologically interesting with the formally attentive by reading Hughes's 1930s poetry as an aesthetic response to a political problem.

The 1930s were a decade of formal awakening and experiment for Hughes, sparked in no small part by his time in Russia and his encounter with postrevolutionary Soviet aesthetics, particularly Russian Constructivism and, most relevantly for this chapter, the Constructivist theater. The major formal innovation of the postrevolutionary period, Constructivism formed a heterogeneous movement whose practitioners worked in various forms of media, from graphic design and photography to cinema and architecture, to conduct their experiments in utility and form. Constructivism attempted to rethink the relationship between art and industry and suture art-making to the principles of engineering and design of the postrevolutionary workers' state. It was a self-reflexive and self-referential movement that underscored the artist's role *as worker*, and Barrett Watten notes that Constructivist aesthetics embody "the imperative in radical literature and art to foreground their formal construction."[7] By reading Hughes alongside this Constructivist vision, we can resituate his 1930s poetry as part of a broader American cultural effort, shaped by the brutalities of Jim Crow America and sharpened by the crisis of the Depression, to create forms that could articulate collective experiences and commitments. Like Ridge, Hughes's political imagination was fundamentally collective and global in orientation. Unlike Ridge, however, who experimented with the flexibility of the lyric poem and its subject by turning to the extended form of the poetic sequence, Hughes embraced experimental, often theatrical forms, developing a style that could articulate the collective struggles of the international working class.

Hughes's efforts in the 1930s to articulate shared struggles and agitate for shared freedom form a signature instance of the Black radical tradition's embrace of new collectives against the social formations of racial capitalism. Cedric Robinson's influential theorization of racial capitalism in *Black Marxism* as a description of entwined processes of social differentiation and accumulation is instructive here.[8] Scholars have taken up the heuristic of racial capitalism to understand how capitalism develops expropriative methods that bring populations into productive labor and simultaneously "relies on exclusion from those same modes of production and accumulation in the form of containment, incarceration, abandonment, and underdevelopment for a racial surplus population."[9] Capitalism is, as Nancy Fraser observes, "a mode of accumulation that is simultaneously a system of domination," and a powerful manifestation of that domination is the social separateness and uneven life chances, naturalized and enforced as race, that are integral to the accumulation process.[10] For Jodi Melamed, racial capitalism names "the disjoining or deactivating of relations between human beings (and human and nature)" that capitalist expropriation requires.[11] Drawing on Ruth Wilson Gilmore, Melamed describes racial capitalism as a technology of "antirelationality" for capital "partitions, divides, and separates groups between political geographies *and* is the dominant relation to flow between and bind them. What is stripped out are other (and other possible) relations to land, resources, activity, community, and other possible social wholes that have been broken up for capital." Against this, in the Black radical tradition, "collective resistance takes the form of (re)constituting collectives."[12]

This chapter focuses on such an instance of forming new collectives. Building on Anthony Reed's description of Black aesthetic experiment in

Freedom Time, I read Hughes's Constructivist poetics as a formally distinct example of how "black experimental poetics set their own agenda, articulate conflicts and politics in the present, posit alternative modes of futurity and community, and require new modes of thinking."[13] The radical poetry that Hughes wrote in the 1930s seeks a language of solidarity for the shared struggles of exploited laborers in the capitalist core and their expropriated brethren in its peripheries. It does this in ways that mark a turning point in Hughes's career, namely, by drawing on and developing the techniques of Russian Constructivism and the Soviet avant-garde, particularly the theater. It is not simply that Hughes's poems are anti-aesthetic or evacuated of "art" but also that they represent a formal response to the shifting landscape of labor politics and what art might do for labor. It was in relation to Constructivism that Hughes participated in two of the key projects for leftist and labor-aligned writers in the 1930s: first, the articulation of a collective subject, a "we"; and second, an emergent spatial understanding of the geographies of international anti-capitalist struggle. In her 2005 book on Constructivist art, Maria Gough sought to challenge the received view that the formalism of the Constructivists of the 1920s was at odds with leftist politics and party ideology. Gough "attempts to demonstrate that the Constructivists' preoccupation with form is never singular—that it is never a preoccupation with *making* at the expense of the ideological meaning of that which is made."[14] This chapter shares a similar motivation to Gough's work but from the other end: reading Hughes through the framework and the formal strategies of Constructivism, I argue that Hughes's socially committed verse is not only a preoccupation with ideology at the expense of form but also a formal intervention into a shifting understanding of both poetic labor and poetry's representation of collective life.

GUESS I'LL QUIT NOW

Before turning to Hughes's 1930s poetry, I want to consider his poetics of labor in the 1920s. Hughes's 1927 sophomore collection, *Fine Clothes to the Jew*, a follow-up to the previous year's *The Weary Blues*, describes the lives of service workers, alcoholics, gamblers, sex workers, and prize fighters. The book was largely praised by the white press but reviewed poorly in the Black press, where Hughes was described as a "sewer dweller," a writer of poems that "reek of the gutter," and the "poet 'low-rate' of Harlem" (a pun on "laureate") who wrote an "unsanitary, insipid and repulsing . . . commentary on the psychology of the 'new Negro.'"[15] Hughes would later claim that the poems originated in his own experience of service work, writing that they were written "while I was dragging bags of wet wash laundry around or toting trays of dirty-dishes to the dumb-waiter of the Wardman Park Hotel in Washington."[16] An elevator attendant in such a hotel appears in "Elevator Boy" from *Fine Clothes*:

> I got a job now
> Runnin' an elevator
> In the Dennison Hotel in Jersey.
> Job ain't no good though.
> No money around.
>   Jobs are just chances
>   Like everything else.[17]

In Hughes's 1930 Bildungsroman *Not Without Laughter*, Sandy, the protagonist, finds work as an elevator attendant after moving from Kansas to Chicago. Hughes details this work in the book's penultimate chapter, "Elevator": "At the hotel Sandy's hours on duty were long, and his legs and back ached with weariness from standing straight in one spot all the time, opening and closing the bronze door of the elevator. He had been assigned the last car in a row of six, each manned by a colored youth standing inside his metal box in a red uniform, operating the lever that sent the car up from the basement grill to the roof-garden restaurant on the fifteenth floor and then back down again all day. Repeating up-down—up-down—up-down interminably, carrying white guests." After two months, "there were times when Sandy felt as though he could stand it no longer." He works with older men, like his coworker Mr. Harris, who have been on this job for decades. The repetition of the job, "the same doors opening at the same unchanging levels hundreds of times each innumerable, monotonous day," looms before Sandy.[18] Unlike Mr. Harris, however, Sandy manages to leave, and by the end of the novel he is planning to return to high school.

The poem promises no such thing. The elevator's rising and falling traps its attendant in a Sisyphean labor that raises the attendant and lands him inexorably back on the ground in sharp monosyllables: "up an' down, / Up an' down." There's a heavy resignation to this poem, in which jobs are "just chances / Like everything else." The elevator's movement makes a game of chance out of the myth of occupational and social mobility. That there will be no end to this or to similar labors is underscored by the speaker's imagining of the next job, consisting of "somebody else's shoes / To shine, / Or greasy pots in a dirty kitchen." "Somebody else's shoes" seems to offer the promise of change by holding on to the idea that the elevator worker might step into somebody else's life. But the line breaks; those shoes will be made "to shine," and labor will continue. The poem's final line reformulates its first line, "I got a job now":

> I been runnin' this
> Elevator too long.
> Guess I'll quit now.[19]

Able to move upward only as far as the elevator rises, then quickly plunged to earth again, the elevator worker chooses to end his trials. John Marsh reads this line optimistically, writing that the "casualness of the sentiment reveals how little is at stake in the decision [to quit]—yet how important the always available strategy of quitting was to make service work manageable."[20] I agree that its sentiment is casual, but it is casual only because the gesture is almost meaningless. The boy can quit abruptly because there will be more interchangeable jobs—more elevators, more shoes, more greasy pots. The decision to quit amounts to no ending at all.

Fine Clothes paints a picture of the racist working conditions of Jim Crow America. In service jobs, Black workers labored as porters, chauffeurs, and servers; in manufacturing plants, white supremacist pseudoscience was harnessed to justify forcing Black workers to perform the most difficult and dangerous work.[21] By 1920, the Black industrial workforce had increased by more than 150 percent, whereas the percentage of Black farmers had decreased by 30 percent.[22] Yet while the numbers of Black workers in industry swelled, the racism of organized white labor meant that Black workers were excluded from unions and largely absent from the strikes that defined the 1910s.[23] Black union representation increased in the 1920s, in part because of Soviet recognition of the oppression of Black laborers and the Soviet conviction that untapped revolutionary potential was to be found outside Western Europe. A homegrown Black labor movement gathered strength from the mid-1920s onward. In October 1925, the American

Negro Labor Congress took place in Chicago with five hundred attendees who aimed to build a militant workers' organization.[24] "Unquestionably," wrote Robert Minor in *Workers Monthly*, "this convention resulted in forming a strong nucleus for a mass movement, and a nucleus which already has the beginnings of mass connections."[25]

Some of the Black labor movement's early successes came from the efforts of the fifteen thousand workers employed as porters for the Pullman Company who organized in the summer of 1925 to form the Brotherhood of Sleeping Car Porters (BSCP). After three years as an independent union, in 1928 they shocked white delegates at the American Federation of Labor convention by applying for an international charter.[26] Porters worked an average of four hundred hours a month for poor wages (the starting salary for regular workers was sixty-seven dollars a month, with the cost of uniform, shoe polish, meals, and so on deducted from their wages); they carried luggage, shone shoes, cut hair, served drinks, and adhered to a strict code of etiquette.[27] This kind of work kept the link between Black working men, servitude, and enslaved labor alive. In their unionization campaigns, the BSCP "drew upon the memories of slavery and emancipation to connect the union's challenge to the Pullman Company to the larger quest for first-class citizenship in the broader political arena."[28] Hughes describes a porter's labor in a poem from *Fine Clothes*:

> I must say
> Yes, sir,
> To you all the time.
> Yes, sir!
> Yes, sir!
> All my days
> Climbing up a great big mountain
> Of yes, sirs!
>
> Rich old white man
> Owns the world.
> Gimme yo' shoes
> To shine.
>
> Yes, sir![29]

Hughes realizes this endless labor, also Sisyphean, vertically as "a great big mountain / Of yes, sirs!" This poem's motivating energy is the repetition of two words—"Yes, sir!"—which register the affective labor of the porter, a labor that demands the workers' obedience and willingness to produce comfort and domination in the person they serve. The "great big mountain" of the porter's work echoes the title of Hughes's famous essay published in *The Nation* the previous year, "The Negro Artist and the Racial Mountain," in which Hughes traced "this urge within the race towards whiteness, the desire to pour racial individuality into the mold of American standardization, and to be as little Negro and as much American as possible."[30] White supremacy is constructed and maintained by Black service work and by the extraction of a social performance of deference. By interjecting the porter's thoughts with the discursively imposed language of his labor ("Yes, sir!"), "Porter" shows how whiteness demands a standardized Black affective labor that enforces racial hierarchies.

The major formal innovation of *Fine Clothes to the Jew* is the stanzaic blues poem. Along with Sterling Brown, Hughes is credited with transforming the rich musical tradition of the blues into a standardized poetic form. In his prefatory "Note on Blues," Hughes defines the form in terms of its "strict poetic pattern: one long line repeated and a third line to rhyme with the first two." To this he adds a reminder that the blues define a distinctive mood, which is "always despondency, but when they are sung people laugh."[31] The blues poem's effect is largely in its handling of repetition followed by modification or change. Hughes suggested that the third line "rhymes" with the repeated first two lines—just as the sound pattern of rhyming shapes meaning, that third line can reinforce, challenge, or modify the preceding two lines. The standard form of the blues poem also means that the poem can be repeated; each individual blues poem is part of a larger body of poems that work through similar themes and experiences, told by similar characters. Take, for example, Sterling Brown's trio of poems, "New St. Louis Blues." The first poem, "Market Street Woman," shows us the life of a down-on-her-luck sex worker; the next, "Tornado Blues" describes the "dirty work" of a tornado that pulverizes a neighborhood; and "Low Down" gives us a man asking for tobacco, "bummin' cut plug from passers by." Aimless, wageless, and unemployed, the speaker of "Low Down" meditates on his lucklessness in a variation on the idea of luck that we saw in Hughes's "Elevator Boy." Here, the "dice are loaded," and the "deck's all marked to hell," as the speaker's path in the afterlife is clear.[32] Where "Elevator Boy" ends with a sudden refusal of labor, Brown's poem underscores the entrapment of the man asking to borrow tobacco, mapping this onto a larger system of inequality and suffering. "New St. Louis Blues" shows us not an individual instance of suffering but a shared experience of Black immobility and unemployment. The repetition with which the blues does its work—both within the individual stanza and as a repeated, repeatable form—indexes Black unfreedom, even as it refuses the myth of social mobility and racial uplift through hard work.

Brent Hayes Edwards reminds us that the blues poems that Brown and Hughes were writing did not constitute "a recognized subgenre, but instead an area of literary experimentation in open concert with a brand of commercial music viewed as licentious or degenerate."[33] The poems were also deemed degenerate for the socially and economically marginalized lives they represented. Their speakers are unemployed or precariously employed and geographically displaced, subject either to forced immobility or migration. The blues poem is frequently poised at the moment of departure, the train pulling away from the station, a life left behind. Brown's poem "Riverbank Blues" limns the contradictions of enforced mobility, with "muddy streams" keeping the speaker "fixed for good" and the river threatening to leave the man "in some ornery riverbank town."[34] In their intertwined immobility and dispossession, the speakers of Hughes's and Brown's blues poems exemplify the "bare life" that Michael Denning, reformulating Marx's account of the surplus population of labor, describes as those who are "disposable in the eyes of state and market." Denning invites us to understand that "'proletarian' is not a synonym for 'wage laborer,' . . . but for dispossession, expropriation, and radical dependence on the market. You don't need a job to be a proletarian: wageless life, not wage labor, is the starting point in understanding the free market."[35] We can see this dispossession and dependence at play in the first stanza of Hughes's poem "Bound No'th Blues":

> Goin' down the road, Lawd,
> Goin' down the road.
> Down the road, Lawd,
> Way, way down the road.
> Got to find somebody
> To help me carry this load.

The poem's speaker is unnamed, one of the millions of Black Southerners who left the South for the North seeking an escape from Jim Crow, white supremacist terror, and coercive labor practices. Margaret Ronda calls on Denning's concept of wageless life in her reading of Paul Laurence Dunbar's 1896 *Lyrics of Lowly Life*, writing that Dunbar's agrarian laborers—at once bound to their work and disposable—elaborate "a plot that runs counter to capitalist economic language of value, measure, exchange, and progress; to the ideology of the work ethic and virtuous wealth; and to racial uplift narratives centered on productive labor."[36] Like Dunbar's speakers, Hughes's dispossessed have no way out, and the poem implicitly refutes optimism regarding the Great Migration and racial progress. Whereas "Elevator Boy" and "Porter" are oriented vertically, here the orientation is primarily flat and horizontal, toward the stretch of "way, way down the road." Its space is at once endless and constricting. The road expands, but it offers nothing beyond this expansion, nothing beyond the point of "way, way down." Itinerancy, mobility, and dispossession are not temporary features but continually reinforced; they are not a line to move across but a space one is forced to sit within. The speaker never makes it North, and the poem refuses even to rehearse the familiar narrative of disappointment in Northern racism. "Road's in front o' me, / Nothin' to do but walk. / Road's in front o' me, / Walk . . . an' walk . . . an' walk." The poem leaves us suspended in the endless walking as movement becomes another constricted condition.

I have indicated that the specific energies of the blues stanza are formed by the repetition of its A-A'-B structure, with a line repeated—Hughes often breaks his into two lines—followed by a third line that resolves, reiterates, or offers a counterpoint to the first two. "Bound No'th Blues" does enormous work with this formal structure of repetition and reformulation. Here is its final stanza:

> Road, road, road, O!
> Road, road . . . road . . . road, road!
> Road, road, road, O!
> On the no'thern road.
> These Mississippi towns ain't
> Fit fer a hoppin' toad.

"Road" is stated twelve times in four lines. In the first three lines, it is the only word, the only linguistic feature besides two ellipses and two exclamatory *Os*, which are vocal but nonverbal. Its repetition is both insistent and emptying; there is (literally) nothing but road in those lines. Here, *road* comes to mean repetition itself. It signifies persistence, predictability, and inescapability, as well as an ironic refusal of progress. "Road" repeated enough becomes the condition of being on the road. Once again, no alternative is presented, for the North exists only as the road's direction, and Southern towns cannot be tolerated; they "ain't / Fit fer a hoppin' toad." The rhyme lands heavily on the "hoppin' toad," which brings out the wry, melancholy humor of the blues. "Hoppin'" registers the speaker's itinerancy (it was contemporary slang for hopping onto a moving train, or getting a ride without paying), but it also gives the speaker a kind of elegance: "hoppin'" suggests a dance or shuffle, as well as a kind of pragmatic light-footedness, which brings us back to the distinctive rhythm of the blues poem. Even as the poem holds the threat of racist dehumanization over the speaker's head, it refuses that in favor of humor and grace.

In a belittling review of *Fine Clothes to the Jew* printed in *New Masses* in 1927, Kenneth Fearing wrote that Hughes's poetry made use of "dialect and jazz rhythm . . . with as much success as anyone has achieved using those limiting devices." "The trouble with these successes," Fearing declared, "is that they are small, the poems are little better than poignant playthings."[37] Fearing's description of Hughes's poems as mere "playthings" is the mirror image of the complaint against Hughes's insufficient lyricism that would be levied by Van Vechten six years later: that the poems are too functional, too *far* from poignant playthings. Fearing missed, of course, the way that Hughes's blues poems develop a political aesthetic. Reading Brown's and Bessie Smith's blues in relation to the 1927 Mississippi floods, Sonya Posmentier writes that the structure of environmental catastrophe "itself provides the aesthetic alternative to teleological narrative" because catastrophe's structure is "repetitive, migratory, circulatory, transformative, dispersive, and connecting."[38] In Brown and Hughes, the devices of the blues poem index the repetitive and dispersive conditions of wageless Black life in the 1920s. But blues irony evokes this stuckness and forced repetition; it doesn't provide a transformative vision. Or, to put it in Anthony Reed's terms, "the blues underscores what needs transformation."[39] It was in the subsequent decade, as we will see, that Hughes would shift his sights to the project of transformation itself.

SPRING BESIDE THE KREMLIN

Scattered throughout the six hundred boxes of the Hughes Papers in Yale University's Beinecke Library are traces of Hughes's time in the Soviet Union and beyond: a list of cities visited and miles traveled, scraps of paper containing addresses in Moscow, his map of Samarkand, as well as a collection of postcards showing socialist realist depictions of May Day demonstrations, photographs of collective farmer workers, and illustrations of Russian airships. In 1932, Hughes traveled to Moscow via Berlin to make a film about race relations in the American South. "I envy you doing a film in Moscow," wrote Ezra Pound to Hughes on July 8, 1932, the same day the Dow Jones plunged to its lowest point of the Great Depression as the Hoover administration lived out its final months and fascism continued to make progress across the European continent. "I won't say I wish I were there," Pound continued, "for I haven't got the stamina to see such a job through, and I have too much to do."[40] Pound need not have doubted his stamina for the film project was canceled before shooting ever began. Hughes was part of a group of twenty-two Black actors and writers hired to make the film, to be produced by a German–Russian studio, the Meschrabpom Film Corporation of the Workers International. Named *Chernye i belye* (*Black and White*) in homage to Vladimir Mayakovsky's poem of the same name, the film focused on the lives of steel mill workers in Birmingham, Alabama, and was designed to be "a kind of trade-union version of the Civil War all over again, intended as a great sweeping panorama of contemporary labor battles in America."[41] In *I Wonder as I Wander*, Hughes describes how the film's protagonist was to be a progressive white labor organizer who campaigned for Black and white unification against the white capitalist antagonists. The plot was to build up to a race riot, in response to which the white workers of the North would rush to the aid of the unionized Southern workers. "It would have looked wonderful on screen," Hughes wrote, "so well do the Russians handle crowds in films" (*IWAW*, 103).

This was about all the praise that Hughes could muster for the script. Despite the Comintern's approval, Hughes deemed the screenplay—written by a Russian, Georgii Eduardovich Grebner, who had never visited the United States—to be "a pathetic hodgepodge of good intentions and faulty facts," and concluded that "the writer's concern for racial freedom and decency had tripped so completely on the stumps of ignorance" (*IWAW*, 101).[42] The German director chosen to work on the film, Karl Junghans, had only directed one movie, *Strange Birds of Africa* (later titled *Fleeting Shadows*), an anti-imperialist documentary set in Africa. Yet *Black and White* was to stumble over more than the script. Despite a series of negotiations with the Comintern, the group was informed that the film would not be completed (*IWAW*, 116). The group returned from Odessa to Moscow, where the more irate members accused Meschrabpom of having betrayed the Black workers of America and having sabotaged the revolution. These complaints were repeated before the Comintern, who ruled that the film should be made after a year of hiatus, but this never eventuated.[43] Although during his year in the Soviet Union Hughes befriended filmmakers and attended parties at Sergei Eisenstein's home, the failed experience of *Black and White* left him with a negative impression of the collaborative production of filmmaking.[44] "O, Movies," he wrote. "Temperaments. Artists. Ambitions. Scenarios. Directors, producers, actors, censors, changes, revisions, conferences. It's a complicated art—the cinema. I'm glad I write poems."[45]

With the film production delayed and eventually abandoned, and the cinemas themselves deemed "ice-cold," poorly ventilated, and "very pungent kennels," Hughes spent his year in Russia at the theater instead, and it was the theater that would leave the deepest imprint.[46] "All of us 'Negro-worker-comrades,' as Muscovites called us," Hughes recounts, "were almost nightly guests of one or another of the great theaters, the Moscow Art Theater, the Vakhtangov, the Meyerhold, the Kamerny, or the Opera, where we saw wonderful performances and met their distinguished actors" (*IWAW*, 101). Hughes writes with admiration of plays by Gorky, Chekhov, and Gogol seen at the Moscow Art Theater, which were subjected to Stanislavsky's "carefully realistic treatment" (*IWAW*, 208). He was invited to rehearsals by Okhlopkov and Meyerhold. In contrast with productions at the more popular Vakhtangov and Kamerny Theaters—"popular with the general public and the run-of-the-mill intellectuals" but nevertheless "expertly done and quite beautiful"—Hughes deemed those of the Okhlopkov and Meyerhold theaters "a little special, even for Moscow" (*IWAW*, 209). While traveling in the USSR he saw a great deal of regional and traditional theater, and he spent some of his last days in Moscow attending the amateur Workers' Theater Olympiad, which began on May 26, 1933, and the Professional Theater Festival, which began on June 1. He described the latter in a letter to Noël Sullivan written en route to China on the Trans-Siberian Express. "Moscow is a hard place to leave," Hughes lamented to Sullivan. "There's always something else one should see or do."[47]

The decade before Hughes's arrival in Moscow saw growing relations of solidarity and cooperation between the Bolsheviki and Black radicals in the United States. In an article written in 1913 and published as "Russians and Negros" in *Krasnaya Niva* in 1925, Lenin compared the United States in the aftermath of enslavement with Russia in the wake of serfdom. He notes the parallel chronologies of slavery and serfdom—two systems of human bondage developed on the borders of early modern Europe in response to shortages of agrarian labor, both abolished in the 1860s. He writes that Black Americans "still bear more than anyone else, the cruel marks of slavery" and deems the formerly slave-holding states "an American 'Russia.'"[48] Lenin argues that full freedom for Black Americans is not possible under capitalism for it "cannot give either complete emancipation or even complete equality," which can be achieved only under communism.[49] In the early 1920s, Lenin was largely responsible for the Communist Party USA's recognition of the plight of Black Americans after raising the issue directly at the Second Congress of the Communist International in 1920. In 1922, Otto Huiswoud and Claude McKay attended the Fourth Congress of the Communist International (Huiswoud as an official delegate and McKay as an unofficial observer) and presented a successful bid to the Comintern for the creation of a "Negro Commission." The work of Black communists "was to be one sector in a world movement against colonialism and imperialism as the contemporary stages of world capitalism."[50] Robin Kelley writes of McKay's address that his "point was clear: the Negro stood at the fulcrum of class struggle; there could be no successful working-class movement without black workers at the center."[51] After 1922, the training of Black American cadres in the Soviet Union was taken more seriously, resulting in the declaration at the Sixth Congress in 1928 that Black Americans constituted an "oppressed nation" in the South and a "national minority" in the North.[52]

Hughes's travels in the Soviet Union took place a decade after Huiswood and McKay's visit, not long before the First All-Union Congress of Soviet Writers held in August 1934. This was a period of transition, when the Writers' Union was increasing its hold over printing, distribution, publishing, radio, film, and theater; when commissions were regularized, and pay for artists was relatively secure. It was the final flush of the avant-garde, as Soviet realism had not yet been cemented as the only state-sanctioned mode of expression, and artistic experimentation had not yet been violently suppressed.[53] Hughes writes with open admiration of the literary culture of the Soviet Union in the early 1930s:

> This is the only place I've ever made enough to live on from writing. Poets and writers in the Soviet Union are highly regarded and paid awfully well; as a class, I judge, the best cared for literary people in the world. And books sell [like] hotcakes. Usually ten days after a new book has appeared, not a copy can be found. And in spite of the paper shortage, they print large editions. Imagine in America, 10,000 copies of anybody's book of poems—as a first edition. And that is common here! And then come the translations into all the minority languages.[54]

This formed a marked contrast with the difficulty that Hughes experienced in gaining regular employment and publication in the United States. While in Moscow, Hughes stayed at the Grand Hotel, where, as a tourist, he would have been insulated from food shortages. Hughes's admiration for the country was due in large part to his sense that the USSR was vastly outpacing Jim Crow America in social and racial progress. He wrote, "Of all the big cities in the world where I've been, the Muscovites seemed to me to be the politest of peoples to strangers. But perhaps that was because we were Negroes and, at that time, with the Scottsboro Case on world-wide trial in the papers everywhere, and especially in Russia, folks went out of their way to show us courtesy. On a crowded bus, nine times out of ten, some Russian would say, '*Negrochanski tovarish*—Negro comrade—take my seat!'" (*IWAW*, 99). It is unsurprising, then, that in 1933 he described the Soviet Union as the "dream of all the poor and oppressed—like us—come true."[55] Even as late as 1956, he would write only ambiguously about the purges and the sweeping violence of Stalinism.[56]

Hughes was not the only Black artist enthusiastic about Soviet racial progress, nor was he the only international traveler to write about the Soviet theater around this time. The American director Norris Houghton's *Moscow Rehearsals: An Account of Methods of Production in the Soviet Theater*, written after he had gained access to Stanislavsky's Moscow Art Theater, exhaustively documents the work of actors, directors, and set designers.[57]

In *The New Spirit in Russian Theater*, the British journalist and art critic Huntly Carter describes "the method of making the theater and people one, the theater free to all, of mixing the people with the dramatic, militant and constructive action of the plays."[58] His book consistently emphasizes the collective spirit of Russian theater, which elaborated the principle of "No personality but mass personality. No spectators but one spectator. No minds but a perception of Bolshevist aims and end in collective liberty."[59] The poet Joseph Macleod traveled to Russia, where he spent time with Paul Robeson "to see for myself what a real collective audience was like."[60] This was an interest echoed by the English actor and director André van Gyseghem, who, in his account of the Soviet theater based on four visits to the USSR between 1933 and 1938, describes the breakdown of the absolute, unimpeachable power of the author.[61] Carter, Macleod, and van Gyseghem's descriptions consistently highlight the change in the relationship between author and audience, as well as the elevation of the audience, no longer only as consumers but also as active producers of meaning. In the words of Lars Kleberg, "the center of gravity shifted from the *producer* viewed as a solitary subject to the *relationship* between producer and audience, and thus to the question of how art exerted its influence."[62]

These observers also wrote with enthusiasm and admiration for the social institutions around the theater: the collaborations between actors, writers, and directors and the close relationship between professional theater groups and amateur workers' theater. Van Gyseghem outlines the community work of staging a play, which involved meetings held in workers' clubs and institutes at which theater directors and club members could exchange thoughts about the play's historical and political significance and ideas for particular interpretations, acting "not only as individuals but as members of a theatrical community who have a common aim and who march in harmony together."[63] He goes on to describe the summertime provincial tours that the large theater groups would take to regional areas and farms. This was a system of mutual exchange in which actors learned more about the workers whom they were tasked with portraying and workers met actors, received theater tickets at reduced rates, and received advice on their amateur productions. There was a thriving culture of amateur workers' theater embodied by the Agit Brigades, the factory groups who made dramatic propaganda. The Olympiad of Autonomous Art, held in Moscow in April 1932, displayed the work of theatrical, choral, and orchestral agit groups from across the Soviet Union.⁶⁴ This culture of workers' theater was hugely attractive to Hughes. In the theater, he witnessed a more successful version of cooperative artistic production than that of the Meschrabpom debacle. If poetry could learn from the theater, then perhaps it could also bring about a new collective spirit.

CHANTS, SCRIPTS, AND BIOMECHANICS

In his 1921 manifesto, "Our Agenda," the avant-garde writer and critic Osip Brik explained how making art could be a collective enterprise:

> [The Bourgeoisie] thought that only an individual could create, that creation by a collective was absurd. The possibility of any artistic or creative achievement was excluded from factory and plant. Only an artist working with brush and chisel, or perhaps an artisan working manually, could lay claim to the status of a creator; the collective of workers in a factory or a plant—never.
> We know this is not the case. We know that the creative force of a collective is incalculably greater than that of single individuals. We know that until now the view that only individuals and not collectives were creative can be explained by the fact that the creative forces of a collective were liberated from the power of exploitative individuals only through the victory of the Communist Revolution. For us, factories and plants are tools of the collective's creativity, and from them we expect miracles incommensurable with the tricks of individual handicraftsmen.⁶⁵

In the immediate aftermath of the revolution, Russian poets experienced great pressure to establish a collective and proletarian mode of verse and to extricate poetry from its association with individualist values and bourgeois idleness. The philosopher and science fiction writer Aleksandr Bogdanov argued for a poetry of proletarian life and labor, away from a lyric poetry associated with the psychology and moods of the individual. Bogdanov's history of poetry and poetic consciousness moves in three phases corresponding to three "spirits": the spirit of authority, the spirit of individualism, and the spirit of fellowship. Proletarian poetry, still in its infancy, would be the verse of that final stage, which would bring into being a new poetic consciousness. "This new consciousness," Bogdanov wrote, "should unfold and enclose the whole of life, the whole of the world, in its creative unity."⁶⁶

In 1938, Hughes published his pamphlet *A New Song*, inspired by his travels throughout that decade. After traveling through Russia and central Asia, he made his way to China in 1933 and then spent time reporting on the Spanish Civil War for the *Baltimore Afro-American* in 1937. *A New Song* was printed by the International Workers Order (IWO), a fraternal benefit society affiliated with the Communist Party founded in 1930 after a split from the Workmen's Circle, a Jewish mutual benefit society.[67] With an introduction by Mike Gold, Hughes's pamphlet had an initial print run of ten thousand and a price tag of fifteen cents. Gold's foreword emphasizes the pamphlet's intended working-class readership and purpose of furthering multiracial solidarity. "The International Workers Order publishes these poems in the desire to make available literature which would otherwise be out of the reach of wage earners," he wrote. "It chose the poetry of Langston Hughes because it considers it as one of its missions to create a better understanding and closer solidarity between nationalities."[68] Its readership was the working class that made up the IWO's membership, which at its height numbered two hundred thousand.[69]

We can feel the imprint of Soviet literature on the poems that make up Hughes's pamphlet. In the thirties, Hughes translated poetry by Mayakovsky and Boris Pasternak, who visited Hughes while in Russia. In particular, Mayakovsky's formal experiments anticipate Hughes's, from his late typographic variations to his hybrid poem-plays.[70] But the real influence on these poems is Soviet performance culture. It is striking that in his March 1 letter to Van Vechten, which accompanied his packet of poems, Hughes does not mention the books or poets he is reading but goes into detail in his discussion of the theater:

> The theaters are very interesting this winter: A new art policy has gone into effect, and the poster-propaganda plays (enormously effective in their way) are giving place to a drama less rigidly stylized and of greater human scope. The new Gorky play, "Egor Bulachev and Others," is very rich and warm and beautifully done at the Vahtango Theater. It is about the decay of a merchant family on the eve of the revolution. . . . The Gypsy Theater is delightful. . . . And I've seen just about everything at Tairov's Kamery, where they do O'Neill, and where they tell me they have invited Paul [Robeson], and that he is interested and is learning Russian in London. It is the most "smart" and "highbrow" of the Russian theaters, brilliant but not as daring as Meyerhold or as solid as some of the others.[71]

Many of the poems that Hughes wrote in the 1930s take the form of chants, scripts, recitations, or performances. Hughes describes "The Colored Soldier" as "a dramatic recitation to be done in the half-dark"; "Broke" is "a complaint to be given by a dejected looking fellow"; "The Big-Timer" is "a moral poem to be rendered by a man in a straw hat"; and "Dark Youth of the U.S.A." is "a recitation to be delivered by a Negro boy." One of the most ambitious of *A New Song*'s theatrical poems is "Chant for May Day." In a letter to Van Vechten, Hughes described the 1933 May Day parade in Moscow: "I had a place on the Red Square. That moment when the military parade is over and the Square is cleared, a sea of workers bearing banners and slogans and emblems above their heads pours into the vast space before Stalin and Kalinin and the other leaders—well, there is nothing else like it to be seen in the world."[72]

Hughes's chant eschews poetic description of an event in favor of participatory script:

CHANT FOR MAY DAY

To be read by a Workman with, for background, the rhythmic waves of rising and re-rising Mass Voices, multiplying like the roar of the sea.

> WORKER: The first of May:
> When the flowers break through the earth,
> When the sap rises in the trees.
> When the birds come back from the South.
> Workers:
> Be like the flowers,
> 10 VOICES: Bloom in the strength of your unknown power,
> 20 VOICES: Grow out of the passive earth,
> 40 VOICES: Grow strong with Union,
> All hands together—
> To beautify this hour, this spring,
> And all the springs to come
> 50 VOICES: Forever for the workers![73]

The other chant in *A New Song*, "Chant for Tom Mooney," is about the labor leader convicted of the 1916 San Francisco Preparedness Day bombing. The poem was inspired by Hughes's time in Los Angeles;

he would later visit Mooney in San Quentin prison.[74] Whereas "Tom Mooney" is a more loosely organized chant that hinges on the repetition of Mooney's name ("remembered forever will be the name: / TOM MOONEY / schools will be named / TOM MOONEY"), "Chant for May Day" takes the form of a carefully directed script resembling the mass theatrical events that became popular after the Russian Revolution. After the lines I have quoted, the voices eventually build to one hundred workers who seize both political power and the "forces of the earth." Like the crowd scenes of the Soviet films that Hughes so admired, "Chant for May Day" choreographs a multitude. We can detect here the twin, intertwined formal and social impulses that characterize Constructivism, that of the formal construction of the text, and that of the utopian construction of a new society that these texts envisage. The voices build, beginning with a single worker and ending with one hundred. But this is not a linear process: the poem progresses from one worker to ten, twenty, forty, and fifty voices before returning to a single worker. The process repeats, until eventually we arrive at the full hundred voices. The nonlinearity means that we dwell in the process of construction that makes up the bulk of the poem. The poem and the voices it comprises gather and build, and so, too, does the poem's vision of the revolutionary future. Indeed, the poem locates the building of this future in the workers' collective voice.

Compare "Chant for May Day" with Claude McKay's poem "Petrograd: May Day, 1923," an early poem collected in *Cities*, comprising mostly poems from the mid-1930s:

> Cities are symbols of man's upward reach,
> Man drawing near to man in close commune,
> And mighty cities mighty lessons teach
> Of man's decay or progress, late or soon,
> And many an iron-towered Babylon,
> Beneath the quiet golden breath of Time
> Has vanished like the snow under the sun,
> Leaving no single mark in stone or rhyme
> To flame the lifted heart of man today,
> As Petrograd upon the First of May.[75]

The poem shares the Communist language of social and organic replenishment with Hughes—"today / All life rejoices in the first of May"—as well as the language of "close commune" and an investment in collective life. Their formal differences are obvious: the Petrograd poem, with its ten-line ABAB-CDCD-EE stanzas, is a sonnet (its regularity stands out from the modified sonnets that make up *Cities*).[76] The more significant difference is less the distance between sonnet and chant and more a difference in mode and where it positions its reader. Where McKay's poem works with the tools of lyric description and allows us to vividly imagine the events of May Day, Hughes's poem scaffolds a collective theatrical event and invites participation.

In a review of *A New Song* published in the *Daily Worker* in April 1938, Anna Peters wrote, "There are chants in this book which lose some of their effectiveness by being read instead of performed by mass choruses."[77] Peters's review raises a key issue: without one hundred other voices, how are we to read a poem like "Chant for May Day"? We know that poems usually register a fiction of spoken language even though they promise the possibility of a vocal reading. Hughes's chant both refuses and amplifies that fiction: it makes the possibility of speaking the poem's script its literal matter, but the gathering of so many voices arranged as they are makes its performance practically and logistically difficult. It is unclear whether Hughes intended the poem to be read aloud or simply to look as though it could with enough people. But it is more important that in the act of reading we are implicated in a choral upsurge of voices that make up the "fellowship" that Bogdanov described. The joining, surging voices conjure what Paolo Virno calls the multitude, with its "complex of breaks, landslides, and innovations," characterized by "the indefinite or *potential* character of its existence."[78] The multitude of voices embodies the "imaginary agent of society's creative *Potenza*," which brings about not just readers joined in unison but also emergent forms of existing together.[79]

A theatrical, self-consciously performative text like "Chant for May Day" asks to be read alongside histories of performance, and here I want to turn to a theorist and practitioner of the theater: Vsevolod Meyerhold, an actor and the director of the Meyerhold Theater, who best provides us with a critical language for reading Hughes's poem-scripts. During his visit to Russia, Hughes attended rehearsals at the Meyerhold Theater at the director's invitation and expressed repeated admiration for his techniques. Born in Penza to a Russian–German family and sentenced to death in 1940 during the purges, Meyerhold is best remembered for developing a program of actor training called biomechanics. His theories were influenced by the work of the poet and theorist of scientific management, Alexei Gastev, one of the architects of postrevolutionary rapid industrialization. In 1920, Gastev founded the Central Institute for Labor in Moscow, and, with the support of Lenin and Trotsky, his institute would attempt to bring Taylorism to the USSR. In his capacity as a poet, Gastev searched "for ways in which poetry can assist in the conversion of the excessiveness of the human body into the restraint and control of the machine."[80] "Chant for May Day" is a poem about not only performance but also, like Meyerhold's acting theory, the management of bodies in space and cultivating an aesthetics of bodily efficiency informed by Soviet Taylorism.

Meyerhold's theory of biomechanics was grounded in the idea that acting could be improved by harnessing industrial techniques of rationalization, productivity, and efficiency. His most extensive statement on biomechanics comes from a report of a lecture at the Moscow Conservatoire in June 1922. The report begins by lamenting the clear division between work and leisure that capitalism creates and by arguing that under socialism, "labor is no longer regarded as a curse but as a joyful, vital necessity."[81] To keep up with these "conditions of ideal labor," art, for Meyerhold, required a new method and a new form that must come from industry. This Taylorization of the theater meant scrapping elaborate costumes and makeup as a waste of time and replacing these trappings with a rigorous program of actor training. Adopted from gymnastics, boxing, and fencing, this "biomechanical" training was intended to cultivate the physical expressiveness of an actor's body and further Meyerhold's campaign against "psychology" in theater. For Meyerhold, "a theater built on psychological foundations is as certain to collapse as a house built on sand," but "a theater which relies on physical elements is at very least assured of clarity."[82] Meyerhold figured the dual labor of the actor thus:

$$N = A_1 + A_2$$

Here, N is the actor; A_1 is the artist who conceives the idea and issues instructions necessary for its execution, developed by intellectual training; and A_2 is the medium that executes the ideas of A_1, the actor's body, cultivated through the practical physical training of biomechanics.[83] The training consisted of compartmentalized physical exercises called études, which nurtured physical expressiveness, flexibility, and control and which

FIGURE 3.1. Vsevolod Meyerhold's students performing the étude "Shooting from the Bow."
Source: Photograph by A. A. Temeren (1926).

clearly take their cue from time and motion studies; figure 3.1 shows the itemized gestures of an étude in practice. The aim of cultivating such physical lucidity was to make the theater more efficient: to reduce the time of a play from four hours to one hour and to make each movement and expression do as much work as possible.

All of this provides a useful vocabulary for a reading of "Chant for May Day." The poem makes use of the language of the organic body—this is not, at face value, the technophilic aesthetics that we might expect from other Constructivist texts. In vernal May Day tradition, the strength of the workers is compared to "the sap rising in the trees," which later modulates into the more embodied "sap of your own strength." That language is also used to point to the end of American racism, "when the birds come back from the South." The voice of the single worker instructs the others to "be like the flowers," which leads, with its own sonic logic, to the rhymes on "power" and "hour" in the final lines. The strictness of that rhyme solidifies the organicism of "flower." This poem's vitality is neither overflowing nor gushing. The lines are mostly clipped imperatives: like Meyerhold's rigorously trained actors, Hughes's rigorously choreographed hundred voices arise from human bodies that are trained, harnessed, and turned to account. The voices of the workers join together to produce not an object but a world.

Like Meyerhold's theater, Hughes's chant has little investment in any lyric subjectivity and interiority, or, in Meyerhold's term, "psychology." There is no effort to individualize the speakers or develop the inner life that we associate with the lyric poem, which is discarded in favor of the mass consciousness of workers. For Hughes, this would be a diversion, and the force of the poem or play's revolutionary vision would suffer at the hands of our need to disentangle the motivations, fears, and desires of the lyric speaker. And it would privilege the needs of the individual above the needs of the collective mass joined in a shared vision. All of this translates into an aesthetic of crispness and clarity, which in this poem looks like simplicity. Yet "Chant for May Day" is not "deceptively simple," to use that hackneyed phrase. Rather, it makes, as Alan Wald suggests, "a virtue of [its] 'simplicity.'"[84] As a mass-distributed poem, it is willfully, deliberately simple in its description but complex in its methods and execution. Like in Meyerhold's algebraic formulation of the relationship between artist and actor, in this poem the intellectual labor has already been performed by the director, and here Hughes himself takes on the role of director. Our role as reader, in turn, becomes that of both receiver and participant, to open ourselves to the text such that we can imagine our voice contributing to the rising chorus, even if that requires putting aside the interpretative moves of lyric reading.

In chapter 13 of *Capital*, Marx outlines the transformation that accompanies the change to cooperative labor and the shift to the capitalist mode of production proper. Drawing together individual workers into a large mass involves "the fusion of many forces into a single force," which results in "the creation of a new collective power." "When the worker co-operates in a planned way with others," Marx writes, "he strips off the fetters of his individuality, and develops the capabilities of his species."[85] Something like this process is registered in Hughes's chant as the move from the single voice to the voice of the masses invokes that mass capability. Something is gained just as something is discarded. Unlike Hughes's early poems, there is no single lyric speaker or blues singer to cling to, however shared and anonymous the identity of that speaker might have been. The lyric "I" is replaced with the building voices of a hundred workers, and with its departure goes a certain lyric sensibility or world view, which T. J. Clark describes as "the illusion in an artwork of a singular voice or viewpoint, uninterrupted, absolute, laying claim to a world of its own," with its own "metaphors of agency, mastery, and self-centeredness that enforce our acceptance of the work as the expression of a single subject."[86] This illusion had to be shattered to clear space for something else, not quite an illusion but not yet a reality either: the poem is the expression and labor of a multiplicity of subjects and voices. Yet we shall see that Hughes's poetry cannot quite give up on the lyric and the project of reforming it; in Clark's words, he returns to it "like a tongue to a loosening tooth."[87]

SPATIAL FORM

In *Marxism and Literature*, Raymond Williams reminds us that for a social theory of literature, the relationship between the individual and the collective is always a question of literary form. "The problem of form," Williams writes, "is a problem of the relations between social (collective) modes and individual projects." Stable, recognizable literary forms are the "common property" of writers and readers; "a specific relationship, of a collective or relatively general kind, is called upon and activated in the very processes of composition and performance."[88] Hughes's inherited form in *A New Song* is the ballad, a term he uses to describe poems that sometimes make vague or no use of traditional ballad stanzaic structures but that retain the ballad's affinity with anonymous and proletarian cultural expression. *A New Song* includes the "Ballad for Ozie Powell," one of the Scottsboro Boys; "Song of Spain"; and "Ballads for Lenin." The latter poem makes use of a ballad's ABCB rhyme scheme and moves between stanzas that appeal directly to Lenin, delivered by an unnamed speaker or various speakers—"Comrade Lenin of Russia, / High in a marble tomb, / Move over, Comrade Lenin, / And give me room"—and stanzas that briefly detail the life and struggle of a worker "type"—"I am Ivan, the peasant, / Boots all muddy with soil"; "I am Chico, the Negro / Cutting cane in the sun"; "I am Chang from the foundries / On strike in the streets of Shanghai." The poem's title is not "Ballad," "A Ballad," or "The Ballad," but "Ballads." The poem's openness, its refusal to settle into the solidity of a first-person lyric address is hinted at in the plurality of its title. But where the poem's speakers are various and international, the stability of the ballad form acts as a binding agent that brings the various speakers together. This conceptual and class unity finds a home in the poem's formal unity and the familiarity of the ballad as a culturally inherited form.

But what about Hughes's use of poetic forms that are not stable and inherited but much more experimental and unfamiliar? Take, for example, a poem from the same period entitled "Wait," published in the first issue of *Partisan*, the magazine of the John Reed Club in Carmel, California:

PICKERS	I am the Silent One,	MEERUT
	Saying nothing,	
CHAPEI	Knowing no words to write,	HAITI
FORD	Feeling only the bullets	KOREA
	And the hunger	
STRIKERS	And the stench of gas	CHILD
ALABAMA	Dying.	LABOR
NEGROES	And nobody knows my name	SUGAR
	But someday,	
CUBA	I shall raise my hand	HAITI
	And break the heads of you	
UNEMPLOYED	Who starve me.	BONUS

The poem maps the geography of global immiseration and anti-capitalist struggle. It continues in the same format, in which the voice of the Silent One is framed by capitalized proper and common nouns: working-class groups ("strikers," "unemployed") mixed among international sites of oppression, conflict, and labor unrest. It concludes by exploding outward, the marginal capitalized places, names, and victims of militarism and capitalism take the stage at last in a single stream:

MINERS	I shall find the words to speak	MEERUT
	Wait!	

HAITI UNEMPLOYED MILLIONS CALIFORNIA CHERRY PICKERS STRIKING MINERS ALABAMA SUGAR BEET WORKERS INDIAN MASSES SCOTTSBORO SHANGHAI COOLIES PATTERSON SUGAR BEET WORKERS COLONIAL ASIA FRICK'S MINERS CUBA POOR FARMERS JAPANESE CONSCRIPTS WORKERS JOHANNESBURG

MINERS CHAPEI ALABAMA NEGROES OXNARD SUGAR
BEET WORKERS INDIAN MASSES BONUS MARCHERS FORD
STRIKERS HAITI[89]

"The militant leaders of the [Black American] intelligentsia must feel and express the spirit of revolt that is slumbering in the inarticulate Negro masses," wrote Claude McKay in his report on attending the Fourth Congress of the Communist International in 1922. "Precisely as the emancipation movement of the Russian masses had passed through similar phases."[90] Here the central poem does the work of articulating the "spirit of revolt." The central lyric moves from silence to articulation before exploding into the people and places of the final stream. This makes an argument for the sort of work that a lyric poem can do—the work of indexicality or compression, of letting the voice of the Silent One stand in for the shared experience of a multitude. But the poem's interest and effect lie in its clear exaggeration of that lyric work. This is primarily achieved through its spatial design, which channels revolutionary collectives into a single undifferentiated lyric. If "Chant for May Day" replaced the individual voice with an amplified chorus, here the individual voice is supplemented and enhanced until it eventually bursts open entirely. "Wait," then, is a lyric that feels the pressure to express collective experience. Or, to see it another way, it is a poem that cannot quite relinquish the impulse toward the lyric and that responds to that impulse with an explosive revolutionary violence.

Contra the governing performative energy of "Chant for May Day," the significant development of "Wait" is its spatial organization. In a chapter on Hughes and documentary photography, Sarah Ehlers offers a rich comparison between this poem and Hughes's scrapbooks and snapshots. "Read as snapshots," Ehlers argues, "the words in the lists illuminate the processes and violence of capitalism by freezing moments and spaces where such violence takes place."[91] Ehlers's observation that the poem freezes spaces where capitalist violence is enacted is suggestive. To carry this spatial idea further, I offer a different aesthetic key to reading "Wait," namely, the spatial aesthetics of Constructivist design in multiple arenas, both two- and three-dimensional. "Our age is an industrial age," wrote Aleksei Gan, "and sculpture must give way to the spatial resolution of an object."[92] That ethos carried over to the way that objects were treated in two-dimensional forms and Constructivist graphic design. Take, for example, Alexander

FIGURE 3.2. Maquette for a trade union poster, "Trade Union Is a Defender of Female Labor," by Alexander Rodchenko (c. 1925).
Source: © 2024 Estate of Alexander Rodchenko / UPRAVIS, Moscow / ARS, NY.

Rodchenko's 1925 maquette for a trade union poster (figure 3.2). In the center a woman reads; she is the focal point, and we are invited to read along with her. On either side are images from factories. Above, the text reads, "Trade union / a blow against women's slavery," and below, "trade union / defender of women's labor." The four quadrants of the poster—two scenes of work, two sentences about the trade union—are gathered together in the central figure of the woman, much like the central speech of the Silent One in "Wait," framed here by women workers. Rodchenko used similar techniques in his 1923 advertisements for the airline Dobrolet. The Dobrolet poster advertises shared ownership of the national airline as a patriotic duty: "He who is not a shareholder in Dobrolet is not a citizen of the USSR." In that poster, an airplane sitting in the center is offered to the viewer as something communally held; the poster implies that the airline's future and success belong to the viewers as well. Constructivist poster design makes frequent use of these central motifs framed by texts.

The effect is participatory and invitational. Both Rodchenko's posters and Hughes's poem organize the relationship between the exemplary individual worker and collective life spatially. Like the central lyric poem of "Wait," the posters are organized around a central object—the reading woman, the plane—that direct the eye inward and gather collective experience and collective investments into a single form.

Still, the poem's spatial arrangement calls for a firmer three-dimensional parallel, and this can be found in Constructivist set design and theatrical staging. Here we can turn to Hughes's interest in the work of Nikolai Pavlovich Okhlopkov, an actor, director, and student of Meyerhold's who starred in Eisenstein's *Alexander Nevsky* in 1938. Okhlopkov's first production was a mass spectacle performed in front of thirty thousand spectators in his hometown of Irkutsk, in Siberia, in 1921; he combined mass spectacle with avant-garde formal experimentation influenced by Meyerhold.[93] Like Hughes, Okhlopkov counted among his favorite poets Mayakovsky and Whitman, and it is no surprise that Hughes recognized some of his own sensibility in the director's work. In *I Wonder as I Wander*, Hughes describes Okhlopkov's Teatr Krasnoi Presni as "the most advanced in production styles of any playhouse I have ever seen" (*IWAW*, 208). He continues, "For each production the entire seating and platform arrangements of the theater were changed, and the whole auditorium was always used as a playing area, front, back and aisles. Sometimes a conventional stage was utilized, too, with perhaps a runway from the stage up to the balcony. Sometimes there were runways along the side walls all the way to the lobby. And one amazing production was so designed that important things were happening all over the place, so the spectators sat in swivel chairs, whirling around at will to catch whatever interested them most" (*IWAW*, 208–9).

"The whole auditorium was always used": with no space wasted, the Okhlopkov theater extends beyond the stage, dissolving the line between observer and observed. Where directors work with and within the space of the theater, poets work with and against the spatial coordinates of the page, the blank space that surrounds the black line. To read a poem is thus to move through the spaces that a poet has organized for us. What is so particular about "Wait" is that our path through the poem is not so clearly charted. The poem is ergodic in asking us to chart our own course. Like the viewers in the spinning chairs, we can turn our attention to the poem's component parts in whichever order we desire. We might read the vertical columns consecutively or relegate them to a choral background voice to be read after the central lyric poem. If we read across the columns horizontally, we create surprising and resonant combinations: "ALABAMA / dying / LABOR," for example. If in "Chant for May Day" our readerly agency exists mostly by our suggested participation in a carefully choreographed mass chorus of voices, here we gain the ability to direct our own experience. The possibility for multiple voices is also offered: one reader might take the central lyric, and two others the flanking columns. But this openness brings agency back to the individual reader for it means that one experience of reading "Wait" might not resemble another. If the poem withholds any easy shared experience of reading, it paradoxically does this at the same time as it affirms the value and necessity of collective expression.

Hughes's 1930s poetry reminds us of the formal challenges that the decade's revolutionary politics and collective labor movements posed for left-wing American poets—especially those whose work was published in large print runs—namely, how to formulate a poetics that would encapsulate this collective energy and agitate for the emancipation of the international working class. In a sense, this is the problem of form keeping up with content, or perhaps with politics. I have suggested that Hughes found a solution by borrowing from and transforming the aesthetic strategies of the Constructivist theater and that we might in turn find vocabulary for reading Hughes by paying closer attention to his Constructivist poetics. If his 1930s experimentalism can be characterized by a poetic work grounded in the bringing together of genres and forms, it is equally marked by an abdication of the figure of the poet as an isolated individual working alone at a desk. These poems foreground their own construction, in the gathering of voices of "Chant for May Day" or the modular building of "Wait," without relying on the image of the individual worker or writer. This is a construction that goes hand in hand with the social reorganization that the poems envision, leaning hopefully, as the 1930s wore on, into the communist future.

DON'T YOU WANT TO BE FREE?

Fifteen years after his time in the Soviet Union, Hughes outlined his reasons for bringing politics and poetry close together:

Poets who write mostly about love, roses and moonlight, sunsets and snow, must lead a very quiet life. Seldom, I imagine, does their poetry get them into difficulties. Beauty and lyricism are really related to another world, to ivory towers, to your head in the clouds, feet floating off the earth.

Unfortunately, having been born poor—and also colored—in Missouri, I was stuck in the mud from the beginning. Try as I might to float off into the clouds, poverty and Jim Crow would grab me by the heels, and right back on earth I would land.[94]

This was written in 1947, while Hughes was under investigation by the FBI and six years before his appearance before Joseph McCarthy's investigative committee.[95] In May 1952, he renounced his membership of the National Council of American–Soviet Friendship on the grounds that his involvement prevented Southern colleges from hiring him to speak, thus jeopardizing a major source of income.[96] Nevertheless, according to Rampersad, Hughes "continued to praise [the Soviet Union's] racial policies, and he once or twice attended cocktail parties at the Soviet Consulate in New York."[97]

Hughes was by no means the only writer for whom the politically fertile ground of the Depression years nurtured an experimental project of reimagining what a collective subject for literature might look like. Richard Wright's *12 Million Black Voices*, a 1941 book of photojournalism and a "folk history" of Black life in America, narrates Black history from the forced transport of enslaved people to the text's present, focusing first on the plantation system and sharecropping and then on service work and urban industrial labor. Wright's historical narrative is paired with photographs selected from Farm Security Administration files; no new photographs were taken for the project, which drew exclusively on existing Depression cultural work (Edwin Rosskam, a white photographer, was responsible for the photo direction). Wright is clear that the problem of making a collective history is a problem of form: "To paint the picture of how we live on the tobacco, cane, rice, and cotton plantations is to compete with mighty artists: the movies, the radio, the newspapers, the magazines, and even the Church. They have painted one picture: charming, idyllic, romantic; but we live another: full of the fear of the Lords of the Land, bowing and grinning when we meet white faces, toiling from sun to sun, living in unpainted wooden shacks that sit casually and insecurely upon the red clay."[98]

"In the absence of fixed and nourishing forms of culture, the Negro has a folklore which embodies the memories and hopes of his struggle for freedom," Wright had written four years earlier in his "Blueprint for Negro Writing."[99] *12 Million Black Voices* blends the style of folklore history with its prophetic voice and inclusive "we" and with the photographic techniques of Depression-era documentary. Both work with authority: folklore as collectively held history expressing a "unified sense of a common life and a common fate" is blended with photographic evidence that conditions are really as described, unidyllic and unromantic. In the generic blending of that book, Wright clears new ground for the formal representation of the history of Black labor in the formation of a Black collective consciousness.

The ballads, recitations, and chants that Hughes composed in the 1930s were one strand of his larger project to revolutionize political performance. In 1932, he published *Scottsboro Limited*, a play and four poems about the Scottsboro trial in Alabama and an important precursor for work later in the decade (the play was also translated into Russian and performed during Hughes's visit to the Soviet Union). In 1935, his play *Mulatto* opened on Broadway; the following year he was in Cleveland, Ohio, writing plays in association with the Karamu Theater. In 1938, Hughes returned from Spain to New York, where he set about opening a theater of his own. Louise Thompson secured the backing of the IWO, which provided space and sponsorship; all of the theater's first members were IWO workers.[100] On April 21, 1938, the Harlem Suitcase Theater, located in a loft on 125th Street, debuted what would be one of its bread-and-butter pieces, the agitprop play *Don't You Want to Be Free?* The play ran on weekends only for 135 performances. Hughes regularly updated the script in line with contemporary events (a 1944 "war version" ends with Black and white workers enlisting together). Building on the techniques Hughes had developed in *Scottsboro Limited*, the play's setting is minimal: "a bare stage, except for a lynch rope and an auction block. No scenery and very few props. No special lighting. Only actors needed—and an audience." In his opening monologue, the Young Man draws attention to this bareness, announcing, "We haven't got any scenery, or painted curtains, because we haven't got any money to buy them."[101] We can feel the imprint of Meyerhold's efficiency here. This choice made the play enormously adaptable and easy to stage. *Don't You Want to Be Free?* resolves some of the generic tensions between poem and performance in "Chant for May Day" by moving fluidly between prose dialogue and lyric performance. After the Young Man introduces the play, he reads a poem:

> I am a Negro:
>   Black as the night is black,
>   Black like the depths of my Africa.
>
> I've been a slave:
>   Caesar told me to keep his door-steps clean.
>   I brushed the boots of Washington.[102]

Hughes's readers will have encountered this poem before as the introductory "Proem" in *The Weary Blues*, printed elsewhere as "Negro." Each stanza begins with a speaker who announces their association with a group ("I've been a worker"; "I've been a singer"; "I've been a victim"), followed by two examples, the first historical and the second contemporary. Thus, American slavery is presented as the continuation of Roman slavery; lynchings in Texas are compared to Belgian colonial violence in the Congo; and the construction of the Woolworth Building, completed in 1912, continues the labor conditions of the construction of the pyramids. This labor history is braided with Black artistic history, the singer who "carried my sorrow songs" and "made ragtime." The poem synthesizes diverse examples of colonial and racist violence into a systemic history of art, racist violence, and coerced labor. In his production notes, Hughes suggested that the play would appeal particularly to Black history groups and Black labor unions. By weaving his poetry with dramatic dialogue, Hughes makes a lyric poetry that is historically situated as well as deeply alive and embodied. Poems are cut, their lines and rhymes shared between characters; they are alternately sung or spoken, delivered by individual or by crowd. Alongside this formal hybridity, Hughes emphasizes, "Whatever form of staging is used, audience-space should still be employed for much of the action of the play, since the idea behind this type of production is to cause the audience to feel that they, as well as the actors, are participating in the drama—and not simply sitting inactively looking at a show."[103] A range of characters begin not on stage but in the audience. The porosity of its movements between character, genre, and history makes a play that is connective and total in outlook.

In "Blueprint for Negro Writing," Wright framed the task of the Black writer in material terms as a project of design and construction:

> We live in a time when the majority of the most basic assumptions of life can no longer be taken for granted. Tradition is no longer a guide. The world has grown huge and cold. Surely this is a moment to ask questions, to theorize, to speculate, to wonder out of what materials can a human world be built.
>
> Each step along this unknown path should be taken with thought, care, self consciousness, and deliberation.[104]

In both the poem that reaches toward performance and the play whose fabric is woven of poetry, Hughes theorizes and speculates about the limits and possibilities of material. Considered together, *Don't You Want to Be Free?* and Hughes's 1930s poems can tell us about both the achievements and limits of forms, as well as the imaginative work that poetry can do. *Don't You Want to Be Free?* was an easily produced, inexpensive, hugely portable form of popular theater that was still bound by the constraints of the theater: real bodies are in rooms, delivering lines, while other bodies sit, watch, and listen. In contrast, there is something unrealizable about a poem like "Chant for May Day," something utopian about the text's vision of a hundred workers in wave-like unison. A blueprint for something difficult but not impossible, "Chant for May Day" withholds the occasion of its reading but insists on its potential. The problem of reading "Chant for May Day" has only two solutions: one is overly literal, of finding one hundred workers to sing the poem together. The other is imaginative, an exercise in conjuring and conducting an imagined collective.

My final Constructivist comparison, then, is a similarly troubled work of imagination: the unrealized work of the architect Vladimir Tatlin. I am thinking less of his famous unrealized tower, *The Monument to the Third International*, than of the *Letatlin* flying machines he constructed between 1929 and 1931 (the name combines the verb *letat*, "to fly," with the artist's name). Closer by far to Leonardo da Vinci's designs than to twentieth-century aircraft, the *Letatlin* was to be powered by the body of its driver, who would lie down inside the machine and ride it like a bicycle, wearing its outer body like wings (figure 3.3). Bringing the body back to flight, it offered a corrective to modern aviation; when wearing the machine, "its rider would discover his or her own promise as well as fulfil his or her timeless dream

FIGURE 3.3. Presentation of the *Letatlin* (1933).

of flight."[105] Tatlin used organic materials for his flying machines, building them from wood, cork, silk, and leather, held together by steel thread.[106] Like "Chant for May Day," the *Letatlin* is physical, muscle-powered, and driven by the body's strength, more like a set of wings than a plane. Tatlin wrote, "I want to give back to man the feeling of flight. This we have been robbed of by the mechanical flight of the aeroplane. We cannot feel the movement of the body in the air."[107]

Of course, the person-powered flying bicycle never flew, functioning instead as "a graceful monument to a dream," an episode in "a very different history of technology, an enchanted technology."[108] The *Letatlin* had disappeared from view by the time one was discovered in the Monino Russian Federation Central Air Force Museum, a military museum next to the Youri-Gagarin cosmonaut training center, fifty kilometers from Moscow. It was restored and displayed at the Tretiakov Gallery in Moscow in 2017. A similar reconstruction was displayed in London at the Royal Academy's revolution centenary show in 2017. It was hung alone in a gallery, enormous and looming, spinning slowly and casting shadows, as viewers walked around the suspended machine, a few directly underneath its wings. Suspended in the gallery is as close as it has yet come to flying—a failure, a compromise, perhaps, or something more like a challenge to the Constructivist imagination. The *Letatlin* is undeniably utopian. Utopia might be "an unrealized, unrealizable ideal" that offers only "the consolations of social critique."[109] But I don't believe that is the case here. Neither the *Letatlin* nor "Chant for May Day" reminds us only of the limitations of the presently possible, and nor do they make a critique of only the present—although they were certainly built from a present that their makers recognized to be violently limiting and inadequate. Nor is "failure" quite right: Hughes and Tatlin left us scripts and plans for a future. Their not-yet-achievable work offers us a horizon to move toward, not abandoning us to critique an inadequate present but pointing us toward a condition of future possibility.

Chapter Four

REPRODUCING GERTRUDE STEIN

A kind of burbling in the waters of inspiration. Because of their recurrence, what had originally seemed merely details of atmosphere became, in time, thematic.
LYN HEJINIAN, "MY LIFE"

In the final two chapters of this book, I consider the poetics of social reproduction in Gertrude Stein and Lorine Niedecker, two vastly different writers whose work is centrally concerned with practices that sustain and reproduce life. "Social reproduction" builds on a Marxist-feminist perspective that has shown how capitalism relies on reproductive labor—"the work that produces the work-force," in Silvia Federici's words—to produce a constant supply of human labor power, while capitalism simultaneously obscures the nature of that work *as work*.[1] "Labor power is a commodity," Mariarosa Dalla Costa and Selma James wrote in their landmark *The Power of Women and the Subversion of the Community*, "produced by women in the home."[2] Understood in a broader sense, social reproduction comprises both the domestic labor that was the focus of the Wages for Housework critique and the many other practices, material and immaterial, waged and unwaged, that together create and recreate a shared social world. This includes the gestating, bearing, and raising of children; the work of cooking, cleaning, mending, and sewing; caring for friends and elders; and the diverse practices of creating and maintaining social bonds and communities. Social reproduction is defined by its separation from economic production, its obscured character, and capitalism's dependence on its continued operations. In Nancy Fraser's words, capitalism "free rides" on social reproduction, without which waged work and the accumulation of surplus value would be impossible, but at the same time the drive to accumulate creates periodic crises of reproduction.[3] This "peculiar relation of separation-cum-dependence-cum-disavowal," as Fraser observes, "is an inherent source of instability," a social contradiction embedded in the structure of capitalism.[4]

Always beginning and beginning again, Stein's major stylistic innovation, her signature repetition, is also the primary experience of the motions and temporality of reproduction. Nothing is ever done; rather, it is done over and over. Yet despite this obvious formal parallel, reading Stein as a writer concerned with work in the first place is to challenge much of her critical reception. There are the facts of her life: Stein enjoyed financial independence that guaranteed her freedom from waged labor; her household relied on racialized domestic service work; and her writing life was made possible by Alice B. Toklas's secretarial and administrative labors. During her lifetime, Stein was associated with leisure and idleness. In a damning 1934 article in *New Masses*, Mike Gold finds in Stein "the same kind of orgy and spiritual abandon that marks the life of the whole leisure class."[5] Much later, critics have seen Stein as the idle partner to Toklas's constant labor. Janet Malcolm describes the division of labor in the Stein–Toklas household as "one doing everything and the other nothing." She extends this description to Stein's writing itself: "Her literary enterprise," Malcolm asserts, "was itself almost entirely work-free."[6] And among Stein's most sensitive literary critics, the consensus is that Stein's writing constitutes a form of play; indeed, if there is one word that critics have uniformly agreed applies to Stein, it is *playful*. For Ulla E. Dydo, Stein was in possession of an "always playful mind," while Dana Cairns Watson writes that for Stein, "the essence of genius" is "talking with the playful human mind."[7] Karen Leick describes Stein's "playful use of Alice as a subjective narrator" in *The Autobiography of Alice B. Toklas*; for Barbara Will, that narrative choice was "playful, camp, self-fracturing."[8] Writing about "Roast potatoes for," Marjorie Perloff argues that Stein was a practitioner of Wittgensteinian language games who engaged in "the game of testing the limits of language, which is, for Stein, *the* game that matters."[9] Astrid Lorange offers a clarifying counter to Perloff, interpreting Stein's play as a broader condition of her writing, "not merely a 'playing with' language but something like *playing-as-writing*."[10] If "playful" is a convention for describing modernist experiment, it also risks reifying the idea that Stein was a writer who played but did not work. Her sphere of production was not the work desk but the playpen.

The problem is that the accusations long leveled against Stein—of idleness, privilege, dependence, and elsewhere of automatism—are terms that the writer herself courts. Stein liked desultory and circular actions: flirting, daydreaming, window-shopping, wandering. She relished her uselessness. "I was the youngest of the children," she writes in *Wars I Have Seen*. "Nobody can do anything but take care of you, that is the way I was and that is the way I still am."[11] Stein insists on the value and effort of her work (the setup: "It takes a lot of time to be a genius") but in the same breath dissolves our expectation of hard labor (the punch line: "You have to sit around so much doing nothing, really doing nothing").[12] In an essay that links Stein's "unreadability" to her poetics of feminized, unwaged labor, Natalia Cecire observes that Stein "insists on the value of repetitive labors without presupposing that that value must come on capital's gendered terms."[13] The question of whether making art consists entirely of working was an active one for Stein. Like Picasso in Stein's portrait of the artist, Stein is at once "one who was working" and "not ever completely working."[14] Stein is "utterly impure," Catherine Stimpson writes of Stein's handling of gender, "linear as well as pluri-dimensional, 'male' as well as 'female,' the fountain as well as the womb."[15] The same can be said of her description of her difficult but unworked genius, of a life of working and not working. And the same can be said of social reproduction. Cleaved from economic production, kept private in the home, naturalized as love, and mystified as gender, the experience of reproduction is always simultaneously that of working and not working. But it is also true that the cooperative practices of social reproduction—of raising children, caring for a partner, building and sustaining community—are not identical to the work of, say, answering telephones in an office. For Kathi Weeks, only preserving the essential antagonism of social reproduction as "the rest of life beyond work that capital seeks continually to harness to its times, spaces, rhythms, purposes, and values" will keep the framework useful for antiwork politics.[16] One reason that social reproduction has emerged as such a generative heuristic for feminist theorists and critics is that, poised on this borderline between work and not-work, social reproduction troubles those categories that structure human activity under capitalism: between work that is visible and invisible; productive and unproductive; valuable and valueless; private and public; queer and straight. It is her sustained challenges to these structuring principles, her simultaneous working and not working, that make Stein an emblematic poet of reproduction.

Stein doesn't simply reflect or document the contradictions of reproduction. In her early writing, she aligns her work with both minute, repetitive, invisible household labors and the social project of the reproduction of the American middle class, making an uneasy alliance between avant-garde experimentation and reproductive labors. I read Stein's interaction with publishers unwilling to print her work against her own descriptions of her writing and show how Stein insists that her writing's similarity to reproduction demonstrates its value and its centrality to human life. Writing at the moment of an emergent Taylorist disciplining of domestic work, the Stein of *Tender Buttons* reconstructs the home as the site of expansive, unruly experiments in observation and experience. In her later long poem *Stanzas in Meditation*, Stein traces the epistemological challenges and intellectual life of long-term queer intimacy. I read the *Stanzas* in relation to the volume of love notes between Stein and Toklas that are kept in their joint archive. Both the poem and the notes, I suggest, are engaged with the daily practices of reproduction that sustain both a relationship and a writing life. Stein asks us to see the repetitions of reproduction not as the remaking of the world as it is but as the dynamic, unsettled process of making life go on.

Both this chapter and the next approach social reproduction from outside the heteronormative family, and neither deals with the gestating, bearing, and raising of children. Many modernist women writers either did not have children or did not raise their children, and my focus on nonmaternal reproductive labors follows the character of literary modernism.[17] Displacing maternity from the center of my analysis, while remaining indebted to the analytical terms that social reproduction theory provides, I explore these poets' non-normative forms of relating to the world, making art, organizing intimacy, and imagining new futures. "Why privilege maternity as the paradigm for a care-taking committed to an alternate futurity," asks Elizabeth Freeman in response to Lisa Baraitser, "when elder care, care of life partners, care of friends, intergenerational eroticism, and teaching and mentoring have been so central to queer life?"[18] Stein prompts us to think of the life of a relationship as a sustained practice of queer reproduction not in the hackneyed sense of constituting "emotional labor" but as the fundamental work of making life—and writing—possible, and then making it possible again.

MAKING AMERICANS

In the mid-1930s, Gertrude Stein was big business. Her return to America was announced in lights circling Times Square; Bergdorf Goodman used a variation on her "rose is a rose is a rose" to advertise hats; she was on the cover of *Time* magazine; she was invited to provide fashion coverage for *Harper's Bazaar*; she had tea with Eleanor Roosevelt; and she gave a lecture attended by a future president, John F. Kennedy.[19] Her first purchases with her new income were an eight-cylinder Ford and "the most expensive coat made to order by Hermes" for her poodle, Basket.[20] Stein's vertiginous rise to fame might be read as a parable about the easy commodification of the avant-garde. "Suddenly it was all different," she writes in *Everybody's Autobiography*. "What I did had a value that made people ready to pay." She continues, "Up to that time everything I did had a value because nobody was ready to pay."[21] But what precisely was the basis of that value? If the late Stein is gesturing toward the literary value of the high avant-garde writer, rejected by the market but embraced by those in the know, her statements about her writing tell a different story. The early Stein understood her writing not as written for small avant-garde circles or a literary elite but as participating in the devalued, daily labors of social reproduction.

The Gertrude Stein and Alice B. Toklas archive at Yale University's Beinecke Rare Book and Manuscript Library contains a remarkable number of rejection letters. Some are famously imitative of her style, turning "Steinese" back onto the writer to declare her unpublishable.[22] Others were blunt, such as when Austin Harrison of the *English Review* writes simply "Dear Madam, I really cannot publish these curious Studies."[23] Most publishers justified their refusal to print Stein's writing on the grounds that it would fail to sell. Stein's intermittent correspondence over several years with Ellery Sedgwick of the *Atlantic Monthly* is a study in her rejection by the popular literary market. In October 1919, Sedgwick told Stein that her poems "would be a puzzle picture to our readers. All who have not the key must find them baffling, and—alack! that key is known to very, very few."[24] A few months later he reiterated his opinion: "Your letter . . . seems to show me that you misjudge our public. Here there is no group of literati or illuminati or cognoscenti or illustrissimi of any kind, who could agree upon interpretations of your poetry. More than this, you could not find a handful even of careful readers who would think it was a serious effort."[25]

That criticism continued until the mid-1920s. On February 27, 1924, Sedgwick told Stein, "The difficulty an American editor must find in your work is that it can of its nature be understood by only a very few people."[26] Sedgwick asked Stein for "some sort of key or syllabus," but in June of that year in response to further letters from Stein, he repeated his refusal: "The simple truth is that not one of our readers in a thousand would understand your essay, regardless of the explanatory note." And he repeated it yet again a few weeks later on July 28: "You are not more sorry than I, and yet I am quite certain that readers generally would be color-blind and music-deaf to your work."[27] In December 1927, Blanche Knopf wrote to Stein about *Lucy Church Amiably*:

> You know how strongly I feel about you and how much we'd like to publish you if it were at all possible. We have all read LUCY CHURCH AMIABLY here and frankly I don't believe that we have progressed enough, even though you think we have, in modern literature to make it possible to sell it for you. There is no use whatever in merely printing a book without a chance in the world of coming out on it financially ourselves or pleasing you, and I don't think that is at all what you would want us to do.[28]

The correspondence between Knopf and Stein is polite and respectful, and Knopf shows a canny flattery in positioning Stein as both unlikely to engage in vanity printing and *trop moderne* for a slow-moving public.[29] In May 1928, an editor at Kegan Paul, Trench, Trubner and Co. also refused to publish *Lucy Church Amiably* because, despite deeming the book "very clever," "we do not think it has any considerable chance of selling remuneratively."[30]

In the face of all these rejections describing her incomprehensibility, Stein insisted that her work could be read by a general audience. She lamented to Carl Van Vechten in April 1916, "Alas about every three months I get sad. I make so much absorbing literature with such attractive titles and even if I could be as popular as Jenny Lind where oh where is the man to publish me in series. Perhaps some day you will meet him. He can do me as cheaply and as simply as he likes but I would so like to be done. Alas."[31] Stein kept a small black notebook of her customary graph paper labeled "Literature" (and subtitled "Book of Short Things," likely to distinguish its contents from her "long thing" in progress, *The Making of Americans*). Here she recorded the status of her works submitted to publishers.[32] By the time the notebook leaves off, most of its entries are marked "returned," often after being submitted to several publishers (one of the only exceptions is *Tender Buttons*, published by Marie Press, a private press in New York). The small act of recordkeeping testifies to Stein's insistence that she could and would be published. While Stein famously did not draft her poems and novels, she did draft at least some of her letters, often on the reverse pages of letters she received. In an undated draft of a letter to an unnamed publisher, Stein wrote a disclaimer to accompany the enclosed manuscript that "the style and manner are peculiar, at least I judge so from the interest it xcites [*sic*] and the difficulty of finding a publisher. I wish you would read them several times before you decide."[33] The letter combines an admission of her formal distinctiveness, curiously understated as "peculiar," with a plea for patient reading. "I am sure there is a public for me," she wrote in a draft to the editor of *Harper's* after the magazine rejected "Accents in Alsace" in November 1919.[34]

Stein's greatest struggle for publication was for *The Making of Americans*, a fifteen-year process that Donald Gallup has documented in detail.[35] Stein wrote the book between 1903 and 1911, when she began to search for a publisher, but it did not appear in print in full until 1925. After her early failed attempts to secure a contract between 1911 and 1913, the idea of publication lay dormant until the summer of 1922, when Carl Van Vechten, whom Stein would later credit as being responsible for the book's eventual appearance, raised the idea of publication again. On March 15, 1923, Stein wrote to Van Vechten that "the idea of getting the Family published that delights me more than I can say. It's a long book 2428 pages of typewriting 19 lines to the page."[36] Van Vechten wrote to Stein in October 1923 of his plans with Alfred Knopf, first to issue a circular announcing the book and inviting subscriptions and eventually to print it in a three- or four-volume edition with large type and portraits of Stein by Picasso and Davidson as frontispieces. The set would be sold for twenty-one dollars—several hundred dollars in today's value—and would be aimed largely at collectors rather than general readers.[37] The idea stalled. In 1924, Ernest Hemingway took up Stein's cause and began to lobby Ford Madox Ford to publish the book. The book began to be serialized in the *Atlantic Monthly* in April 1924, and Stein received her first check of 450 francs for fifteen pages.[38] Still, the prospect of full publication eluded Stein, with Liveright refusing to bring the book out in full and Jane Heap's attempts to convince Eliot to serialize the book in the *Criterion* coming to nothing. By the beginning of 1925, Stein appeared to have a promising publisher in the shape of Robert McAlmon, then living in Paris and publishing under the Contact Editions imprint, associated with William Bird and the Three Mountains Press. While the novel was eventually published in both ordinary and deluxe editions, Stein's relationship with McAlmon quickly soured, with McAlmon ultimately threatening to pulp all books that remained unsold within a year of its publication. *The Making of Americans* found only a few devoted readers. Marianne Moore wrote to Stein in July 1926 to express her admiration for the book as "one of the most eager and enriching experiences that I have ever had."[39] By and large, and despite Moore's advocacy, *The Making of Americans* was a commercial and critical failure. By the end of December 1926, only one deluxe copy, twenty-eight leather-bound copies, and seventy-four paperbound copies had been sold and paid for. Over one hundred more copies were sent to bookstores, but, according to McAlmon, "it is certain that a relatively small number of copies actually reached the hands of readers."[40]

The Making of Americans is an epic of social reproduction. I mean this in two senses: first, that the book unfolds a family narrative that is also a narrative of class formation; second, that the book's sheer vastness and its formal repetition model the texture and temporality of social reproduction. As she follows the Hersland and Dehning families, Stein limns the work of subjectivation and the creation of social bonds that are the work of social reproduction: "They are doing something, living, working, loving, dressing, dreaming, waking, cleaning something, being a kind of a one, looking like some one, going to be doing something, being a nice one, being a not nice one, helping something, helping some one, winning, conquering, losing, forgetting, being an influence in being a living one being a dead one, having courage to be going on living, having a troubled living, being a worried one, cleaning themselves all their living, learning something, beginning something."[41] Here, the accumulation of practices of living evokes the sheer expanse of social reproduction's work. In passages like these, *The Making of Americans* negotiates "the nature of wholeness," as Jennifer Ashton describes one of Stein's principal concerns: what counts as whole and how we know it to be whole.[42] The question here is what makes up a whole social life. This is work that is not just "cleaning something" or "dressing" but also "being an influence" or "having courage to be going on living." The expansiveness of *The Making of Americans* approaches the totality of the work that produces human subjects.

In her meta-critical reflections on the book's progress, Stein positions herself as performing the invisible daily labor of reproduction. The second chapter opens with an extraordinary passage that reflects on the conditions and methods of the book's composition and the task the book assigns its readers. "Bear it in your mind my reader," Stein writes. "Truly I never feel it that there ever can be for me any such a creature":

> No it is this scribbled and dirty and lined paper that is really to be to me always my receiver,—but any how reader, bear it in your mind—will there be for me ever any such a creature,—what I have said always before to you, that this that I write down a little each day here on my scraps of paper for you is not just an ordinary kind of novel with a plot and conversations to amuse you, but a record of a decent family progress respectably lived by us and our fathers and our mothers, and our grandfathers, and grandmothers, and this is by me carefully a little each day to be written down here; and so my reader arm yourself in every kind of a way to be patient, and to be eager, for you must always have it now before you to hear much more of these many kinds of decent ordinary people, of old, grown, grand-fathers and grand-mothers, of growing old fathers and growing old mothers, of ourselves who are always to be young grown men and women for us, and then there are still to be others and we must wait and see the younger fathers and young mothers bear them for us, these younger fathers and young mothers who always are ourselves inside us, who are to be always young grown men and women to us. And so listen while I tell you all about us, and wait while I hasten slowly forwards, and love, please, this history of this decent family's progress.[43]

Stein theorizes her work as a minor labor, written on "scraps of paper" that act as a "record," a kind of accounting ledger that registers the family's history. Here, Stein positions herself as a secretary whose job is not to create but record. The writing is done on "scraps," dashed away, "scribbled," as if in the margins of the day; the paper is "dirty," which situates the work's production among the ephemera of daily life (the "scraps") and conjures the labor of cleaning. Stein fastens that minor daily labor to the reproduction of class. What is being made is not only the book, the ledger, or the laundry but also a "decent family," a life "respectably lived by us and our fathers and our mothers," as Stein twice lists generational reproduction. Like the unsent note to a publisher, Stein pleads for a certain kind of patient and slow reading that is also framed in intimate terms: we are asked to "love, please, this history of this decent family's progress."[44] The slowness of her writing demands a patient readership for Stein describes her object in terms that make it incompatible with fast-paced consumption and aligns it closely with reproductive daily household labors of the kind that produce family lineages.

If the book's writing is a daily labor, its story of the family's progress is the progress of the American nation and the American middle class with its "simple monotonous tradition," which for Stein is "the one thing always human, vital, and worthy."[45] If Stein moves between scales, from the large-scale reproduction of the middle class and the emergence of an American nation to the small, invisible daily labors of reproduction, so, too, does the book's attitude switch between aggrandizing self-announcement—it is a history, a record, a landmark in the development of a national literature—and the self-doubt of asking, "Will there be for me ever any such a creature" as a reader? Later, in the book's sixth chapter, Stein describes the shame of writing the book: "You write a book and while you write it you are ashamed for every one must think you are a silly or a crazy one and yet you write it and you are ashamed, you know you will be laughed at or pitied by every one and you have a queer feeling and you are not very certain and you go on writing." In an interview with Robert Haas in 1946, the last year of her life, Stein reflected on the psychic toll of her early difficulty with publishing. Writers like her "spend thirty years of our life in being made fun of and laughed at and criticized and having no existence and being without a cent of income. The work needs concentration, and one is often exhausted by it."[46] Stein's readers understood her career to be bifurcated into two incompatible kinds of value: the market value attached to the *Autobiography*, and the literary and aesthetic value of her earlier writing, when "nobody was ready to pay."[47] "I know you won't let your great success in America stop the flow of your serious work," wrote James Laughlin to Stein in 1935. "*Tender Buttons* is more important to me than the *Autobiography*. I mean to say there are lots of good raconteurs and very few writers who can verbally raise Lazarus."[48] But Stein's own figuration of her value, in *The Making of Americans* and elsewhere, tells a different story. This is not the story of an avant-garde appreciated by the discerning few but of the devalued, exhausting, and totally ordinary labors of social reproduction. The writing and publication of *The Making of Americans* together reflect the contradictory character of reproductive work. Its sheer repetitive volume registers the vast labor of social reproduction, while its unpublishability indexes that labor's effacement.

THE UNORGANIZED INDUSTRIES

Monotonous, repetitive, refined into smaller and smaller verbal units, Stein's writing evokes modern work processes and the atomized tasks of the industrial assembly line.[49] The verbal modulations and repetitions of Stein's "Portraits" engage the rhythms of a Taylorist work discipline that breaks the labor process into concise and optimally efficient operations and organizes workers' bodies by the rhythms of the machine. The shuddering motion of the body at work, performing its strictly delineated task, is encoded into the motions of the subjects of Stein's portraiture. Stein's 1909 portrait of Picasso is a portrait of an artist at work. Or maybe not, for while Picasso is insistently "one who was working," he is simultaneously "not ever completely working," and, more insistently again, he "certainly was not completely working."[50] What is "not completely working"? Does it register time, success, functionality, completion, partiality? Is he working part time or in a distracted manner? Stein's "Picasso" negotiates the line between the purposive action of work and the unwilled demands of the human body, indicated by the active verb "working" against the passive construction of being "one having something coming out of him": "Some were certainly following and were certain that the one they were then following was one working and was one bringing out of himself then something. Some were certainly following and were certain that the one they were then following was one bringing out of himself then something that was coming to be a heavy thing, a solid thing and a complete thing."[51]

The "coming thing" might be ejaculatory, gestational, or defecatory. Stein situates her writing in an unspecified zone of bodily emission. Peristalsis, as Jean Walton points out, names a zone of bodily uncertainty. It cannot be willed, but nor is it as automatic as breathing or the heartbeat; it thus "marks the *in*distinction between the organic and the psychological, between fuel and waste in the body-machine, between natural and technological operations, between the compulsive and the compulsory."[52]

Peristalsis is also a gendered issue, and Walton notes that women's bodies in the early twentieth century were targeted by a new emphasis on streamlining, waste reduction, and efficiency that moved from the shop floor to the home and to the body in what Walton calls the "peristaltic imperative."[53] The heaviness and solidity of the "something coming out" of Picasso, and that he is "bringing out of himself," requires some effort. The body must be worked on or pressed in some way to bring the thing that is inside of it out. But this work is only brief; for the rest of the portrait, Picasso is described in a more passive figuration as "one having something coming out of him." Stein's "Picasso" writes a theory of artistic making as an irrepressible force and as a metabolic process that straddles the line between automatic and willed, organic and disciplined activities. It thus conjures the bodily processes that maintain and reproduce life—including ingestion and egestion, procreation, even breastfeeding—and locates art-making in this zone.

In *Time and Western Man* (1927), Wyndham Lewis wrote a characteristically venomous description of Stein's "thick, monotonous prose-song." He writes, "What is the matter with it is that it is so 'dead'": "Gertrude Stein's prose-song is a cold, black suet-pudding. We can represent it as a cold suet-roll of fabulously-reptilian length. Cut it at any point, it is the same thing; the same heavy, sticky, opaque mass all through, and all along. It is weighted, projected, with a sibylline urge. It is mournful and monstrous, composed of dead and inanimate material. It is all fat, without nerve. Or the evident vitality that informs it is vegetable rather than animal. Its life is a low-grade, if tenacious, one; of the sausage, by-the-yard variety."[54] Or, as Jessica Burstein memorably glosses this passage, for Lewis, rather than "a thick stew," Stein "was serving up something like modernist tofu."[55] Lewis describes Stein's prose as "monstrous, desperate, soggy *lengths* of primitive mass-life," which is "jumbled, cheap, slangy, and thick to suit."[56] For Lewis, Stein represents "a technical problem." This is the problem of writing brought too close to factory production in its "fabulously-reptilian length," writing that is at the same time overly, or incorrectly, bodily—"all fat, without nerve"; writing that is at once ultra-modern in its invocation of "mass-life" and "primitive," "reptilian," evoking some earlier evolutionary stage. For Lewis, Stein's writing sits uncomfortably on the boundaries of human and animal, modern and atavistic, mechanical and organic. But for all his acridity, Lewis is not far off the mark. Lewis's "heavy, sticky, opaque mass" sounds a lot like the "heavy thing, a solid thing, and a complete thing" of Stein's Picasso. In writing scenes of artistic labor that recall both the digestive, metabolic functions of the body and modern forms of industrial work discipline, Stein poises her writing precisely on the place where these forms of discipline enter spheres ostensibly outside the realm of capitalist production: the body, but more importantly for this section, also the home.

In the early twentieth century, Taylorism sought a new stage for its experiments in efficiency, which had already revolutionized manufacture. It found new territory in the domestic sphere, which increasingly came to be seen as a site that could be managed, rationalized, and made efficient, with the house worker's labor disciplined just as that of the factory laborer. This transformation was part of broader cultural and economic debates over the structure and fate of the modernizing home. The late nineteenth century saw home arts become the new field of home economics, formalized in 1893 when the National Household Economic Association was founded with the aim of incorporating household management into school curricula.[57] The significance of home economics for the future of the organization and meaning of household and women's work was the subject of much debate. Would home economics professionalize the home and thereby destroy the sanctity of the domestic sphere that had been carefully preserved in the "perpetual mothers' day," to borrow Ann Douglas's phrase, of the sentimental nineteenth century?[58] Or would it further dignify the home as a site of work performed by an expert, skilled laborer?

Charlotte Perkins Gilman's 1903 book, *The Home: Its Work and Influence*, advanced an early critique of the confinement of the woman, the "inexhaustible laborer," within the home. Gilman harnessed the language of industrial progress to argue against the separation of women as individual caretakers of individual homes, a process that naturalizes housework as the purview of women (an argument that the Wages for Housework campaign would later take up and extend).[59] Gilman writes,

> Our efforts to "lift the standard of household industry" ignore the laws of industry. We seek by talking and writing, by poetising and sermonising, and playing on every tender sentiment and devout aspiration, to convince the housewife that there is something particularly exalted and beautiful, as well as useful, in her occupation. This shows our deep-rooted error of sex-distinction in industry. We consider the work of the woman in the house as essentially feminine, and fail to see that, as work, it is exactly like any other kind of human activity, having the same limitations and the same possibilities.[60]

In Gilman's analysis, the separation of the home from capitalist production demarcates it as a uniquely private sphere and prevents its full socialization. "Our houses are threaded like beads on a string," she writes, "tied, knotted, woven together, and in the cities even built together; one solid house from block-end to block-end; their boasted individuality maintained by a thin partition wall." But for Gilman, more than simply isolating, the home as it is currently constructed is *inefficient*. Gilman argues that the domestic industries involve "an enormous waste of labor," as well as a waste of space; fuel; food, both purchased and left over after cooking; and tools. She proposes instead collective kitchens and eating houses. For Gilman, only when women's work is more completely socialized will the home regain its position as "the recognised base and background of our lives."[61]

Against Gilman's arguments for women's further socialization and their release from the private labors of the home, the 1910s saw efforts to modernize the private home through the rigorous adoption of Taylorist principles that would streamline domestic labor while reaffirming its status as uniquely the responsibility of the housewife.[62] Christine Frederick reacted to Gilman's vision of the socialization of housework by seeking to move the "efficiency gospel" of scientific management from the shop floor to the kitchens and drawing rooms of the "Rational Household." Frederick was an editor at *Ladies' Home Journal* who in 1912 began writing a series of articles called "The New Housekeeping," which were gathered into a book by the same name in 1913. A bestseller in both Europe and the United States, the book was reissued in 1919. Like Mary E. Dillon and Lillian Gilbreth, Frederick aimed to bring the developments of scientific management and motion studies into the "very unorganized industries" of the home.[63] "I was sitting by the library table, mending," begins Frederick's account of her introduction to scientific management, setting us firmly in a scene that reaffirms gendered hierarchies of labor. Frederick overhears her husband and a male guest repeat several talismanic words: "efficiency," "scientific management," "motion studies," "standard practice." Guiding the reader, she narrates her initial disbelief that the rationalization of the factory could be at all transferable to the sheer range of tasks performed in the home: "'That sounds like a fairy tale!' I laughed skeptically. 'What else wonderful can they do with this magic wand of "efficiency"?'"[64] Drawing on motion studies, Frederick describes the efficiently organized kitchen with optimized countertop and cabinet heights for women of different physicalities and advises ways of reducing waste motions in household tasks. The book includes advice on the use of efficient tools, including fuel-saving devices ("Device Utilizing One Burner for Baking"), time-saving devices ("A Double Pan Which Cooks Two Foods at Once") and labor-saving devices ("Dish Drainer Allows Dishes to Dry Themselves"), and tips for the efficient management of household finances, bringing the techniques of office regulation into household recordkeeping. Frederick encapsulates the new merging of house and factory and the transformation of the mechanics of private life, while reaffirming its essential privacy, when she describes the optimally efficient organization—contra Gilman's socialized vision—of "*my* factory, *my* business, *my* home."[65]

The New Housekeeping shares a surprising contemporary: Stein's 1914 collection of prose poems and an ode to her newfound lesbian domesticity, *Tender Buttons*. Like Frederick's housekeeping guides, Stein catalogs the objects that populate the bourgeois home. Frederick: "A Carafe Which Keeps Beverages Iced Many Hours"; Stein: "A Carafe, That Is a Blind Glass." Frederick: "Coffee Pot Permits Making Coffee Hours in Advance"; Stein: "A Piece of Coffee." Writing about the "unorganized industries" of the home, Stein both organizes and disorganizes, or reorganizes, domestic objects and uses. The animating tension of *Tender Buttons* is between its drive to categorization through its inventory of objects and the radical dismantling of those objects' forms and functions as soon as they are invoked. *Tender Buttons* takes the rigid order of the household management guide and gives us instead the object seen otherwise, in its radically dissected form. Stein takes useful things and imagines them otherwise, as commodities disburdened of their use values:

A BOX.

Out of kindness comes redness and out of rudeness comes rapid same question, out of an eye comes research, out of selection comes painful cattle.[66]

Stein doesn't describe objects as they already are but rather breaks them into colors, forms, and shapes that are both like and unlike the box, coat, hat, umbrella, or gloves and that conjure what the object resembles or is related to. Use is constantly subject to Stein's interrogations: "What is the use of a covering to a door." And more suggestively, "What is the use in a violent kind of delightfulness." "What is the use" is "asked rhetorically, indicating uselessness," as Mia You observes, even though, in Stein's rearrangement of words into homophones and puns, "the used is rendered useless, the useless finds new uses."[67] She describes objects as they might be and language as it might be used, the latter an imaginative act generated by the word "suppose." To suppose is to imagine something into being: "Suppose it is within a gate which open is open at the hour of closing summer that is to say it is so." Sometimes uses aren't proposed but negated: "Go lack go lack use to her" begins "Orange In." "Act so that there is no use in a center" begins "Rooms." And even more severely drained of usefulness in "Roastbeef," the human body itself is evacuated of its use: "There is no use there is no use at all in smell, in taste, in teeth, in toast, in anything, there is no use at all."

The New Housekeeping also describes objects invested with new or multiple uses, labor-saving devices that present maximal efficient use: "Stationary Egg-Beater Prevents Waste Motion"; "Hot Mangle Which Replaces Hand Labor." Like Frederick's study of newly manufactured, useful tools, Stein breaks household items into their functions:

A SELTZER BOTTLE.

> Any neglect of many particles to a cracking, any neglect of this makes around it what is lead in color and certainly discolor in silver. The use of this is manifold. Supposing a certain time selected is assured, suppose it is even necessary, suppose no other extract is permitted and no more handling is needed, suppose the rest of the message is mixed with a very long slender needle and even if it could be any black border, supposing all this altogether made a dress and suppose it was actual, suppose the mean way to state it was occasional, if you suppose this in August and even more melodiously, if you suppose this even in the necessary incident of there certainly being no middle in summer and winter, suppose this and an elegant settlement a very elegant settlement is more than of consequence, it is not final and sufficient and substituted. This which was so kindly a present was constant.[68]

For the first two sentences, we are broadly in the mode of object description: particles, cracking, lead, and discolor; here, we are in the laboratory—or in the bottle itself—witness to the process of carbonating water. If the "neglect" (and "cracking") of the first sentence position us momentarily within a negative mode, the first transformative verb, "makes," moves us from the negative to the positive, to the concretely visible, to color and discolor. With the second sentence, "the use of this is manifold," we move into the issue of use. Stein offers to unveil the manifold uses of the seltzer bottle, yet what she gives us is not an answer but a series of suggestions ("suppose"). What is made is not only carbonated water but also language, "the mean way to state it" and the "elegant settlement." The new use of the seltzer bottle is the production of language—almost limitlessly for as the pun on "present" in the final line tells us, the proposals that we can tease out from the seltzer bottle ("suppose") are "constant." This rearrangement of use and usefulness central to Stein's writing takes on new meaning in the context of the training and rationalizing of the home and women's work. Read against Frederick's arguments for Taylorization, *Tender Buttons* comes to look like a perverse counterpart to *The New Housekeeping*. Stein takes the rigid order of the household management guide and gives us instead the object seen otherwise, in its radically rearranged form. The book is fascinated with the form and function of things, and with efforts to catalog the home, while unleashing those objects from their containers. In *Tender Buttons*, the restraining efforts of the reformers of the "unorganized industries" are evoked only to insist on the household's unruliness and its refusal to be contained. That unruliness, Stein tells us, is an occasion for almost limitless work with language.

I began with Stein's "Picasso" as an instance of how Stein invokes the discipline of modern industrial labor while simultaneously assigning creative production to the amorphous zones of human digestion and egestion. Like "Picasso," *Tender Buttons* evokes the disciplining of the home; "what is the use" constantly brings us back to use value and the commodity's useful purpose even as it transforms those uses. In a Steinian vein, Sara Ahmed imagines queer use as ingestion and attention:

> You might have to refuse to ingest what would lead to your disappearance: the words, the ways, the worlds. Queer use can be about not ingesting something; spitting it out, putting it about. If queer use is not ingesting something, not taking it in, queer use can also be about how you attend to something. To queer use can be to linger on the material qualities of that which you are supposed to pass over; it is to *recover* a potential from materials that have been left behind, all the things you can do with paper if you do not follow the instructions.[69]

Ahmed's queer use designates a "potential for an explosion, how small deviations, a loosening of a requirement, the creation of an exit point, opening a door to allow something to escape, can lead to more and more coming out."[70] *Tender Buttons* luxuriates in the object world of the domestic sphere. It finds there an endless source of intellectual fascination; each object is an occasion for elastic experiments in observation and transformative redescription. Stein lingers "on the material qualities of that which you are supposed to pass over," but she supplements those material qualities with immaterial experiences, sensory impressions, or proposals ("suppose") for new ways of seeing. One of Stein's signature moves is to turn the ordinary spheres of reproduction into "occasions" for intellectual experiment and adventure; I will go on to show how Stein applies this pressure to the sustained experience of queer intimacy. *Tender Buttons* reframes the object world of the domestic sphere not as newly efficient and value-producing but as generating new impressions, new ways of seeing, and new and useless uses. Stein's reproduction consists of "regeneration, not self-replication," to borrow a phrase from the feminist theorist Sophie Lewis.[71] For Stein, reproduction does not consist of making the same thing over and over, simply with greater efficiency, but of the ordinary world's capacity to generate, seemingly endlessly, new uses and impressions. In expanding the bounds of reproduction, *Tender Buttons* proposes a new, unruly housekeeping of its own.

STANZAS IN MEDITATION AND QUEER REPRODUCTION

Stein was interested in what happened inside houses, behind the closed doors of kitchens and drawing rooms and in the daily patterns that constitute life with another person. The early prose piece "Miss Furr and Miss Skeene" describes the shared life of the titular pair as they go about their day and are "regularly gay": "To be regularly gay was to do every day the gay thing that they did every day. To be regularly gay was to end every day at the same time after they had been regularly gay. They were regularly gay. They were gay every day. They ended every day in the same way, at the same time, and they had been every day regularly gay."[72] Miss Furr and Miss Skeene practice a regular gayness, every single day marked by the periodic motions of the clock. Their regular gayness makes them all the more socially irregular as they cultivate their lesbian life together.

For Stein, being gay is not a static existence or state of being but a practice that is repeated every day; indeed, the word she uses is *working*: Miss Furr and Miss Skeene "were both gay then and both working there then."[73] Queerness, and queer intimacy, are iterative and accretive. Stein reframes queer togetherness, "to be regularly gay" and "to do every day the gay thing that they did every day," as a work of reproduction, a form of life produced and reproduced every day.

That life with another person is an exercise in reproduction was a preoccupation for the Stein of the early 1930s, two decades into the life she shared with Toklas. In 1932, Stein wrote two major books that are so different in style a reader would be forgiven for assuming they were the work of different writers. The gossipy romp and biographical trickery of *The Autobiography of Alice B. Toklas* launched Stein's literary celebrity. However, that book has a shadowy twin in another work: the long, austere poetic sequence *Stanzas in Meditation*, which pushes Stein's experiments with abstraction to new extremes. Where the *Autobiography* is all subject and action and a full social world, the *Stanzas* are all grammar and wandering thought, consisting, as John Ashbery writes, mostly of "colorless connecting words."[74] *Stanzas in Meditation* marks a formal development from Stein's early verses. Its vocabulary is remarkably spare, consisting for the most part of mono- and disyllabic words and a limited set of pronouns whose referents are frequently unclear. We can move through long stretches of the *Stanzas* before coming across a concrete noun. "The result," Ashbery suggests, "is like certain monochrome de Kooning paintings in which isolated strokes of color take on a deliciousness they never could have had out of context, or a piece of music by Webern in which a single note on the celesta suddenly irrigates a whole desert of dry, scratchy sounds in the strings."[75] Where the *Autobiography* brought Stein notoriety, the *Stanzas* gained little attention.[76] Where the *Autobiography* develops a posture of simultaneous concealment and self-exposure, the *Stanzas* hunker down into extreme reticence. Ulla E. Dydo has called the *Stanzas* the "other autobiography," while Joan Retallack describes the book as "a kind of negative (in the photographic sense) of what *The Autobiography of Alice B. Toklas* will become."[77] "This is her autobiography one of two," Stein writes, the poem itself seeming to acknowledge its twinned relationship with the other, more visible book.[78]

Both books are bound up with Stein's marriage to Toklas and with Toklas's status as both voice and addressee across Stein's work, her immense secretarial and editorial labors, and her presence in the archive. Where in the *Autobiography* Stein postures as Toklas posturing as Stein's biographer, in the *Stanzas* the dynamic between the two women is both the book's implied subject and woven into the problem of its editing history. Dydo, whose archival discovery has determined the *Stanzas*' critical reception, lays out the story this way: in the summer of 1932 in Bilignin, Stein wrote the six notebooks of the *Stanzas*, which Toklas then prepared into a typescript. In December 1932, Toklas read the newly rediscovered manuscript of *Q.E.D.*, Stein's early novella about a lesbian love triangle. The discovery brought to light Stein's earlier relationship with May Bookstaver, which Stein had not revealed in the "confessions" the couple had made to each other at the beginning of their relationship. The revelation sparked a long quarrel that lasted, in an impressive act of lesbian grudge-bearing, until 1935.[79] While preparing a second typescript, Toklas insisted that Stein eliminate all uses of the word *may*. The word is blacked out, corrected, or changed, most often to *can*. Dydo's discovery was justification enough for a corrected edition, edited by Susannah Hollister and Emily Setina, which removes the corrections. Hollister and Setina describe the corrected edition as embracing "the variety of works in their multiple, distinct forms."[80] Still, the restoration of Stein's original manuscript, every "may" intact, speaks to a demand for Stein's writing to reach us unmediated. Toklas's presence is acceptable as typist but no further than that, and the trustworthy Stein text is the unedited one. In her preface to the edition, Retallack writes that an "issue of textual integrity" was "put right," having finally undone "the biographical cleansing that Toklas had demanded."[81]

Yet the restored edition, having reversed Toklas's changes, performs its own act of "biographical cleansing." There is no reading Stein without reading Toklas—quite literally, in the sense that Toklas typed almost every piece of Stein's writing, and Stein's writing reaches us, her readers, only because of Toklas's labors. This is where the masquerade of the *Autobiography* is deadly serious. Stein-as-Toklas-narrating-Stein reminds us that there is no version of Stein's life that isn't filtered through Toklas, that in some meaningful sense the two women are inseparable. Nowhere is this more keenly felt than in Stein's archive—which is, of course, also Toklas's archive. As Melanie Micir notes of modernism's "intimate archives," of which the Gertrude Stein and Alice B. Toklas Papers in the Beinecke library is one, "the intimacy of their relationships has been built into the structure of their physical archives."[82] Like reading any printed work of Stein's, to leaf through her archival papers is to handle Toklas's labor. Any typescript in the archive encompasses both the secretarial labor that Toklas performed in their long collaborative practice, as well as the archival work that Toklas performed after Stein's death when she collected Stein's archive for donation to Yale according to the terms of Stein's will (a will that, because of the lack of legal provision for queer relationships and despite Stein's effort to provide for Toklas after her death, left Toklas at the mercy of Stein's blood relations until her death in poverty in 1967).[83] It is a critical commonplace to see Stein and Toklas's marriage as aping the heteronormative relationship dynamics of the genius-husband and secretary-wife, a criticism that itself imports normative ideas of relationships into Stein and Toklas's lifelong negotiation of queer intimacy and gender expansiveness.[84] Reading the *Stanzas* as an intimate archive entangled with the material presence of Toklas in the Beinecke archive, I suggest, allows us to see both the poem and the papers as forming a queer collaborative practice that makes a shared life possible.

We do not need to know anything of the *Stanzas'* editorial history to know that we are reading a kind of love poem. The first line evokes Toklas, Stein's "little bird": "I caught a bird which made a ball," as if taking us back to their first meeting:

> Once now I will tell all which they tell lightly.
> How were we when we met.
> All of which nobody not we know
> But it is so.
> (1, V, 63–64)

Often the poem switches into direct address:

> Out from the whole wide word I chose thee
> (1, VIII, 69)

> I forgive you everything and there is nothing to forgive
> (4, I, 139)

The speaker is often reminded of the presence of a loved one in the background of her thoughts:

> Full well I know that she is there
> (2, I, 80)

The long passages of pronoun-driven poetry both open the question of how the self can exist in relation to others and form a larger textual landscape that works its way through sense, perception, and extended concentration. The poem embraces stretches of time during which little happens. The *Stanzas* are interested in the extended, restless, sometimes attentive but frequently wandering habits of thought provoked by a shared life. In tracing these thought processes, the poems make an implicit argument about the intellectual life of shared experience. That the *Stanzas* are a love poem is a source of complication and instability as the poem traces the ambivalences and epistemic knots formed by the complicated relations of loving:

> Tell me darling tell me true
> Am I all the world to you
> And the world of what does it consist
> May they be a chance to may they be desist
> This came to a difference in confusion
> Or do they measure this with resist with
> Not more which.
> (3, X, 117–18)

We open with the trochaic rhythms of the nursery rhyme. The stanza moves from that seemingly small nursery rhyme question—she-loves-me-she-loves-me-not—to the much larger epistemological problem of the third line as "does she loves me" opens onto "what is the world and what is it made of"? But perhaps this risks diminishing the importance of the first couplet. While its singsong rhythm might seem to openly undermine itself and its own gravity, it also asserts itself as the well from which serious thought springs: loving prompts a question about the nature of the world. Nor do the two modes, the nursery rhyme and the meditative, ask altogether different questions. The second question shades that first question, adding another layer of meaning to the question about whether the speaker is loved. To put it another way, replacing "the world" for "significance in the life of another person," the passage might be rephrased as something like "tell me darling / am I significant to you / and what does it mean to be significant to another person?" This undoes any clear hierarchical difference between the two subjects in play and creates a generative, unsettled relationship between love and knowledge, a relationship that is also "a difference in confusions," restless and unsettled.

The next lines move into a much knottier problem in which the relations between lines and thoughts are less easily untangled:

> Than a conclusion
> May they come with may they in with
> For which they may need needing
> It is often by the time that not only
> Which waiting as an considerable
> And not only is it in importance
> That they could for an instance
> Of made not engaged in rebound
> They could indeed care
> For which they may not only
> Be very often rested in as much
> Would they count when they do
> Is which which when they do
> Making it do.
> (3, X, 118)

This is one single, complete sentence which begins almost in reverse. "Than a conclusion" enters the poem because of the logic of Stein's rhymes; the "confusion" earlier demands the settled "conclusion" here. Not only is its syntax much knottier than the poem's opening lines, its nouns—"importance," "instance"—are abstract nouns of emphasis, and the grammatical function of words, such as in "need needing," are left unclear: is that second "needing" a noun or a verb? When the poem detaches from the codified and digestible rhythms of thought ("Tell me darling tell me true") and breaks across the bounds of lines, it becomes harder to find something to cling to. It is as if the questions raised—What is the world? What does it mean to be loved?—make it impossible to return to the clear and easy sense of previous ways of thinking.

The romantic lines of the *Stanzas* bear a striking resemblance to a more intimate correspondence. Stein wrote hundreds of love notes to Toklas, which are held in the Beinecke library in a folder labeled "Autrespondence," as if to signal their difference from Stein's vast correspondence with others. The folder is impressive for its sheer volume; this was no small part of Stein's writing life. Many are short good-night notes written as Toklas went to sleep early and Stein stayed up to write.[85] Nor are they merely evidence of the first flush of a love affair: several of the notes are dated to 1940, when Stein was sixty-six years old. Their duration suggests that this form of intimate writing was part of how the relationship lasted over decades. Usually signed "Y. D." for "Your Darling," the notes were often hidden around the house for Toklas to find. This practice of daily writing was also an occasion for Stein and Toklas to engage in gender-expansive play. Stein pledges her devotion and fidelity to her "wifey" and "baby," and Stein often appears as a husband, a "Jewish gentleman," a "hubby," but a husband of a pleading, beseeching kind, rather than one of patriarchal power. Every night Stein pledges her devotion for Toklas to read in the morning. One note reads in its entirety "Baby precious, / all hers / always / always" (figure 4.1).[86]

Toklas throughout is described as a baby: "baby precious," "blessed baby," Stein's "sweet baby," while Toklas calls Stein her "baby boy." Stein doodles rows of small baby figures on the notes, sometimes in pairs and sometimes in continuous lines. On the note that reads "Baby precious, / all hers / always / always," two drawn baby figures sit together in a rectangle, as if they are in bed, in the upper right corner of the note, where a stamp would be placed on an envelope. Stein is also a maker of babies: "I made so many babies," she offers to her wife.[87] On the reproductive dynamics of the love notes and Stein's offerings to Toklas, Hannah Roche comments that "Toklas is thus by no means a mere typist or amanuensis: from the distance of her bed, she possesses the power to impregnate Stein with work—or, to put it another way, with labor."[88] Stein describes writing with Toklas's pen and with Toklas in mind. "Baby precious I write with

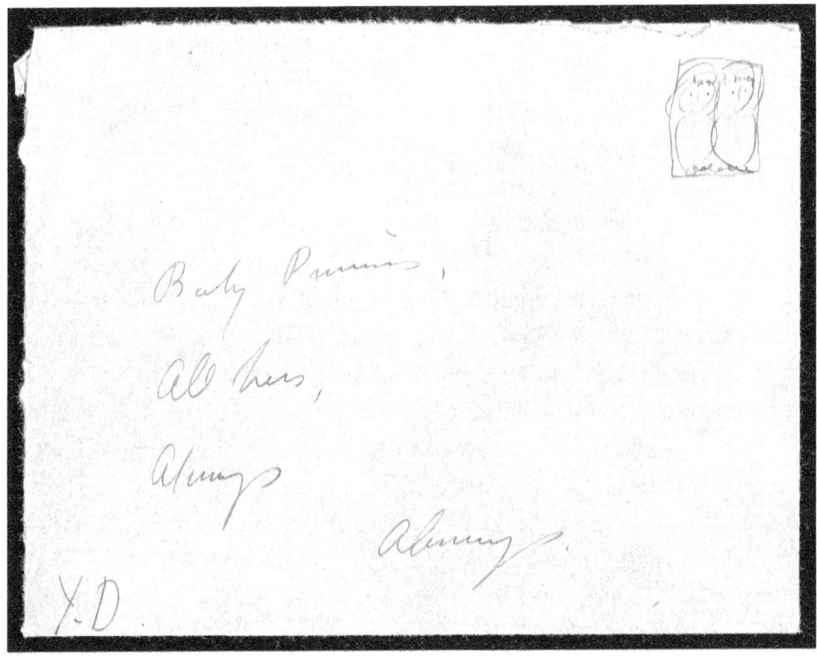

FIGURE 4.1. Note from Gertrude Stein to Alice B. Toklas.
Source: Beinecke Rare Book and Manuscript Library, Yale University.

my baby's / pen," Stein writes in one, Toklas having provided the tools for composition. "The stars are bright and I love / my baby," Stein writes in another. "I made lots of literature / and I loved my baby." One note ends with Stein admonishing herself: "and now / concentrate concentrate concentrate." Toklas in turn writes to Stein, "You made / lots of literature / last night didn't / You." Toklas frames the notes as a literary art, writing to Stein, "Notes are a very beautiful form of literature; they are never too frequent, do not fear to overwhelm me."[89]

Toklas had not meant to give the notes to the Beinecke; at first she asked that they be destroyed. Instead, they were locked away and made unavailable to researchers until 1981, and they were not included in the Beinecke's catalog until 1995.[90] And yet the notes share enough ground with Stein's published writings that any easy boundary between the public poet and the private note writer cannot hold. The notes themselves are small poems.

Many of the poems make use of the repetitions and rhythms characteristic of both the *Stanzas* and Stein's writing more generally:

> when this you see you know I love but thee,
> you are all to me and I am all yours, precious
> baby precious girl as pretty as pretty can
> be and all to me, and I am all she[91]

Among the notes is an undated, two-page one titled "A Command Poem," which opens "commanded by wifee, written by hubbie." Here, Stein takes the role of the secretary, normally attributed to Toklas, who in this case commands Stein's writing. In the poem's managerial and submissive dynamic, we see how Toklas made Stein's writing possible not only by providing the material conditions for Stein's ongoing life but also by prompting (commanding) Stein's ongoing production. The latter part of "A Command Poem" uses the same counting that we find in the *Stanzas*: "Once is a this / Twice is a this / Three times and four times / Five times and six times / All times and more times."[92] Here, the countable numbers open out into infinity, describing a shared love in these expansive terms. The *Stanzas*, the love notes, and the *Autobiography* all hover over the space between the intimate and the public. The *Stanzas* are neither the private face of the *Autobiography*, nor are they the public face of the private language of the notes. Like the slippage between Stein and Toklas encoded in the authorship of the *Autobiography*, Stein's poetry works with both the meta-discourse of her conversations with Toklas and the public language with which we structure our lives. In their reticence, they usher our attention toward the unseen, unnoticed, and privately held, and, in their collaborative history with Toklas, they gesture toward the reproductive work that sustains a relationship, which in turn makes writing possible.

For all their length, the *Stanzas* refuse to give too much away; their reticence is one of their signature stylistic features. Lauren Berlant observes that intimacy has its own ways of speaking lowly and sparely. "To intimate," they write in the introduction to a special issue of *Critical Inquiry*, "is to communicate with the sparest of signs and gestures"; intimacy has "the quality of eloquence and brevity." Berlant's description resonates with the sparseness of the *Stanzas*, whose reticence paradoxically speaks in an intimate mode. The spareness of intimate communication is also an assumption of shared language, of a shorthand that the intimists have built together. But intimacy is never simply private; the scripts and institutions of intimacy register "an aspiration for a narrative about something shared, a story about both oneself and others." If intimacy provides the plot or script for a life, if it "builds worlds," it is also destabilizing and ambivalent for "its potential failure to stabilize closeness always haunts its persistent activity, making the very attachments deemed to buttress 'a life' seem in a state of constant if latent vulnerability." Intimacy "only rarely makes sense of things," Berlant tells us, and in *Stanzas in Meditation* intimacy often appears as the thing to untangle.[93] Stein puts it in terms of thought against feeling: "What do I think when I feel," she asks, in a line that encapsulates the book's project (3, XXII, 136).

As the *Stanzas* progress, they trouble over order, neatness, and certainty, mulling over the possibility of "a diffusion but not a confusing," as Stein described letter writing in her lectures on narration.[94] The poem repeatedly returns to units of measurement and quantity and to the actions of sifting, sorting, and counting, which might be able to grant some order and certainty to "the messiness of intimacy," both its physical messiness—the messy wetness of bodies and fluids that Stein describes both here and in other poems—and the experiential and emotional uncertainties of intimate relationships.[95] Jennifer Cooke observes that "literature reflects the fact that our intimate relationships with others are more messy and incoherent, more unanticipated and unscripted, than the ways we are expected to react to them."[96] Stein's poem tests the possibility of restraining or disciplining that messiness. The poem has two primary tools and sets of vocabulary for dealing with and attempting to arrange this messiness: naming and number. The two are brought together in Stanza VI of the first section:

> It is the day when we remember two.
> We two remember two two who are thin
> Who are fat with glory too with two
> With it with which I have thought twenty fair
> If I name names if I name names with them.
> I have not hesitated to ask a likely block
> Of which they are attributed in all security
> As not only why but also where they may
> Not be unclouded just as yes to-day
> They call peas beans and raspberries strawberries or two

They forget well and change it as a last
That they could like all that they ever get
As many fancies for which they have asked no one.
Might any one be what they liked before
Just may they come to be not only fastened
It should be should be just what they like
This May in unison
All out of cloud. Come hither. Neither
Aimless and with a pointedly rested displeasure
She may be glad to be either in their resigning
That they have this plan I remember.
(1, VI, 65–66)

The "day when we remember two" locates the stanza perhaps on an anniversary or other shared significant date. The only concrete nouns that appear in this passage are "peas," "beans," "raspberries," "strawberries," and "clouds." Other nouns—such as "name" and "Tuesday"—have no physicality. The poem leans on the proper nouns even though it allows them only brief airtime. The poem subjects those nouns to its questions of naming and description: "They call peas beans and raspberries strawberries or two." Beans are called peas, and raspberries are called strawberries or "two." As readers, we are left uncertain whether the speaker has encountered and is referring to peas or beans or raspberries or strawberries. Next, we move from the problem of name to number, which also navigates a dynamic of stability and instability: "Shall we be three I wonder now." Number might be stabilizing—the knowledge of "being" one or two or three—but here that stabilizing knowledge is withheld. The poem attempts to come to terms with the available categories of being, either as a raspberry or a strawberry, or as one, a solitary individual, or two, a couple, or three, with all the emotional or experiential uncertainty that the addition of another figure might provoke. The ordering and restraining work of number fails to do its job, creating only further uncertainty.

While we get the sense that the *Stanzas* are about ordinary life lived together, they are not *Tender Buttons*, with its flush of enthusiasm for a new household; they lack the early poems' delight in cataloging the home and its objects. More than the material of household life, these poems are interested in the extended, restless, sometimes attentive but frequently wandering habits of thought provoked by a shared life. The poems make an implicit argument about the intellectual character of such shared experience. One way the poems do this is by their investment in extended attention, which has a great deal of space within it for wandering and inattention. "In one direction there is the sun and the moon," she writes. "In the other direction here are cumulus clouds and the sky / In the other direction there is why" (1, XV, 76). The poem wanders into meditations on sensory confusion:

> It is very often very strange
> How hands smell of woods
> And hair smells of tobacco
> And leaves smell of tea and flowers
> (2, II, 81)

Here, the surprising relationship is of a sensory kind, of hands smelling like plants and hair smelling like smoke. The poem's task, then, is to make sense of the crossed wires of sensory experience. The poem subjects its sensory observations to the pressures of its thought to make a broader comprehensible map of knowledge, just as we move from contemplating a lover to contemplating the entire world, and back again. It is this wandering habit that Ashbery finds remarkably true to life. Reading the *Stanzas*, he writes, it often "seems not so much as if we were reading as living a rather long period of our lives with a houseful of people," who "sometimes make no sense and sometimes make perfect sense; or they stop short in the middle of a sentence and wander away, leaving us alone for awhile in the physical world, that collection of thoughts, flowers, weather, and proper names."[97]

In the last chapter of *The Alice B. Toklas Cookbook*, Toklas describes the fourteen summers tending her garden at Bilignin, where Toklas managed the vegetable garden and Stein looked after the flower boxes and box hedges. Growing vegetables, Toklas makes clear, "was a full-time job and more," as anyone who has cultivated a garden will know; it took "an hour to gather a small basket [of strawberries] for Gertrude Stein's breakfast."[98] Toklas's garden provides some of the few concrete descriptions in the *Stanzas*. "They shell peas and of the pea shell they make a soup to eat and drink," Stein writes (4, I, 139). The garden is present as an offering: "And vegetables and pumpkins and pansies too / She knew she grew all these through to you" (1, XV, 77); "She has left roses and the rose trees"

(5, LVIII, 230). Toklas's account of gardening at Bilignin each summer rhymes with the surprises and confusions described in the *Stanzas*. Situated near the Alps, a late frost could ruin string beans and green peas, and the berries posed their own problems:

> Besides all the strawberries there were the raspberries. . . . When one came upon them unexpectedly, one did not know what all the pendent clusters of colour could be. They never seemed real to me, but a new and joyous surprise each morning.[99]

Toklas characterizes the repetitions of daily life not as exact replicas but as daily, continual revelations. This could be a description of the operations of Steinian repetition. Lyn Hejinian reminds us that Stein's repetitions are fundamentally inclusive rather than corrective. "Key elements," she tells us, "coexist with their alternatives in the work. Nothing is superseded. A phrase or sentence is not obliterated when an altered or even contradictory version of it appears."[100] If, as Berlant suggests, the intimate work of building a life with another person has the potential to destabilize as much as structure a life, then writing becomes a way of attending to, and perhaps making sense of, that confusion.

Reading Stein means staying in the unfixed zones where a strawberry might be a raspberry, where language is at once public and private, where the poet is always working and not ever completely working. It is that attention to the unfixed in Stein that allows her to pose such a sustained challenge to the divisions that structure life under capital's regime—there is life over here, and work on the other side; there is work here, and the home elsewhere; there is the body just here, and the brain somewhere else. Which is not to say that she settles the issue for us; Stein rarely, if ever, settles an issue. *Stanzas in Meditation* ends abruptly: "These Stanzas are now done," she announces. But that final stanza leaves us suspended in the present:

> Why am I if I am uncertain reasons may inclose.
> Remain remain propose repose chose.
> I call carelessly that the door is open
> Which if they may refuse to open
> No one can rush to close.
> (5, LXXXIII, 249)

A resistance to closure is as much a hallmark of avant-garde indeterminacy as of the "open mesh of possibilities" signified for decades now by the word *queer*.[101] The *Stanzas* are nothing if not generally queer in their "refusal to signify monolithically," which could describe all of Stein's writing, and they are specifically, precisely queer in their sustained attention to the reproduction of queer life. We might describe Stein's queer labor as the creation and handling of misused objects, as in the seltzer bottle that becomes an occasion for a fizzing, unsettled language. Or we might describe it as her sustained attention to the contours of queer life over time. Writing about "Melanctha," one of the stories in *Three Lives*, Elizabeth Freedom names Stein's mode of "defective, imperfect, queer chronicity *chronocatachresis*," which, drawing on the literary term *catachresis*—the misuse of a word—designates "an individual's 'perverse' deregulation of temporality." Stein's *chronocatachresis* "names a way of misusing, or even misunderstanding, the principles of control over a condition, the management of wayward affects, and the discipline of self-production."[102] Reading Stein as a poet of social reproduction, we can follow throughout her writing a perverse dissolution of divisions of labor, even as she obliquely engages with the disciplinary structures of her time. Again and again, Stein points us back to the fundamental condition of experience that makes life possible at all. Steinian reproduction, like Steinian repetition, does not simply reproduce the world as it is. Again and again, Stein sutures her writing to reproduction to open alternative, queer, perverse ways of making life happen.

Toklas, for her part, described successfully growing vegetables in the garden at Bilignin as akin to maternal feeling: "The first gathering of the garden in May of salads, radishes and herbs made me feel like a mother about her baby—how could anything so beautiful be mine. And this emotion of wonder filled me for each vegetable as it was gathered every year. There is nothing that is comparable to it, as satisfactory or as thrilling, as gathering the vegetables one has grown." At the end of the season, Stein and Toklas would pack their harvest into baskets to return with them to Paris. The beauty of this harvest was a point of pride for Toklas. The baskets full of carrots, squash, and eggplants, Toklas wrote, "made for me more poignant color than any post-Impressionist picture."[103] The gardener is an artist and a mother; the work of reproduction expands into its other life-giving forms. For Toklas, and for Stein, the experience of making something beautiful and the experience of making something for and with another person are inseparable. The labors of daily life are various; they are often unnoticed. The *Stanzas* map the textures of life that are not eventful or particular but ordinary. That work is registered elsewhere as making beds or brewing coffee. Here, the ordinary work of life is its wandering attention, the thought that cannot be fully disciplined by number, time, measure, or naming—even as the poem subjects those disciplinary systems to the pressures of its thought—and the work of understanding a relationship with another. The *Stanzas* are a whole book made up of the in-between and unremarked thoughts, the thinking that makes up the spaces between encounters and action and does not come to any point or product. Attention is also a kind of work, and a way of serving others—to direct attention toward them while simultaneously meditating about the forms of that attention. Thought makes possible more thought, more interrogations, more of the same life. Like Toklas's garden, the intellectual work of the *Stanzas* is a kind of world-making—of continually making life with another person possible, and then making it possible again.

For poets coming after her, Stein opened up repetition as a way of mapping the rhythms of life, of acknowledging how life both repeats and changes. Perhaps no writer has offered a clearer interpretation of Steinian repetition than Lyn Hejinian, whose poem "My Life" matches Oulipian constraint with a formal openness that reflects a "vast and overwhelming" world where each moment is "potent with ambiguity, meaning-full, unfixed, and certainly incomplete."[104] "My Life" seeks a form for the dynamic and recursive process through which subjectivity is formed. "Long time lines trail behind every idea, object, person, pet, vehicle, and event," Hejinian writes; people, and the world in which people live, are the accumulation of time.[105] But this accumulation does not simply move forward. Moving from childhood to adulthood, "My Life" maps the reproduction that creates the self as not a linear but a recursive and dynamic process. "We take the great parts of human life to be distinct," Hejinian writes, "but childhood and adulthood, youth and age, are never juxtaposed."[106] Against the specificity of impressions and memories—snapdragons among the cineraria, husked corn and shelled peas, her father's typewriter—is the sweep of the poem, unfolding, then folding back in on itself. Certain lines surface and resurface in "My Life." The Steinian line "A rose, a pause, something on paper" punctuates the poem at several points, but its meaning changes as the line is constelled with different surrounding lines—here, as part of a "nature scrapbook"; later, after a letter has been opened; still later, a pause in the speed of New York City—and as it repeats, it becomes more and more part of the poem's, and life's, architecture while never settling into a stable meaning. "I heard it anew not again," Hejinian tells us. "My Life" theorizes an interaction between the specificity of its impressions and the temporality of its repetitions: "The sudden brief early morning breeze, the first indication of a day's palpability, stays high in the trees, while flashing silver and green the leaves flutter, a bird sweeps from one branch to another, the indistinct shadows lift off the crumpled weeds, smoke rises from the gravel quarry—all this is metonymy. The 'argument' is the plot, proved by the book. Going forward and coming back later."[107] For Hejinian, poetic language "opens—makes variousness and multiplicity and possibility articulate and clear."[108] Repetition does not reproduce the same thing over and over. Nor does reproduction. Reproduction, like a life, is not a plot; it does not start here and end there, a to c via b, never looking over its shoulder. It rebounds on itself, it repeats, and in doing so it creates the startlingly new. Stein, and Hejinian after and with her, remind us that the work of reproduction is breathlessly generative, that it is nothing less than the dynamic process that makes up the full, boundless possibility of a life.

Chapter Five

LORINE NIEDECKER
AND THE WORK OF RESTRAINT

Lorine N., Janitor of Wisconsin
—KEVIN DAVIES, *THE GOLDEN AGE OF PARAPHERNALIA*

Late in 1948, an article was published in the *Jefferson County Union* that celebrated the local industries of Fort Atkinson, Wisconsin, a flood-prone town on the Rock River a few miles upstream from Lake Koshkonong. The town and its six thousand inhabitants boasted an economy that included "the manufacture of hose, dairy equipment, canned goods, barn equipment, poultry supplies, and saws," as well as "the famous 'Little Pig Sausages'" produced by a resident, Milo Jones II. Jones the sausage maker was not Fort Atkinson's only local celebrity: in addition to the "father of the 'Little Pig Sausages,'" the town claimed as one of its own "the poet, Loraine [*sic*] Niedecker."[1] Niedecker wrote to Louis Zukofsky with ambivalence about her inclusion in the newspaper: "The worst is to have the ordinary person look at you as tho you wrote of moonlight and roses and were a simpleton in general but never stir himself to find out otherwise." She hoped that the piece might help her writing find a wider audience but doubted that her fellow inhabitants of Fort Atkinson would bother to acquaint themselves with her verse. "Such is fame," she joked, "that I'm linked to a sausage maker."[2]

Niedecker spent her life working. A middle-class childhood became an adult life marked by poverty, financial insecurity, and low-paid work. After leaving Beloit College early to care for her ill mother, Niedecker took a job as an assistant librarian in Fort Atkinson but was laid off during the

Depression. In 1938, she began working as a writer and research editor for the Works Progress Administration's *Wisconsin: A Guide to the Badger State*. After a stint of unemployment, between 1944 and 1950 she worked as a stenographer and proofreader for the local dairy industry journal, *Hoard's Dairyman*. When her deteriorating eyesight made proofreading impossible, Niedecker survived on typing work, a small disability pension, and occasional assistance from Zukofsky.[3] She was employed finally as a cleaner at the Fort Atkinson Memorial Hospital from 1957 to 1963. In 1963, she left that job and moved to Milwaukee with her second husband, Al Millen, whom she described in a letter to Zukofsky as "in the labor movement."[4] When Niedecker married Millen, she listed her occupation on her marriage license as simply "laborer."

Niedecker's writing life was difficult to reconcile with her labor, and with the people—the ordinary "folk"—among whom she lived. While her poetry is firmly planted in community and place, it is filled with ambiguity around its own illegibility and invisibility. Niedecker sometimes mourns the difficulties of a life spent writing slowly; she sometimes relishes poetry's incommensurability with the drudgery of everyday labors. In the poem quoted in this book's introduction, Niedecker at the printshop observes "the folk from whom all poetry flows / and dreadfully much else."[5] The speaker acknowledges her indebtedness to the folk even as she asserts poetry's difference:

> But what vitality! The women hold jobs—
> clean house, cook, raise children, bowl
> and go to church.
>
> What would they say if they knew
> I sit for two months on six lines
> of poetry?
> (CW, 143)

Here, Niedecker is the "broody hen," in Rachel Blau DuPlessis's words, "hatching the potential of a folk whose manner she finds both dreadful and admirable."[6] Niedecker describes a complicated entanglement characterized by simultaneous dependence and estrangement. Poetic language may come from the folk, but poetic work is fundamentally alien to them.

Niedecker describes a poet at work who is still, solitary, moving as little as possible:

> I learned
>   to sit at desk
>   and condense
> (CW, 194)

In an earlier poem she ventriloquizes her mother, a woman "moored to this low shore by deafness," her life populated by "floor, pump, wash machine," as she compares herself to her poet daughter:

> I've wasted my whole life in water.
> My man's got nothing but leaky boats.
> My daughter, writer, sits and floats.
> (CW, 107)

The poet sits at her desk; she sits and drifts on the river; she sits on two lines of poetry. Whatever production she undergoes in her stillness makes for very little: six months for two lines. Niedecker paints the passive anti-productivity of poetry as something that requires enormous effort but leaves the body involuntarily:

> Now in one year
>   a book published
>   and plumbing—
> took a lifetime
>   to weep
>   a deep
>   trickle
> (CW, 195)

Written in 1962, the poem brings together Niedecker's belated domestic modernity—the installation of plumbing and a pressure pump in her home—with her writing life.[7] It applies two pressures of diminishment, one of time and one of scale: the slowness of a lifetime and the littleness of a trickle. Perhaps the poem is wept from crying, the product of intense feeling. Or perhaps it is a weeping sore or wound, a deep cut. Or perhaps it is a spring. That "deep," the poem's only rhyme, marks the trickle as something that though small and slow is significant, a thing that surfaces from the depths.

Reading Niedecker's "little barely audible poems," as George Oppen once described them, involves a practice of attunement, of orienting ourselves toward the barely audible or visible.[8] She is most frequently associated with the Objectivist poets—comprising Oppen, Zukofsky, Charles Reznikoff, and Carl Rakosi—although usually with qualification. She was the only woman among the group, the only gentile; she lived in the middle of the continent far from any metropolitan cultural center and was deeply concerned with the rhythms of rural life. Acknowledging the looseness of the group's connection, DuPlessis and Peter Quartermain use the term "nexus" to describe the Objectivists, a term they suggest "embraces contradiction, variousness, and dispute."[9] My focus in this chapter will be what Ron Silliman has called "third-phase Objectivism," that is, the period after the Second World War when the Objectivist poets were at their productive height.[10] By the 1960s, however, these were mature writers, and it makes little sense to retain their 1930s grouping. Outside of the Objectivist nexus, scholars have struggled to position Niedecker, a writer seemingly sui generis connected only tangentially to literary movements. She is a writer of folk poetry, a surrealist, an environmentalist poet. And because she has received so little attention until recently, efforts to write about her have often necessarily entailed arguing for her place in literary history.

As Elizabeth Willis has shown, Niedecker worked from an affinity with the late nineteenth-century Arts and Crafts movement of Ruskin and Morris, a movement that fused art with the dignity of human labor and articulated a vision of anticapitalist social transformation through aesthetic production.[11] Building on Willis's reading of this Arts and Crafts influence, I suggest that we might fruitfully understand Niedecker's work in relation to the turn to craft techniques by feminist artists in the decades after the Second World War. Working with methods that had been associated with hobbyism and gendered domestic work—sewing, knitting, crochet, quilting, scrapbooking, and collage—artists such as Lenore Tawney, Eva Hesse, Sheila Hicks, and Cecilia Vicuña developed bodies of work that refused the denigration of women's reproductive labor and participated in a broader feminist effort to designate the home as a fully politicized site of class and antipatriarchal struggle.[12] At the same time that these craft methods gained new political urgency, feminist activists and theorists engaged in a program that "located gender relations on the terrain of political economy" and expanded that terrain to include sexuality, care, housework, and reproduction more broadly.[13]

In this chapter, I read Niedecker's late poetry in relation to the custodial labor that she performed as a hospital cleaner and the domestic labors—cooking, cleaning, sewing—that she describes in her later poems. Reproductive labor, with its values of care, preservation, and self-effacement, provide us with the vocabulary to understand Niedecker's late poetry. I bring this analysis of reproduction into conversation with the poems' material forms by focusing my analysis on archival versions of the homemade books of poetry that Niedecker wrote, decorated, and sent to her friends. These books embrace the aesthetics of handicraft and practices of amateurism, which, as Julia Bryan-Wilson and Benjamin Piekut note, are practices "of cultural making 'from below' that are distinct from 'fine art' and its institutions that produce criteria around expertise, education and training."[14] Niedecker had no allegiance with any feminist movement, and her close friendships were all with men. She often found herself in the role of amanuensis, typing Zukofsky's manuscripts until his marriage to Celia Thaew. Her turn to craft names her exclusion from formal and institutional literary production and publishing and toward homemade forms of creation and informal distribution that take their coordinates from devalued forms of gendered reproductive labor. Moreover, Niedecker's late poetry refigures what reproduction itself might mean—not as boundless creation, but as a practice of restriction and restraint.

HOMEMADE, HANDMADE

In the fall and winter of 1964, Niedecker sent three books of poems to friends. She mailed the first book of thirty verses, called "Homemade Poems," to the poet and translator Cid Corman in Kyoto in October.[15] In December she sent two versions, both titled "Handmade Poems," to Louis Zukofsky and the poet Jonathan Williams. The three versions share twenty-two poems in common, with some revisions made in the intervening months. *Homemade/Handmade Poems*, as the editions are named in

LORINE NIEDECKER AND THE WORK OF RESTRAINT

Jenny Penberthy's *Collected Works*, collects short lyrics about Niedecker's domestic life on Blackhawk Island and in Milwaukee, poems that detail her idiosyncratic canon—Mary Shelley, Bashō, John Ruskin, Margaret Fuller, George Santayana—and poems about the spring and fall, chicory, muskrats, birch forests, sumac trees, and wild strawberries.

The version Niedecker sent to Corman, now held in the New York Public Library, consists of a slim autograph book that the poet covered in dark gold wrapping paper decorated with a pale gold circular pattern (figure 5.1). In the center of the page, Niedecker pasted a rectangle of white and bronze striped paper to frame the book's title, written in the poet's hand. On the first page, Niedecker covered the paper completely with a thick, woven blue card. Pasted onto that is a hand-painted watercolor, inside carefully measured margins, of her cottage on Blackhawk Island (figure 5.2). Still visible are the pencil outlines of the house with its crosshatched roof. Flowers line the path to the house and shore, trees are painted with black trunks and green foliage, and a small pink boat sits tethered to a black wharf. Niedecker left the image unsigned. The watercolor of her home occupies the place where we would expect to find the

FIGURE 5.1. Cover of *Homemade Poems*.
Source: Permission is given by Bob Arnold, Literary Executor for the Estate of Lorine Niedecker.

FIGURE 5.2. Watercolor of Blackhawk Island in *Homemade Poems*.
Source: Permission is given by Bob Arnold, Literary Executor for the Estate of Lorine Niedecker.

copyright page. The publisher is Niedecker and the publishing house her home. The book combines the cheap, easily available material of wrapping paper with Niedecker's amateur watercolors. She wrote the poems by hand, in blue pen.

"I somehow feel compelled to send you the product of the last years, just to keep in touch," Niedecker wrote to Corman. "I know you're not printing. I even braved school kids' paints to show you where we live! It's been—ah—years!"[16] We can hear a note of anxiety about her limited access to publishing in this description, though she insists on her cheerful lack of expertise. She similarly writes to Zukofsky in October 1964, "Sure I'm dabbling in water colors!"[17] "Homemade Poems" is a distinctive object in Niedecker and Corman's correspondence. For the most part, Niedecker typed her letters to Corman, only occasionally writing them by hand. The version she sent to Zukofsky is dated September 1964 but signed "Merry Christmas '64."[18] That version is a simple autograph book with a cover decorated with a small strip of wrapping paper in Christmas colors.

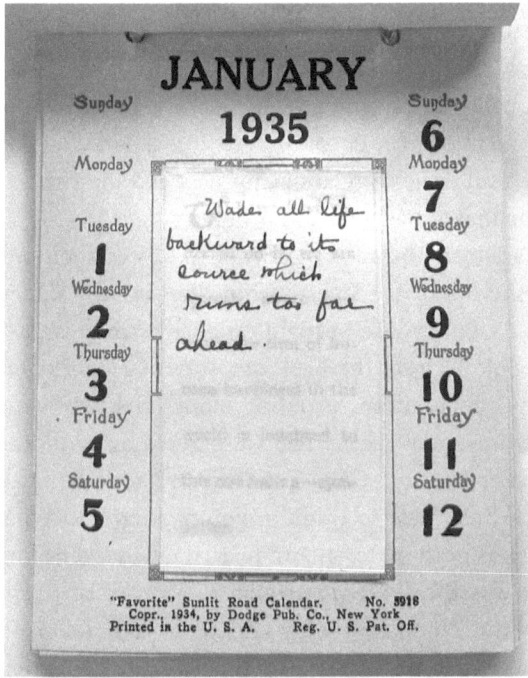

FIGURE 5.3. "Next year, or, I fly my rounds, tempestuous."
Source: Permission is given by Bob Arnold, Literary Executor for the Estate of Lorine Niedecker.

The book begins with a similar watercolor to the one she sent to Corman. In the bottom left corner she has written, in all capitals, "WHERE WE LIVE."

Niedecker sent many photographs, sketches, and watercolors to friends during this period of her life. Her homemade bookmaking builds on a decades-long practice of gift-giving. Thirty years earlier, for Christmas 1934, she sent Zukofsky a copy of "The Favorite Sunlit Road Calendar," a small tearaway biweekly calendar tied together at the top with an orange ribbon (figure 5.3). She retitled the calendar "Next year, or, I fly my rounds, tempestuous." Over the calendar's inspirational quotations from scripture and notable people—Robert Louis Stevenson, Marcus Aurelius—Niedecker pasted small strips of paper on which she wrote her own small poems. Some comment on the year's markers. The first entry, for the new year, reads "Wade all life / backward to its / source which / runs too far / ahead" (*CW*, 41).[19] Niedecker ran a line of paste along the top edge of her strips of paper, keeping the bottom edge loose so that the reader could flip up her poem and see the original quotation underneath—a relational reading not possible in the two-dimensional version of the calendar reprinted in Niedecker's *Collected Works*. In doing so, she reforms a mass market commodity into a handcrafted object. More than that, she establishes a relationship between the two, entangling the poetic with the mass-produced and ordinary.

Niedecker's letters to the Zukofskys are full of such small gifts. On scrap paper, she doodled scenes—a hot dog stand, a dance, her house; she painted a Canada goose in flight on a Christmas card; she wrote letters to Celia Zukofsky on the back of issues of *Hoard's Dairyman*, as if to show the products of her proofing labor. The two women also sent each other homemade gifts: "The little red box with the red flower came," Niedecker wrote to Celia Zukofsky in December 1949. "I like the pin very much but I hate to think of you making it, all that time etc."[20] This practice was both material and textual. Niedecker's longest exercise in gift-giving was the *For Paul* sequence, a series of poems written in large part for the Zukofsky family and their young son, Paul, between 1949 and 1956, which describes a writing process dependent on mutual exchange. "I've been away from poetry many months," she writes in one poem, "and now I must rake leaves / with nothing blowing / between your house / and mine" (*CW*, 157). Niedecker's feminist critics have tended to see her practice of exchange as a project of claiming her individual freedom against the commercial literary market. For DuPlessis, the "poetics of gift exchange" that Niedecker constructed with Zukofsky and Corman "made a familial economy of affiliation that rejects the feedback loop of impersonal publication, prizewinning poetry, and fame."[21] Willis notes that Niedecker "clearly saw the abjection of the poet within American culture, but she also saw it somehow counterweighted by the dizzying freedom of working with others almost entirely beyond the bounds of the market economy."[22] While it is certainly true that Niedecker arranged her life outside the literary economy, in no small part by necessity, the idea of "dizzying freedom" is difficult to reconcile with the minor forms of this material and with Niedecker's accounts of her restricted writing and working life. I suggest that these restricted conditions were important to her poetry. It is in relation to these minor forms of making that she articulates what poetic work might be for.

Homemade/Handmade Poems opens with an invitation:

> Consider at the outset:
> to be thin for thought
> or thick cream blossomy
>
> Many things are better
> flavored with bacon
>
> Sweet Life, My love:
> didn't you ever try
> this delicacy—the marrow
> in the bone?
>
> And don't be afraid
> to pour wine over cabbage[23]
> (*CW*, 200)

The poem delivers some basic truths of cooking. "Consider," it tells us, but the pun in the following line takes away the object of our consideration. "Thin" has a larger function beyond reforming a platitude for it sets up the poem's concern with the spare and simple. Those opening lines stage the book's first disappointment. An invitation is extended ("consider"), but once accepted we find that it leads to very little: to the restricted "thin for thought," the ponderous generosity of "consider" having been quickly rescinded. In this way the poem invites us to reorient our sense of scale and value to diminishment. The shift from the first to the second stanza stages the book's second disappointment in the fall from the Yeatsian beauty of "blossomy" to the rough, coarse (though still thick, sensuous) bacon. This motion of disappointment recurs in the poem's second half. The move to "Sweet Life, My love" extends an offer of an illicitly tasted "delicacy" contained "in the bone." When the penultimate line breaks on "And don't be afraid," anything—or nothing—at all might come next; the poem could reasonably stop there, advising us not to be afraid in general. But we end with another tumble, this time onto the unlovely, unpoetic "cabbage." By asking us to suspend our fear, the poem implicitly promises us something to be feared, but all it offers is the daring to make wine-soaked cabbage.

The poem takes us through disappointments and tonal frustrations; small inflations—"Sweet life, My love"—are followed by small deflations: cabbage and bacon. Little jokes are lined up one after the other. *Homemade/Handmade Poems* delights in the smallness of domestic dramas. The year before Niedecker compiled her books of homemade poems, she retired from her job at the hospital. Much of the tonal lightness of *Homemade/Handmade Poems* is rooted in her release from paid labor after a lifetime of working. She enthused about her newfound freedom to Corman: "There is something in me these free days—free from working for a living—so filled with the life I've always wanted."[24] Her retirement was the most productive period of her life, but still she wrote that she was "afraid of feeling *busy*." "No, I won't be writing for awhile," she told Corman, "and I need time, like an eon of limestone or gneiss, time like I used to have, with no *thought* of publishing. I'm very slow anyhow, you know."[25] "Consider at the outset" presents reproductive domestic labor not as a necessary daily trial but as a source of fascination and delight, one that only the space of retirement from labor makes possible.

Just before her marriage and retirement, Niedecker's home life was thrown into disarray. In 1959, a devastating flood on Blackhawk Island forced her to evacuate; when she returned, her cabin was "writhing with fish and worms."[26] The flood prompted her to sell the two small houses left to her by her father, but when the buyers defaulted she was forced to foreclose, a knotty legal experience that she documents in letters and verse:

FORECLOSURE

Tell em to take my bare walls down
my cement abutments
their parties thereof
and clause of claws

Leave me the land
Scratch out: the land

May prose and property both die out
and leave me peace
(*CW*, 291)

It's a sharp little poem. The pun on "property," which encodes the word "poetry," entangles the trials of home ownership with the difficulties of writing. "Houses mean nothing much to me anymore," she wrote to Zukofsky in November 1963.[27] That same month, Niedecker left her job at the hospital and moved to Milwaukee with Millen. The pair spent weeks in the city and weekends and vacations on Blackhawk Island. "What an adjustment for me," Niedecker had written to Zukofsky earlier that year after the pair's initial meeting. "Too bad for me to become used to daily companionship, to deep affection, to human (!) happiness."[28] Millen's Milwaukee apartment required intensive cleaning before it was habitable for the couple. "I don't know what has been biggest here—the cooking," she wrote to Zukofsky, "or the cleaning of the first four days—such filth you could not possibly experience even in New York in the old days." The couple furnished the apartment with furniture from Goodwill and settled into a routine in

FIGURE 5.4. Polaroid photograph by Lorine Niedecker of her new home on Blackhawk Island.
Source: Permission is given by Bob Arnold, Literary Executor for the Estate of Lorine Niedecker.

which Al worked night shifts and cooked when possible, they visited the laundromat together, and Niedecker explored Milwaukee on foot during the day.[29] They sold Niedecker's cottage on Blackhawk Island and set about building a new one on land that she owned (figure 5.4). It is this house she painted with watercolors and photographed for Zukofsky. Niedecker described building and moving into the house in unpublished letters to Zukofsky. "This month so far—and part of last—compresses within it the excitement of a lifetime. We've signed a contract for a house to be built out there on the river as soon as they can get out on the land—no flooding this year." She conjured in detail the house's construction, its mahogany walls, double closets, birch kitchen cabinets, and gas stove. "I do hope we'll never regret it," she wrote.[30] She sewed new curtains for the bedroom and slip covers for the house chairs.[31]

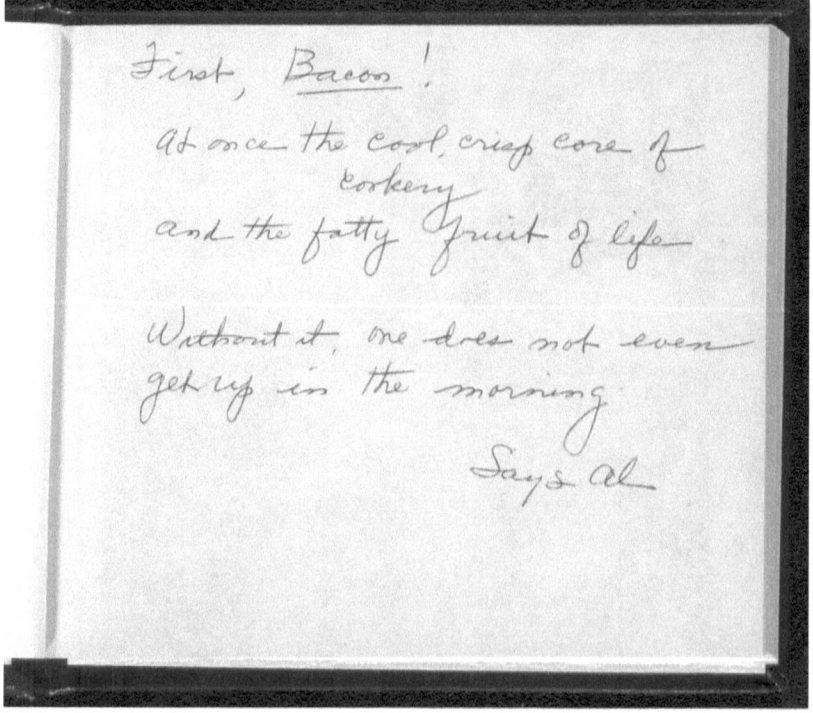

FIGURE 5.5. "A Cooking Book."
Source: Permission is given by Bob Arnold, Literary Executor for the Estate of Lorine Niedecker.

To write about her new home life, Niedecker turned to domestic genres. In December 1964, she filled an autograph book with short meditations and anecdotes about cooking and sent it as a Christmas present to her cousin, Maude Hartel. In the first pages of the book, Niedecker jokes about what she lacks. "The fact that I don't know much about the subject of cooking should entitle me to write a book about it," she writes, deferring to Al, who "ate from the soil."[32] She advises on the virtue of cooking with bacon: "At once the cool, crisp core of cookery / and the fatty fruit of life / Without it, one does not even get up in the morning / Says Al" (figure 5.5).

Later, the book records the conversation from "Consider at the outset":

Al : You (looking at me) should eat cooked marrow—
L : What's marrow?
Al : Beef marrow in the bone—there is no delicacy in the world like this.

Niedecker embraces her position as a cheerfully inexpert member of the household economy. The book delights in thrifty uses ("Cook the carcass of chicken for soup after it's been roasted") and home remedies, advising its reader to save goose fat "to use with turpentine for rubbing on the chest— for chest colds." Some of the notes are lineated into little poems. A page titled "Old Remedies / *from Al's Childhood*" tells us:

> He
> speaks also of winter-green
> leaves for tea and Queen
> Anne's Lace (wild carrot)
> for tea and nasturtiums
> for salad.[33]

"A Cooking Book" collects the traces of daily life. It melds poetry with minor genres, domestic ephemera, and everyday household labors. But Niedecker also alters our expectation that a cooking book written by a woman will share the domestic expertise she has acquired over decades of labor. Roles are inverted: the recipes and remedies are all Al's. Once again, Niedecker is in the position of the happy amateur.

Homemade/Handmade Poems likes to frustrate expectations. It is full of little jokes at the expense of poetic self-seriousness:

SANTAYANA'S

For heaven's sake, dear Cory,
poetry?—I like somewhat
the putrid Petrarch
and the miserable Milton.
I don't have books,
don't meet important persons
only an occasional stray student
or an old Boston lady.
(*CW*, 203)

The poem reworks a letter from George Santayana to Daniel Cory. While Santayana was living in Italy and being harangued by Pound, he wrote to Cory that he wished "to see only people and places that suggest the normal and the beautiful: not abortions or eruptions like E. P.":[34]

> For heaven's sake, dear Cory, do stop Ezra Pound from sending me his book. Tell him that I have no sense for true poetry, admire (and wretchedly imitate) only the putrid Petrarch and the miserable Milton; that I don't care for books, hardly have any, and would immediately send off his precious volume to the Harvard library or to some other cesspool of infamy. That is, if he made me a present of it. If he sent it only for me to look at and return, I would return it unopened; because I abhor all connection with important and distinguished people, and refuse to see absolutely anyone except some occasional stray student or genteel old lady from Boston.[35]

Niedecker noted her hesitation about the poem: "I might never use this—too much his own words" (*CW*, 427). In compressing Santayana's letter, she changes a joke about Pound's brash social presence to a joke on poetry in general. But it is no accident that she chose a letter about Pound, who hovers just behind this poem. We might read this as a self-directed nod toward the ridiculousness of choosing to be a poet. But I think we can read this poem as speaking to us with a straight face, as written by a person *really* frustrated with poetry. The poem's second half is supposed to describe a life with no investment in poetry, but the world of the life of the "old Boston lady" isn't all that far removed from Niedecker's ordinary life in Wisconsin. DuPlessis observes of Niedecker's orientation toward anonymity that she "worked to claim the non-elite, nonhegemonic literary career (anonymity, erasure, loss) as a cultural identity" and that, further, "she embraced, worked toward, and improvised playfully on the condition of anonymity."[36] If we read the poem as speaking to us with a straight face, then its sympathies and allegiances land on the poem's unnamed and unpoetic subjects, its stray students and old ladies. And so, "*Santayana's*" becomes an exercise in corrupting poetry, deflating it from the extraordinary to the ordinary. Its fall is staged, from its title and the quasi-mystical authority of Santayana's name to the anonymous characters at its end, and in that fall it takes poetry down with it.

In another poem Niedecker braids domestic and blue-collar labor with literary history:

> I knew a clean man
> but he was not for me.
> Now I sew green aprons
> over covered seats. He
>
> wades the muddy water fishing,
> falls in, dries his last pay-check
> in the sun, smooths it out
> in *Leaves of Grass*. He's
> the one for me.
> (*CW*, 208)

"Sewing new slip covers for me new house chairs," Niedecker wrote to Zukofsky in August 1964. "I'm putting slip covers over slip covers, a kind of apron over the regular covers so that when Al comes in from looking at a fish pole or cutting another tree down he can sit down without my worrying. He can cover himself with more sand and/or mud and new cut grass etc."[37] The poem turns away from the "clean man" and, by implication, the world of white-collar work divorced from water, mud, and physical labor. In doing so, it also turns away from a bourgeois poetry that sees itself as separate from working-class life and the wage relation. The poem declares its preference for the unruliness of the muddy fisherman via the repurposing of two objects: the aprons sewn into seat covers and the copy of *Leaves of Grass*. In the wet, corrupted book and the erotics of working-class masculinity, Niedecker draws on the Whitmanian ideal of the physical and spiritual alignment of the poet and worker. This is an alignment that he mediates via wet paper in the 1855 version of "A Song for Occupations":

> Come closer to me,
> Push close my lovers and take the best I possess,
> Yield closer and closer and give me the best you possess.
>
> This is unfinished business with me . . . how is it with you?
> I was chilled with the cold types and cylinder and wet paper between us.[38]

In an elegant reading of Whitman's evocation of the animal and human bodily labors of the printshop, Peter Riley suggests that Whitman's speaker "lingers mid-production with that wetness," creating "a fantasy print shop assemblage of bodies, cylinders, and ink."[39] Riley reads in these lines an alternative to Marx's emphasis on the deformed, alienated body of the industrial worker and suggests that Whitman finds in the printshop a new social contract based on bodily intimacy and contact. Where Whitman leaves us suspended, Niedecker makes a decisive trade in favor of the unclean man. This is also a definitive move in favor of a poetry muddied by association with two bodily acts: the labor indicated by the fishing body and the paycheck, and the poem's suggestive eroticism in which one man is traded for another. An apron becomes a seat cover, a copy of Whitman smooths out a paycheck, and a calendar or autograph book become a handcrafted collection of poems. Niedecker invests commodities with new use values. At the same time, she brings poetry into contact with these objects and renders it thrifty, scrappy, and domestic. Here, we are far from the Poundian practice of craft as seriousness and expertise that I traced in chapter 1, the practice that Jasper Bernes, writing about Oppen, describes as "an artisanal grammar of tool, matter, environment, a grammar of the dignity of materials and makers, and a potential reciprocity between bodies and objects that is not possible in fully industrialized capitalism."[40] Craft, for Niedecker, designates not perfectibility, seriousness, and mastery but rather tampering, repurposing, and bodily eroticism via compromised materials that are put to new uses.

This tampering is material, but it also operates at the level of tone and pace. One of Niedecker's signature modes is bathos, but a bathos of a controlled kind. Its falls are small and frequent; we don't plummet and sink so much as stumble and trip. Niedecker's motion is always softly and quietly downward, landing us on bacon or cabbage, an old Boston lady, or her quiet but firm declaration that "he's the one for me." John Wilkinson's description of how bathos works in the poetry of James Schuyler, a poet who shares some affinities with Niedecker in style and subject, is apt: "Bathos does not figure as a fall from a high lyric tone but as a principled steadiness and soundness of nerve. The collapse it performs may be evident not so much at the level of the individual poem relative to an oeuvre, as in a poetical rhetoric which starts in the mud and stays there, or gently rises and lowers. Its collapse in such a case is from general cultural assumption about how lyric should do its business."[41] How should the lyric do its business? Where should it direct its attention? Who and what should it value? These are questions asked by both the poems' tonal deflations and Niedecker's choice of material. Similar questions were asked by women artists of the same era working with the vocabulary of handicraft and domestic traditions. In 1955, the artist Ann Wilson layered acrylic paint onto a found quilt (figure 5.6). The quilt's forms and fabric are still visible in some places

FIGURE 5.6. *Moby Dick* by Ann Wilson (1955).
Source: Digital image © Whitney Museum of American Art / Licensed by Scala / Art Resource, NY.

under the paint's uneven layers. She titled the quilt "Moby Dick." Drawing on the historical quilts of her childhood in Pennsylvania, Wilson layers American literary history with the occluded history of women's domestic work. "It was American history that I was dealing with," Wilson explained five and a half decades later, "and the woman's part in it."[42]

Wilson was part of a group of artists—along with Robert Indiana, Agnes Martin, and Lenore Tawney—who lived and worked together in the late 1950s and early 1960s in Coenties Slip, an old seaport in Lower Manhattan with views of the Brooklyn Bridge and the East River. The location, at the south end of the island of Manhattan, where the land meets the rivers and the sea—an urban counterpart to the flooded banks of the Rock River where Al fished and Niedecker sewed her slip covers to protect her chairs from mud and water—proved generative for the group's experiments with tampered material and refuse. Wilson's quilt trades in both what passes away and what can be salvaged and repurposed. Like Niedecker's repurposed apron and wet copy of *Leaves of Grass*, *Moby Dick* remakes both the quilt and Melville's novel, which stands in synecdochically for American literary history. Wet, layered, and rewritten, Melville and Whitman are interwoven with women's work. Craft in this sense not only insists on the value of devalued labors but also navigates relationships of preservation and passing. It turns to the occluded and partial history of gendered work and creates new objects from that history's tattered, sodden forms.

HOUSING CONDITIONS: NIEDECKER IN THE DEPRESSION

The thrifty domestic economy and handcrafted aesthetics of *Homemade/Handmade Poems* have their roots in Niedecker's Depression-era writing. In 1946, Niedecker published *New Goose* with the Press of James A. Decker, later renamed simply the Decker Press, a small but prolific poetry press run out of Prairie City, Illinois. The press also published Zukofsky's *55 Poems* in 1941 and *Anew* in 1946, Kenneth Rexroth's *The Art of Worldly Wisdom* in 1949, and books by August Derleth and Hubert Creekmore.[43] *New Goose* runs to fifty pages. Cheaply produced, in a small "pocket poetry" format of 6 by 4.5 inches, its paper is roughly cut and unevenly copied. Several pages are cut in such a way that the poems are broken off prematurely; other poems are hard to read, their lines drifting into the book's margins and gutters.

LORINE NIEDECKER AND THE WORK OF RESTRAINT

New Goose wasn't published until just after the war but is clearly a document of the Depression. Its themes are the dispossession, hunger, poverty, debt, unemployment, and speed-up experienced by the rural working class in the 1930s. The book's historical characters lead us back to contemporary poverty; we find John James Audubon jailed "twice for debt" (*CW*, 107) and Van Gogh hungry, "the family's shoes / patched and worn" (*CW*, 108). Its poems about local legend and natural history draw on Niedecker's time working in Madison on *Wisconsin: A Guide to the Badger State*, part of the Federal Writers' Project *American Guide* series. Many of the poems adopt the rhythms of the nursery rhyme:

> I'm a sharecropper
> down here in the south.
> Housing conditions are grave.
>
> We've a few long houses
> but most folks, like me,
> make a home out of barrel and stave.
> (*CW*, 98)

The poem riffs on the nursery rhyme trope of surprising housing; in place of the old woman who lived in a shoe, we find a worker in a barrel. Its referent is the visual trope of the "bankruptcy barrel," common in newspapers in the 1930s, of a destitute man, naked except for a barrel around his body held up by suspenders. The housing conditions are "grave," as the barrel comes to look like a coffin, and the "stave"—the wooden planks that make up the side of a barrel—staves off hunger or death by starvation. The "few long houses" also evoke Indigenous dwelling structures, linking twentieth-century tenant labor to broader histories of colonial dispossession. Other poems work with the distortions and surprises of the nursery rhyme:

> The land of four o'clocks is here
> the five of us together
> > looking for our supper.
> Half past endive, quarter to beets,
> seven milks, ten cents cheese,
> > lost, our land, forever.
> (*CW*, 111)

Time is measured by food and hunger in a poem in which enough to eat is not a promise but a peril. Much of the poem's effect is in the tonal change at its end and the move to the slow finality of the heavily demarcated line "lost, our land, forever." The rhyme on "supper" and "forever" extends the poem's clock, as we lengthen from "four o'clocks" to all of time. Niedecker repurposes the nursery rhyme's associations with domesticity and early life to interrogate the shared shape of home life in a Depression landscape of tenant farming, food shortages, and dispossession. Drawing on the anonymous authorship and collective knowledge of the nursery rhyme, Niedecker writes lyrics in which domesticity is not a matter of private life but a collective experience of loss.

Land is lost forever, sharecroppers die, working people are swindled out of their stock by crooked financiers. Each poem ends with a severe disappointment:

> To see the man who took care of our stock
> as we slept in the dark, the blackbirds flying
> high as the market out of our pie,
> I travel now at crash of day
> on the el, a low rush of geese over those below,
> to see the man who smiled
> and gave us a first-hand country shake.
> (CW, 103)

The "blackbirds flying / high as the market of our pie" rewrite the blackbirds of "Sing a Song of Sixpence." The undead birds that sing when the pie is opened, despite having been baked—the song's central horror—fly instead of sing, soaring like a market that produces pie for some. That nursery rhyme is a fable of ruling class consumption: "Wasn't that a tasty dish / to set before a king?" it ends. In Niedecker's poem, the king becomes a smooth, smiling stockbroker who delivers a "first-hand country shake." "Hand" slips into "shake": perhaps the man's handshake is "first-hand," a genuine and shared country sociality that sits in opposition to what is secondhand or sold off. But the poem's irony settles on that final line and in the disjunction between the speaker who "slept in the dark" and the eerie reassurance of the man's smile and too-sure handshake. I also hear a suggestion of "shakedown" in that final word. If we read it this way—if "country shake" becomes "country shakedown"—then the poem registers how rural economies and rural citizens were "shaken down" by urban finance. Marx's word for the accumulation of fictitious capital was "swindle." When writing about the English commercial crash of 1847, he describes the "entire business world of a country being seized by such swindling."[44] In *New Goose*, people are swindled out of their land, the products of their labor, and the livelihood they are due.

Nursery rhymes work with a child's understanding of the world, which they elaborate into verses that are uncanny, strange, surreal, and frequently violent. Niedecker's rhymes draw on this tradition, asking us to sit with the deliberately withheld knowledge and obfuscation that was keenly felt at the depths of the Depression, which she links to historical violence. "Winnebagoes knew nothing of government purchase of their land," Niedecker writes in "Pioneers." Like the Indigenous inhabitants who "knew nothing," Niedecker uses the nursery rhyme to elaborate a problem of knowledge and of things whose scale, whether of speed or duration, is beyond comprehension. We find asparagus that "grows too fast to stop it," the loss of land "forever," and stock markets that suddenly crash. For Ruth Jennison, writing about the Depression, poetry is a genre whose "force ... resides in the figural and the unseen," which makes it "uniquely suited to represent a world financial system that is increasingly conducted in an invisible manner."[45] Niedecker's handling of the nursery rhyme stages the swindling and trickery of rural populations by financial interests as a problem of both ordinary life and poetic knowledge.

The stakes of this swindling are both world-historical and personal. In *New Goose*, the home is always at risk of disappearing out of sight, being stolen, washed away. Spring "overflows the land"; an old woman must bid "good-bye to lilacs by the door / and all I planted for the eye" (*CW*, 107), while an old man "lived to be eighty-four / then left everything":

> Heirs rush in—lay one tree bare
> claiming a birdhouse, leave
> wornout roof hanging there
> nothing underneath.
> (*CW*, 93)

Margaret Ronda writes that "Niedecker's representations of agrarian life highlight the prehistory of these changes and the consistent logics of property and profit that drive them, attending to what is almost and wholly lost as they occur."[46] "Home" is not a settled or stable space in these poems, nor is access to shelter, food, or land. Rather, the domestic—and the loss of the domestic—is a historicized experience, subject to colonial violence, ecological catastrophe, and economic crisis. It is part of a pattern of longer histories, just as here the devastations of the man's heirs connect the poem to larger instances of ecological violence. What is so distinctive about Niedecker's handling of the nursery rhyme is how she uses it to situate the genre's associations of domesticity within collective history. In this bridging of the local and the historical, Niedecker is deeply attuned to how the very possibility of a "home" is shaped, lost, or stolen by violent transformations of labor and land.

HOSPITAL KITCHEN

At the end of 1963, Niedecker retired from her last job. From 1944 to 1950, she worked as a proofreader and stenographer at *Hoard's Dairyman*. She handed in her resignation in June 1950, writing to Zukofsky, "Hoards has become a sweatshop with bad working physical conditions, each girl doing the work of two and no thanks and no raise in pay for over a year and a half."[47] Meanwhile Niedecker's deteriorating eyesight made reading fine print impossible. She began to receive disability payments in 1950, but her vision wasn't poor enough to qualify for a permanent pension. In addition to disability support, she lived off an allowance from her father of eighty dollars a month and occasional five-dollar checks from Zukofsky, as well as sporadic typing work.[48] She worked briefly in the Fort Atkinson library mending and shelving books but was described by a coworker, Phyllis Walsh, as a "good worker, but with little training, [she] had to perform menial jobs."[49] She applied to work at Moe Light as a switchboard operator soon after, and she would describe this job search in a short prose piece, "Switchboard Girl," first published in *New Directions* in 1951. Niedecker describes leaving *Hoard's*: "Nystagmus ('The poet's eye, in a fine frenzy rolling'), the searching movement, combined with 80 percent vision. You'll have to use a magnifying glass, we can't give you glasses to reach print. Good-bye to proof reading. Good-bye to a living" (*CW*, 335).

The piece documents the process of applying for a job at midlife—in 1951, she was forty-eight years old and had a disability. She writes, "I was the September dandelion—forty, female—seeking a place among the young fluorescent petunias" (*CW*, 335). She didn't get the job: "I lost. 'No natural aptitude.'"

The job that would stick for the longest was as a cleaner in the dietary unit at the Fort Atkinson Memorial Hospital. On workdays Niedecker was awake by 5 a.m., left the house at 6:15 a.m., and returned at 5 p.m. She relied on neighbors for rides or walked the five miles into town. She described her labors in a letter to Zukofsky:

> I should draw a picture of myself covered with dust mops, pails, kitchen cleanser, cloths, broom etc. wondering where I am down those long halls past all those doors. Not really hard—the floor is, most important thing is to wear spongy soles. Arms and feet feel it. Noon hour not a working time but paid for it and given the meal so really 7 hrs. on time sheet. I take care of the dining room so far as cleaning but someone is always coming in to sit there and talk and I have to watch and wait till I can get back in to finish up before the next meal. Hospital convention bids me sit at table at coffee break in morning (15 min.) and at noon with other cleaning ladies—elderly cripples already drawing social security checks (they're allowed to earn a little money besides s.c.) but one of them is a woman I know—used to come down to see Runkes—everyone trembles a bit before and behind Miss Gobel, the Superintendent (and on Tuesday mornings I have to make her bed and dust her apartment—some things observed as senseless as the stiff white caps on the nurses' heads. Pretty democratic system, tho, at that—office girls on easy terms with cleaning women, at least with me, but I dunt keer—what happens to me after I get home and a little rested and Sat. and Sun. is all that matters to me—have not been able to get hold of an anthology of Haiku from the Univ. Library.[50]

Institutional cleaning rose sharply across the twentieth century, from fewer than 80,000 workers in 1900 to 3.5 million in 1990, the numbers rising most steeply after 1950.[51] Like millions of other workers by the end of the 1950s, Niedecker was working a job in the expanding health care industry amid the shift to a service economy in the United States.[52] The work of cleaning hospitals is a non-nurturant form of "institutional service work" that forms the unseen counterpart to the care that hospitals provide.[53] Women of color are overrepresented in cleaning jobs and other "heavy, dirty, 'back-room' chores"—cooking and serving food in restaurants and cafeterias and caring for the ill and elderly in hospitals and nursing homes, whereas white women are generally favored for jobs that require social and physical contact with the public, such as nursing and teaching.[54] One of the central insights of feminist labor theory is that some aspects of jobs performed primarily by women are either invisible or not fully visible *as* work.[55] Patriarchal capital has an extensive set of techniques for maintaining the invisibility of women's work: reproductive labor is naturalized as love; the emotional content of service work is subsumed into social norms of warmth, generosity, and service; mothering is privatized as a matter of home and family; much reproductive labor is unwaged, outside the objectification of the wage relation. Institutional reproductive work exists somewhere in the invisible terrain between the public and private spheres as the waged counterpart to the unwaged labor of cleaning (which no doubt most cleaning women perform in addition to their waged work as a "second shift," to use Arlie Russell Hochschild's term).[56] The hospital and home are related as sites of care. The home can function as an extension of the hospital, as Nona Y. Glazer has shown in her analysis of how a work transfer shifts the responsibility for discharged patients onto the unwaged work of women in the home who take on the labor of nurses.[57] The workers overrepresented in public cleaning are often less visible socially—they are the elderly, disabled women that Niedecker describes or women of color; they are often multiply socially overlooked. So, too, must these workers cultivate invisibility as part of the job for cleaners are mostly required to be absent when other workers, clients, or patients are around, and they often work at night. Cleaning carries a final invisibility in the nature of the labor. The work of cleaning is a work of removal (of dirt, waste, marks upon a space), as well as a work of preservation. The cleaned space is one that has been returned to a neutral, unmarked state. The labor leaves no evidence of itself behind. Caring for a space, not for people: hospital cleaning is the invisible but still semipublic face of caring labor that makes further care possible.

In her letter to Zukofsky, Niedecker describes her hospital work as managing this invisibility; she must "watch and wait" for the dining room to empty so she can clean it in time for the next service. The invisibility of her hospital labor is registered in her poetry, appearing paradoxically in its absence. In her letter, she characteristically cordons off her hospital work from her reading and writing life, and it is the margins of time that flank the working day—the weekend, the time spent with library books—that matter. To the invisible labor of the hospital cleaner is added the invisibility of writing poetry. Just once does her time in the hospital appear in *Homemade/Handmade Poems*. This is the only poem in which she mentions the job explicitly:

HOSPITAL KITCHEN

Return
the night women's
gravy

to the cleaned
stove
(*CW*, 205)

We know where we are; the poem is deliberate about its location. The whole poem is an instruction that Niedecker and the other cleaners may well have been given in their early days on the job. Five lines in total, it slightly, subtly condenses as it progresses, moving from the 2/4/2 syllabic structure of the first tercet to the 3/1 syllables of the concluding couplet, in which "gravy" is whittled to the single syllable of "stove." Niedecker's condensery takes on a new meaning in this poem for this formal diminishment coincides with an erasure of human presence and action. The "night women" are registered only in the gravy that they have left behind. They are otherwise invisible, occupying the separate, unseen space of the night shift. The cleaning woman enters the poem only in an impersonal imperative and a past-tense verb, in the stove that has been "cleaned." That passive construction underscores the invisible character of custodial work, but, importantly, it doesn't correct it. A different first-person, attributive poem, "I returned / the night woman's gravy" or "I cleaned the stove" might insist on the cleaner's presence and her labor. We land on the cleaned stove, and it is the preserved and tended object, not the person doing the preserving, that is underlined. It is also tonally flat. Unlike her poems that lightly rise and fall into bathos, this poem begins low and stays there. The imperative and the passivity freeze the poem and, like the haiku Niedecker was trying to find at the library, create an arrested image of a single scene.

"Hospital Kitchen" might be the only time Niedecker explicitly acknowledges her job, but other homemade poems share that poem's ethos. Another instructional verse from *Homemade/Handmade Poems* is as follows (figure 5.7):

> For best work
> you ought to put forth
>   some effort
>   to stand
> in north woods
> among birch
> (*CW*, 210)

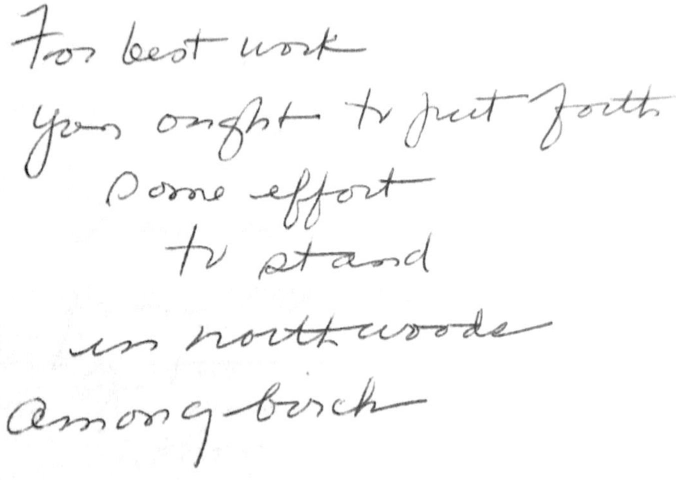

FIGURE 5.7. "For Best Work" from *Homemade Poems*.
Source: Permission is given by Bob Arnold, Literary Executor for the Estate of Lorine Niedecker.

This poem suggests rather than commands. Its first line sets us up to receive advice or counsel, but that expectation is soon shattered as the "best" work deflates to advice to do nothing at all, to stand still enough to pale into the white bark and lenticels of a birch tree. So much of this poem's impact lives in its assonance and half-rhymes. The phrase "best work" shares a long central vowel with "forth" and "effort," setting up our expectation that the work will be arduous. "Stand" snaps us back to attention; it stands out with its difference before the poem returns to its alliterative pattern ("work"/"woods") and closes out the near rhyme on "work"/"birch" that bookends the poem. The poem's series of near rhymes, never quite achieving anything as solid as a perfect match, are central to its minimalism. The poet Rae Armantrout observes that the poem turns admonitions—do your best, try harder—into parody, writing, "It sounds as if she thinks the valuable work is being done by trees and what humans should do is imitate them *exactly*, i.e., stand still, out-of-doors, and put forth. The little joke is that such behavior, if maintained, would cause humans to die of exposure."[58] I agree with Armantrout that the poem subordinates human labor to the real work done by trees of cleaning air and maintaining environmental equilibrium. Even if it isn't precisely a joke about death by exposure, the poem turns the idea of human effort into one of human erasure. In this sense, it isn't quite parody. It doesn't send up the imperative to put forth effort so much as reformulates what counts as effort and what effort might be for. It advises us to direct our energy not toward acting upon or imposing on the world but toward existing within it. The most surprising and essential words of the poem are its final prepositions: "in north woods / among birch."

"For Best Work" also rewrites the craft principles that uphold the integration of material making and the articulation of selfhood. Take, for example, George Oppen's poem "Product" from 1962's *The Materials*, which describes the boats of New England: "Fresh from the dry tools / And the dry New England Hands." That poem moves from the crafted object at one with its environment—the white-painted body of the boat dipping in the waves of the Atlantic—to a moment of self-recognition: "What I've seen / Is all I've found: myself."[59] But we might not want to trust this repair between self and world too easily for beneath Oppen's narrative of craft-based integration is an anxiety about irreducible strangeness. Niedecker's poem, in contrast, insists on such separation and the loss of self involved in standing still among the trees. "For Best Work" speaks to some of the volume's anxieties about reproduction, expressed most insistently in the penultimate poem of *Homemade/Handmade Poems*, a biography of Mary Shelley:

> Who was Mary Shelley?
> What was her name
> before she married?
>
> She eloped with this Shelley
> she rode a donkey
> till the donkey had to be carried.
> (*CW*, 212)

The questions of the first lines perform a double erasure for the answer to those questions—"Who was Mary Shelley? / What was her name / before she married?"—is Mary Wollstonecraft, a name shared by mother and daughter. Marriage, the poem suggests from the outset, can be an obliterating force, not just for individual women but also for their legacy. The poem's ethos resonates with Anahid Nersessian's arguments about Romantic adjustment, which she describes as "a formal as well as an ethical operation that allows human beings to accommodate themselves to the world by minimizing the demands they place upon it."[60] The Mary Shelley poem stands out in the volume for its formal evenness, its regular tercets, and its length (it is the longest poem in the book) and joins a lineage of Niedecker's antimarriage poems.[61] Elizabeth Willis interprets the poem as emerging from Niedecker's "household industry" of vexed collaborative practice with Zukofsky and as a meditation on *Frankenstein*, which recounts "the traumas of textual production in the context of both personal loss and the author's failure to produce a culturally accepted model of the maternal."[62] Even if we don't read the poem as rehearsing older pain about disappointed maternity, the poem registers a division of labor that designates women as carers rather than writers or thinkers. The second time that it is posed, in the poem's penultimate stanza, the question "Who was Mary Shelley?" is settled:

She read Greek, Italian
She bore a child

Who died
and yet another child
who died.
(*CW*, 213)

These lines are striking for how plainly, almost brutally, they state the fact of the infants' deaths. "Who was Mary Shelley?," asked twice in the poem, is answered in the compounding negative: she is someone who created dead children, which is to say that she is someone who failed to create. Her reproduction is continually offered and disappointed. "She bore a child" is stopped short by "Who died"; it expands into potential again—"and yet another child"—but then disappoints again, with yet another terminating spondee: "Who died." Four lines end with a heavy and final /d/ as "child" is reformulated into "died." This repetition propels the poem forward. The reproduction of these spondees in the palindromic final stanza sits at odds with the restriction that the stresses enforce. These repetitions make a corrupted reproduction that produces only more dead ends. It is worth noting that the poem abridges Shelley's biography: the son who lived to adulthood is never mentioned. It makes Shelley's maternity unsuccessful. Why does Niedecker insist on the failure of Shelley's labor?

The heavy stresses of the final stanza not only disappoint but also restrain. They both restrain the poetic line, and they restrain Shelley's production. Further, the final stanza performs an act of emotional restraining by stating a devastation plainly and refusing to elaborate on it. In its refusal to console, the poem asks us to adjust to this restrained reproduction. Nersessian reads against the grain of "a mass idealization of the unrestrained and inexhaustibly available" world to find in Romantic poetry an emphasis on limit for Romanticism "functions as utopian thought insofar as it takes its own formalism to mime a minimally harmful relationship between human beings and a world whose resources are decidedly finite."[63] Both "Hospital Kitchen" and "For Best Work" direct their attention not to people but to nonhuman forms—to the cleaned stove, the paper birch. This is a custodial worldview that values preservation. It also values limit, mounting a deflationary idea of poetic work that turns from an ethos of productivity to embrace antiproductivity and restriction. In the Mary Shelley poem, that restriction is sharpened to a brutal point.

Yet Shelley, however restricted her maternity, remains alive in the poem and in her writing. The insistence on loss is essential to Niedecker's view of what reproduction is. Niedecker reformulates reproduction to mean accommodating the self in the service of others and to the world as it is. This dynamic necessarily embraces loss:

> O my floating life
> Do not save love
>   for things
>   Throw *things*
> to the flood
>
> ruined
> by the flood
>   Leave the new unbought—
>   all one in the end—
> water
> (*CW*, 268)

Glossing Marx on alienation as labor put into objects, which, when they become commodities, are taken away from the worker, Sara Ahmed notes that "the worker is bound to a lost object: capitalism as such might rest on melancholia." The more the worker produces, Ahmed notes, "the more the worker suffers" for alienation is a "feeling-structure, a form of suffering that shapes how the worker inhabits the world."[64] In her dialectic of preservation and loss, Niedecker proposes an equally melancholy solution for the suffering worker. Only by rendering ourselves minimally present and minimally productive, she suggests, can we better attend to the world around us.

WHEN ECSTASY CAN'T BE CONSTANT

Against the spare, evacuated lyrics of *Homemade/Handmade Poems*, one poem registers a sudden and effusive feeling:

LAUNDROMAT

Casual, sudsy
social love
at the tubs

After all, ecstasy
can't be constant
(*CW*, 202)

It's almost dismissive, that slouching first word, "casual," which opens the poem onto an ordinary scene. "Casual, sudsy," two trochees (or possibly a dactyl on "casual") that feel easily dashed off, their ease extends to the second line with the slant rhyme on the first words of each, "casual" and "social." We luxuriate in the thick, sensuous onomatopoeia of "sudsy." Its thick diphthongs drop into the monosyllables of the third line. The slant rhyme on "love" and "tubs" brings love down to the tubs, or perhaps it brings us to the tubs to see what kind of love is possible there. The seeming ease of the sonic echoes in these short lines, the sibilance that puts every syllable in this thirteen-word poem to work, gives us the sense of glimpsing a snippet of a small experience that would otherwise go unnoticed. The poem opens itself up to ecstasy, then takes us back in again to the point of ecstasy's retreat. In the couplet, we move from the enclosure of the tubs outward. With "after all," the poem announces that it will deliver a verdict on the scene. But its ending withholds as much as it resolves, presenting us with an experience only to remind us that it cannot last.

In a letter to Zukofsky, Niedecker described her and Al's weekly washing trips in Milwaukee:

> We take our wash to a laundromat. We had 3 shopping bags full, a large white laundry bag and a bushel basket—a week ago—never again—we now go with 2 shopping bags once a week. It's a fraternity. Al goes around showing newcomers how to operate the machines, especially the big one that we washed the living room rug in. I take a newspaper to glance at and somebody asks me if he (most of the people who frequent laundromats here are men) may borrow part of it for a few minutes. Some of the people are definitely from houses that do not lean.[65]

Like hospitals, laundromats are borderline spaces that sit between private and public life as a site of work that is neither the industrial laundry nor the private laundry of the middle-class American home.[66] Niedecker celebrates the small encounters and frequent attachments of the laundromat as a site of urban social life. Earlier in the letter she had described their apartment as "leaning"; the laundromat's users, from houses that do and do not lean, are from varied class positions. In the poem, the "tubs" call to mind earlier technologies of washing, namely, the tub or basin and scrub board, and an echo of the social forms of preindustrialized washing lingers in the poem. The poem's formal slightness underscores the fragility of the occasional bonds of the social spaces of washing. Laundromats trouble the private–public boundary in the way they bring items from the domestic world, normally unseen, into a public space, creating a compromised intimacy. The sheets that protect beds are brought to be washed; clothing, which is normally the boundary between self and world, is brought in dirty and vulnerable; and underwear, which is normally hidden under outer layers, is brought out into the open. In her letter, Niedecker calls the laundromat a "fraternity"; it is mostly men who wash in public. While the poem is not clearly gendered, its sexual suggestiveness—the "casual" love—brings us back to the eroticism of work in poems like "I knew a clean man." The intimacy of the laundromat is introduced in the poem's first word, "casual," which leads into the sexuality of "ecstasy," which, after all, cannot be "constant," which might be faithful or unfaithful, and which suggests attachments beyond the bounds of spouse and family.

The ecstasy that "can't be constant" carries a vague threat of insanity or spiritual transport beyond return. In an unpublished letter to Zukofsky in 1964, Niedecker typed five notes about a painting she was completing, then added, in handwriting at the end of the letter, a note about the distinction between writing and painting: where "painting (for me) is creating ecstasy in the act of the painting," writing "is toning down the ecstasy that 'came.'"[67] Writing is an effort to control ecstasy, an experience so threatening it demands toning down. The inconstancy of ecstasy also offers a rejoinder to the normal and routine. More than that, "After all, ecstasy / can't be constant" presents the sudden and unexpected eruption of intense social feeling as unable to be contained or subjected to the time management of work discipline. Ecstasy is preserved in ordinary tasks of labor. Neither happiness nor satisfaction, ecstasy is larger and less containable. Because it is uncontainable, it troubles labor rather than maintaining it (no one asks us to be ecstatic on the job; there is no "job ecstasy"). Niedecker's small poem tracks a form of ecstatic experience and social life that transports us temporarily beyond work.

The ecstasy poem, sudsy and wet, describes an experience of physicality that transports us beyond the physical. This transport is something Niedecker referred to repeatedly as "metaphysical" or "metaphysics." This is another of her rare cleaning poems, which appeared in *Origin* in 1967:

> Cleaned all surfaces
> and behind all solids
> and righted leaning things
>
> Considered then, becurtained
> the metaphysics
> of flights from housecleanings
> (CW, 231)

As in "Hospital Kitchen," there is no subject here, and human presence is withheld, though its activity, cleaning, is registered. Where the first stanza sits in the material world of surfaces and solids, the second moves beyond solidity. What are "the metaphysics / of flights from housecleanings"? Is it the mental freedom proposed by the tending of surfaces and things—that to right a leaning thing is an invitation to ask what makes a thing lean and what rightness is? *Flight* was not a word Niedecker used with particular frequency, and the "flights from housecleanings" call to mind the "flight's end or flight's beginning" of one of Niedecker's earliest poems, "When Ecstasy if Inconvenient." That poem opens with the speaker instructing herself to "feign a great calm" and control her ecstasy:

> Know amazedly how
> often one takes his madness
> into his own hands
> and keeps it.
> (CW, 25)

These lines are quietly ecstatic despite the speaker's efforts at self-restraint. That final stanza resolves the inconvenience of that ecstasy not by diminishing or erasing it but by keeping it close. In the later poem, the "flights from housecleanings" offers another ecstatic escape. Those flights are still only proposed, still only "considered," and we end, after all, back where we started, from "Cleaned" to "housecleanings." Like the ecstasy that cannot be constant, flights of imaginative freedom cannot be sustained for long. Nor do they need to be for the work of cleaning is regular and repeated and proposes further ecstasies in the future. Ecstasy is inconvenient precisely because it intrudes on, and is indeed generated by, an ordinary scene: an afternoon spent tidying a house or washing clothes.

George Oppen got his facts wrong when he described Niedecker's life in a letter to his sister in 1963:

> Mary [Oppen] was talking to you about Lorine Niedecker. She came to NY for a few days in 1930 or so, and we met her. She must be 60 by now; a tiny little person, very, very near sighted always. She had graduated from Wisconsin but was too timid to face almost any job. She took a job scrubbing floors in a hospital near the run-down farm she had inherited, and she is still living in that crumbling farm house and scrubbing floors. Someone in Scotland printed a tiny little book of her poems, which are little barely audible poems, not without loveliness.[68]

Niedecker never attended Wisconsin, never graduated, did not live on a farm, and no amount of timidity excused her from facing many jobs. Although Oppen quotes two of Niedecker's poems with some admiration, he writes with pity about the circumstances of her life: "And yet poor Lorine, of course, too. Surely people are not easily or naturally happy."[69]

Oppen pities Niedecker for her lonely rural life of drudge work, of scrubbing floors at home and in the hospital. He is most insightful when he describes her "little barely audible poems." The littleness of Niedecker's poems does immense work; the refinement of that smallness is the primary way that the poet thinks about her relation to her world and her labor. She also navigates this smallness materially. In the form of *Homemade/Handmade Poems* and in poems like "I knew a clean man," Niedecker embraces amateur crafted objects, as well as corrupted and repurposed commodities. Poems like "Hospital Kitchen" and "For Best Work" ask for a hard-won stillness and self-erasure in the service of preservation. Finally, we find sudden, fleeting ecstasies and metaphysical transport within moments of ordinary labor that cannot, and should not, be contained. Niedecker asks for a material attention to what should be tampered with, what should be preserved, and what we should glimpse and let pass.

Niedecker writes "little barely audible poems, not without loveliness": contained within this qualified compliment is a sense that her poems are always somewhat difficult to hear, and that their loveliness is surprising in a poem so withholding and possibly so negligible. The craft forms she embraces are also conscious of their own negligibility. Julia Bryan-Wilson writes, "The pervasive idea that craft might be utilized for strategic or polemical purpose . . . has been shadowed by an even more prevalent story within the twentieth century regarding textile techniques such as sewing, knitting, or quilting, which is that they are fundamentally *trivial*. In fact, 'hobbyist' methods of textile handmaking have long been castigated as inconsequential, particularly because they have traditionally been gendered female. As Simone de Beauvoir wrote in 1949, 'With the needle or the crochet hook, woman sadly weaves the very nothingness of her days.' "[70]

The sticking point with Niedecker is that she doesn't insist that her poems are important or consequential but thinks through and insists on the value of that inconsequentiality. Her idea of "best work," after all, is to stand perfectly still, work that looks very much like weaving nothingness. Niedecker asks us what attuning ourselves to the inconsequential might do, both ethically and aesthetically. This turn to amateur craft forms and compromised materials decenters the ideal of mastery core to the artisanal model of literary work. In her powerful decolonial argument, *Unthinking Mastery*, Julietta Singh describes the link between the mastery of colonization and the mastery of aesthetics. Mastery, she writes, "aims for the full submission of an object," and in so doing, it "requires a rupturing of the object being mastered, because to be mastered means to be weakened to a point of fracture."[71] Niedecker displays considerable mastery of concision, precision, and observation in her "little barely audible poems." But as Oppen's phrasing reminds us, her handling of these qualities and methods cannot easily be reconciled with available ideas of formal and poetic mastery. Instead, Niedecker's reformulation of mastery in both her material practices and the ethics of her late poems names a commitment to maintaining the integrity of the world.

After her retirement, Niedecker and Millen took several vacations around northern Wisconsin and the Great Lakes. That landscape contours the poet's late writing. Her travels with Millen were also an occasion for gift-making. At the end of 1963, Niedecker sent Zukofsky a Duo-Tang folder filled with materials from the couple's trip to the Upper Mississippi River near Al's childhood home of Swan River, Minnesota. A Polaroid photo shows Millen standing above the river. The book begins with a first-person elegy for a lost world. "We stood and looked at that the spot where the Millen place was supposed to be," Niedecker writes. "No sign of habitation. A small clump of pines. Gone back to nature."[72] Niedecker's poetry from the late 1960s navigates dynamics of loss, preservation, and renewal. "Wintergreen Ridge," published in *Caterpillar* in 1968, traces ecological history and land preservation against the threat of "the grand blow-up" of nuclear annihilation. We follow the speaker "where the arrows / of the road sign / lead us," her cascading tercets structuring her meditations:

> Man
>   lives hard
>   on this stone perch
>
> by sea
>   imagines
>   durable works
>
> (*CW*, 247)

Written against a background of environmental devastation and nuclear threat, the possibility of the transhistorical durability of the art object is cast into doubt, even though it remains a focus of human desire and imagination. The poet "gawks / lusting / after wild orchids," then quotes a sign (the text's italics indicates that she is quoting from signage), which itself forms a small rhyming poem: "*Flowers / loveliest / where they grow // Love them enjoy them / and leave them so*" (*CW*, 248–49). "Let's go!" announces the poet, as both speaker and poem move on, leaving the wild orchids alone. If we are to imagine "durable works," if we are to decide that there will be life on this planet for years to come, then we must practice these forms of restriction. This is another way of affirming the poet's primary role as the observer, whose difficulty is in maintaining a position of rigorous self-removal.

    The questions that occupied Niedecker in the late 1960s have become only more pressing for poets writing in an era of accelerating climate crisis. The late work of Bernadette Mayer, a poet often associated with the second generation of the New York School, turns its attention to the weird rhythms of disrupted seasonal change around her home in East Nassau, New York. 2016's *Works and Days* incorporates a "Spring Journal" that spans from the spring equinox to the summer solstice, functioning, like the Hesiod poem from which Mayer takes her book's title, as a kind of farmer's almanac. Buds appear on the lilac bush, hepatica emerges, the weather seems to warm enough to plant beans and peas, a field is suddenly full of dandelions, and late snow returns, all watched over by cardinals, goldfinches, and grackles. But this is a twenty-first century almanac in which the irregularly warming season heralds more than summer's approach. "A gloomy warmth," Mayer writes. "A glimpse of the future?"[73] Hope arrives and is quickly dashed. "There's an ominous wind blowing," Mayer writes. "Wait, everything's looking a little brighter / Oh, no, it's darkening" (*WD*, 61). "Isn't every day weird?" she asks (*WD*, 91). The book returns to fantasies of self-erasure and secrecy. "In the woods, I can build things / Without anybody seeing me" (*WD*, 15). "Yielding can be a good thing," Mayer tells us (*WD*, 29); "I vanish into the universe like a wave" (*WD*, 81).

In *Milkweed Smithereens*, published in the final month of Mayer's life, she anticipates her own death. "*So what if I die? Will the hepatica? The hepatica will never die,*" she writes, transposing, like Niedecker, the timeline of human life against that of plant life. Of her burial, she imagines a reintegration with the earth: "*I could cover myself with seeds or even a mat of heirloom tomatoes. or heirloom weeds.*"[74] These are poems more of old age than apocalypticism; Mayer doesn't indulge in fantasies of a world without people. But the poems worry over what will persist and how capitalism's mastery of the world forms a new enclosure of biological life. Mayer muses on sunflower seeds:

> maybe our seeds are genetically engineered.
> Genetically engineering plants is like sterilization.
> Let the plants reproduce! says my sign. I carry it
> To all the demonstrations of the past, present and emu
>
> (*WD*, 26)

It's a typical Mayer twist: the future replaced with that most surprising bird, the emu. The genetic engineering of seeds—the replacement of open-pollinated seeds with hybrids, owned by petrochemical companies, that cannot be collected and planted by farmers the following season—is here described as a refusal of reproduction. Mayer is best known as a poet of social reproduction, and her earlier books *Midwinter Day* and *The Desires of Mothers to Please Others in Letters* trace in intimate detail the work of gestating and raising children while making art.[75] Here, Mayer extends that concern with reproduction to the natural world under late capitalism. Plants, too, have the *right* to reproduce, to create themselves anew through their seeds. In this late poem, Mayer makes clear that the struggle for reproductive possibilities under capitalism is limited not to maternity alone, that the concerns of social reproduction and the struggle for a lasting natural world are one and the same.

If anyone makes "durable works" in "Wintergreen Ridge," it is the women who protest development. "Who saved it?" Niedecker asks, then answers:

> Women
> > of good wild stock
>
> > stood stolid
> > > before machines
> > > > They stopped bulldozers
>
> > cold
> > > We want it for all time
> > > > they said
>
> > and here it is—

(*CW*, 249–50)

This form of refusal is women's work, and it is reproductive work. The lineage of the women "from good wild stock"—as if they were raised by the land itself—is placed on the line as they calmly stand down the bulldozers. Their "stock" is at stake, and so is the world's. In the "stolid" stance of the women on the land, they refuse to cede to the destruction that "durable works" might consist of, imperiling their own solidity for the endurance of something else. How can we embrace the discomfort of self-removal and self-loss as a condition for the reproduction of a world under threat? Niedecker's pressing claim on us—one that grows more pressing with every passing year—is to ask, What might be saved if we committed to standing still before the bulldozers, among the birch?

CODA

Drafting Modernism

> There is no "ending" exactly
> but maybe processes,
> —RACHEL BLAU DUPLESSIS, "DRAFT 114: EXERGUE AND VOLTA"

This book has found in modernist poetry a set of powerful counterimpulses that challenge the governing social and economic mandate of the modern world: the demand to work for a living. I have assembled an archive of poets who rethought the terms and structures of working life, who imagined alternative cultural and social values to those defined and reinforced by work, and who looked ahead to a world where the disciplining function of labor would no longer restrict freedom or constrain social life. Throughout the pages of this study, we have traveled diverse terrain: from the fantasies of integrated agrarian worlds of Pound's late cantos to Langston Hughes's vision of global revolution; from the factories and tenements of the Lower East Side documented by Lola Ridge, through the patterns and textures of everyday queer intimate life in Stein, to Niedecker's handling of the hospital kitchens and birch forests of rural Wisconsin. We have also ranged in scale, from the global imaginaries of Hughes to the domestic interiors of Stein, and we have roamed formally, from the epic expanse of Pound to Niedecker's whittled miniatures. The writers in this study share more in their concerns than in the conclusions they drew, but resonances emerge nevertheless. Hughes and Ridge both imagined new forms of international solidarity. Niedecker and Stein, seemingly so disparate, were both concerned with non-normative reproductive practices. By turning to labor, these writers imagined new ways of writing, new political practices, and new forms of social life.

This book has approached labor as a phenomenon that creates social and cultural values—including those that enforce normative standards of race and gender—and it has sought an analytic for how labor creates subjectivities and social worlds. For the poets I have read, the question of work is more than a question of technique or method, of how to write a poem. It is also a question of what it means to write a poem in a world structured by work, and of what other worlds might be possible. But this book has also made an argument about the development of modernist poetic form, and about the material practices that enrich and challenge these forms. Literary modernism's intermediality—its magpie-like habit of borrowing from film, music, and painting—is more various than scholars have often acknowledged, spanning from workers' theater to homemade books. These intermedial relationships shaped the distinctive textures of modernist poetics, which constitute the primary way that poetry does its thinking.

This book has also approached value in an expansive, cultural sense, rather than one that is strictly economic. Labor creates and reinforces values, and so poets turn to labor to challenge those values and to imagine new ones in their wake. These poets ask why some activities have been rendered invisible and therefore valueless; they sense and articulate how labor enforces restrictive values of gender and race. Some of these new values offer a cautionary tale. Pound's fantasy of unalienated labors under the direction of the insightful mind, and the values on which he insists—efficiency, clarity, action—slide quickly into a dictatorial fantasy and coalesce into the hardened fascism of his late poems. For other poets, poetic labor resists and recasts the normative values of the work society. Stein's experiments implicitly resist an emergent disciplining of women's domestic work, while Niedecker develops a practice of attunement to the minimally small and still, a practice through which she asks us to rethink what *productivity* means and embrace instead a stance of resolute unproductivity. In my choice of poets and in the broad historical and geographical terrain of this study, I have sought to challenge modernist studies' winnowing, narrowing tendencies. The horizon of the totality has both guided my choice of local readings and my ambitions for this project, even as it remains a horizon. By working toward seeing modernism as a totality, this book offers an invitation for future scholars of modernism to keep the total web of social relations in sight. The ambitions of this book are utopian, but I have sought a rigorously historical utopianism that resurrects the conditions and commitments of the past to understand how they might speak to us today, and, if they do speak, what demands they might make and what questions they might ask.

The questions that animate this study are alive for poets writing today. In the poetry of Anne Boyer, Tongo Eisen-Martin, Jill Magi, Mark Nowak, Rodrigo Toscano, and the Commune Editions poets, among many others, the problems of how work arranges social life and how to build a society beyond labor are central to their work. I want to end by turning to a poet who has asked similar questions and who is also one of poetic modernism's most thoughtful interpreters. Rachel Blau DuPlessis has spent a life shaping and reshaping modernism's legacy on multiple fronts as a scholar, essayist, and poet. As a scholar, her work has been transformative in articulating a feminist rereading of the literary canon for "the whole of culture and cultural product would have to be reconceptualized," as she writes of the initial moment of her feminist education.[1] In her scholarship, DuPlessis unearths the gendered stakes of modernist world-making, providing a language for this book's understanding of poetry's aesthetic and political stakes. Riffing on Adorno on art's world-imagining ambitions, DuPlessis writes that poetry is "a theorizing practice, a practice of thinking, and . . . a commitment to the thought that emerges in the subtle concreteness of segmented, saturated language."[2]

In 1986, DuPlessis began writing a long poem called *Drafts*, a title that signals the poem's embrace of provisionality, plurality, and endless revision. In 2013, DuPlessis published the final installment of her "poem of a life." *Surge* contains its long-projected terminus: the 114th draft. But this ending soon proved to be open-ended, as 2014 saw the appearance of *Interstices*, in which the long poem finds new "ways of exceeding itself" for "things are first tied, / and then untied, / first raveled, then unraveled."[3] *Drafts* "closes without ending"; it "ends, but doesn't end."[4] DuPlessis's practice of repeating titles—multiple drafts are called "Gap," for example—allows the later poems to revise, reconsider, and return to the earlier poems. This practice also turns the earlier poems into antecedents, ancestral attempts at later versions, even though it resists a narrative of linear progression. Each installment is a draft, and the poem as a whole constitutes one great draft. DuPlessis has insisted on the importance of sitting with the polarities of finished and unfinished, drafted and revised, and closed and open, for the poem "manifests an endless dialogue between closed and open" and attempts to "over-pass any number of opposites." DuPlessis's goal was to make a poem that resists totalizing despite embracing "totalizing temptations," a poem that "as a whole ruptures the binaries that might contain it."[5] Antimodernist in its ambitions, even though modernism lives in its DNA, the modernist long poem becomes one of the forms that DuPlessis describes in "Draft 14: Conjunctions" as "at once perfect *and* incomplete."[6]

Like the long poems of modernism, the primary subject of *Drafts* is itself. Endlessly self-referential and weaving its own history, the poem both describes and interprets the conditions of its making and makes an archive of these conditions. One of its earliest poems, "Draft 6: Midrush," begins as follows:

>   Works
>   thru the dead   to circle
>
>   the living flood-
>
> flung expectations   lit wreathes,
> and came to meet the cowering   wassail
> pairs   doors and houses
> in a tarred ark.   edged in blinking.
> (*TOLL*, 33)

DuPlessis takes us back to Adam's curse and the very beginning of labor, "when the living began / to 'labor' (as S. wrote, / rushed) 'to die'"—an unending toil paramount to death. The poem's focus is not the curse that God in his disappointment in Adam casts upon the earth but rather Noah's gathering of the "cowering / pairs" into his ark. The "wassail" of the second column places the poem in the long history of medieval seasonal rites. If the scriptures and the rituals make this scene historical, it is also contemporary for this is a "living flood" that might drown us today. The poem describes itself as an "epyllion," an epic in miniature: "Some epyllion—/ pastoral, reclusive, elegiac: flooded / shards drifted up "forever / thru the clay."

The flood of Noah forms an image of the accumulated weight of centuries of labor that bears upon the living:

> It is they that speak
> silt
> we weep
> silt
> the flood-bound
> written over and under with their
> muddy marks
>
> of writing under the writing.
> (*TOLL*, 36)

As we move through the poem, we are constantly brought back to the silt, to what has passed into the water and to what the flood, never fully receding, continues to surface. Writing is listening to silt and producing—or "weeping," as DuPlessis writes in a Niedeckerian image—your own silt, bound in a flood that will not end, "over and under," the curse never lifted. There is "always another little something—/ a broken saucer" to be dredged up. "Midrush," the practice of "overlaying stories" (*Toll*, 37), makes a secular version of *midrash*, the interpretation of the Hebrew scripts. DuPlessis describes her poetic midrash as "doubled and redoubled commentary, poetry with its own gloss built in. My idea was sidebars, visuals, anything to create 'otherness inside otherness.'"[7] This flooded epyllion is haunted by the modernist epic. "Wraithes of poets, Oppen and oddly / Zukofsky / renew their open engagement with me / wreathing smoke-veils" (*Toll*, 35). In her critical writing, DuPlessis argues that her feminist practice focuses less on explicit feminist statements than on material engagements with culture, consisting of "the research of cultural materials" or "a feminism of critique."[8] In this rushing history of labor from Noah to now, one thick sedimentary layer through which the poet must wade is the masculine lineage of the modernist poem.

If "Midrush" limns a relationship with high modernism, it also names a more prosaic labor as a "nonce word meaning the rushing around one experiences in midlife."[9] "Midrush" brings together the critical work of unpicking modernism's legacy with the ordinary, daily work of middle age:

raising children, teaching and grading essays, and being endlessly pressed for time. What kind of a life deserves the sustained labor of a long poem? At its end, "Draft 6" funnels inward to show us the circumstances of its composition. "I get so homeless," DuPlessis writes. "I will never survive / all this":

> I'm just trying to make
> whatever rushed
> arrangements
> I can and can't
> even hear
> long distance
>
> because nearer louder
> "mommy don't go mommy don't go"
> while I have to
> work at understanding even
> nominally
> crossing out and re-
> writing odd scraps
> in the little ticket square, of days.
> (*TOLL*, 38–39)

The poet is "homeless" in literary history, trying to make a space for herself in a modernist lineage, and homeless again in her midrush, out the door and away from the child pleading with her not to go. "Where is my place?" she asks, the final lines capturing her between the labor of care and the work of writing. The poem quickens its pace. Gone are its twin columns of text; instead we rush forward into the present. The child's voice is an intrusion into the poem that rushes us from the pairs on the ark to the twinned needs to care for children and make a living in the present. We hear the child's voice only once, but once recorded it is paraliptically present until the poem's end and in subsequent readings. Not writing about care is a way of writing about being drawn away from care. The pressures of this poem are great: historical, daily, living, flooded, material, immaterial, and immediate. The poem responds to those pressures with an extraordinary bathos as the final lines scale down drastically from the great labors of the scriptures and the epics of modernity to the desultory work of "nominally / crossing out and re- / writing," swapping out historical time for "little ticket squares." As a self-declared epyllion, the poem both rejects and embraces the heroic ideals of the epic. It engages the epic but pins it to the marginal and local, to those odd scraps of paper and little squares that mark a calendar's days, and to what elsewhere she calls, riffing on a rhyme she might sing to her child, "these pinholes we live / in, the little / songs we sing / stars; twinkling."

Drafts ends but is not complete; it stops but does not close. The one hundredth draft, "Gap," registers the desire for an ending and the resistance to this desire. Punctured by gaps, words and phrases are excised or withheld ("silence. _____"). "Gap" reminds us that "the complete / is never complete" (*Surge*, 46). "Draft 114: Exergue and Volta"—the concluding poem of *Drafts* but not the "final" poem—takes us deep into this desire and its resistance. That draft makes a thick collage of modernist citations about ending from Stein, Silliman, and many from DuPlessis herself, situating us in the "tidal surge of writing" while also restlessly looking for material corollaries for the writer's practice that might help her understand the poem at the moment of its completion: "It's how to read / works haptic as a nest of quipu / where strung knots twist / their tangled fullness, / changing over into under, / under to over," DuPlessis writes, layering Poundian pedagogy onto quipu, an Incan device for numerical recordkeeping made from cotton or camelid fiber strings. It is as if, this late in the day, the poem remains resistant to DuPlessis's own comprehension. Elsewhere the poem is a sand mandala, on the edge of disappearing ("Thrown with joy / into the flowing water," DuPlessis writes, echoing Niedecker's injunction to "throw *things* / to the flood"), or else the poem is "transparent ribbons—/ little strips blowing towards each other—." Finally the poem returns us to paper:

> That this began
> that this ends
> that this refused to begin
> (though it started)
> that it refuses to end
> (though it is folding itself up)
> (*SURGE*, 159)

The paper of the poem can be folded into one shape, then undone and refolded into other forms along the lines of old and new creases. "Look at it!" DuPlessis marvels at her poem, "how many words and torquing shapes / can be made" (*Surge*, 154). This is a way to describe an ending to a poem that by its own structural principles cannot end. But it is also a way to think about a relationship with the intellectual legacy of poetic modernism. The poem lives inside modernism but rejects the parameters of modernism; it takes the modernist architecture of the long poem but bridles against the rigid lines of that architecture; it makes a modernist monument that refuses its own monumentality. Modernism here is not a calcified tradition but a living art that continues to make claims on us and that gives us a language with which to write and think, even if that language is only ever provisional. The labor of the writer of long poems is not the carving of great monuments in stone, and the labor of their readers is not—to paraphrase Basil Bunting on reading Pound—the project of scaling the Alps.[10] Rather, this labor is a mutual making of provisional objects, by writer and reader, to be formed and reformed from a shared history—like ribbons gathered from the air.

NOTES

INTRODUCTION

1. Lorine Niedecker, "Poet's Work," in *Collected Works*, ed. Jenny Penberthy (University of California Press, 2002), 194.
2. Ezra Pound, *ABC of Reading* (Faber and Faber, 1991), 36.
3. Pound, *ABC of Reading*, 36.
4. Modernism's new literary-professional developed alongside broader transformations in industry that saw the formation of a new managerial class, or what James Burnham famously termed "the managerial revolution." See James Burnham, *The Managerial Revolution* (John Day, 1941; Reprint, University of Indiana Press, 1960).
5. A. R. Orage, *Readers and Writers* (George Allen & Unwin, 1922), 59. John Keats to John Taylor, February 27, 1818, in *Complete Poems and Selected Letters of John Keats* (Modern Library Classics, 2001), 282.
6. For the classic account of how modernism was "shaped and legitimated" by the discourse of professionalism, see Thomas Strychacz, *Modernism, Mass Culture, and Professionalism* (Cambridge University Press, 1993), 5; see also Mary Ann Gillies, *The Professional Literary Agent in Britain, 1880–1920* (University of Toronto Press, 2007).
7. A spate of recent books argue that the legacy of modernism is one of institutionalization and new professional values. Evan Kindley studies the rise of the poet-critic and cultural administration, and Christopher Kempf traces the incorporation of the term *workshop* into higher education. For Kimberly Quiogue Andrews, the story of poetry in the twentieth century is its institutionalization in the academy; Kamran Javadizadeh's forthcoming book complicates this story by attending to academia as well as psychiatric institutionalization. See Evan Kindley, *Poet-Critics and the Administration of Culture* (Harvard University Press, 2017); Christopher Kempf, *Craft Class: The Writing Workshop in American Culture* (Johns Hopkins University Press, 2022); Kimberly Quiogue Andrews, *The Academic Avant-Garde:*

INTRODUCTION

Poetry and the American University (Johns Hopkins University Press, 2023); Kamran Javadizadeh, *Institutionalized Lyric: American Poetry at Midcentury* (Oxford University Press, forthcoming).
8. Leigh Claire La Berge, *Wages Against Artwork: Decommodified Labor and the Claims of Socially Engaged Art* (Duke University Press, 2019), 19.
9. Michael Denning, *Culture in the Age of Three Worlds* (Verso, 2004), 224.
10. John Hollander, *Melodious Guile: Fictive Pattern in Poetic Language* (Yale University Press, 1988), 86.
11. Fredric Jameson, *A Singular Modernity: Essay on the Ontology of the Present* (Verso, 2002), 159.
12. Karl Marx, *Capital*, vol. 1, trans. Ben Fowkes (Penguin, 1990), 284.
13. Marx, *Capital*, 1:283–84.
14. Jennifer Bajorek, *Counterfeit Capital: Poetic Labor and Revolutionary Irony* (Stanford University Press, 2009), 48. Or, as David Harvey puts it, "What we do 'out there' is very much about us 'in here.'"
15. Karl Marx, "Estranged Labor," from *Economic and Philosophic Manuscripts of 1844*, trans. Martin Milligan, Marx-Engels Archive, 1959 (updated 2009), https://www.marxists.org/archive/marx/works/1844/manuscripts/labour.htm. Emphasis in the original.
16. Nancy Fraser, "Expropriation and Exploitation in Racialized Capitalism: A Reply to Michael Dawson," *Critical Historical Studies* 3, no. 1 (2016): 165, 166. Emphasis in the original.
17. Marx, *Capital*, 1:315.
18. Michael Hardt and Antonio Negri, *Labor of Dionysus: A Critique of the State-Form* (University of Minnesota Press, 1994), 14–15.
19. Hardt and Negri, *Labor of Dionysus*, 22.
20. Karl Marx, *The German Ideology*, Marx-Engels Archive, 1845, https://www.marxists.org/archive/marx/works/1845/german-ideology/ch01a.htm#p28.
21. Barbara Foley, *Marxist Literary Criticism Today* (Pluto, 2019), 4.
22. Kathi Weeks, *The Problem with Work: Feminism, Marxism, Antiwork Politics, and Postwork Imaginaries* (Duke University Press, 2011), 19.
23. Fredric Jameson, *The Political Unconscious: Narrative as a Socially Symbolic Act* (Cornell University Press, 1981), 18–19. Emphasis in the original.
24. T. J. Clark, *Farewell to an Idea: Episodes from a History of Modernism* (Yale University Press, 1999), 3.
25. Jameson, *The Political Unconscious*, 236–37, 291.
26. See Carolyn Lesjak, "Reading Dialectically," *Criticism* 55, no. 2 (2013): 233–77.
27. Ruth Jennison, "29|73|08: Poetry, Crisis, and a Hermeneutics of Limit," *Mediations: Journal of the Marxist Literary Group* 28, no. 2 (2015): 39.
28. Virgil in his *Georgics*, punning on *versus*—a field's furrow and also a line of verse—implicitly figures the poet's crafting of lines within a larger world of cultivation. Scholars of earlier periods have drawn comparisons between literary labor and the work of early modern housewives and between Romantic poetry and its leech gatherers, mowers, and reapers. See Katie Kadue, *Domestic Georgic: Labors of Preservation from Rabelais to Milton* (University of Chicago Press, 2020); Anne Janowitz, *Lyric and Labor in the Romantic Tradition* (Cambridge University Press, 1998).

INTRODUCTION

29. David Harvey, "The Geography of Capitalist Accumulation: A Reconstruction of the Marxian Theory," *Antipode* 7, no. 2 (1975): 9.
30. Harry Braverman, *Labor and Monopoly Capital: The Degradation of Work in the Twentieth Century* (Monthly Review, 1998), 317.
31. See Christine Frederick, *The New Housekeeping: Efficiency Studies in Home Management* (Doubleday, 1913), 10, viii.
32. Despite being unequally represented by an organized labor movement frequently hostile to women, unionized women were on the front line of strikes and labor militancy. In 1920, only 7 percent of women workers belonged to unions, compared to a quarter of male workers. See Sharlene Nagy Hesse-Biber and Gregg Lee Carter, *Working Women in America: Split Dreams* (Oxford University Press, 2000), 29–30. See also Alice Kesler-Harris, "Problems of Coalition-Building: Women and Trade Unions in the 1920s," in *Women, Work and Protest: A Century of US Women's Labor History*, ed. Ruth Milkman (Routledge, 1985), 110–38. A racist division of labor continued to determine the working lives of women, and in 1910 more than 90 percent of working Black women worked as agricultural laborers or domestic workers—as maids, cooks, or children's nurses—compared with just under 30 percent of working white women. Delores Aldridge, "Black Women in the Economic Marketplace: A Battle Unfinished," *Journal of Social and Behavioural Sciences* (1975): 53. See also Evelyn Nakano Glenn, *Unequal Freedom: How Race and Gender Shaped American Citizenship and Labor* (Harvard University Press, 2002).
33. Jodi Melamed, "Racial Capitalism," *Critical Ethnic Studies* 1, no. 1 (2015): 77.
34. Destin Jenkins and Justin Leroy, introduction to *Histories of Racial Capitalism*, ed. Destin Jenkins and Justin Leroy (Columbia University Press, 2021), 3.
35. Lisa Lowe, *The Intimacies of Four Continents* (Duke University Press, 2015), 150.
36. Harvey, "The Geography of Capitalist Accumulation," 9.
37. See Michael Denning, *The Cultural Front: The Laboring of American Culture in the Twentieth Century* (Verso, 2011).
38. Joseph North, *Literary Criticism: A Concise Political History* (Harvard University Press, 2017), 6–7.
39. This tendency is perhaps best exemplified in Alex Goody and Ian Whittington, eds., *The Edinburgh Companion to Modernism and Technology* (Edinburgh University Press, 2022), given its individual chapters on electricity, clocks, radio, automobiles, and so on. See also Melissa Dinsman, *Modernism at the Microphone: Radio, Propaganda, and Literary Aesthetics During World War II* (Bloomsbury, 2015); Jennifer Lieberman, *Power Lines: Electricity in American Life and Letters, 1882–1952* (MIT Press, 2017); David Trotter, *The Literature of Connection: Signal, Medium, Interface, 1850–1950* (Oxford University Press, 2020).
40. Take, for example, Jonathan Wild, *The Rise of the Office Clerk in Literary Culture, 1880–1939* (Palgrave Macmillan, 2006); Leah Price and Pamela Thurschwell, eds., *Literary Secretaries/Secretarial Culture* (Ashgate, 2005); or Celia Marshik, *At the Mercy of Their Clothes: Modernism, the Middlebrow, and British Garment Culture* (Columbia University Press, 2016).
41. Harry Harootunian, *Marx After Marx: History and Time in the Expansion of Capitalism* (Columbia University Press, 2015), 19.
42. Warwick Research Collective, *Combined and Uneven Development: Towards a New Theory of World Literature* (Liverpool University Press, 2015), 8.

INTRODUCTION

43. Hannah Arendt, *The Human Condition* (University of Chicago Press, 1998), 100.
44. Weeks's observation that Arendt places too much distance between labor/work and "the legitimate business of the political" informs this choice. Weeks, *The Problem with Work*, 15.
45. W. B. Yeats, *Collected Poems* (Macmillan, 1951), 78.
46. "Thereupon emerges the modernist cliché par excellence: a certain kind of aesthetic elegance and investigative intelligence 'went with' heterosexual, homosocial maleness; a certain kind of middle-brow and mimetic, inadequate modernist-realism, and/or sentimentalism 'went with' femaleness; an overarching unbalanced exaggeration, errant playfulness, and unbalanced sensibility 'went with' gayness." Rachel Blau DuPlessis, *Purple Passages: Pound, Eliot, Zukofsky, Olson, Creeley, and the Ends of Patriarchal Poetry* (University of Iowa Press, 2012), 9.
47. Mariarosa Dalla Costa and Selma James, *The Power of Women and the Subversion of the Community* (Falling Wall, 1975), 33. Emphasis in the original. For other writers, such as Margaret Benston, women's labor is "pre-capitalist," and this designation means that the category of "women" stand in a different relation to production than the category of "men." Margaret Benston, "The Political Economy of Women's Liberation," in *The Politics of Housework*, ed. Ellen Malos (Allison & Busby, 1982), 121.
48. Dalla Costa and James, *The Power of Women and the Subversion of the Community*, 3.
49. Marx, *Capital*, 1:644.
50. Silvia Federici, "Wages Against Housework," in *Revolution at Point Zero: Housework, Reproduction, and Feminist Struggle* (PM, 2012), 16–17.
51. Dalla Costa and James, *The Power of Women and the Subversion of the Community*, 28. Emphasis in the original.
52. Federici, "Wages Against Housework," 16.
53. Silvia Federici, "Counterplanning from the Kitchen," in *Revolution at Point Zero: Housework, Reproduction, and Feminist Struggle* (PM, 2012), 30.
54. Federici, "Wages Against Housework," 18. Emphasis in the original.
55. Federici, "Counterplanning from the Kitchen," 34.
56. Denise Riley, *"Am I That Name?" Feminism and the Category of "Women" in History* (University of Minnesota Press, 1988), 5.
57. Weeks, *The Problem with Work*, 1, 7, 3.
58. See Morag Shiach, *Modernism, Labour, and Selfhood in British Literature and Culture, 1890–1930* (Cambridge University Press, 2004); Katherine Mullin, *Working Girls: Fiction, Sexuality, and Modernity* (Oxford University Press, 2016); Juno Jill Richards, "Oceans, Archives, Perverts: Sex Work in the Colonial Port City," *GLQ* 28, no. 4 (2022): 541–66.
59. DuPlessis, *Purple Passages*, 3.
60. Amy De'Ath, "Hidden Abodes and Inner Bonds: Literary Study and Marxist-Feminism," in *After Marx: Literature, Theory, and Value in the Twenty-First Century*, ed. Colleen Lye and Christopher Nealon (Cambridge University Press, 2022), 230.
61. Silvia Federici, preface to *Revolution at Point Zero: Housework, Reproduction, and Feminist Struggle* (PM, 2012), 2–3.
62. For example, Alva Gotby writes that Federici "raise[s] questions of what it would mean to reclaim a radical, pre-capitalist history without romanticising it. . . . Such history is important in denaturalising capitalism and its attendant relations of gender and family. However, a non-romanticised vision of the past must emphasise

INTRODUCTION

the struggle and conflict in these histories, rather than assuming that pre-capitalist communities lived in harmony. Despite good intentions, in these works Federici sometimes falls short of this." Alva Gotby, "Book Review: *Witches, Witch-Hunting and Women* by Silvia Federici and *Re-enchanting the World: Feminism and the Politics of the Commons* by Silvia Federici," *Feminist Review* 124 (2020): 206.
63. Silvia Federici, "Feminism and the Politics of the Common in an Era of Primitive Accumulation," in *Revolution at Point Zero: Housework, Reproduction, and Feminist Struggle* (PM, 2012), 148.
64. T. S. Eliot, *The Waste Land and Other Poems* (Faber and Faber, 1999), 25.
65. E. P. Thompson, "Time, Work-Discipline, and Industrial Capitalism," *Past & Present* 38 (1967): 90.
66. Marx, *Capital*, 1:367.
67. One could identify earlier moments of transformation in global higher education, such as the replacement of free tuition with the Higher Education Contributions Scheme in Australia in 1989; the changes to university funding in New Zealand in 1991; and the introduction of university tuition in the United Kingdom in 2006, as well as its tripling in 2012. Taken together, the neoliberal transformations of university education globally have created both a new precarity and a new militancy.
68. Peter Riley, *Whitman, Melville, Crane, and the Labors of American Poetry: Against Vocation* (Oxford University Press, 2019), 6.
69. Jasper Bernes, *The Work of Art in the Age of Deindustrialization* (Stanford University Press, 2017), 2.
70. John Marsh, *Hog Butchers, Beggars, and Busboys: Poverty, Labor, and the Making of Modern American Poetry* (University of Michigan Press, 2011).
71. Margaret Ronda, "'Not Much Left': Wageless Life in Millennial Poetry," *Post45*, October 9, 2011, https://post45.org/2011/10/not-much-left-wageless-life-in-millenial-poetry/.
72. Douglas Mao and Rebecca Walkowitz, "The New Modernist Studies," *PMLA* 123, no. 3 (2008): 737.
73. Tyrus Miller, *Late Modernism: Politics, Fiction, and the Arts Between the World Wars* (University of California Press, 1999), 7.
74. John Attridge, "An Introduction to Modernist Work," in *Modernist Work: Labor, Aesthetics, and the Work of Art*, ed. John Attridge and Helen Rydstrand (Bloomsbury, 2019), 2. Similarly, James Purdon notes that the "informatic revolution" described by N. Katherine Hayles and Donna Haraway "was as much a legacy of early twentieth-century bureaucracies as a post-industrial achievement." James Purdon, *Modernist Informatics: Literature, Information, and the State* (Oxford University Press, 2016), 6.
75. Douglas Mao, introduction to *The New Modernist Studies*, ed. Douglas Mao (Cambridge University Press, 2021), 12.
76. Michael North, "The Afterlife of Modernism," *New Literary History* 50, no. 1 (2019): 96.
77. Susan Stanford Friedman, *Planetary Modernisms: Provocations on Modernity Across Time* (Columbia University Press, 2015).
78. Paul Saint-Amour, "Weak Modernism, Weak Theory," *Modernism/Modernity* 25, no. 3 (2018): 454.
79. See Alys Moody and Stephen Ross, eds., *Global Modernists on Modernism* (Bloomsbury, 2020).

INTRODUCTION

80. Or perhaps "weak," a word that Saint-Amour claims as important for this field's overturning of the superseded "strong" theory of modernism. Saint-Amour, "Weak Modernism, Weak Theory."
81. See Paula Rabinowitz, *Labor and Desire: Revolutionary Women's Fiction in Depression America* (University of North Carolina Press, 1991); Barbara Foley, *Spectres of 1919: Class and Nation in the Making of the New Negro* (University of Illinois Press, 2003); Cary Nelson, *Revolutionary Memory: Recovering the Poetry of the American Left* (Routledge, 2001); Alan Wald, *Exiles from a Future Time: The Forging of the Mid-Twentieth-Century Literary Left* (University of North Carolina Press, 2002).
82. Christopher Nealon, *The Matter of Capital: Poetry and Crisis in the American Century* (Harvard University Press, 2011), 35.
83. Ruth Jennison, *The Zukofsky Era: Modernity, Margins, and the Avant-Garde* (Johns Hopkins University Press, 2012), 10.
84. See Mark Steven, *Red Modernism: American Poetry and the Spirit of Communism* (Johns Hopkins University Press, 2017).
85. Mao, introduction to *The New Modernist Studies*, 15.
86. See Sarah Ehlers, *Left of Poetry: Depression America and the Formation of Modern Poetics* (University of North Carolina Press, 2019); Amy Elkins, *Crafting Feminism from Literary Modernism to the Multimedia Present* (Oxford University Press, 2023).
87. Nealon, *The Matter of Capital*, 2–3.
88. Lorine Niedecker, "In the great snowfall before the bomb," in *Collected Works*, ed. Jenny Penberthy (University of California Press, 2002), 142.
89. Niedecker, "In the great snowfall before the bomb," 143.

1. EZRA POUND'S WORK ETHIC

1. Ezra Pound, *The Cantos* (New Directions, 1993). Hereafter, canto and page number are cited parenthetically.
2. The marble original is held in the National Gallery of Art in Washington, DC, some six miles from where the poet was incarcerated.
3. In a stomach-churning image in his "Translator's Postscript" to Remy de Gourmont's *The Natural Philosophy of Love*, Pound glosses de Gourmont: "Thought is a chemical process, the most interesting of all transfusions in liquid solution. The mind is an upspurt of sperm, no, let me alter that; trying to watch the process: the sperm, the form-creator, the substance which compels the ovule to evolve in a given pattern, one microscopic, minuscule particle, entering the 'castle' of the ovule." Ezra Pound, "Translator's Postscript," in *The Natural Philosophy of Love*, by Remy de Gourmont, trans. Ezra Pound (Boni and Liveright, 1922), 300.
4. Ezra Pound to Howard Mumford Jones, September 1935. Ezra Pound Papers, Yale Collection of American Literature, Beinecke Rare Book and Manuscript Library, Yale University, YCAL MSS 43, box 23, folder 1001. Hereafter, "EPP," followed by box and folder numbers.
5. My use of *protofascism* to describe impulses in Pound's early poetics that are more fully realized in his later poetry differs from Jameson's use of the term

1. EZRA POUND'S WORK ETHIC

in his description of Wyndham Lewis's reactionary stance against Marxism. See Fredric Jameson, *Fables of Aggression: Wyndham Lewis, the Modernist as Fascist* (University of California Press, 1979).

6. *Craft* is dominant in creative writing pedagogy and in contemporary writing's self-description. Indeed, the contemporary genre of the "craft essay" points to craft's dominance today. Christopher Kempf traces that genre's roots to the modernist moment and the craft books by Pound and Stein. For Kempf, while the figuration of practical aesthetic education as a workshop has its historical roots in the American Arts and Crafts movement, that metaphorization now "transcodes professional-managerial soft skills—linguistic facility, social and emotional discernment, symbolic fluency—in the language of manual labor." Christopher Kempf, *Craft Class: The Writing Workshop in American Culture* (Johns Hopkins University Press, 2022), 6.
7. It is common to describe Pound's embrace of fascism as a "conversion." Matthew Feldman, for example, draws on Emilio Gentile's theories of "political faith" to detail Pound's "conversion." In an effort to place Pound's nascent fascism earlier than his wholehearted embrace of Mussolini, I use the language of development rather than conversion. See Matthew Feldman, *Ezra Pound's Fascist Propaganda, 1935–45* (Palgrave Macmillan, 2013), 3.
8. Alberto Toscano, *Late Fascism: Race, Capitalism, and the Politics of Crisis* (Verso, 2023), 4.
9. Tim Redman, *Ezra Pound and Italian Fascism* (Cambridge University Press, 1991), 10.
10. By August 1913, the magazine had a weekly circulation of 4,500, significantly larger than the typical circulation of modernism's little magazines. See Ann L. Ardis, "The Dialogics of Modernism(s) in the *New Age*," *Modernism/Modernity* 14, no. 3 (2007): 417.
11. A. J. Penty, "The Restoration of Beauty to Life," part 1, *New Age* 1, no. 1 (1907): 5.
12. A. J. Penty, "The Restoration of Beauty to Life," part 2, *New Age* 1, no. 2 (1907): 21.
13. William Morris, *Signs of Change*, Marxists Internet Archive, 1896, https://www.marxists.org/archive/morris/works/1888/signs/index.htm.
14. "Guild Socialism: The Moral Foundations of Existing Society," *New Age* 11, no. 24 (1912): 559.
15. Pound briefly identified as a syndicalist. Despite confessing himself in October 1912 to be "ignorant of the detail of Syndicalist tenets," in 1914 he wrote that "as a Syndicalist, somewhat atrabilious, I disbelieve vigorously in any recognition of political institutions." Ezra Pound, "Patria Mia," part 6, *New Age* 11, no. 24 (1912): 564; Ezra Pound [Bastien Von Helmholtz, pseud.], "Suffragettes," *Egoist* 1, no. 13 (1914): 254. See David Kadlec, "Pound, BLAST, and Syndicalism," *ELH* 60, no. 4 (1993): 1015–31.
16. Ezra Pound, "Through Alien Eyes," part 1, *New Age* 12, no. 11 (1913): 252.
17. A. R. Orage, "Notes of the Week," *New Age* 10, no. 23 (1912): 529. Lenin, a keen observer of the miners' strike, argued that it "definitely marked an epoch" and asserted that "the British proletariat is no longer the same. The workers have learned to fight. They have come to see the path that will lead them to victory." Vladimir Ilyich Lenin, "The British Labor Movement in 1912," *Pravda* 1 (1913). Reprinted in Vladimir Ilyich Lenin, *Lenin: Collected Works*, vol. 18, trans. Stepan Apresyan, ed. Clemens Dutt (Progress, 1975), 467–68.

1. EZRA POUND'S WORK ETHIC

18. Ezra Pound, "Through Alien Eyes," part 3, *New Age* 12, no. 13 (1913): 301. Lee Garver reads Pound's poem "The Seafarer" in relation to the strikes of 1911 and 1912. See Lee Garver, "Seafarer Socialism: Pound, *The New Age*, and Anglo-Medieval Radicalism," *Journal of Modern Literature* 29, no. 4 (2006): 2.
19. *Nascitur ordo*: "A new order is born." Pound, "Through Alien Eyes," part 3, 300.
20. Ezra Pound, *Gaudier-Brzeska: A Memoir* (New Directions, 1970), 111.
21. See Robert Casillo, "The Italian Renaissance: Pound's Problematic Debt to Burckhardt," *Mosaic: An Interdisciplinary Critical Journal* 22, no. 4 (1989): 13–29.
22. Ezra Pound, "I Gather the Limbs of Osiris: A Rather Dull Introduction," part 2, *New Age* 10, no. 6 (1911): 130, 131.
23. Cecire names these principles "flash" and traces their origins to the development of flash photography in the late nineteenth century. The specific kind of knowledge that flash secures is "population knowledge," bound up "in the virtues of public-mindedness, investigative or journalistic integrity ('sunshine is the best disinfectant'), and concern for the health of the social body." Natalia Cecire, *Experimental: American Literature and the Aesthetics of Knowledge* (Johns Hopkins University Press, 2019), 73, 50.
24. Ezra Pound, "I Gather the Limbs of Osiris: On Technique," part 9, *New Age* 10, no. 13 (1912): 298.
25. Kadlec, "Pound, *BLAST*, and Syndicalism," 1015.
26. Pound, "I Gather the Limbs of Osiris," part 2, 130.
27. Ezra Pound "The Serious Artist," part 1, *New Freewoman* 1, no. 9 (1913): 161, 162.
28. Pound "The Serious Artist," part 1, 162.
29. Pound "The Serious Artist," part 1, 163.
30. See also Bruce Fogelman, "The Evolution of Pound's 'Contemporania,'" *Journal of Modern Literature* 15, no. 1 (1988): 93–103.
31. Ezra Pound to Harriet Monroe, October 13, 1912, in Ezra Pound, *Selected Letters of Ezra Pound 1907–1941*, ed. D. D. Paige (Faber and Faber, 1982), 11.
32. Ezra Pound, "A Pact," *Poetry* 2, no. 1 (1913): 12.
33. Ezra Pound, "What I Feel About Walt Whitman," in *Selected Prose 1909–1965*, ed. William Cookson (New Directions, 1973), 145.
34. Ezra Pound, "Pax Saturni," *Poetry* 2, no. 1 (1913): 8.
35. John Reed, "A Word to Mr. Pound," *Poetry* 2, no. 3 (1913): 112.
36. Steffens narrates the McNamara trial in his autobiography. See Lincoln Steffens, *The Autobiography of Lincoln Steffens* (Harrap, 1931).
37. John Reed, "Sangar," *Poetry* 1, no. 3 (1912): 71–74.
38. Reed wrote to Pound, "If your criticism had been one of poetic form, I should have respected it, at any rate." Reed, "A Word to Mr. Pound," 112.
39. See, for example, S. Verdad, "S. Verdad and Foreign Politics," *New Age* 9, no. 26 (1911): 620.
40. Ezra Pound to Harriet Monroe, March 30, 1913, in Pound, *Selected Letters*, 17. Here Pound is referring to the American advertising and marketing pioneer John Wanamaker.
41. Ezra Pound, "Patria Mia," part 8, *New Age* 11, no. 26 (1912): 611.
42. Ezra Pound, "Epilogue," in *Collected Early Poems of Ezra Pound*, ed. Michael John King (New Directions, 1976), 209.

1. EZRA POUND'S WORK ETHIC

43. Daniel Tiffany, *Radio Corpse: Imagism and the Cryptaesthetic of Ezra Pound* (Harvard University Press, 1995), 101.
44. Jessica Berman, *Modernist Commitments: Ethics, Politics, and Transnational Modernism* (Columbia University Press, 2012), 25.
45. Pound, *Gaudier-Brzeska*, 87–89.
46. T. S. Eliot, "Tradition and the Individual Talent," in *Selected Prose*, ed. Frank Kermode (Faber and Faber, 1975), 23.
47. "We can produce at this moment goods and services at a rate very considerably greater than the possible rate of consumption in the world." C. H. Douglas, *Social Credit* (Cecil Palmer, 1924), 18–19. Douglas argued that the working poor did not have enough money to consume the surplus of goods produced, whereas the wealthy had neither the need nor the ability to consume the surplus. In his view, unemployment created a group of people who were less likely or able to consume goods. Yet if more workers are laid off and demand continues to fall, then profit will fall correspondingly, unless more workers are also laid off to reduce costs, which in turn reduces demand even further. The burden of cost then shifts to the public, who, in funding unemployment benefits, support the maintenance of private profit. For more on Douglas and Pound, see Alec Marsh, *Money and Modernity: Pound, Williams, and the Spirit of Jefferson* (University of Alabama Press, 1998), 91.
48. Douglas, *Social Credit*, 110–11.
49. Douglas, *Social Credit*, 132–33.
50. Ezra Pound, "Credit and the Fine Arts: A Practical Application," *New Age* 30, no. 22 (1922): 284–85.
51. Ezra Pound to Scofield Thayer, April 23, 1922, in T. S. Eliot, *The Letters of T. S. Eliot*, vol. 1, ed. Valerie Eliot and Hugh Haughton (Faber and Faber, 2009), 665; Pound, "Credit and the Fine Arts," 285.
52. T. S. Eliot to Richard Aldington, June 30, 1922, in Eliot, *The Letters of T. S. Eliot*, 688. Eliot cautioned Pound against including any mention of Lloyd's in announcements of the scheme: "If it is stated so positively that Lloyds Bank interfered with literature, Lloyds Bank would have a perfect right to infer that literature interfered with Lloyds Bank". T. S. Eliot to Ezra Pound, July 28, 1922, in Eliot, *The Letters of T. S. Eliot*, 712.
53. Eliot's letter to the editor was printed in *The Liverpool Daily Post and Mercury* on November 30, 1922: "The circulation of untrue stories of this kind cause me profound astonishment and annoyance and may also do me considerable harm" (Eliot, *The Letters of T. S. Eliot*, 794). The editor apologized with some qualification, writing, "We are quite sure that nothing except a tribute to Mr. Eliot's high position as a critic and poet was intended in what our contributor wrote" (Eliot, *The Letters of T. S. Eliot*, 795).
54. T. S. Eliot to Ottoline Morrell, December 12, 1922, in Eliot, *The Letters of T. S. Eliot*, 806.
55. Lawrence Rainey, *Institutions of Modernism: Literary Elites and Popular Culture* (Yale University Press, 1998), 75.
56. Ezra Pound to Wyndham Lewis, April 1922, in Ezra Pound, *Pound/Lewis*, ed. Timothy Materer (Faber and Faber, 1985), 130.

1. EZRA POUND'S WORK ETHIC

57. Ezra Pound to William Carlos Williams, March 18, 1922, in Ezra Pound, *Pound/Williams*, ed. Hugh Witemeyer (New Directions, 1996), 55. Emphasis in the original. Pound wrote to his father two months later, "If you *want* to spend money spend it on Bel Esprit." Ezra Pound to Homer Pound, May 22, 1922, in Ezra Pound, *Ezra Pound to His Parents*, ed. Mary de Rachewiltz, A. David Moody, and Joanna Moody (Oxford University Press, 2010), 499.
58. For the composition and textual history of the Malatesta cantos and a comprehensive examination of Pound's historical sources, see Lawrence Rainey, *Ezra Pound and the Monument of Culture: Text, History, and the Malatesta Cantos* (University of Chicago Press, 1991), 29–57.
59. Mary Hollingworth points out that one of the most persistent myths surrounding artistic production in the Renaissance is the idea that artists were free to explore their own ideas because they enjoyed the support of generous and enlightened patrons intent on acquiring works of genius. The patron played a crucial role not only in providing funds but also in determining the form and content of artworks: they were "not passive connoisseurs" but rather "active consumers," and it was the patron, rather than the artist, who was seen by contemporaries as being the creator of the artistic project. Mary Hollingworth, *Patronage in Renaissance Italy: From 1400 to the Early Sixteenth Century* (John Murray, 1994), 1.
60. For more on Pound's use of Plethon, see Peter Liebregts, *Ezra Pound and Neoplatonism* (Fairleigh Dickinson University Press, 2004), 160.
61. Hugh Kenner, *The Pound Era* (Faber and Faber, 1972), 419.
62. Peter Brooker, "London," in *Ezra Pound in Context*, ed. Ira B. Nadel (Cambridge University Press, 2010), 235.
63. Peter Wilson, *A Preface to Ezra Pound* (Longman, 1997).
64. Sean Pryor, *W. B. Yeats, Ezra Pound, and the Poetry of Paradise* (Ashgate, 2011), 121.
65. Donald Davie, "The Poet as Sculptor," in *Studies in Ezra Pound* (Carcanet, 1991), 203.
66. Davie, "The Poet as Sculptor," 203.
67. Adrian Stokes, quoted in Davie, "The Poet as Sculptor," 202.
68. Sean Pryor, "Canto 17," in *Readings in the Cantos*, vol. 1, ed. Richard Parker (Clemson University Press, 2018), 163.
69. Kenner, *The Pound Era*, 420.
70. Adrian Stokes, quoted in Davie, "The Poet as Sculptor," 202.
71. Pound, typescript for Canto XVII, quoted in Liebregts, *Ezra Pound and Neoplatonism*, 174.
72. Louis Zukofsky, "Sincerity and Objectification: With Special Reference to the Work of Charles Reznikoff," *Poetry* 37, no. 5 (1931): 274.
73. Ezra Pound, "Pound Joins the Revolution!," *New Masses* 2, no. 2 (1926): 3. In response, Pound wrote in an unpublished essay, "I naturally want the revolution to join me." "Revolution," typescript, EPP, box 135, folder 5837.
74. Ezra Pound, "Workshop Orchestration," *New Masses* 2, no. 5 (1927): 21.
75. Pound, "Workshop Orchestration," 21.
76. Ezra Pound, *Machine Art and Other Writings: The Lost Thought of the Italian Years*, ed. Maria Luisa Ardizzone (Duke University Press, 1996), 78; subsequently cited parenthetically. Pound echoes this idea in *ABC of Economics*: "As mechanical efficiency increases, production will require progressively less human time and effort." Ezra Pound, *ABC of Economics* (Peter Russell, 1953), 14.

1. EZRA POUND'S WORK ETHIC

77. It is reasonable to question how many noises, disagreeable or otherwise, Pound had heard in factories.
78. Pound was not alone in this thought: Harry Braverman points out that the engineer is an inheritor of the craftsman: "The profession of engineering is a relatively recent development. Before the engineer, the conceptual and design functions were the province of craftsmanship, as were the functions of furthering the industrial arts through innovation. . . . The working craftsman was tied to the technical and scientific knowledge of his time in the daily practice of his craft. Apprenticeship commonly included training in mathematics, including algebra, geometry, and trigonometry, in the properties and provenance of the materials common to the craft, in the physical sciences, and in mechanical drawing. . . . The craft provided a daily link between science and work." Harry Braverman, *Labor and Monopoly Capital: The Degradation of Work in the Twentieth Century* (Monthly Review, 1998), 91–92.
79. Ezra Pound, *Jefferson and/or Mussolini: L'Idea Statale: Fascism as I Have Seen It* (Stanley Nott, 1932), 33–34.
80. Pound, *Jefferson and/or Mussolini*, 66.
81. Pound, *Jefferson and/or Mussolini*, 36.
82. Ezra Pound, "Mussolini Defines State as 'Spirit of the People': Fascism Analyzed by Ezra Pound, Noted American Writer," *Chicago Tribune*, April 9, 1934, 5.
83. Pound, *ABC of Economics*, 26.
84. Peter Nicholls, *Ezra Pound: Politics, Economics, and Writing—A Study of the Cantos* (Macmillan, 1984), 57.
85. Nicholls, *Ezra Pound*, 56.
86. Ezra Pound, "The Individual and His Milieu: A Study of Relations and Gesell," *Criterion* 15, no. 58 (1935): 30–45.
87. For a full account of Pound, Marx, and the historical rhetorical method, see Mark Steven, "Reading Capital, Writing History: Pound's Marx," *Modernism/Modernity* 24, no. 4 (2017): 771–90.
88. Ezra Pound to Harriet Monroe, March 30, 1913, in Pound, *Selected Letters*, 17.
89. Marx describes the development of these laws and the campaigns led against them in detail in chapter 10 of *Capital*, "The Working Day." In 1825, an act was passed limiting the working hours of children; it was amended in 1829 and again in 1831 to apply only to children working in cotton mills. "The new Factory Act of 8 June 1847 enacted that on 1 July 1847 there should be a preliminary reduction of the working day for 'young persons' (from thirteen to eighteen) and all females to eleven hours, but that on 1 May 1848 there should be a definite limitation of the working day to ten hours." See Karl Marx, *Capital*, vol. 1, trans. Ben Fowkes (Penguin, 1990), 395. Marx describes the Printworks Act of 1845, which limited the working day for women and children to sixteen hours and allowed men over thirteen to be worked any time of the day or night, as "a parliamentary abortion." See Marx, *Capital*, 1:408.
90. Ezra Pound, "Patria Mia," part 4, *New Age* 11, no. 22 (1912): 515.
91. Ezra Pound, "The Revolt of Intelligence," *New Age* 26, no. 18 (1920): 287; Alec Marsh, "Thaddeus Coleman Pound's 'Newspaper Scrapbook' as a Source for *The Cantos*," *Paideuma* 24, nos. 2–3 (1995): 163–93.
92. The line about sweating blood is delivered by Pound's maternal grandfather, a Wadsworth.

1. EZRA POUND'S WORK ETHIC

93. Ezra Pound, radio speech 34, May 9, 1942. Ezra Pound, *Ezra Pound Speaking: Radio Speeches of WWII* (Greenwood, 1978), 121.
94. Redman, *Ezra Pound and Italian Fascism*, 49.
95. Odon Por, *Fascism*, trans. E. Townshend (Labour, 1923), 3.
96. A. J. Penty, *Tradition and Modernism in Politics* (Sheed & Ward, 1937), 49.
97. Ezra Pound, "What Is Money For?," in *Selected Prose*, 263.
98. In an unpublished letter to Joseph Macleod, Pound blamed the failure of guilds on usury, writing that "fascism is a higher degree of ORGANIZATION than the ang/sax is capable of reaching OR comprehending. Guild systems did WORK/and the century of usury that shat on all terms and mingled them in one shitten soup." Ezra Pound to Joseph Macleod, April 1938, EPP, box 32, folder 1332.
99. See Alessandra Anatola Swan, "The Iconic Body: Mussolini Unclothed," *Modern Italy* 21, no. 4 (2016): 361–81; Simonetta Falasca-Zamponi, *Fascist Spectacle: The Aesthetics of Power in Mussolini's Italy* (University of California Press, 1997), 152.
100. Edward Coke, *The Second Part of the Institutes of the Laws of England* (E. and R. Brooke, 1797), 643.
101. Ian F. A. Bell, "Middle Cantos XLII–LXXI," in *The Cambridge Companion to Ezra Pound*, ed. Ira B. Nadel (Cambridge University Press, 1999), 104.
102. Zhaoming Qian, "Painting into Poetry: Pound's Seven Lakes Canto," in *Ezra Pound and China*, ed. Zhaoming Qian (University of Michigan Press, 2003), 72. I am grateful to Mary de Rachewiltz for generously allowing me to look at the screen book in her collections at Brunnenburg.
103. Canto LXIX, typescript, no date, EPP, box 74, folder 3311.
104. Canto LXIX, typescript, no date, EPP, box 74, folder 3312.
105. Laurence Binyon, preface to *A Short History of Chinese Civilisation*, by Tsui Chi (Victor Gollancz, 1942), 8.
106. Ezra Pound, *Guide to Kulchur* (Peter Owen, 1972), 272. For a full history of Pound's relationship with Confucius, see Mary Paterson Cheadle, *Ezra Pound's Confucian Translations* (University of Michigan Press, 2003), 9–28. See also Zhaoming Qian, *Orientalism and Modernism: The Legacy of China in Pound and Williams* (Duke University Press, 1995). On Pound's relationships with Chinese friends and scholars, see Ezra Pound, *Ezra Pound's Chinese Friends: Stories in Letters*, ed. Zhaoming Qian (Oxford University Press, 2008).
107. For Pound, China around 1900 is "a chaos wherein [Confucian] ideas have long been abused," but he maintains that the "degradation" will be "temporary" because "a nucleus of sanity still exists in China." Ezra Pound, "Mang Tsze," in *Selected Prose*, 109–10. Pound makes occasional references to China, and to Chiang Kai-Shek in particular, in his radio broadcasts. See Pound, *Ezra Pound Speaking*, 9, 20, 147. In 1956, Pound would write of "the abyss of Chinese politics as of 1956." Ezra Pound to David Wang, October 11, 1956, in Pound, *Ezra Pound's Chinese Friends*, 179.
108. W. B. Yeats, introduction to *The Oxford Book of Modern Verse, 1892–1935* (Clarendon, 1936), xxiv.
109. On Pound and the *Mostra*, see Catherine E. Paul, "Italian Fascist Exhibitions and Ezra Pound's Move to the Imperial," *Twentieth Century Literature* 51, no. 1 (2005): 64–97. See also Miranda Hickman, *The Geometry of Modernism: The Vorticist Idiom in Lewis, Pound, H. D., and Yeats* (University of Texas Press, 2005), 105.

1. EZRA POUND'S WORK ETHIC

Peter Nicholls also identifies the visit as a powerful influence on Pound's turn to fascism. See Peter Nicholls, "Bravura or Bravado?," in *Modernism and Masculinity*, ed. Julian Murphet and Natalya Lusty (Cambridge University Press, 2014), 239–40.

110. Claudia Lazzaro and Roger J. Crum, introduction to *Donatello Among the Blackshirts: History and Modernity in the Visual Culture of Fascist Italy*, ed. Claudia Lazzaro and Roger J. Crum (Cornell University Press, 2005), 4.
111. Marla Stone, "Staging Fascism: The Exhibition of the Fascist Revolution," *Journal of Contemporary History* 28, no. 2 (1993): 230–31.
112. Harry Harootunian, "A Fascism for Our Time," *Massachusetts Review* (2022): 13–14.
113. Richard Sieburth, "In Pound We Trust: The Economy of Poetry/The Poetry of Economy," *Critical Inquiry* 14, no. 1 (1987): 166.
114. Donald Davie, "The Rock-Drill Cantos," in *Studies in Ezra Pound*, 178. The line "in pochi" means "in a few"; "causa motuum" means "cause of motion" (or emotion).
115. For a detailed reading of the opening lines of this canto, see Sean Pryor, "So Slow: Canto CVI," in *Glossator: Practice and Theory of the Commentary*, vol. 10, *Astern in the Dinghy: Commentaries on Ezra's Pound's* Thrones de los Cantares XCVI–CIX, ed. Alexander Howard (Glossator, 2018), 287–308.
116. Massimo Bacigalupo, *The Forméd Trace: The Later Poetry of Ezra Pound* (Columbia University Press, 1980), 335.
117. Chao promoted Kuan as "the greatest statesman and economist of China." Tze-chiang Chao to Ezra Pound, June 16, 1957, in Pound, *Ezra Pound's Chinese Friends*, 169.
118. Carroll F. Terrell, *A Companion to the Cantos of Ezra Pound*, vol. 2 (University of California Press, 1980), 624.
119. See Ernst Bloch, *Heritage of Our Times*, trans. Neville Plaice and Stephen Plaice (University of California Press, 1991).
120. Peter Nicholls, "Lost Object(s): Ezra Pound and the Idea of Italy," in *Ezra Pound and Europe*, ed. Claus Melchior and Richard Taylor (Rodopi, 1993), 173.
121. Hugh Kenner, "Under the Larches of Paradise," *Hudson Review* 9, no. 3 (1956): 459.
122. Peter Nicholls, "'2 Doits to a Boodle': Reckoning with *Thrones*," *Textual Practice* 18, no. 2 (2004): 233.
123. Dudley Fitts, "Prelude to Conclusion," *Saturday Review of Literature* 39 (1956): 18.
124. Randall Jarrell, "Five Poets," *Yale Review* (1956): 103; John Wain, "The Shadow of an Epic," *Spectator* (1960): 360.
125. Wain, "The Shadow of an Epic," 360.
126. Nicholls, "'2 Doits to a Boodle,'" 245.
127. Stone, "Staging Fascism," 230.
128. See, for example, Bacigalupo, who argues that the ideograms "preserve their magic appeal" as a result of their visual-material presence, or R. John Williams, who superimposes Canto LXXXV onto a sketch of Jacob Epstein's sculpture *Rock Drill*. Bacigalupo, *The Forméd Trace*, 233; R. John Williams, *The Buddha in the Machine: Art, Technology, and the Meeting of East and West* (Yale University Press, 2014), 125–26.

1. EZRA POUND'S WORK ETHIC

129. Ernest Fenollosa, *The Chinese Written Character as a Medium for Poetry: A Critical Edition*, ed. L. Klein, H. Saussy, and J. Stalling (Fordham University Press, 2008), 45.
130. Rebecca Beasley, *Ezra Pound and the Visual Culture of Modernism* (Cambridge University Press, 2007), 207.
131. Ezra Pound, "A Few Don'ts by an Imagiste," *Poetry* 1, no. 6 (1913): 201.

2. THE SOCIAL LIFE OF SEWING: LOLA RIDGE

1. The previous year broke records for arrival: in 1907 just over one million arrivals passed through New York; in 1908 that number was 585,970. *Annual Reports of the Commissioner General of Immigration*, 1892–1924 (Washington, DC: U.S. Department of Justice, Immigration, and Naturalization Service).
2. Virginia Jackson, *Dickinson's Misery* (Princeton University Press, 2005), 8.
3. Virginia Jackson, "Lyric," in *The Princeton Encyclopedia of Poetry and Poetics*, 4th ed., ed. Stephen Cushman et al. (Princeton University Press, 2012), 826.
4. Matthew Bevis, "Unknowing Lyric," *Poetry*, March 2017, https://www.poetry foundation.org/poetrymagazine/articles/92372/unknowing-lyric.
5. Silvia Federici, *Re-enchanting the World: Feminism and the Politics of the Commons* (PM, 2019), 110.
6. Andrea Brady, *Poetry and Bondage: A History and Theory of Lyric Constraint* (Cambridge University Press, 2021), 148.
7. Sarah Ehlers, *Left of Poetry: Depression America and the Formation of Modern Poetics* (University of North Carolina Press, 2019), 8.
8. Amelia M. Glaser, *Songs in Dark Times: Yiddish Poetry of Struggle from Scottsboro to Palestine* (Harvard University Press, 2020), 4.
9. Oren Izenberg, *Being Numerous: Poetry and the Ground of Social Life* (Princeton University Press, 2011), 39.
10. Rachel Blau DuPlessis, "Lorine Niedecker, the Anonymous: Gender, Class, Genre and Resistances," *Kenyon Review* 14, no. 2 (1999): 99. Ridge has received more attention in recent years, thanks in no small part to the following works: Lola Ridge, *To the Many: Collected Early Works*, ed. Daniel Tobin (Little Island, 2018); Terese Svoboda, *Anything That Burns You: A Portrait of Lola Ridge, Radical Poet* (Schaffner, 2016); and Lola Ridge, *The Ghetto, and Other Poems: An Annotated Edition*, ed. Lawrence Kramer (Fordham University Press, 2023).
11. Cristanne Miller, "'Tongues Loosened in the Melting Pot': The Poets of Others and the Lower East Side," *Modernism/Modernity* 14, no. 3 (2007): 463. Caroline Maun places Ridge within a uniquely American modernism alongside Evelyn Scott, Charlotte Wilder, and Kay Boyle, while Nancy Berke situates her among similarly neglected leftist women poets, including Genevieve Taggard and Margaret Walker. See Caroline Maun, *Mosaic of Fire: The Work of Lola Ridge, Evelyn Scott, Charlotte Wilder, and Kay Boyle* (University of South Carolina Press, 2012); Nancy Berke, *Women Poets on the Left: Lola Ridge, Genevieve Taggard, Margaret Walker* (University Press of Florida, 2001).
12. Juno Jill Richards, *The Fury Archives: Female Citizenship, Human Rights, and the International Avant-Gardes* (Columbia University Press, 2020), 21, 1.

2. THE SOCIAL LIFE OF SEWING

13. Kenyon Zimmer, *Immigrants Against the State: Yiddish and Italian Anarchism in America* (University of Illinois Press, 2015). See also Andrew Cornell on the political function of the term *anarchism* in the establishment of the 1924 reforms: "anarchism: was used as a racializing epithet to challenge the rights of eastern and Southern European immigrants to claim the privileges of national belonging and whiteness, and this helped build support for the immigration reforms of 1924." Andrew Cornell, *Unruly Equality: U.S. Anarchism in the Twentieth Century* (University of California Press, 2016), 16.
14. Zimmer, *Immigrants Against the State*, 16. The composition of the industry changed with waves of immigration: before the arrival of Eastern European Jews, the garment trades had employed mostly German laborers; later in the century, Black, Puerto Rican, Chinese, and Dominican workers would labor in the industry in significant numbers. For more on the international character of New York City's garment industry, see Daniel Soyer, ed., *A Coat of Many Colors: Immigration, Globalization, and Reform in New York City's Garment Industry* (Fordham University Press, 2004).
15. Susan A. Glenn, *Daughters of the Shtetl: Life and Labor in the Immigrant Generation* (Cornell University Press, 1990), 92.
16. Daniel E. Bender, *Sweated Work, Weak Bodies: Anti-Sweatshop Campaigns and Languages of Labor* (Rutgers University Press, 2004), 24.
17. Glenn, *Daughters of the Shtetl*, 93.
18. Margaret M. Chin, *Sewing Women: Immigrants and the New York City Garment Industry* (Columbia University Press, 2005), 8.
19. Marie Ganz, with Nat J. Ferber, *Rebels; Into Anarchy—and Out Again* (Dodd, Mead, 1920), 93–94.
20. Glenn, *Daughters of the Shtetl*, 58.
21. Nancy L. Green, *Ready to Wear and Ready to Work: A Century of Industry and Immigrants in Paris and New York* (Duke University Press, 1997), 54.
22. Tony Michels, *A Fire in Their Hearts: Yiddish Socialists in New York* (Harvard University Press, 2005), 5. Gus Tyler characterizes the Lower East Side as an "informational, inspirational classroom." Gus Tyler, *Look for the Union Label: A History of the International Ladies' Garment Workers' Union* (Routledge, 2016), 20.
23. In the early twentieth century, anarchists were more likely to speak and write Yiddish, Italian, Russian, or Spanish, rather than English, as their primary language. For more on the multilingual character of American anarchism, see Cornell, *Unruly Equality*, 22.
24. Lola Ridge Papers, Smith College Special Collections, Smith College, SSC-MS-00131, box 1.
25. Her second husband, David Lawson, disputed this claim; Svoboda implicitly supports Ridge's account. Svoboda, *Anything That Burns You*, 101.
26. "Observations and Comments," *Mother Earth* 3, no. 8 (1908): 310.
27. "Lola Ridge, Poet, Dies in Brooklyn," *New York Times*, May 21, 1941.
28. See Laura Hapke, *Sweatshop: The History of an American Idea* (Rutgers University Press, 2004), 31–32.
29. See Keith Gandal, *The Virtues of the Vicious: Jacob Riis, Stephen Crane, and the Spectacle of the Slum* (Oxford University Press, 1997).

2. THE SOCIAL LIFE OF SEWING

30. Milton Regenstein, "Pictures of the Ghetto," *New York Times*, November 14, 1897.
31. "The peripatetic philosopher comes to New York with the flowers that bloom in the Spring. You find him, or her, in all the poorer parts of the city, more or less, but especially in three or four neighbourhoods. Little groups of them dot the sidewalk all Summer long, strolling up and down, discussing art, literature, drama, Socialism, Anarchy, women's suffrage, child labor, the nature of evil, pragmatism, restricted immigration, Milwaukee politics, and any number of other subjects to the number of seventy times seven." "Peripatetic Philosophers of This Many-Sided Town," *New York Times*, May 29, 1910.
32. Bernard G. Richards, "A Lower East Side Vacation," *Boston Evening Transcript*, 1903, reprinted in Tony Michels, ed., *Jewish Radicals: A Documentary History* (New York University Press, 2012), 162, 164.
33. Ridge, *The Ghetto, and Other Poems*, 3. Hereafter cited parenthetically as *TG*.
34. Lola Ridge, "Women and the Creative Will," in *To the Many: Collected Early Works*, ed. Daniel Tobin (Little Island, 2018), 147.
35. "The term *lyric sequence* is most accurately applied to works that maintain a sense of tension between the unity or interrelation of the whole and the independent workings of each part." *The Princeton Encyclopedia of Poetry and Poetics*, 4th ed., 835.
36. M. L. Rosenthal and Sally M. Gall, *The Modern Poetic Sequence: The Genius of Modern Poetry* (Oxford University Press, 1983), 3, 9. Emphasis in the original.
37. Babette Deutsch, "Two First Books," *Little Review* 16, no. 1 (1919): 66.
38. Lola Ridge Papers, Smith College Special Collections, Smith College, SSC-MS-00131, box 9.
39. Linda Kinnahan reads Ridge's representation of women in "The Ghetto" in relation to depictions of working women in modern visual culture: the documentary photography of workers in binderies and ragpickers in tenements by Jacob Riis and Lewis Hine, as well as photographs of women's strikes in newspapers and illustrations in radical magazines like *The Masses*. See Linda Arbaugh Kinnahan, "Portraits of Working Women: Lola Ridge's 'The Ghetto' and the Visual Record," *Humanities* 11, no. 5 (2022): 117–61.
40. Joshua Logan Wall, *Situating Poetry: Covenant and Genre in American Modernism* (Johns Hopkins University Press, 2022), 102.
41. Morris Rosenfeld, "The Sweatshop," in *Sing, Stranger: A Century of American Yiddish Poetry: A Historical Anthology*, trans. Benjamin Harshav and Barbara Harshav, ed. Benjamin Harshav (Stanford University Press, 2006), 21.
42. The quotation as it appeared in the press was a translation of Lemlich's speech described as a "philippic in Yiddish." The text of the speech was as follows: "I am a working girl, one of those who are on strike against intolerable conditions. I am tired of listening to speakers who talk in general terms. What we are here for is to decide whether we shall or shall not strike. I offer a resolution that a general strike be declared now." Tyler, *Look for the Union Label*, 57.
43. Glenn, *Daughters of the Shtetl*, 154.
44. Rose Pesotta, *Bread Upon the Waters* (Dodd, Mead, 1944), 12.
45. *Landsleit* here refers to fellow Jews from the same region. As most factories did not observe Shabbat, choosing to work uptown meant negotiating with one's religious observance and familial pressure.
46. Pesotta, *Bread Upon the Waters*, 11.

2. THE SOCIAL LIFE OF SEWING

47. See Paul Avrich, *An American Anarchist: The Life of Voltairine de Cleyre* (AK, 2018). Goldman wrote to Ridge, planning to introduce her to de Cleyre, although this may or may not have eventuated. Gussie Denenberg, another anarchist, described Ridge as "fragile looking and intense." Ridge reminded her "of Voltairine de Cleyre. She had the same spirit." Svoboda, *Anything That Burns You*, 90–92.
48. Voltairine de Cleyre, "Anarchism," in *Exquisite Rebel: The Essays of Voltairine de Cleyre, Feminist, Anarchist, Genius*, ed. Sharon Presley and Crispin Sartwell (State University of New York, 2005), 67.
49. de Cleyre, "Anarchism," 80.
50. de Cleyre, "The Political Equality of Women," in *Exquisite Rebel: The Essays of Voltairine de Cleyre, Feminist, Anarchist, Genius*, ed. Sharon Presley and Crispin Sartwell (State University of New York, 2005), 242. Emphasis in the original.
51. See Joshua Logan Wall, "Family Business: Charles Reznikoff in Text and Textile," *Studies in American Jewish Literature* 37, no. 1 (2018): 37–55.
52. Charles Reznikoff, *Family Chronicle* (Universe, 1971), 8.
53. Reznikoff, *Family Chronicle*, 99.
54. Saidiya Hartman, *Wayward Lives, Beautiful Experiments: Intimate Histories of Riotous Black Girls, Troublesome Women, and Queer Radicals* (Norton, 2019), 229.
55. Hartman, *Wayward Lives, Beautiful Experiments*, 230.
56. Richards, *The Fury Archives*, 2.
57. Alexander Berkman did not learn Yiddish until he arrived in New York, nor did the poet David Edelstadt or Emma Goldman (who sometimes delivered lectures in Yiddish but more often in Russian, German, or English) ever became fully fluent. See Michels, *A Fire in Their Hearts*; Zimmer, *Immigrants Against the State*.
58. Jacob Riis, *How the Other Half Lives: Studies Among the Tenements of New York* (Dover, 1971), 94–95.
59. Raymond Williams, *The Politics of Modernism: Against the New Conformists* (Verso, 1989), 45–46.
60. "Lola Ridge's Poetry," *New Republic* 17, no. 211 (1918): 76.
61. Alfred Kreymborg, "A Poet in Arms," *Poetry* 13, no. 6 (1919): 337.
62. Miller, "'Tongues Loosened in the Melting Pot,'" 464.
63. Ezra Pound, *Gaudier-Brzeska: A Memoir* (New Directions, 1970), 46.
64. Emma Goldman was shocked by the surveillance of her first factory job in Rochester: "The work here was harder, and the day, with only half an hour for lunch, seemed endless. The iron discipline forbade free movement (one could not even go to the toilet without permission), and the constant surveillance of the foreman weighed like stone on my heart." Emma Goldman, *Living My Life* (Penguin, 2006), 13.
65. Andrew Godley, "Selling the Sewing Machine Around the World: Singer's International Marketing Strategies, 1850–1920," *Enterprise and Society* 7, no. 2 (2006): 266–314. Paula A. de la Cruz-Fernández has traced how the firm marketed ornamental embroidery—"women's work"—as art, distinct from factory sewing, thus locating the home as a site where global capitalism was constructed. See Paula A. de la Cruz-Fernández, "Marketing the Hearth: Ornamental Embroidery and the Building of the Multinational Singer Sewing Machine Company," *Enterprise and Society* 15, no. 3 (2014): 442–71.

2. THE SOCIAL LIFE OF SEWING

66. René Depestre, "*La machine Singer*," in *Anthologie personelle* (Actes Sud, 1993), 28. "A singer machine in a Black household / Arab, Indian, Malay, Chinese, Annamese / Or in any wayward third-world home." Translation mine.
67. Aimé Césaire, *Journal of a Homecoming/Cahier d'un retour au pays natal* (Duke University Press, 2017), 89.
68. Karl Marx, *Capital*, vol. 1, trans. Ben Fowkes (Penguin, 1990), 342.
69. Marx, *Capital*, 1:344.
70. Bruce Robbins, "The Sweatshop Sublime," *PMLA* 117, no. 1 (2022): 92.
71. Maria Mies, *Patriarchy and Accumulation on a World Scale: Women in the International Division of Labor* (Zed, 2014), 3.
72. Juliana Spahr, *Well Then There Now* (Black Sparrow, 2011), 14, 147–48.
73. Anne Boyer, *Garments Against Women* (Ahsahta, 2015), 29.
74. As Lindsay Turner has written, Boyer's "not writing" "underscores the absence of what it is not, paraliptically recognizing global populations of workers and recognizing the difficulty of thinking about—acknowledging, sensing, feeling—those workers." Lindsay Turner, "Writing/Not Writing: Anne Boyer, Paralipsis, and Literary Work," *ASAP/Journal* 3, no. 1 (2018): 136–37.
75. Christopher Oakey, "Prose Poetry and Purposiveness in Anne Boyer's *Garments Against Women*," *Contemporary Literature* 61, no. 2 (2020): 217.
76. Silvia Federici, "Commons Against and Beyond Capitalism," in *Re-enchanting the World: Feminism and the Politics of the Commons* (PM, 2019), 86.
77. Gail Jones sees the poem's achievement as one of scale: "In the twenties, American anarchism was a hotchpotch of Proudhonist mutualism, collectivism, and bolshevism—with a bit of Stirnerist individualism and Tolstoyan mysticism thrown in; finding the nuanced small scale of a single man's suffering was no easy thing." Gail Jones, "'Growing Small Wings': Walter Benjamin, Lola Ridge, and the Political Affect of Modernism," *Affirmations: of the Modern* 1, no. 2 (2014): 136.
78. Lola Ridge, *To the Many: Collected Early Works*, ed. Daniel Tobin (Little Island, 2018), 274.
79. Anahid Nersessian, *The Calamity Form: On Poetry and Social Life* (Chicago University Press, 2020), 51.
80. Jacques Rancière, "A Few Remarks on the Methods of Jacques Rancière," *Parallax* 15, no. 3 (2009): 122.

3. LANGSTON HUGHES'S CONSTRUCTIVIST POETICS

1. Langston Hughes to Carl Van Vechten, March 1, 1933, in Langston Hughes, *Remember Me to Harlem: The Letters of Langston Hughes and Carl Van Vechten, 1925–1964*, ed. Emily Bernard (Knopf, 2001), 101.
2. Van Vechten to Hughes, April 3, 1933, in Hughes, *Remember Me to Harlem*, 103–4.
3. Hughes to Van Vechten, May 23, 1933, in Hughes, *Remember Me to Harlem*, 104.
4. Arnold Rampersad, *The Life of Langston Hughes*, vol. 1, *1902–1941, I, Too, Sing America* (Oxford University Press, 1986), 339. In contrast, he praises *Fine Clothes to the Jew* in no uncertain terms as "his most brilliant book of poems, and one of the more astonishing books of verse ever published in the United States—comparable in the black world to *Leaves of Grass* in the white." Rampersad, *The Life of Langston Hughes*, 1:141.

3. LANGSTON HUGHES'S CONSTRUCTIVIST POETICS

5. Anthony Dawahare, "Langston Hughes's Radical Poetry and the 'End of Race,'" *MELUS* 23, no. 3 (1998): 22.
6. In general, Hughes has been treated as a choric background voice in the history of Black American literature and leftist politics. Dawahare and others have argued for the significance of Hughes's work in the history of Black radical literature from the 1920s to the Cold War. Meanwhile, Barbara Foley locates Hughes's radical period somewhat earlier than his contact with the USSR, arguing that in the years before 1926 and well before the Great Depression, Hughes was already writing radical verse, while Michael Denning mentions Hughes's 1938 pamphlet, *A New Song*, in passing but focuses largely on his proletarian fiction. Hughes is a relatively minor figure in William J. Maxwell's *New Negro, Old Left: African American Writing and Communism Between the Wars* (Columbia University Press, 1999). Elsewhere, writers have situated the aesthetics of Hughes's 1930s poetry within the formal techniques of Anglo-American modernism. James Smethurst considers Hughes's radical poetry, prose, and theatrical work in relation to its polyvocal qualities and its formal relationship with literary modernism. Similarly, Alan Wald discusses Hughes's Depression-era poetry and the significance of his use of "simple" techniques and his strategies of "familiarization" (such as Hughes's friendly, personified revolution in "Good Morning Revolution"), arguing that these form "an odd parallel" to the more familiar modernist techniques of defamiliarization. See Barbara Foley, *Spectres of 1919: Class and Nation in the Making of the New Negro* (University of Illinois Press, 2003), 58; Michael Denning, *The Cultural Front: The Laboring of American Culture in the Twentieth Century* (Verso, 2011), 228; James Edward Smethurst, *The New Red Negro: The Literary Left and African American Poetry, 1930–46* (Oxford University Press, 1999), 93–115; Alan Wald, *Exiles from a Future Time: The Forging of the Mid-Twentieth-Century Literary Left* (University of North Carolina Press, 2002), 314.
7. Barrett Watten, *The Constructivist Moment: From Material Text to Cultural Poetics* (Wesleyan University Press, 2003), xv.
8. See Cedric J. Robinson, *Black Marxism: The Making of the Black Radical Tradition* (University of North Carolina Press, 2000).
9. Destin Jenkins and Justin Leroy, introduction to *Histories of Racial Capitalism*, ed. Destin Jenkins and Justin Leroy (Columbia University Press, 2021), 3.
10. Nancy Fraser, "Expropriation and Exploitation in Racialized Capitalism: A Reply to Michael Dawson," *Critical Historical Studies* 3, no. 1 (2016): 164–78.
11. Jodi Melamed, "Racial Capitalism," *Critical Ethnic Studies* 1, no. 1 (2015): 78.
12. Melamed, "Racial Capitalism," 78, 81, 80.
13. Anthony Reed, *Freedom Time: The Poetics and Politics of Black Experimental Writing* (Johns Hopkins University Press, 2014), 8.
14. Maria Gough, *The Artist as Producer: Russian Constructivism in Revolution* (University of California Press, 2005), 14.
15. William M. Kelley [W. M. K., pseud.], "Langston Hughes: The Sewer Dweller," *New York Amsterdam News*, February 9, 1927, 22; reprinted in Tish Dace, ed., *Langston Hughes: The Contemporary Reviews* (Cambridge University Press, 1997), 91. "Under the Lash of the Whip: A Column of Constructive Criticism of Men and Measures in the Hope of Correcting Errors and Evils," *Chicago Whip*, February 25, 1927; reprinted in Dace, *Langston Hughes*, 100.

3. LANGSTON HUGHES'S CONSTRUCTIVIST POETICS

16. Langston Hughes, *The Collected Works of Langston Hughes*, vol. 13, *The Big Sea*, ed. Joseph McLaren (University of Missouri Press, 2002), 207.
17. Langston Hughes, *The Collected Works of Langston Hughes*, vol. 1, *The Poems: 1921–1940*, ed. Arnold Rampersad (University of Missouri Press, 2001), 89.
18. Langston Hughes, *Not Without Laughter* (Canongate, 1998), 216.
19. Hughes, *The Collected Works*, 1:89.
20. John Marsh, *Hog Butchers, Beggars, and Busboys: Poverty, Labor, and the Making of Modern American Poetry* (University of Michigan Press, 2011), 154.
21. Steven A. Reich, *A Working People: A History of African American Workers Since Emancipation* (Rowman & Littlefield, 2013), 70–71.
22. Earl Ofari Hutchinson, *Blacks and Reds: Race and Class in Conflict, 1919–1990* (Michigan State University Press, 1995), 9.
23. On the construction of whiteness and the American working class, the classic text is David Roediger, *Wages of Whiteness* (Verso, 1991).
24. Hutchinson, *Blacks and Reds*, 29.
25. Robert Minor, "The First Negro Workers' Congress," *Workers Monthly* 5 (1925): 70.
26. See Philip S. Foner, *Organized Labor and the Black Worker, 1619–1981* (Haymarket, 2017), 177–87.
27. Reich, *A Working People*, 83.
28. Beth Tompkins Bates, *Pullman Porters and the Rise of Protest Politics in Black America, 1924–1945* (University of North Carolina Press, 2001), 5.
29. Hughes, *The Collected Works*, 1:89–90.
30. Langston Hughes, "The Negro Artist and the Racial Mountain," *Nation* 122 (1926): 692.
31. Langston Hughes, "A Note on Blues," in *The Collected Works of Langston Hughes*, vol. 1, *The Poems: 1921–1940*, ed. Arnold Rampersad (University of Missouri Press, 2001), 73.
32. Sterling A. Brown, *The Collected Poems* (Harper & Row, 1980), 69.
33. Brent Hayes Edwards, *Epistrophies: Jazz and the Literary Imagination* (Harvard University Press, 2017), 63.
34. Brown, *The Collected Poems*, 90.
35. Michael Denning, "Wageless Life," *New Left Review* 66 (2010): 80, 81.
36. Margaret Ronda, "'Work and Wait Unwearying': Dunbar's Georgics," *PMLA* 127, no. 4 (2012): 873.
37. Kenneth Fearing, "Limiting Devices: A Review of *Fine Clothes to the Jew*," *New Masses* 3, no. 5 (1927): 29.
38. Sonya Posmentier, *Cultivation and Catastrophe: The Lyric Ecology of Modern Black Literature* (Johns Hopkins University Press, 2017), 157.
39. Reed, *Freedom Time*, 136.
40. Ezra Pound to Langston Hughes, July 8, 1932, quoted in David Roessel, "'A Racial Act': The Letters of Ezra Pound and Langston Hughes," in *Ezra Pound and African American Modernism*, ed. David Coyle (University Press of New England, 2001), 220–21. One of modernism's most surprising friendships, Pound and Hughes's epistolary relationship began in 1931 after both were published in the journal *Contempo*. The two met for the first and last time in September 1950, when Hughes gave a reading at St. Elizabeths. Pound read Hughes attentively, as did most of the Pound family. In 1932, Pound wrote to Hughes, "My father has read yr. novel with interest.

My wife has read yr. novel with interest. Finally I have read yr. n. with interest." Pound to Hughes, in Roessel, "'A Racial Act,'" 223. In a radio broadcast late in 1941, Pound mentioned that "Langston Hughes has a book in press, probably out by now . . . which is allus a good thing." Ezra Pound, "This War on Youth—On a Generation" (radio broadcast, November 6, 1941), in *Ezra Pound Speaking: Radio Speeches of WWII* (Greenwood, 1978), 15.

41. Langston Hughes, *The Collected Works of Langston Hughes*, vol. 14, *I Wonder as I Wander*, ed. Joseph McLaren (University of Missouri Press, 2003), 103. Hereafter cited parenthetically as *IWAW*.
42. Steven S. Lee has recently drawn attention to significant inconsistencies in Hughes's postwar representation of the script, which, Lee suggests, can be understood as Hughes's attempt "to figure the script as a Soviet straw man to affirm his postwar turn from radicalism." Lee points out that in Grebner's script, the climax of the film is a multiracial labor demonstration in protest of a lynching, followed by an attack by the Ku Klux Klan (KKK) on a Black neighborhood. Lee reports that the film ends with local white workers attempting to help but with victory by the police and the KKK and the arrest or murder of most of the characters. Steven S. Lee, "Langston Hughes's 'Moscow Movie': Reclaiming a Lost Minority Avant-Garde," *Comparative Literature* 67, no. 2 (2015): 187.
43. Rampersad, *The Life of Langston Hughes*, 1:247–51. The film's cancellation was shrouded in mystery. It caused a rancorous split in the group between those who believed the film had been abandoned because of its poor script and Meschrabpom's inefficiency and those who insisted the cause was political (because the film threatened either the USSR's possibility of gaining diplomatic recognition from the United States or the construction of the Dnieprostroi dam, whose construction was overseen by an American engineer) and that the failure constituted a betrayal of the Revolution and the Black workers. The two groups published "minority" and "majority" statements about the status of the film; Hughes was among those who signed the majority statement condemning the charge of political intrigue and sabotage against the Revolution. He also praised Meschrabpom's treatment of the American travelers. Meanwhile, the American press published hyperbolic accounts of the group's suffering. See Rampersad, *The Life of Langston Hughes*, 1:247–51. Langston Hughes, *Letters from Langston: From the Harlem Renaissance to the Red Scare and Beyond*, ed. Evelyn Louise Crawford and MaryLouise Patterson (University of California Press, 2016), 88–91.
44. Hughes writes, "Sergei Eisenstein, after Potemkin at the height of his fame as a film director, gave a party for us shortly after our arrival in Moscow" (*IWAW*, 105).
45. Langston Hughes, "Moscow and Me," in *The Collected Works of Langston Hughes*, vol. 9, *Essays on Art, Race, Politics, and World Affairs*, ed. Christopher C. De Santis (University of Missouri Press, 2002), 59.
46. "The motion-picture theaters, except for a few expensive first-run houses, were ice cold. To go to the movies, one put on more clothing than to go into the street. At the cinema, it was often difficult to see the screen for waves of white vapour rising from the mouths and noses of the spectator like a mist. Lacking heat, these houses also lacked ventilation. Every crack was kept tightly closed against the weather. Full of seldom-bathed comrades, the motion-picture theaters in Moscow smelled like very pungent kennels. I seldom went to the movies that winter" (*IWAW*, 209–10).

3. LANGSTON HUGHES'S CONSTRUCTIVIST POETICS

47. Hughes wrote to Sullivan of the Professional Theater Festival that "all-star casts played. . . . About two hundred theater people from Europe and America came to Moscow." Langston Hughes to Noël Sullivan, June 12, 1933, in Langston Hughes, *Selected Letters of Langston Hughes*, ed. Arnold Rampersad and David E. Roessel (Knopf, 2015), 147.
48. Vladimir Ilyich Lenin, "Russians and Negroes," *Krasnaya Niva*, no. 3 (1925). Reprinted in V. I. Lenin, *Collected Works*, vol. 18, trans. Stepan Apresyan (Progress, 1975), 543–44. Comparative historians made similar claims about the similar trajectory and function of serfdom and slavery. See, for example, Peter Kolchin, *Unfree Labor: American Slavery and Russian Serfdom* (Belknap, 1987).
49. Lenin, "Russians and Negros," 543.
50. Robinson, *Black Marxism*, 222.
51. Robin D. G. Kelley, *Freedom Dreams: The Black Radical Imagination* (Beacon, 2002), 47.
52. For more on the "oppressed nation" thesis, see Robinson, *Black Marxism*, 219–27.
53. See James von Geldern, "Culture, 1900–1945," in *The Cambridge History of Russia*, vol. 3, *The Twentieth Century*, ed. Ronald Grigor Suny (Cambridge University Press, 2006), 594–96. See also Matthew Cullerne Bown and Brandon Taylor, introduction to *Art of the Soviets: Painting, Sculpture, and Architecture in a One-Party State, 1917–1992*, ed. Matthew Cullerne Bown and Brandon Taylor (Manchester University Press, 1993), 1–15.
54. Langston Hughes to Noël Sullivan, January 31, 1933, in Hughes, *Selected Letters*, 139.
55. Hughes, "Moscow and Me," 57.
56. Hughes addresses the purges in his autobiography, providing a response of noncommittal ambiguity and no mention of Meyerhold's torture and death: "As to the purges, trials, the liquidations, the arrests and censorship, deplorable as these things were, I felt about them, in relation to their continual denunciation in the European and American press, much as Frederick Douglass felt before the Civil War when he read in the slave-holding papers that the abolitionists were anarchists, villains, devils and atheists. Douglass said he had the impression that 'Abolition—whatever else it might be—was not unfriendly to the slave.' After all, I suppose, how anything is seen depends on whose eyes look at it" (*IWAW*, 219).
57. See Norris Houghton, *Moscow Rehearsals: An Account of Methods of Production in the Soviet Theater* (Allen & Unwin, 1938).
58. Huntly Carter, *The New Spirit in Russian Theater, 1917–1928* (Brentano's, 1929), 6.
59. Carter, *The New Spirit in Russian Theater*, 6–7.
60. Joseph Macleod, *The New Soviet Theater* (Allen & Unwin, 1943), 8.
61. "The immediate emotions of the audience, their tastes and appreciations, their powers of assimilation—these became the markings of a new barometric chart whereby the director and author in a theater worked." André van Gyseghem, *Theater in Soviet Russia* (Faber and Faber, 1943), 146–47.
62. Lars Kleberg, *Theater as Action: Soviet Russian Avant-Garde Aesthetics*, trans. Charles Rougle (Macmillan, 1993), 26.
63. van Gyseghem, *Theater in Soviet Russia*, 149.
64. See Houghton, *Moscow Rehearsals*, 29–31.
65. Osip Brik, "Our Agenda" (1921), trans. Natasha Kurchanova, *October* 134 (2010): 83.
66. Alekansdr Bogdanov, "Proletarian Poetry," *Labor Monthly* 4, no. 6 (1923): 362.

67. Not to be confused with the Industrial Workers of the World, or "Wobblies," the International Workers Order provided low-cost health and life insurance to its members; it also supported medical clinics, cultural organizations, publications, and even summer camps for members. It was listed as a subversive organization from 1947 and was disbanded in 1954 following a court case with the New York State Insurance Department. See Arthur J. Sabin, *Red Scare in Court: New York Versus the International Workers Order* (University of Pennsylvania Press, 1993).
68. Michael Gold, introduction to *A New Song*, by Langston Hughes (International Workers Order, 1938).
69. At the time of its formation in 1930, the group had between three and five thousand members; by 1938, at the time of the publication of *A New Song*, its membership numbered 141,000. The International Workers Order's membership was extraordinarily diverse, with thirteen ethnic groups represented and a "general" group of anglophone members. Sabin, *Red Scare in Court*, 15–17.
70. For a full account of Hughes's translation, see Ryan James Kernan, *New World Maker: Radical Poetics, Black Internationalism, and the Translations of Langston Hughes* (Northwestern University Press, 2022).
71. Hughes to Van Vechten, March 1, 1933, in Hughes, *Remember Me to Harlem*, 102.
72. Hughes to Van Vechten, May 23, 1933, in Hughes, *Remember Me to Harlem*, 105.
73. Langston Hughes, *A New Song* (International Workers Order, 1938), 14–15.
74. "Chant for Tom Mooney" was inspired by the time Hughes spent in Los Angeles before his trip to the Soviet Union. In a letter forwarded to Hughes from Anna Damon, acting secretary of the International Labor Defense, Mooney wrote, "Langston Hughes visited me at San Quentin prison a few years ago and left a copy of his poem for me at the prison at the time, and I was permitted to receive it and was touched to the very depths of my heart by his sympathetic treatment of my case and my service to the working class movement. Hughes is one of the creative forces in the working class movement and I certainly appreciate the warm sympathetic esteem in which he holds me in his fine verse." Tom Mooney, quoted in Anna Damon to Langston Hughes, February 7, 1936. Langston Hughes Papers, Beinecke Rare Book and Manuscript Library, Yale University, JWJ MSS 26, box 84, folder 1625. Hereafter, "LHP," followed by box and folder numbers.
75. Claude McKay, "Petrograd: May Day, 1923," in *Complete Poems*, ed. William J. Maxwell (University of Illinois Press, 2004), 230.
76. For more on the form of these sonnets, see David B. Hobbs, "Lyric Commodification in McKay's Morocco," *English Language Notes* 59, no. 1 (2021): 181–200.
77. Anna Peters, "Books of the Day," *Daily Worker*, April 30, 1938, 11.
78. Paolo Virno, *A Grammar of the Multitude*, trans. Isabella Bertoletti, James Cascaito, and Andrea Casson (Semiotext[e], 2004), 97, 8. For Hardt and Negri, the multitude is a more expansive category than the industrial working class, made up of "all those who labor and produce under the rule of capital," an idea based "not so much on the current empirical existence of the class but rather on its conditions of possibility." Michael Hardt and Antonio Negri, *Multitude: War and Democracy in the Age of Empire* (Penguin, 2006), 107, 105.
79. Joel Nickels, *The Poetry of the Possible: Spontaneity, Modernism, and the Multitude* (University of Minnesota Press, 2012), 11–12.

80. Julia Vaingurt, "Poetry of Labor and Labor of Poetry: The Universal Language of Alexei Gastev's Biomechanics," *Russian Review* 67, no. 2 (2008): 210.
81. Vsevolod Meyerhold, "Biomechanics," in *Meyerhold on Theater*, trans. and ed. Edward Braun (Bloomsbury, 2016), 243.
82. Meyerhold, "Biomechanics," 245.
83. Meyerhold, "Biomechanics," 244.
84. Wald, *Exiles from a Future Time*, 314.
85. Karl Marx, *Capital*, vol. 1, trans. Ben Fowkes (Penguin, 1990), 443, 447.
86. T. J. Clark, *Farewell to an Idea: Episodes from a History of Modernism* (Yale University Press, 1999), 401.
87. Clark, *Farewell to an Idea*, 401.
88. Raymond Williams, *Marxism and Literature* (Oxford University Press, 1977), 187, 188.
89. Hughes, *The Collected Works*, 1:234–35.
90. Claude McKay, "Soviet Russia and the Negro," *Crisis* 27 (1923): 61–65.
91. Sarah Ehlers, *Left of Poetry: Depression America and the Formation of Modern Poetics* (University of North Carolina Press, 2019), 49.
92. Aleksei Gan, *Constructivism*, trans. Christina Lodder (Tenov, 2013), 36.
93. Nick Worrall, *Modernism to Realism on the Soviet Stage: Tairov, Vakhtangov, Okhlopkov* (Cambridge University Press, 1989), 140.
94. Langston Hughes, "My Adventures as a Social Poet," *Phylon* 8, no. 3 (1947): 205–12; reprinted in *The Collected Works of Langston Hughes*, vol. 9, *Essays on Art, Race, Politics, and World Affairs*, ed. Christopher C. De Santis (University of Missouri Press, 2002), 269–70.
95. A synopsis of a 1943 FBI report reads, "Two poems apparently of a Communist nature written by subject set forth. A publication entitled 'A New Song' by LANGSTON HUGHES and published by the INTERNATIONAL WORKERS ORDER, INC., 80 Fifth Ave., N.Y.C., has been secured." "Langston Hughes," Federal Bureau of Investigation, https://vault.fbi.gov/langston-hughes, accessed February 2025. For more on Hughes's investigation by the FBI, his 1953 appearance before McCarthy's Senate Permanent Subcommittee on Investigations, and his subsequent self-removal from the left, see Mary Helen Washington, *The Other Blacklist: The American Literary and Cultural Left of the 1950s* (Columbia University Press, 2014), 213–14; Rampersad, *The Life of Langston Hughes*, 2:221–31; Jonathan Scott, "Advanced, Repressed, and Popular: Langston Hughes During the Cold War," *College Literature* 33, no. 2 (2006): 30–51.
96. "A major portion of my income is derived from lecturing in the Negro schools and colleges of the South. As you no doubt know, many of these institutions are now being forced by state boards or local politicians to screen their speakers according to the highly controversial Attorney General's list. As I am sure you know, too, Negro speakers do not have the vast area of white women's clubs (with their teas and other social aspects) from which to secure engagements. So our fees must come almost entirely from Negro institutions. Most Negro college heads are certainly not in sympathy with censorship or blacklisting, but seemingly must at this period submit to it in order to maintain their already decreasing grants. And some colleges now ask speakers to indicate on signing of contracts that they do not belong to 'listed' organizations." Langston Hughes to Richard Morford, executive

director of the National Council of American-Soviet Friendship, May 27, 1952. LHP, box 118, folder 224.
97. Rampersad, *The Life of Langston Hughes*, 2:122.
98. Richard Wright, *12 Million Black Voices: A Folk History of the Negro in the United States* (Viking, 1941), 35.
99. Richard Wright, "Blueprint for Negro Writing," in *Within the Circle: An Anthology of African American Literary Criticism from the Harvard Renaissance to the Present*, ed. Angelyn Mitchell (Duke University Press, 1994), 100.
100. Langston Hughes, *The Collected Works of Langston Hughes*, vol. 5, *The Plays to 1942: Mulatto to The Sun Do Move*, ed. Leslie Catherine Sanders and Nancy Johnston (University of Missouri Press, 2002), 538.
101. Hughes, *The Collected Works*, 5:540.
102. Hughes, *The Collected Works*, 5:540.
103. Hughes, *The Collected Works*, 5:570.
104. Wright, "Blueprint for Negro Writing," 106.
105. Julia Vaingurt, *Wonderlands of the Avant-Garde: Technology and the Arts in Russia of the 1920s* (Northwestern University Press, 2013), 108.
106. Maria Tsantsanoglou, "The Soviet Icarus: From the Dream of Free Flight to the Nightmare of Free Fall," in *Utopian Reality: Reconstructing Culture in Revolutionary Russia and Beyond*, ed. Christina Lodder, Maria Kokkori, and Maria Mileeva (Brill, 2013), 44.
107. Vladimir Tatlin, quoted in Vaingurt, *Wonderlands of the Avant-Garde*, 108.
108. Svetlana Boym, *Another Freedom: The Alternative History of an Idea* (University of Chicago Press, 2010), 214.
109. Joshua Kotin, *Utopias of One* (Princeton University Press, 2017), 1.

4. REPRODUCING GERTRUDE STEIN

1. Silvia Federici, "Social Reproduction Theory: History, Issues and Present Challenges," *Radical Philosophy* 204 (2019): 55.
2. Mariarosa Dalla Costa and Selma James, *The Power of Women and the Subversion of the Community* (Falling Wall, 1975), 18.
3. Nancy Fraser, "Contradictions of Capitalism and Care," *New Left Review* 100 (2016): 101.
4. Fraser, "Contradictions of Capitalism and Care," 103. For more on this contradiction, see Lise Vogel, *Marxism and the Oppression of Women: Toward a Unitary Theory* (Brill, 2013).
5. Michael Gold, "Gertrude Stein: A Literary Idiot," in *Change the World!* (Lawrence and Wishart, 1937), 26.
6. Janet Malcolm, *Two Lives: Gertrude and Alice* (Yale University Press, 2007), 40.
7. Ulla E. Dydo, *Gertrude Stein: The Language That Rises 1923–1934* (Northwestern University Press, 2003), 10; Dana Cairns Watson, *Gertrude Stein and the Essence of What Happens* (Vanderbilt University Press, 2005), 110.
8. Karen Leick, *Gertrude Stein and the Making of an American Celebrity* (Routledge, 2009), 154; Barbara Will, *Gertrude Stein, Modernism, and the Problem of "Genius"* (Edinburgh University Press, 2000), 161.

9. Marjorie Perloff, *Wittgenstein's Ladder: Poetic Language and the Strangeness of the Ordinary* (University of Chicago Press, 1996), 85.
10. Astrid Lorange, *How Reading Is Written: A Brief Index to Gertrude Stein* (Wesleyan University Press, 2014), 160.
11. Gertrude Stein, *Wars I Have Seen* (B. T. Batsford, 1945), 1.
12. Gertrude Stein, *Everybody's Autobiography* (William Heinemann, 1938).
13. Natalia Cecire, "Ways of Not Reading Gertrude Stein," *ELH* 82, no.1 (2015): 304.
14. Gertrude Stein, "Picasso," in *Portraits and Prayers* (Random House, 1934), 20.
15. Catharine R. Stimpson, "The Somagrams of Gertrude Stein," *Poetics Today* 6, nos. 1–2 (1985): 78.
16. Kathi Weeks, *The Problem with Work: Feminism, Marxism, Antiwork Politics, and Postwork Imaginaries* (Duke University Press, 2011), 29.
17. As I discussed in chapter 2, to Lola Ridge, we can add Mina Loy and H. D. to the list of modernist women who left their children in the care of others; the list of queer modernist women who did not have children is much longer.
18. Elizabeth Freeman, "Committed to the End: On Caretaking, Rereading, and Queer Theory," in *Long Term: Essays on Queer Commitment* (Duke University Press, 2021), 37."
19. Kennedy wrote to Stein, "I want to thank you for the extremely interesting evening last night. Though in some ways, it may have been a case of pearls before swine, I can assure you that the swine could not have enjoyed himself more. Thank you again." John F. Kennedy to Gertrude Stein, Gertrude Stein and Alice B. Toklas Papers, Yale Collection of American Literature, Beinecke Rare Book and Manuscript Library, Yale University, box 113, folder 2322 (hereafter "GSP," followed by box and folder numbers). In August 1934, Carmel Snow of *Harper's Bazaar* asked Stein whether she could "be tempted to do a fashion article" because the "fashions shown in the new couture collections are tremendously interesting and amusing, featuring picture dresses of 1880 and romantic styles." Carmel Snow to Gertrude Stein, August 20, 1934, GSP, box 110, folder 2218. For a full account of Steine's glittering return to America, see Roy Morris Jr., *Gertrude Stein Has Arrived: The Homecoming of a Literary Legend* (Johns Hopkins University Press, 2019).
20. Stein, *Everybody's Autobiography*, 28.
21. Stein, *Everybody's Autobiography*, 32.
22. A rejection letter from Alfred C. Fifield is frequently the subject of popular essays: "Being only one, having only one pair of eyes, having only one time, having only one life, I cannot read your M.S. three or four times. Not even one time. Only one look, only one look is enough. Hardly one copy would sell here. Hardly one. Hardly one." See, for example, Caitlin Schneider, "Read a Publisher's Rejection Letter to Gertrude Stein," *Mental Floss*, June 30, 2015, https://www.mentalfloss.com/article/65717/read-publishers-rejection-letter-gertrude-stein.
23. Austin Harrison to Gertrude Stein, January 29, 1912, GSP, YCAL MSS 76, box 105, folder 2082.
24. Ellery Sedgwick to Gertrude Stein, October 25, 1919, GSP, box 97, folder 1825.
25. Sedgwick to Stein, December 4, 1919, GSP, box 97, folder 1825.
26. Sedgwick to Stein, February 27, 1924, GSP, box 97, folder 1825.
27. Sedgwick to Stein, May 1, June 30, and July 28, 1924, GSP, box 97, folder 1825. He emphasizes, "I am afraid that the decision which I conveyed to you in my last letter ought to be final."

4. REPRODUCING GERTRUDE STEIN

28. Blanche Knopf to Gertrude Stein, December 7, 1927, GSP, box 113, folder 2335.
29. Stein had had *Three Lives* printed at her own expense with the vanity press Grafton Press. Over a decade later, Stein and Toklas would sell a Picasso painting to fund the establishment of Plain Edition, which printed five of Stein's works.
30. Kegan Paul, Trench, Trubner and Co. to Gertrude Stein, May 1 and May 4, 1928, GSP, box 113, folder 2317.
31. Gertrude Stein to Carl Van Vechten, April 18, 1916, in *The Letters of Gertrude Stein and Carl Van Vechten*, ed. Edward Burns (Columbia University Press, 2013), 53.
32. Notebook, "Literature": notes on status of writings submitted to publishers, GSP, box 92, folder 1707. The Beinecke librarians have dated the notebook 1920.
33. Gertrude Stein, handwritten draft of a letter, undated, GSP, box 134, folder 2955.
34. Stein, handwritten draft of a letter, undated, GSP, box 110, folder 2217.
35. Donald Gallup, "The Making of *The Making of Americans*," in *Fernhurst, Q.E.D., and Other Writings*, by Gertrude Stein (Liveright, 1971), 185–214.
36. Stein to Van Vechten, March 15, 1923, in Burns, *The Letters of Gertrude Stein and Carl Van Vechten*, 68.
37. Van Vechten to Stein, October 22, 1923, in Burns, *The Letters of Gertrude Stein and Carl Van Vechten*, 90.
38. Gallup, "The Making of *The Making of Americans*," 185.
39. Marianne Moore to Stein, July 13, 1926, GSP, box 104, folder 2039. Moore became one of Stein's occasional publishers. Over the following two years, *The Dial* would publish Stein's essay "Composition as Explanation," reimbursing her eighty dollars, and excerpts from *A Long Gay Book*, for which Stein was paid fifty-five dollars.
40. Gallup, "The Making of *The Making of Americans*," 213.
41. Gertrude Stein, *The Making of Americans* (Dalkey, 1995).
42. Jennifer Ashton, "Gertrude Stein for Anyone," *ELH* 64, no. 1 (1997): 289.
43. Stein, *The Making of Americans*, 34.
44. Stein, *The Making of Americans*, 34.
45. Stein, *The Making of Americans*, 34.
46. Gertrude Stein, "A Transatlantic Interview," January 5–6, 1946, in *A Primer for the Gradual Understanding of Gertrude Stein*, ed. Robert Bartlett Haas (Black Sparrow, 1971), 32.
47. Stein, *Everybody's Autobiography*, 32.
48. James Laughlin to Stein, fall 1935, GSP, box 114, folder 2356.
49. But also, crucially, the camera shutter. Michael Davidson writes that "while Stein was skeptical about Futurism's fetish of the machine, she drew upon new modes of mechanical reproduction—like the cinema—to extend and refine her characterological interests. Modern portraiture, like the automobile, translates the dynamic motion of the internal combustion engine into forward motion." Michael Davidson, *Ghostlier Demarcations: Modern Poetry and the Material Word* (University of California Press, 1997), 47. Similarly, Barrett Watten writes that "Stein saw in Ford's modern poetics of repetition a mode of production that was, in explicitly literary terms, analogous to her modernist one." Barrett Watten, *The Constructivist Moment: From Material Text to Cultural Poetics* (Wesleyan University Press, 2003), 1.
50. Stein, "Picasso," 20.
51. Stein, "Picasso," 19.
52. Jean Walton, "Female Peristalsis," *differences* 13, no. 2 (2002): 58

4. REPRODUCING GERTRUDE STEIN

53. Walton, "Female Peristalsis," 59.
54. Wyndham Lewis, *Time and Western Man* (Chatto & Windus, 1927), 61.
55. Jessica Burstein, *Cold Modernism: Literature, Fashion, Art* (Pennsylvania State University Press, 2012), 34. Juliana Chow sees the mechanical motions of Stein's "Portraits" as a project of interrogating labor in terms of its "going" or its "power to live or give life." For Chow, Stein turns to the machine for how the mechanical poses the question of what life or energy is and to value labor in terms of its ability to create further life. Juliana Chow, "Vitalism in Gertrude Stein's Work," *Arizona Quarterly* 69, no. 4 (2013): 81.
56. Lewis, *Time and Western Man*, 78. Emphasis in the original.
57. Janice Williams Rutherford, *Selling Mrs. Consumer: Christine Frederick and the Rise of Household Efficiency* (University of Georgia Press, 2003), 37. In the late nineteenth century schools began offering instruction in home economics, and by 1905 thirty-six land-grant institutions in the West and Midwest offered home economics courses.
58. Ann Douglas, *The Feminization of American Culture* (Papermac, 1996), 6.
59. Charlotte Perkins Gilman, *The Home: Its Work and Influence* (William Heinemann, 1903), 89.
60. Gilman, *The Home*, 97.
61. Gilman, *The Home*, 330, 117, 347.
62. As Suzanne Raitt points out, this framing preserves a gender hierarchy in which, despite the entrance of masculine factory management into the feminine world of domestic labor, "men are still in charge of the conceptualization of the private sphere." Suzanne Raitt, "The Rhetoric of Efficiency in Early Modernism," *Modernism/Modernity* 13, no. 1 (2006): 842.
63. Christine Frederick, *The New Housekeeping: Efficiency Studies in Home Management* (Doubleday, 1913), viii. For more on Frederick's influence on modernism, see Victoria Rosner, *Machines for Living* (Oxford University Press, 2020).
64. Frederick, *The New Housekeeping*, 5.
65. Frederick, *The New Housekeeping*, 10.
66. Gertrude Stein, *Tender Buttons* (Claire Marie, 1914), 11.
67. Mia You, "Buttons and Holes: Picasso and Stein at the Bon Marché," *ELH* 87, no. 3 (2020): 820.
68. Stein, *Tender Buttons*, 16–17.
69. Sara Ahmed, *What's the Use? On the Uses of Use* (Duke University Press, 2019), 207–8.
70. Ahmed, *What's the Use?*, 215.
71. Sophie Lewis, *Full Surrogacy Now!* (Verso, 2019), 167.
72. Gertrude Stein, "Miss Furr and Miss Skeene," in *Writings 1903-32* (Library of America, 1998), 307.
73. *The Oxford English Dictionary* lists Miss Furr and Miss Skeene as the earliest use of "gay" to mean homosexual. The sexualized meaning of the word was not widely current until the 1950s, and Stein's use of the term is ambiguous, even though the portrait is clearly about intimacy between two women. *Oxford English Dictionary*, "gay (*adj.*, *adv.*, & *n.*)," https://doi.org/10.1093/OED/9277815405, accessed February 2025.
74. John Ashbery, "The Impossible," *Poetry* (1957): 250.

4. REPRODUCING GERTRUDE STEIN

75. Ashbery, "The Impossible," 250.
76. During Stein's lifetime, the poem was published only in excerpts in *Poetry*, *Orbes*, and in *Life and Letters Today* in 1936 and 1937, and in the *Muse Anthology of Poetry* in 1938. Stanza LXI was printed in the catalog for a 1932 Francis Picabia exhibition with a French translation by Marcel Duchamp.
77. Ulla E. Dydo, "How to Read Gertrude Stein: The Manuscript of 'Stanzas in Meditation,'" *TEXT: Transactions of the Society for Textual Scholarship*, vol. 1, ed. D. C. Greetham and W. Speed Hill (AMS, 1981): 275–78; Joan Retallack, "On Not Not Reading *Stanzas in Meditation*," in Gertrude Stein, *Stanzas in Meditation: The Corrected Edition*, ed. Susannah Hollister and Emily Setina (Yale University Press, 2012), 19.
78. Stein, *Stanzas in Meditation*, part 4, Stanza XIV, line 17. Hereafter, section, stanza, and page number are cited parenthetically.
79. Dydo paints a compelling picture of an intense and long-lasting fight between Stein and Toklas and of Stein's dependence on Toklas's approval. "One gets the impression," she writes, "that during the summer of 1932 each of the two women goaded and hurt the other wherever possible." Ulla E. Dydo, "'Stanzas in Meditation': The Other Autobiography," *Chicago Review* 35, no. 2 (1985): 13.
80. Susannah Hollister and Emily Setina, preface to Stein, *Stanzas in Meditation*, ix.
81. Retallack, "On Not Not Reading *Stanzas in Meditation*," 9.
82. Melanie Micir, *The Passion Projects: Modernist Women, Intimate Archives, Unfinished Lives* (Princeton University Press, 2019), 10.
83. Micir documents the battle over Stein's estate and the disinheritance of Toklas. Micir, *The Passion Projects*, 88–94.
84. Hannah Roche makes a compelling version of this argument by attending to the "female labor" carried out by Stein, the "little hubby" who "gave birth to the writing." See Hannah Roche, *The Outside Thing: Modernist Lesbian Romance* (Columbia University Press, 2019), 66.
85. A selection of the letters were edited by Kay Turner; see Kay Turner, ed., *Baby Precious Always Shines: Selected Love Notes Between Gertrude Stein and Alice Toklas* (St. Martin's, 2000). The remaining unpublished poems are held in the Beinecke library.
86. Gertrude Stein to Alice Toklas, GSP, YCAL MSS 76, box 133, folder 2920.
87. Stein to Toklas, GSP, box 133, folder 2925.
88. Roche, *The Outside Thing*, 66.
89. Stein to Toklas, GSP, box 133, folder 2920; Stein to Toklas, GSP, box 133, folder 2925; Toklas to Stein, GSP, box 133, folder 2925; Toklas to Stein, GSP, box 133, folder 2929; Toklas to Stein, GSP, box 133, folder 2929.
90. Kay Turner, "This Very Beautiful Form of Literature: An Introduction to the Love Notes Between Gertrude Stein and Alice B. Toklas," in *Baby Precious Always Shines*, 7.
91. Stein to Toklas, GSP, box 133, folder 2920.
92. Stein to Toklas, GSP, box 133, folder 2924.
93. Lauren Berlant, "Intimacy: A Special Issue," *Critical Inquiry* 24, no. 2 (1998): 281, 282, 286.
94. Gertrude Stein, *Narration: Four Lectures* (University of Chicago Press, 1935), 55.
95. Julie Taylor, "On Holding and Being Held: Hart Crane's Queer Intimacy," *Twentieth Century Literature* 60, vol. 3 (2014): 312.

4. REPRODUCING GERTRUDE STEIN

96. Jennifer Cooke, "Making a Scene: Towards an Anatomy of Contemporary Literary Intimacies," in *Scenes of Intimacy: Reading, Writing and Theorizing Contemporary Literature*, ed. Jennifer Cooke (Bloomsbury, 2013), 7.
97. Ashbery, "The Impossible," 251.
98. Alice B. Toklas, *The Alice B. Toklas Cookbook* (Lyons, 1984), 266.
99. Toklas, *The Alice B. Toklas Cookbook*, 277.
100. Lyn Hejinian, "Two Stein Talks," in *The Language of Inquiry* (University of California Press, 2000), 117.
101. Eve Kosofsky Sedgwick, *Tendencies* (Duke University Press, 1993), 8.
102. Elizabeth Freeman, *Beside You in Time: Sense Methods and Queer Sociabilities in the American Nineteenth Century* (Duke University Press, 2019), 154, 5, 155.
103. Toklas, *The Alice B. Toklas Cookbook*, 266, 280.
104. Lyn Hejinian, "The Rejection of Closure," in *The Language of Inquiry* (University of California Press, 2000), 41.
105. Lyn Hejinian, *My Life and My Life in the Nineties* (Wesleyan University Press, 2013), 3.
106. Hejinian, *My Life and My Life in the Nineties*, 133.
107. Hejinian, *My Life and My Life in the Nineties*, 48.
108. Hejinian, "The Rejection of Closure," 56.

5. LORINE NIEDECKER AND THE WORK OF RESTRAINT

1. From an article by August Derleth in the *Jefferson County Union*, cited in *Niedecker and the Correspondence with Zukofsky*, ed. Jenny Penberthy (Cambridge University Press, 1993), 156.
2. Lorine Niedecker to Louis Zukofsky, dated by Zukofsky December 8, 1948, in Penberthy, *Niedecker and the Correspondence*, 156.
3. In the early 1950s, Zukofsky asked Mark Van Doren to recommend Niedecker for a National Institute Award; she received a $200 check with "Writers' and Artists' Relief Fund" written on the reverse. Penberthy, *Niedecker and the Correspondence*, 204.
4. Niedecker to Zukofsky, April 3, 1963, in Penberthy, *Niedecker and the Correspondence*, 331.
5. Lorine Niedecker, *Collected Works*, ed. Jenny Penberthy (University of California Press, 2002), 142. Hereafter cited parenthetically as *CW*.
6. Rachel Blau DuPlessis, *Blue Studios: Poetry and Its Cultural Work* (University of Alabama Press, 2006), 150.
7. Niedecker did not have plumbing installed in her house until 1962. In a 1947 letter to Zukofsky she writes, "Nights I hang over the porch filling my small oil can to fill oil heater. I go to folks for my drinking water as my own well water isn't clear yet—I'm not home enough to pump it to the stage fit for using." Niedecker to Zukofsky, undated (probably November 1947), in Penberthy, *Niedecker and the Correspondence*, 143.
8. George Oppen to June Degnan Oppen, October 31, 1963, in George Oppen, *Selected Letters*, ed. Rachel Blau DuPlessis (Duke University Press, 1990), 93.
9. Rachel Blau DuPlessis and Peter Quartermain, introduction to *The Objectivist Nexus: Essays in Cultural Poetics*, ed. Rachel Blau DuPlessis and Peter Quartermain (University of Alabama Press, 1999), 17.

10. The timeline proposed here by Silliman hangs on Oppen's twenty-eight years of silence after 1934's *Discrete Series*. The first phase of Objectivism is its emergence in the 1930s; the second is its silence; the third is its postwar reemergence. For Silliman, third-phase Objectivism is both more various and more cohesive than its poets' early work. He writes that Oppen's return to poetry transformed Objectivist poetics "from the aesthetically radical and oppositional poetry of the early thirties to a more conservative (aesthetically, if not politically)" version of itself, which is not a judgment I hold to. Ron Silliman, "Third-Phase Objectivism," *Paideuma* 10, no. 1 (1981): 85–91.
11. See Elizabeth Willis, "The Poetics of Affinity: Lorine Niedecker, William Morris, and the Art of Work," *Contemporary Literature* 46, no. 4 (2005): 579–603.
12. For an extensive analysis of both the techniques and the political stakes of this movement, see Julia Bryan-Wilson, *Fray: Art + Textile Politics* (University of Chicago Press, 2017).
13. Nancy Fraser, *Fortunes of Feminism: From State-Managed Capitalism to Neoliberal Crisis* (Verso, 2013), 159.
14. Julia Bryan-Wilson and Benjamin Piekut, "Amateurism," *Third Text* 34, no. 1 (2020): 14.
15. A facsimile edition of the version Niedecker sent to Cid Corman, edited by John Harkey, was published in 2012 by Lost & Found. Lorine Niedecker, "Homemade Poems," City University of New York Graduate Center, Center for the Humanities, https://centerforthehumanities.org/product/lorine-niedecker-homemade-poems/, accessed February 2025.
16. "Homemade Poems," holograph manuscript, October 1964, Cid Corman Collection of Papers, Henry W. and Albert A. Berg Collection of English and American Literature, New York Public Library.
17. Niedecker to Zukofsky, October 13, 1964. She and Al had just returned from Blackhawk Island to Millen's apartment in Milwaukee. "Then yesterday," Niedecker writes, "I painted storm windows while Al did other painting. I painted pictures, tho, too!" Penberthy, *Niedecker and the Correspondence*, 350.
18. "Handmade Poems," holograph manuscript, September 1964, Louis Zukofsky Collection, Harry Ransom Center, University of Texas at Austin, box 33, folder 6. Hereafter, "LZC," followed by box and folder numbers.
19. The calendar poems were written deep in Niedecker's surrealist period. For more on her surrealism, see Ruth Jennison, "Scrambling Narrative: Niedecker and the White Dome of Logic," *Journal of Narrative Theory* 41, no. 1 (2011): 53–81.
20. Lorine Niedecker to Celia Zukofsky, December 19, 1949, LZC, box 33, folder 5.
21. DuPlessis, *Blue Studios*, 153.
22. Willis, "The Poetics of Affinity," 585.
23. In the October "Homemade Poems" edition, line eight read, "A delicacy—the marrow." It was revised to the present text and published in a group of five poems in *Poetry* in August 1965. Niedecker, *Collected Works*, 426.
24. Lorine Niedecker to Cid Corman, postmarked June 8, 1965, in *Between Your House and Mine: The Letters of Lorine Niedecker to Cid Corman, 1960–1970*, ed. Lisa Pater Faranda (Duke University Press, 1986), 59.
25. Niedecker to Corman, July 16, 1966, in Faranda, *Between Your House and Mine*, 59, 91.

26. Margot Peters, *Lorine Niedecker: A Poet's Life* (University of Wisconsin Press, 2011), 130.
27. Niedecker to Zukofsky, November 4, 1963, in Penberthy, *Niedecker and the Correspondence*, 336.
28. Niedecker describes their meeting earlier that year to Zukofsky: "The first time Al Millen came (about the house—wanted to buy it, the one in trouble) I thought: if this relationship grows it would be something like Lady Chatterley's lover. By this time, I see there's more and more actually in common between us—he really reads, knows who I mean by Voltaire, Bertrand Russell, likes H. G. Wells' fiction, knows who Robert Frost was (when I tried to tell him what meant so much to me, poetry).... And he has a lovely, lovely humour. *I know this is it.* What an adjustment for me—too bad for me to become used to daily companionship, to deep affection, to human (!) happiness. I fear it, upsetting to the other thing I've built up in me that, give me another couple of years, would withstand the world, would never need any other life but itself and things like money, peoples' follies and hatreds and all the silly coming and going wouldn't even be there.... What—what—what? I'll marry him. Somehow I'll work it out, time and space for poetry." Niedecker to Zukofsky, April 10, 1963, in Penberthy, *Niedecker and the Correspondence*, 331. In her subsequent letter, Niedecker answers Zukofsky's query: "No, not *sure*,—is anyone ever?" Niedecker to Zukofsky, "Mon" (probably April 1963), in Penberthy, *Niedecker and the Correspondence*, 332.
29. Niedecker to Zukofsky, December 13, 1963, in Penberthy, *Niedecker and the Correspondence*, 338. "We had fun in a Good Will Industries store—a person can sometimes pick up antiques there—saw nothing in that way but the old flatirons that get heated on the range. But we bought a very solid, new-looking card table for 89c plus 4c tax. We like this to eat on at suppertime in the living room in front of the TV. I like funny things like The Flintstones or the Danny Thomas show or Benny Goodman." The acceptance of TV shows a change of heart; in May 1954, Niedecker wrote to Zukofsky, "Tornado warnings here—one yesterday evening but I stayed put in my peanut shell cottage. I could have gone to the McA's who are eternally watching TV in their basement (really only ground floor) room. It shows where I stand with TV—prefer a tornado to it." Niedecker to Zukofsky, May 3, 1954, LZC, box 25, folder 1.
30. Niedecker to Zukofsky, March 11, 1964, LZC, box 25, folder 9.
31. "Sewing bedroom curtains—you'd love that room." Niedecker to Zukofsky, June 12, 1964, LZC, box 25, folder 9.
32. A facsimile of the cooking book is available online from the University of Wisconsin. Lorine Niedecker, "A Cooking Book," University of Wisconsin Digital Collections, https://search.library.wisc.edu/digital/AGUYGSTZFBI4CV9C, accessed February 2025. A transcribed version was published in 1992 by Bob and Suzan Arnold at Longhouse Press.
33. Niedecker, "A Cooking Book."
34. In *Santayana: The Later Years*, Cory omitted the paragraph that this sentence concludes, likely because Pound was still alive at the time. See John McCormick, *George Santayana: A Biography* (Knopf, 1987), 399–401.
35. George Santayana to Daniel MacGhie Cory, in George Santayana, *The Letters of George Santayana*, vol. 5, book 6, ed. W. G. Holzberger (MIT Press, 2004), 48.

36. DuPlessis, *Blue Studios*, 142.
37. Niedecker to Zukofsky, August 25, 1964, LZC, box 25, folder 9.
38. Walt Whitman, *Leaves of Grass* (1855 version), in Walt Whitman, *Complete Poetry and Collected Prose* (Library of America, 1982) 89.
39. Peter Riley, *Whitman, Melville, Crane, and the Labors of American Poetry: Against Vocation* (Oxford University Press, 2019), 58.
40. Jasper Bernes, "John Ashbery's Free Indirect Labor," *Modern Language Quarterly* 74, no. 4 (2013): 521.
41. John Wilkinson, "Jim the Jerk: Bathos and Loveliness in the Poetry of James Schuyler," in *On Bathos: Literature, Art, Music*, ed. Sara Crangle and Peter Nicholls (Continuum, 2010), 71.
42. Jonathan Katz, "Oral History Interview with Ann Wilson, 2009 April 19–2010 July 12," Smithsonian Archives of American Art, April 19, 2009–July 12, 2010, https://www.aaa.si.edu/collections/interviews/oral-history-interview-ann-wilson-15968.
43. The press came to a dramatic end in 1950 when James Decker's younger sister, Dorothy, shot Ervin Tax, who had purchased the press in 1948, and then herself.
44. Karl Marx, *Capital*, vol. 3, part 5, trans. David Fernbach (Penguin, 1992), 274.
45. Ruth Jennison, "29|73|08: Poetry, Crisis, and a Hermeneutics of Limits," *Mediations: Journal of the Marxist Literary Group* 28, no. 2 (2015): 37–46.
46. Margaret Ronda, *Remainders: American Poetry at Nature's End* (Stanford University Press, 2018), 28.
47. Peters, *Lorine Niedecker*, 100.
48. "No, don't send me money," she objected to Zukofsky, "I'm eating off the folks and staying alive." Niedecker to Zukofsky, February 5, 1951, in Penberthy, *Niedecker and the Correspondence*, 176. In March 1956, she was paid twenty dollars for typing a story about early farm life in her region: "My writin' man—Banker is his name—sent me $20 worth of typing to do last month and yesterday a story about early farm life in this community. Said on his folks' farm, a watch was plowed down (it had cost $1.00) for a year and on recovery ran again. Also described one of our first stores—raisins or dried grapes in that day were kept in an open barrel in the store." Niedecker to Zukofsky, March 19, 1956, LZC, box 25, folder 2. After she started at the hospital, Niedecker did occasional typing work for Banker on evenings and weekends.
49. Peters, *Lorine Niedecker*, 100.
50. Niedecker to Zukofsky, February 4, 1957, in Penberthy, *Niedecker and the Correspondence*, 232–33.
51. Mignon Duffy, "Doing the Dirty Work: Gender, Race, and Reproductive Labor in Historical Perspective," *Gender and Society* 21, no. 3 (2007): 322.
52. For an account of the rise of care work as interwoven with industrial decline, see Gabriel Winant, *The Next Shift: The Fall of Industry and the Rise of Health Care in Rust Belt America* (Harvard University Press, 2021).
53. The term "institutional service work" is Evelyn Nakano Glenn's. Evelyn Nakano Glenn, "From Servitude to Service Work: Historical Continuities in the Racial Division of Paid Reproductive Labor," *Signs* 18, no. 1 (1992): 20. The terminology of "nurturant" and "non-nurturant" is Duffy's. See Duffy, "Doing the Dirty Work."
54. The racial division of labor is particularly sharp in cleaning. Nakano Glenn writes that cleaning and building services (i.e., work done by maids, housemen, janitors,

and cleaners), which she calls "prototypically 'dirty work,'" are at the sharpest end of this. In Memphis in 1980, one of every twelve Black women (8.2 percent) did this kind of work, and of the women doing this work, 88.1 percent were Black. In contrast, one of every two hundred white women (0.5 percent) were so employed. Nakano Glenn, "From Servitude to Service Work," 20.

55. The classic text on the invisible burden of emotional labor remains Arlie Russell Hochschild, *The Managed Heart: Commercialisation of Human Feeling* (University of California Press, 1983).
56. Arlie Russell Hochschild, *The Second Shift: Working Parents and the Revolution at Home* (Viking, 1989).
57. See Nona Y. Glazer, "The Home as Workshop: Women as Amateur Nurses and Medical Care Providers," *Gender and Society* 4, no. 4 (1990): 479–99.
58. Rae Armantrout, "Darkinfested," in *Radical Vernacular: Lorine Niedecker and the Poetics of Place*, ed. Elizabeth Willis (University of Iowa Press, 2008), 105.
59. George Oppen, *New Collected Poems* (New Directions, 2008), 61.
60. Anahid Nersessian, *Utopia, Limited: Romanticism and Adjustment* (Harvard University Press, 2015), 3.
61. A poem from *For Paul and Other Poems* describes a woman as "united for life to serve / silver. Possessed." Niedecker, *Collected Works*, 170.
62. Willis, "The Poetics of Affinity," 581, 583.
63. Nersessian, *Utopia, Limited*, 12, 16.
64. Sara Ahmed, *The Promise of Happiness* (Duke University Press, 2010), 166, 167.
65. Niedecker to Zukofsky, December 13, 1963, in Penberthy, *Niedecker and the Correspondence*, 339.
66. The history of laundry is particular, a "rare example of a domestic process, once industrialized, that returned to the home." The industrial laundries that had largely replaced communal washing by the late nineteenth century (and largely ousted the live-in laundress) waned with the manufacture of mechanized washing machines targeted at women consumers beginning in the 1920s and 1930s and escalating in the postwar mania for domestic goods. Arwen Palmer Mohun, "Laundrymen Construct Their World: Gender and the Transformation of a Domestic Task to an Industrial Process," *Technology and Culture* 38, no. 1 (1997): 120.
67. Niedecker to Zukofsky, Armistice Day, 1964, LZC, box 25, folder 9.
68. George Oppen to June Degnan Oppen, October 31, 1963, in Oppen, *Selected Letters*, 93.
69. Oppen to Degnan Oppen, October 31, 1963, in Oppen, *Selected Letters*, 94.
70. Bryan-Wilson, *Fray*, 20. Emphasis in the original.
71. Julietta Singh, *Unthinking Mastery: Dehumanism and Decolonial Entanglements* (Duke University Press, 2017), 10.
72. Lorine Niedecker, typed manuscript, "Upper Mississippi River Vacation," July 1963, LZC, box 25, folder 8.
73. Bernadette Mayer, *Works and Days* (New Directions, 2016), 30. Hereafter cited parenthetically as *WD*.
74. Bernadette Mayer, *Milkweed Smithereens* (New Directions, 2022), 82, 77. Italics in the original.
75. For more on Mayer, feminization, and social reproduction, see Amy De'Ath, "Manly Things," *Post45*, July 27, 2021, https://post45.org/2021/07/manly-things/.

CODA: DRAFTING MODERNISM

1. Rachel Blau DuPlessis, *Blue Studios: Poetry and Its Cultural Work* (University of Alabama Press, 2006), 4.
2. DuPlessis, *Blue Studios*, 5.
3. Rachel Blau DuPlessis, *Interstices* (Subpress, 2014), 11.
4. Rachel Blau DuPlessis, *Surge: Drafts 96–114* (Salt, 2013), 1.
5. DuPlessis, *Surge*, 1–2.
6. Rachel Blau DuPlessis, *Drafts 1–38: Toll* (Wesleyan University Press, 2001), 99.
7. DuPlessis, *Blue Studios*, 210. For more on DuPlessis's practice of midrash, see Paul Jaussen, "The Poetics of Midrash in Rachel Blau DuPlessis's *Drafts*," *Contemporary Literature* 53, no. 1 (2012): 114–42.
8. DuPlessis, *Blue Studios*, 210.
9. DuPlessis, *Surge*, 13.
10. Basil Bunting, "On the Fly Leaf of Pound's Cantos," in *Collected Poems*, 2nd ed. (Fulcrum, 1970), 122.

BIBLIOGRAPHY

UNPUBLISHED AND ARCHIVAL MATERIAL

Cid Corman Collection of Papers. Henry W. and Albert A. Berg Collection of English and American Literature. New York Public Library. Berg Coll MSS Corman.

Ezra Pound Papers. Yale Collection of American Literature. Beinecke Rare Book and Manuscript Library, Yale University. YCAL MSS 43.

Gertrude Stein and Alice B. Toklas Papers. Yale Collection of American Literature. Beinecke Rare Book and Manuscript Library, Yale University. YCAL MSS 76.

Langston Hughes Papers, 1862–1980. James Weldon Johnson Collection, Yale Collection of American Literature. Beinecke Rare Book and Manuscript Library, Yale University. JWJ MSS 26.

Lola Ridge Papers. Smith College Special Collections, Smith College. SSC-MS-00131.

Louis Zukofsky Collection. Harry Ransom Center, University of Texas at Austin. MS-04641.

PUBLISHED MATERIAL

Adorno, Theodor W. *Aesthetic Theory*. Translated by Robert Hullot-Kentor. Continuum, 2002.

Adorno, Theodor W. *Notes to Literature*. Translated by Rolf Tiedemann. Columbia University Press, 1991.

Ahmed, Sara. *The Promise of Happiness*. Duke University Press, 2010.

Ahmed, Sara. *What's the Use? On the Uses of Use*. Duke University Press, 2019.

Aldridge, Delores. "Black Women in the Economic Marketplace: A Battle Unfinished." *Journal of Social and Behavioural Sciences* (1975): 48–62.

Altieri, Charles. "The Objectivist Tradition." *Chicago Review* 5, no. 3 (1979): 5–22.

Altieri, Charles. *Self and Sensibility in Contemporary American Poetry*. Cambridge University Press, 1984.
Anderson, Perry. *The Origins of Postmodernity*. Verso, 1998.
Anderson, Sherwood. "The Work of Gertrude Stein." In *Geography and Plays*, by Gertrude Stein. University of Wisconsin Press, 1993.
Andrews, Kimberly Quiogue. *The Academic Avant-Garde: Poetry and the American University*. Johns Hopkins University Press, 2023.
Annual Reports of the Commissioner General of Immigration, 1892–1924. Washinton, DC: U.S. Department of Justice, Immigration, and Naturalization Service.
Ardis, Ann L. "The Dialogics of Modernism(s) in the *New Age*." *Modernism/Modernity* 14, no. 3 (2007): 407–34.
Arendt, Hannah. *The Human Condition*. University of Chicago Press, 1998.
Armantrout, Rae. "Darkinfested." In *Radical Vernacular: Lorine Niedecker and the Poetics of Place*. Edited by Elizabeth Willis, 103–12. University of Iowa Press, 2008.
Aronowitz, Stanley. *The Death and Life of American Labor: Toward a New Workers' Movement*. Verso, 2014.
Ashbery, John. "The Impossible." *Poetry* (1957): 250–54.
Ashton, Jennifer. "Gertrude Stein for Anyone." *ELH* 64, no. 1 (1997): 289–331.
Ashton, Jennifer. "Labor and the Lyric: The Politics of Self-Expression in Contemporary American Poetry." *American Literary History* 25, no. 1 (2013): 217–30.
Attridge, John, and Helen Rydstrand, eds. *Modernist Work: Labor, Aesthetics, and the Work of Art*. Bloomsbury, 2019.
Avrich, Paul. *An American Anarchist: The Life of Voltairine de Cleyre*. AK, 2018.
Bacigalupo, Massimo. *The Forméd Trace: The Later Poetry of Ezra Pound*. Columbia University Press, 1980.
Bajorek, Jennifer. *Counterfeit Capital: Poetic Labor and Revolutionary Irony*. Stanford University Press, 2009.
Bates, Beth Tompkins. *Pullman Porters and the Rise of Protest Politics in Black America, 1924–1945*. University of North Carolina Press, 2001.
Beasley, Rebecca. *Ezra Pound and the Visual Culture of Modernism*. Cambridge University Press, 2007.
Bell, Ian F. A. "Middle Cantos XLII–LXXI." In *The Cambridge Companion to Ezra Pound*. Edited by Ira B. Nadel, 92–108. Cambridge University Press, 1999.
Bender, Daniel E. *Sweated Work, Weak Bodies: Anti-Sweatshop Campaigns and Languages of Labor*. Rutgers University Press, 2004.
Benjamin, Walter. "The Author as Producer." In *Selected Writings*. Vol. 2, part 2. Translated by Edmund Jephcott, 768–82. Belknap, 1999.
Benjamin, Walter. *Illuminations*. Translated by Harry Zorn. Schocken, 2007.
Benjamin, Walter. *One-Way Street*. Translated by Edmund Jephcott and Kingsley Shorter. Verso, 2006.
Benston, Margaret. "The Political Economy of Women's Liberation." In *The Politics of Housework*. Edited by Ellen Malos. Allison & Busby, 1982.
Berke, Nancy. "'Electric Currents of Life:' Lola Ridge's Immigrant Flaneuserie." *American Studies* 51, nos. 1–2 (2010): 27–47.
Berke, Nancy. *Women Poets on the Left: Lola Ridge, Genevieve Taggard, Margaret Walker*. University Press of Florida, 2001.
Berlant, Lauren, ed. *Intimacy*. University of Chicago Press, 2000.

BIBLIOGRAPHY

Berlant, Lauren. "Intimacy: A Special Issue." *Critical Quarterly* 24, no. 2 (1998): 281–88.
Berman, Jessica. *Modernist Commitments: Ethics, Politics, and Transnational Modernism.* Columbia University Press, 2012.
Bernes, Jasper. "John Ashbery's Free Indirect Labor." *Modern Language Quarterly* 74, no. 4 (2013): 517–40.
Bernes, Jasper. *The Work of Art in the Age of Deindustrialization.* Stanford University Press, 2017.
Bevis, Matthew. "Unknowing Lyric." *Poetry*, March 2017. https://www.poetryfoundation.org/poetrymagazine/articles/92372/unknowing-lyric.
Binyon, Laurence. Preface to *A Short History of Chinese Civilisation*, by Tsui Chi. Victor Gollancz, 1942.
Bloch, Ernst. *Heritage of Our Times.* Translated by Neville Plaice and Stephen Plaice. University of California Press, 1991.
Bogdanov, Aleksandr. "Proletarian Poetry." *Labor Monthly* 4, no. 6 (1923): 357–62.
Bolden, Tony. *Afro-Blue: Improvisations in African American Poetry and Culture.* University of Illinois Press, 2004.
Boltanski, Luc, and Ève Chiapello. *The New Spirit of Capitalism.* Translated by Gregory Elliott. Verso, 2018.
Bontemps, Arna. *American Negro Poetry.* Hill and Wang, 1963.
Bottici, Chiara. *A Philosophy of Political Myth.* Cambridge University Press, 2007.
Bown, Matthew Cullerne, and Brandon Taylor, eds. *Art of the Soviets: Painting, Sculpture, and Architecture in a One-Party State, 1917–1992.* Manchester University Press, 1993.
Boyer, Anne. *Garments Against Women.* Ahsahta, 2015.
Boym, Svetlana. *Another Freedom: The Alternative History of an Idea.* University of Chicago Press, 2010.
Brady, Andrea. *Poetry and Bondage: A History and Theory of Lyric Constraint.* Cambridge University Press, 2021.
Braverman, Harry. *Labor and Monopoly Capital: The Degradation of Work in the Twentieth Century.* Monthly Review, 1998.
Brik, Osip. "Our Agenda" (1921). Translated by Natasha Kurchanova. *October* 134 (2001): 82–83.
Brooker, Peter. "London." In *Ezra Pound in Context.* Edited by Ira B. Nadel, 231–40. Cambridge University Press, 2010.
Brown, Nicholas. *Autonomy: The Social Ontology of Art Under Capitalism.* Duke University Press, 2019.
Brown, Sterling A. *The Collected Poems.* Harper & Row, 1980.
Bryan-Wilson, Julia. *Fray: Art + Textile Politics.* University of Chicago Press, 2017.
Bryan-Wilson, Julia, and Benjamin Piekut. "Amateurism." *Third Text* 34, no. 1 (2020): 1–21.
Bunting, Basil. *Collected Poems.* 2nd ed. Fulcrum, 1970.
Burnham, James. *The Managerial Revolution.* John Day, 1941; Reprint, University of Indiana Press, 1960.
Burns, Edward, ed. *The Letters of Gertrude Stein and Carl Van Vechten.* Columbia University Press, 2013.
Burstein, Jessica. *Cold Modernism: Literature, Fashion, Art.* Pennsylvania State University Press, 2012.
Bush, Ronald L. *The Genesis of Ezra Pound's Cantos.* Princeton University Press, 1989.

Cairns Watson, Dana. *Gertrude Stein and the Essence of What Happens*. Vanderbilt University Press, 2005.
Calinescu, Matei. *Five Faces of Modernity: Modernism, Avant-Garde, Decadence, Kitsch, Postmodernism*. Duke University Press, 1987.
Carnegie, Andrew. *The "Gospel of Wealth" Essays and Other Writings*. Penguin, 2006.
Carnevali, Emanuel. "Review of *Sun-Up*." *Poetry* 17, no. 6 (1921): 332–34.
Carr, Julie. "Women and War, Love, Labor: The Legacy of Lorine Niedecker." In *Poetics and Praxis 'After' Objectivism*. Edited by W. Scott Howard and Broc Rossell, 132–48. University of Iowa Press, 2018.
Carson, Luke. *Consumption and Depression in Gertrude Stein, Louis Zukofsky, and Ezra Pound*. Macmillan, 1999.
Carter, Huntly. *The New Spirit in the Russian Theater, 1917–1928*. Brentano's, 1929.
Casillo, Robert. "The Italian Renaissance: Pound's Problematic Debt to Burckhardt." *Mosaic: An Interdisciplinary Critical Journal* 22, no. 4 (1989): 13–29.
Cecire, Natalia. *Experimental: American Literature and the Aesthetics of Knowledge*. Johns Hopkins University Press, 2019.
Cecire, Natalia. "Marianne Moore's Precision." *Arizona Quarterly* 67, no. 4 (2011): 83–110.
Cecire, Natalia. "Ways of Not Reading Gertrude Stein." *ELH* 82, no. 1 (2015): 281–312.
Césaire, Aimé. *Journal of a Homecoming/Cahier d'un retour au pays natal*. Duke University Press, 2017.
Chan, Evelyn Tsz Yan. *Virginia Woolf and the Professions*. Cambridge University Press, 2014.
Cheadle, Mary Paterson. *Ezra Pound's Confucian Translations*. University of Michigan Press, 2003.
Chin, Margaret M. *Sewing Women: Immigrants and the New York City Garment Industry*. Columbia University Press, 2005.
Chinitz, David. "Literacy and Authenticity: The Blues Poems of Langston Hughes." *Callaloo* 19, no. 1 (1996): 177–92.
Chow, Juliana. "Vitalism in Gertrude Stein's Work." *Arizona Quarterly* 69, no. 4 (2013): 77–109.
Clark, T. J. *Farewell to an Idea: Episodes from a History of Modernism*. Yale University Press, 1999.
Clarke, Bruce. *Dora Marsden and Early Modernism: Gender, Individualism, Science*. University of Michigan Press, 1996.
Clover, Joshua. "Unfree Verse." Poetry Foundation, April 15, 2016. https://www.poetryfoundation.org/harriet/2016/04/unfree-verse.
Coke, Edward. *The Second Part of the Institutes of the Laws of England*. E. and R. Brooke, 1797.
Cooke, Jennifer, ed. *Scenes of Intimacy: Reading, Writing and Theorizing Contemporary Literature*. Bloomsbury, 2013.
Cornell, Andrew. *Unruly Equality: U.S. Anarchism in the Twentieth Century*. University of California Press, 2016.
Costello, Bonnie. *The Plural of Us: Poetry and Community in Auden and Others*. Princeton University Press, 2017.
Cowan, Ruth Schwartz. *More Work for Mother: The Ironies of Household Technology from the Open Hearth to the Microwave*. Basic Books, 1983.

BIBLIOGRAPHY

Cowie, Jefferson. *Stayin' Alive: The 1970s and the Last Days of the Working Class.* New Press, 2010.
Crain Marion G., Winifred R. Poster, and Miriam A. Cherry, eds. *Invisible Labor: Hidden Work in the Contemporary World.* University of California Press, 2016.
Cushman, Stephen, Clare Cavanagh, Jahan Ramazani, and Paul Rouzer, eds. *The Princeton Encyclopedia of Poetry and Poetics.* 4th ed. Princeton University Press, 2012.
Dace, Tish, ed. *Langston Hughes: The Contemporary Reviews.* Cambridge University Press, 1997.
Dalla Costa, Mariarosa, and Selma James. *The Power of Women and the Subversion of the Community.* Falling Wall, 1975.
Daniels, Arlene. "Invisible Work." *Social Problems* 34, no. 5 (1987): 403–15.
Davidson, Michael. *Ghostlier Demarcations: Modern Poetry and the Material Word.* University of California Press, 1997.
Davie, Donald. *Ezra Pound: Poet as Sculptor.* Oxford University Press, 1964.
Davie, Donald. *Studies in Ezra Pound.* Carcanet, 1991.
Davies, Kevin. *The Golden Age of Paraphernalia.* Edge, 2000.
Dawahare, Anthony. "Langston Hughes's Radical Poetry and the 'End of Race.'" *MELUS* 23, no. 3 (1998): 21–41.
de la Cruz-Fernández, Paula A. "Marketing the Hearth: Ornamental Embroidery and the Building of the Multinational Singer Sewing Machine Company." *Enterprise and Society* 15, no. 3 (2014): 442–71.
De'Ath, Amy. "Hidden Abodes and Inner Bonds: Literary Study and Marxist-Feminism." In *After Marx: Literature, Theory, and Value in the Twenty-First Century.* Edited by Colleen Lye and Christopher Nealon, 225–39. Cambridge University Press, 2022.
De'Ath, Amy. "Manly Things." *Post45*, July 27, 2021. https://post45.org/2021/07/manly-things/.
Deamer, Peggy. "Work." In *The Architect as Worker: Immaterial Labour, the Creative Class, and the Politics of Design.* Edited by Peggy Deamer, 61–81. Bloomsbury Academic, 2015.
Denning, Michael. *The Cultural Front: The Laboring of American Culture in the Twentieth Century.* Verso, 2011.
Denning, Michael. *Culture in the Age of Three Worlds.* Verso, 2004.
Denning, Michael. "Wageless Life." *New Left Review* 66 (2010): 79–97.
Depestre, René. *Anthologie personelle.* Actes Sud, 1993.
Deutsch, Babette. "Two First Books." *Little Review* 16, no. 1 (1919): 65–68.
Diepeveen, Leonard. *The Difficulties of Modernism.* Routledge, 2003.
Dinsman, Melissa. *Modernism at the Microphone: Radio, Propaganda, and Literary Aesthetics During World War II.* Bloomsbury, 2015.
Dolinar, Brian. *The Black Cultural Front: Black Writers and Artists of the Depression Generation.* University Press of Mississippi, 2012.
Douglas, Ann. *The Feminization of American Culture.* Papermac, 1996.
Douglas, C. H. *Social Credit.* Cecil Palmer, 1924.
Du Bois, W. E. B. *Black Reconstruction in America.* Harcourt, Brace, 1935.
Dubofsky, Melvyn, and Foster Rhea Dulles. *Labor in America: A History.* Harlan Davidson, 2010.
Duffy, Mignon. "Doing the Dirty Work: Gender, Race, and Reproductive Labor in Historical Perspective." *Gender and Society* 21, no. 3 (2007): 313–36.
Duncan, Robert. *Fictive Certainties: Essays.* New Directions, 1985.

DuPlessis, Rachel Blau. *Blue Studios: Poetry and Its Cultural Work*. University of Alabama Press, 2006.
DuPlessis, Rachel Blau. *Drafts 1–38: Toll*. Wesleyan University Press, 2001.
DuPlessis, Rachel Blau. *Interstices*. Subpress, 2014.
DuPlessis, Rachel Blau. "Lorine Niedecker, the Anonymous: Gender, Class, Genre and Resistances." *Kenyon Review* 14, no. 2 (1999): 96–116.
DuPlessis, Rachel Blau. "Lorine Niedecker's 'Paean to Place' and Its Fusion Poetics." *Contemporary Literature* 46, no. 3 (2005): 393–421.
DuPlessis, Rachel Blau. *Purple Passages: Pound, Eliot, Zukofsky, Olson, Creeley, and the Ends of Patriarchal Poetry*. University of Iowa Press, 2012.
DuPlessis, Rachel Blau. *Surge: Drafts 96–114*. Salt, 2013.
DuPlessis, Rachel Blau, and Peter Quartermain, eds. *The Objectivist Nexus: Essays in Cultural Poetics*. University of Alabama Press, 1999.
Dydo, Ulla E. "Composition as Meditation." In *Gertrude Stein and the Making of Literature*. Edited by Shirley Neuman and Ira B. Nadel, 42–60. Macmillan, 1988.
Dydo, Ulla E. *Gertrude Stein: The Language That Rises 1923–1934*. Northwestern University Press, 2003.
Dydo, Ulla E. "How to Read Gertrude Stein: The Manuscript of 'Stanzas in Meditation.'" *TEXT: Transactions of the Society for Textual Scholarship*. Vol. 1. Edited by D. C. Greetham and W. Speed Hill, 271–303. AMS, 1981.
Dydo, Ulla E. "'Stanzas in Meditation': The Other Autobiography." *Chicago Review* 35, no. 2 (1985): 4–20.
Edwards, Brent Hayes. *Epistrophies: Jazz and the Literary Imagination*. Harvard University Press, 2017.
Ehlers, Sarah. *Left of Poetry: Depression America and the Formation of Modern Poetics*. University of North Carolina Press, 2019.
Einzig, Paul. *The Economic Foundations of Fascism*. Macmillan, 1933.
Eliot, T. S. *The Letters of T. S. Eliot*. Edited by Valerie Eliot, John Haffenden, and Hugh Haughton. 5 vols. Faber and Faber, 2009.
Eliot, T. S. *Selected Prose*. Edited by Frank Kermode. Faber and Faber, 1975.
Eliot, T. S. *The Waste Land and Other Poems*. Faber and Faber, 1999.
Elkins, Amy. *Crafting Feminism from Literary Modernism to the Multimedia Present*. Oxford University Press, 2023.
Epstein, Josh. "The Antheil Era: Pound, Noise, and Musical Sensation." *Textual Practice* 28, no. 6 (2014): 989–1014.
Esteve, Mary. *The Aesthetics and Politics of the Crowd in American Literature*. Cambridge University Press, 2003.
Falasca-Zamponi, Simonetta. *Fascist Spectacle: The Aesthetics of Power in Mussolini's Italy*. University of California Press, 1997.
Faranda, Lisa Pater, ed. *Between Your House and Mine: The Letters of Lorine Niedecker to Cid Corman, 1960–1970*. Duke University Press, 1986.
Fearing, Kenneth. "Limiting Devices: A Review of *Fine Clothes to the Jew*." *New Masses* 3, no. 5 (1927): 29.
Federici, Silvia. *Re-enchanting the World: Feminism and the Politics of the Commons*. PM, 2019.
Federici, Silvia. *Revolution at Point Zero: Housework, Reproduction, and Feminist Struggle*. PM, 2012.

BIBLIOGRAPHY

Federici, Silvia. "Social Reproduction Theory: History, Issues and Present Challenges." *Radical Philosophy* 204 (2019): 55–57.
Feldman, Matthew. *Ezra Pound's Fascist Propaganda, 1935–45*. Palgrave Macmillan, 2013.
Fenollosa, Ernest. *The Chinese Written Character as a Medium for Poetry: A Critical Edition*. Edited by L. Klein, H. Saussy, and J. Stalling. Fordham University Press, 2008.
Field, G. C. *Guild Socialism: A Critical Examination*. Wells Gardner, Darton, 1920.
Filreis, Alan. *Modernism from Right to Left: Wallace Stevens, the Thirties, and Literary Radicalism*. Cambridge University Press, 1994.
Fitts, Dudley. "Prelude to Conclusion." *Saturday Review of Literature* 39 (1956): 18–19.
Fogelman, Bruce. "The Evolution of Pound's 'Contemporania.'" *Journal of Modern Literature* 15, no. 1 (1988): 93–103.
Foley, Barbara. *Jean Toomer: Race, Repression, and Revolution*. University of Illinois Press, 2014.
Foley, Barbara. *Marxist Literary Criticism Today*. Pluto, 2019.
Foley, Barbara. *Spectres of 1919: Class and Nation in the Making of the New Negro*. University of Illinois Press, 2003.
Foner, Eric. *Free Soil, Free Labor, Free Men: The Ideology of the Republican Party Before the Civil War*. Oxford University Press, 1995.
Foner, Philip S. *Organized Labor and the Black Worker, 1619–1981*. Haymarket, 2017.
Fraser, Nancy. "Contradictions of Capitalism and Care." *New Left Review* 100 (2016): 99–117.
Fraser, Nancy. "Expropriation and Exploitation in Racialized Capitalism: A Reply to Michael Dawson." *Critical Historical Studies* 3, no. 1 (2016): 163–78.
Fraser, Nancy. *Fortunes of Feminism: From State-Managed Capitalism to Neoliberal Crisis*. Verso, 2013.
Frederick, Christine. *The New Housekeeping: Efficiency Studies in Home Management*. Doubleday, 1913.
Freeman, Elizabeth. *Beside You in Time: Sense Methods and Queer Sociabilities in the American Nineteenth Century*. Duke University Press, 2019.
Freeman, Elizabeth. "Committed to the End: On Caretaking, Rereading, and Queer Theory." In *Long Term: Essays on Queer Commitment*. Duke University Press, 2021.
Gallup, Donald. "The Making of *The Making of Americans*." In *Fernhurst, Q.E.D., and Other Early Writings*, by Gertrude Stein, 175–214. Liveright, 1971.
Gan, Aleksei. *Constructivism*. Translated by Christina Lodder. Tenov, 2013.
Gandal, Keith. *The Virtue of the Vicious: Jacob Riis, Stephen Crane, and the Spectacle of the Slum*. Oxford University Press, 1997.
Ganz, Marie, with Nat J. Ferber. *Rebels; Into Anarchy—and Out Again*. Dodd, Mead, 1920.
Garver, Lee. "Seafarer Socialism: Pound, *The New Age*, and Anglo-Medieval Radicalism." *Journal of Modern Literature* 29, no. 4 (2006): 1–21.
Gelphi, Albert. *American Poetry After Modernism: The Power of the Word*. Cambridge University Press, 2015.
Gesell, Silvio. *The Natural Economic Order: A Plan to Secure the Uninterrupted Exchange of the Products of Labor, Free from Bureaucratic Interference, Usury and Exploitation—Land Part*. Translated by Philip Pye. Free-Economy, 1936.
Giddens, Anthony. *The Transformation of Intimacy: Sexuality, Love and Eroticism in Modern Societies*. Polity, 1992.

Gillies, Mary Ann. *The Professional Literary Agent in Britain, 1880–1920*. University of Toronto Press, 2007.
Gilman, Charlotte Perkins. *The Home: Its Work and Influence*. William Heinemann, 1903.
Giordano, Claire, and Fernando Giuliano. "A Tale of Two Fascisms: Labour Productivity Growth and Competition Policy in Italy, 1911–1951." *Banca d'Italia* 28 (2012).
Glaser, Amelia M. *Songs in Dark Times: Yiddish Poetry of Struggle from Scottsboro to Palestine*. Harvard University Press, 2020.
Glazer, Nona Y. "The Home as Workshop: Women as Amateur Nurses and Medical Care Providers." *Gender and Society* 4, no. 4 (1990): 479–99.
Glenn, Evelyn Nakano. "From Servitude to Service Work: Historical Continuities in the Racial Division of Paid Reproductive Labor." *Signs* 18, no. 1 (1992): 1–43.
Glenn, Evelyn Nakano. *Unequal Freedom: How Race and Gender Shaped American Citizenship and Labor*. Harvard University Press, 2002.
Glenn, Susan A. *Daughters of the Shtetl: Life and Labor in the Immigrant Generation*. Cornell University Press, 1990.
Godley, Andrew. "Selling the Sewing Machine Around the World: Singer's International Marketing Strategies, 1850–1920." *Enterprise and Society* 7, no. 2 (2006): 266–314.
Gold, Michael. "Carnevali and Other Essays." *New Masses* 2, no. 2 (1926): 3.
Gold, Michael. "Gertrude Stein: A Literary Idiot." In *Change the World!* Lawrence and Wishart, 1937.
Gold, Michael. "Notes of the Month." *New Masses* 6 (1930): 4.
Golding, Alan. "Experimental Modernisms." In *The Cambridge Companion to Modern American Poetry*. Edited by Walter Kalaidjian, 37–49. Cambridge University Press, 2015.
Goldman, Emma. *Living My Life*. Penguin, 2006.
Goldstone, Andrew. *Fictions of Autonomy: Modernism from Wilde to de Man*. Oxford University Press, 2013.
Goody, Alex, and Ian Whittington, eds. *The Edinburgh Companion to Modernism and Technology*. Edinburgh University Press, 2022.
Gotby, Alva. "Book Review: *Witches, Witch-Hunting and Women* by Silvia Federici and *Re-enchanting the World: Feminism and the Politics of the Commons* by Silvia Federici." *Feminist Review* 124 (2020): 204–6.
Gough, Maria. *The Artist as Producer: Russian Constructivism in Revolution*. University of California Press, 2005.
Green, Nancy L. *Ready to Wear and Ready to Work: A Century of Industry and Immigrants in Paris and New York*. Duke University Press, 1997.
Grieve, Thomas F. *Ezra Pound's Early Poetry and Poetics*. University of Missouri Press, 1997.
"Guild Socialism: The Moral Foundations of Existing Society." *New Age* 11, no. 24 (1912): 559–61.
"Guild Socialism: A Working Model." *New Age* 11, no. 27 (1912): 632.
Haas, Robert Bartlett, ed. *A Primer for the Gradual Understanding of Gertrude Stein*. Black Sparrow, 1971.
Haider, Carmen. "Capital and Labour Under Fascism." PhD diss., Columbia University, 1930.
Hapke, Laura. *Sweatshop: The History of an American Idea*. Rutgers University Press, 2004.

Hardt, Michael, and Antonio Negri. *Commonwealth*. Harvard University Press, 2009.
Hardt, Michael, and Antonio Negri. *Labor of Dionysus: A Critique of the State-Form*. University of Minnesota Press, 1994.
Hardt, Michael, and Antonio Negri. *Multitude: War and Democracy in the Age of Empire*. Penguin, 2006.
Harley, J. H. *Syndicalism*. T. C. & E. C. Jack, 1912.
Harootunian, Harry. "A Fascism for Our Time." *Massachusetts Review* (2022): 13–14.
Harootunian, Harry. *Marx After Marx: History and Time in the Expansion of Capitalism*. Columbia University Press, 2015.
Hartman, Saidiya. *Scenes of Subjection: Terror, Slavery, and Self-Making in Nineteenth-Century America*. Oxford University Press, 1997.
Hartman, Saidiya. *Wayward Lives, Beautiful Experiments: Intimate Histories of Riotous Black Girls, Troublesome Women, and Queer Radicals*. Norton, 2019.
Harvey, David. *A Companion to Marx's Capital*. Verso, 2010.
Harvey, David. "The Geography of Capitalist Accumulation: A Reconstruction of the Marxian Theory." *Antipode* 7, no. 2 (1975): 9–21.
Hastings, Beatrice. *The Old "New Age": Orage—and Others*. Blue Moon, 1936.
Hejinian, Lyn. *The Language of Inquiry*. University of California Press, 2000.
Hejinian, Lyn. *My Life and My Life in the Nineties*. Wesleyan University Press, 2013.
Hesse-Biber, Sharlene Nagy, and Gregg Lee Carter, *Working Women in America: Split Dreams*. Oxford University Press, 2000.
"Hester Street Market." *New York Times*, July 27, 1895.
Hickman, Miranda. *The Geometry of Modernism: The Vorticist Idiom in Lewis, Pound, H. D., and Yeats*. University of Texas Press, 2005.
Hobbs, David B. "Lyric Commodification in McKay's Morocco." *English Language Notes* 59, no. 1 (2021): 181–200.
Hochschild, Arlie Russell. *The Managed Heart: Commercialisation of Human Feeling*. University of California Press, 1983.
Hochschild, Arlie Russell. *The Second Shift: Working Parents and the Revolution at Home*. Viking, 1989.
Hollander, John. *Melodious Guile: Fictive Pattern in Poetic Language*. Yale University Press, 1988.
Hollingsworth, Mary. *Patronage in Renaissance Italy: From 1400 to the Early Sixteenth Century*. John Murray, 1994.
Houghton, Norris. *Moscow Rehearsals: An Account of Methods of Production in the Soviet Theater*. Allen & Unwin, 1938.
Hughes, Langston. *The Collected Works of Langston Hughes*. Edited by Arnold Rampersad. 16 vols. University of Missouri Press, 2001–2003.
Hughes, Langston. *Letters from Langston: From the Harlem Renaissance to the Red Scare and Beyond*. Edited by Evelyn Louise Crawford and MaryLouise Patterson. University of California Press, 2016.
Hughes, Langston. *Montage of a Dream Deferred*. Henry Holt, 1951.
Hughes, Langston. "The Negro Artist and the Racial Mountain." *Nation* 122 (1926): 692–94.
Hughes, Langston. *A New Song*. International Workers Order, 1938.
Hughes, Langston. *Not Without Laughter*. Canongate, 1998.
Hughes, Langston. *Remember Me to Harlem: The Letters of Langston Hughes and Carl Van Vechten, 1925–1964*. Edited by Emily Bernard. Knopf, 2001.

BIBLIOGRAPHY

Hughes, Langston. *Selected Letters of Langston Hughes*. Edited by Arnold Rampersad and David E. Roessel. Knopf, 2015.
Hughes, Langston. "Walt Whitman and the Negro." *Nocturne* 7 (1955): 9.
Hutchinson, Earl Ofari. *Blacks and Reds: Race and Class in Conflict, 1919–1990*. Michigan State University Press, 1995.
Huyssen, Andreas. *After the Great Divide: Modernism, Mass Culture, Postmodernism*. Indiana University Press, 1986.
Izenberg, Oren. *Being Numerous: Poetry and the Ground of Social Life*. Princeton University Press, 2011.
Jackson, Paul. *Great War Modernisms and the New Age Magazine*. Bloomsbury, 2013.
Jackson, Virginia. *Dickinson's Misery*. Princeton University Press, 2005.
Jameson, Fredric. *Fables of Aggression: Wyndham Lewis, the Modernist as Fascist*. University of California Press, 1979.
Jameson, Fredric. *The Modernist Papers*. Verso, 2007.
Jameson, Fredric. *The Political Unconscious: Narrative as a Socially Symbolic Act*. Cornell University Press, 1981.
Jameson, Fredric. *A Singular Modernity: Essay on the Ontology of the Present*. Verso, 2002.
Janowitz, Anne. *Lyric and Labour in the Romantic Tradition*. Cambridge University Press, 1998.
Jarrell, Randall. "Five Poets." *Yale Review* (1956): 103–6.
Jaussen, Paul. "The Poetics of Midrash in Rachel Blau DuPlessis's *Drafts*." *Contemporary Literature* 53, no. 1 (2012): 114–42.
Javadizadeh, Kamran. *Institutionalized Lyric: American Poetry at Midcentury*. Oxford University Press, forthcoming.
Jenkins, Destin, and Justin Leroy, eds. *Histories of Racial Capitalism*. Columbia University Press, 2021.
Jennison, Ruth. "29|73|08: Poetry, Crisis, and a Hermeneutics of Limit." *Mediations: Journal of the Marxist Literary Group* 28, no. 2 (2015): 37–46.
Jennison, Ruth. "Scrambling Narrative: Niedecker and the White Dome of Logic." *Journal of Narrative Theory* 41, no. 1 (2011): 53–81.
Jennison, Ruth. *The Zukofsky Era: Modernity, Margins, and the Avant-Garde*. Johns Hopkins University Press, 2012.
Johnson, James Weldon. *Writings*. Library of America, 2004.
Jones, Gail. "'Growing Small Wings': Walter Benjamin, Lola Ridge, and the Political Affect of Modernism." *Affirmations: of the Modern* 1, no. 2. (2014): 120–42.
Jones, Howard Mumford. *Gargoyles and Other Poems*. Cornhill, 1918.
Kadlec, David. "Pound, BLAST, and Syndicalism." *ELH* 60, no. 4 (1993): 1015–31.
Kadue, Katie. *Domestic Georgic: Labors of Preservation from Rabelais to Milton*. University of Chicago Press, 2020.
Katz, Jonathan. "Oral History Interview with Ann Wilson, 2009 April 19–2010 July 12." Smithsonian Archives of American Art, April 19, 2009–July 12, 2010. https://www.aaa.si.edu/collections/interviews/oral-history-interview-ann-wilson-15968.
Keats, John. *Complete Poems and Selected Letters of John Keats*. Modern Library Classics, 2001.
Kelley, Robin D. G. *Freedom Dreams: The Black Radical Imagination*. Beacon, 2002.
Kelley, William M. [W. M. K, pseud.]. "Langston Hughes: The Sewer Dweller." *New York Amsterdam News*, February 9, 1927, 22.

Kempf, Christopher. *Craft Class: The Writing Workshop in American Culture*. Johns Hopkins University Press, 2022.
Kenner, Hugh. *The Pound Era*. Faber and Faber, 1972.
Kenner, Hugh. "Under the Larches of Paradise." *Hudson Review* 9, no. 3 (1956): 457–65.
Kermode, Frank. *Romantic Image*. Routledge, 2002.
Kernan, Ryan James. *New World Maker: Radical Poetics, Black Internationalism, and the Translations of Langston Hughes*. Northwestern University Press, 2022.
Kesler-Harris, Alice. "Problems of Coalition-Building: Women and Trade Unions in the 1920s." In *Women, Work and Protest: A Century of US Women's Labor History*. Edited by Ruth Milkman, 110–138. Routledge, 1985.
Kimball, Dexter S. *Industrial Economics*. McGraw-Hill, 1929.
Kindley, Evan. *Poet-Critics and the Administration of Culture*. Harvard University Press, 2017.
Kinnahan, Linda Arbaugh. "Portraits of Working Women: Lola Ridge's 'The Ghetto' and the Visual Record." *Humanities* 11, no. 5 (2022): 117–61.
Kirsch, Sharon J. *Gertrude Stein and the Reinvention of Rhetoric*. University of Alabama Press, 2014.
Kleberg, Lars. *Theater as Action: Soviet Russian Avant-Garde Aesthetics*. Translated by Charles Rougle. Macmillan, 1993.
Kluge, Alexander, and Oskar Negt. *History and Obstinacy*. Translated by Richard Langston. MIT Press, 2014.
Kolchin, Peter. *Unfree Labor: American Slavery and Russian Serfdom*. Belknap, 1987.
Kotin, Joshua. *Utopias of One*. Princeton University Press, 2017.
Kreymborg, Alfred. "A Poet in Arms." *Poetry* 13, no. 6 (1919): 335–40.
La Berge, Leigh Claire. *Scandals and Abstraction: Financial Fiction of the Long 1980s*. Oxford University Press, 2015.
La Berge, Leigh Claire. *Wages Against Artwork: Decommodified Labor and the Claims of Socially Engaged Art*. Duke University Press, 2019.
"Langston Hughes." Federal Bureau of Investigation. https://vault.fbi.gov/langston-hughes. Accessed February 2025.
Lazzarato, Maurice. "Immaterial Labor." In *Radical Thought in Italy: A Potential Politics*. Translated by Paul Colilli and Ed Emery. Edited by Paolo Virno and Michael Hardt, 142–57. University of Minnesota Press, 1996.
Lazzaro, Claudia, and Roger J. Crum, eds. *Donatello Among the Blackshirts: History and Modernity in the Visual Culture of Fascist Italy*. Cornell University Press, 2005.
Lee, Steven S. "Langston Hughes's 'Moscow Movie': Reclaiming a Lost Minority Avant-Garde." *Comparative Literature* 67, no. 2 (2015): 185–206.
Leick, Karen. *Gertrude Stein and the Making of an American Celebrity*. Routledge, 2009.
Lenin, Vladimir Ilyich. "The British Labour Movement in 1912." *Pravda* 1 (1913). Reprinted in Vladimir Ilyich Lenin. *Lenin: Collected Works*. Vol. 18. Translated by Stepan Apresyan. Edited by Clemens Dutt. Progress, 1975.
Lenin, Vladimir Ilyich. "Russians and Negroes." *Krasnaya Niva*, no. 3 (1925). Reprinted in Lenin, V. I. *Collected Works*. Vol. 18. Translated by Stepan Apresyan, 543–44. Progress, 1975.
Lesjak, Carolyn. "Reading Dialectically." *Criticism* 55, no. 2 (2013): 233–77.
Lewis, Sophie. *Full Surrogacy Now!* Verso, 2019.
Lewis, Wyndham. *Time and Western Man*. Chatto & Windus, 1927.

Lieberman, Jennifer. *Power Lines: Electricity in American Life and Letters, 1882–1952.* MIT Press, 2017.
Liebregts, Peter. *Ezra Pound and Neoplatonism.* Fairleigh Dickinson University Press, 2004.
Lodder, Christina, Maria Kokkori, and Maria Mileeva, eds. *Utopian Reality: Reconstructing Culture in Revolutionary Russia and Beyond.* Brill, 2013.
"Lola Ridge, Poet, Dies in Brooklyn." *New York Times,* May 21, 1941.
"Lola Ridge's Poetry." *New Republic* 17, no. 211 (1918): 76–77.
Longenbach, James. *The Resistance to Poetry.* University of Chicago Press, 2004.
Lorange, Astrid. *How Reading Is Written: A Brief Index to Gertrude Stein.* Wesleyan University Press, 2014.
Lowe, Lisa. *The Intimacies of Four Continents.* Duke University Press, 2015.
Lowell Field, G. *The Syndical and Corporative Institutions of Italian Fascism.* AMS, 1968.
Luker, Ed, and Jo Lindsay Walton. *Poetry and Work: Work in Modern and Contemporary Anglophone Poetry.* Palgrave, 2019.
Macleod, Joseph. *The New Soviet Theater.* Allen & Unwin, 1943.
Malcolm, Janet. *Two Lives: Gertrude and Alice.* Yale University Press, 2007.
Malos, Ellen, ed. *The Politics of Housework.* Allison & Busby, 1982.
Mao, Douglas, ed. *The New Modernist Studies.* Cambridge University Press, 2021.
Mao, Douglas. *Solid Objects: Modernism and the Test of Production.* Princeton University Press, 1998.
Mao, Douglas, and Rebecca Walkowitz, eds. *Bad Modernisms.* Duke University Press, 2006.
Mao, Douglas, and Rebecca Walkowitz. "The New Modernist Studies." *PMLA* 123, no. 3 (2008): 737–48.
Marcuse, Herbert. *Collected Papers of Herbert Marcuse.* Vol. 1, *Technology, War, and Fascism.* Routledge, 1998.
Marcuse, Herbert. *An Essay on Liberation.* Allen Lane, 1969.
Marsh, Alec. *Money and Modernity: Pound, Williams, and the Spirit of Jefferson.* University of Alabama Press, 1998.
Marsh, Alec. "Thaddeus Coleman Pound's 'Newspaper Scrapbook' as a Source for *The Cantos.*" *Paideuma* 24, nos. 2–3 (1995): 163–93.
Marsh, John. *Hog Butchers, Beggars, and Busboys: Poverty, Labor, and the Making of Modern American Poetry.* University of Michigan Press, 2011.
Marsh, Margaret S. *Anarchist Women 1870–1920.* Temple University Press, 1981.
Marshik, Celia. *At the Mercy of Their Clothes: Modernism, the Middlebrow, and British Garment Culture.* Columbia University Press, 2016.
Marx, Karl. *Capital.* Vol. 1. Translated by Ben Fowkes. Penguin, 1990.
Marx, Karl. *Capital.* Vol. 3. Translated by David Fernbach. Penguin, 1992.
Marx, Karl. "Estranged Labor." From *Economic and Philosophic Manuscripts of 1844.* Translated by Martin Milligan. Marx-Engels Archive, 1959 (updated 2009). https://www.marxists.org/archive/marx/works/1844/manuscripts/labour.htm.
Marx, Karl. *The German Ideology.* Marx-Engels Archive, 1845. https://www.marxists.org/archive/marx/works/1845/german-ideology/ch01a.htm#p28.
Marx, Karl. *The Poverty of Philosophy.* Translated by Harry Quelch. Cosimo, 2008.
Marx, Karl. *Selected Works.* Progress, 1970.
Marx, Karl. *Theories of Surplus Value.* Translated by G. A. Bonner and Emile Burns. Lawrence and Wishart, 1951.

BIBLIOGRAPHY

Maun, Caroline. *Mosaic of Fire: The Work of Lola Ridge, Evelyn Scott, Charlotte Wilder, and Kay Boyle*. University of South Carolina Press, 2012.
Mauro, Evan. "The Death and Life of the Avant-Garde." *Mediations* 26, nos. 1–2 (2012–2013): 119–42.
Maxwell, William J. *New Negro, Old Left: African American Writing and Communism Between the Wars*. Columbia University Press, 1999.
Mayakovsky, Vladimir. *Vladimir Mayakovsky & Other Poems*. Translated and edited by James Womack. Carcanet, 2016.
Mayer, Bernadette. *Milkweed Smithereens*. New Directions, 2022.
Mayer, Bernadette. *Works and Days*. New Directions, 2016.
McCall, Leslie. "Increasing Class Disparities Among Women and the Politics of Gender Equity." In *The Sex of Class: Women Transforming American Labor*. Edited by Dorothy Sue Cobble, 15–34. Cornell University Press, 2007.
McCormick, John. *George Santayana: A Biography*. Knopf, 1987.
McCray, W. Patrick. *Glassmaking in Renaissance Venice: The Fragile Craft*. Routledge, 2017.
McGurl, Mark. *The Program Era*. Harvard University Press, 2009.
McKay, Claude. *Complete Poems*. Edited by William J. Maxwell. University of Illinois Press, 2004.
McKay, Claude. "Soviet Russia and the Negro." *Crisis* 27 (1923): 61–65.
Melamed, Jodi. "Racial Capitalism." *Critical Ethnic Studies* 1, no. 1 (2015): 76–85.
Menand, Louis. *Discovering Modernism: T. S. Eliot and His Context*. Oxford University Press, 1987.
Meyer, Steven. *Irresistible Dictation: Gertrude Stein and the Correlations of Writing and Science*. Stanford University Press, 2002.
Meyerhold, Vsevolod. *Meyerhold on Theater*. Translated and edited by Edward Braun. Bloomsbury, 2016.
Michels, Tony. *A Fire in Their Hearts: Yiddish Socialists in New York*. Harvard University Press, 2005.
Michels, Tony, ed. *Jewish Radicals: A Documentary History*. New York University Press, 2012.
Micir, Melanie. *The Passion Projects: Modernist Women, Intimate Archives, Unfinished Lives*. Princeton University Press, 2019.
Middleton, Peter. "Folk Poetry and the American Avant-Garde: Placing Lorine Niedecker." *Journal of American Studies* 31, no. 2 (1997): 203–18.
Mies, Maria. *Patriarchy and Accumulation on a World Scale: Women in the International Division of Labor*. Zed, 2014.
Miller, Cristanne. "'Tongues Loosened in the Melting Pot': The Poets of Others and the Lower East Side." *Modernism/Modernity* 14, no. 3 (2007): 455–76.
Miller, Tyrus. *Late Modernism: Politics, Fiction, and the Arts Between the World Wars*. University of California Press, 1999.
Mills, Jean. "Gertrude on the Block: Writing, Love, and Fame in *Stanzas in Meditation*." *Philological Quarterly* 63, no. 2 (2010): 197–210.
Minor, Robert. "The First Negro Workers' Congress." *Workers Monthly* 5 (1925): 68–73.
Mitchell, Angelyn, ed. *Within the Circle: An Anthology of African American Literary Criticism from the Harvard Renaissance to the Present*. Duke University Press, 1994.

Mohun, Arwen Palmer. "Laundrymen Construct Their World: Gender and the Transformation of a Domestic Task to an Industrial Process." *Technology and Culture* 38, no. 1 (1997): 97–120.
Moody, Alys, and Stephen Ross, eds. *Global Modernists on Modernism*. Bloomsbury, 2020.
Morris, Roy, Jr. *Gertrude Stein Has Arrived: The Homecoming of a Literary Legend*. Johns Hopkins University Press, 2019.
Morris, William. *Signs of Change*. Marxists Internet Archive, 1896. https://www.marxists.org/archive/morris/works/1888/signs/index.htm.
Morrisson, Paul. *The Poetics of Fascism: Ezra Pound, T. S. Eliot, Paul de Man*. Oxford University Press, 1996.
Mullen, Bill V., and James Smethurst, eds. *Left of the Color Line: Race, Radicalism, and Twentieth-Century Literature of the United States*. University of North Carolina Press, 2003.
Mullin, Katherine. *Working Girls: Fiction, Sexuality, and Modernity*. Oxford University Press, 2016.
Nealon, Christopher. "Camp Messianism, or, the Hopes of Poetry in Late-Late Capitalism." *American Literature* 76, no. 3 (2004): 579–602.
Nealon, Christopher. *Foundlings: Lesbian and Gay Historical Emotion Before Stonewall*. Duke University Press, 2001.
Nealon, Christopher. *The Matter of Capital: Poetry and Crisis in the American Century*. Harvard University Press, 2011.
Nealon, Christopher. "Three Militants." *Lana Turner Journal*, January 22, 2017. http://www.lanaturnerjournal.com/blog/three-militants.
Nelson, Cary. *Revolutionary Memory: Recovering the Poetry of the American Left*. Routledge, 2001.
Nersessian, Anahid. *The Calamity Form: On Poetry and Social Life*. Chicago University Press, 2020.
Nersessian, Anahid. *Utopia, Limited: Romanticism and Adjustment*. Harvard University Press, 2015.
Ngai, Sianne. *Our Aesthetic Categories: Zany, Cute, Interesting*. Harvard University Press, 2012.
Nicholls, Peter. "'2 Doits to a Boodle': Reckoning with *Thrones*." *Textual Practice* 18, no. 2 (2004): 233–49.
Nicholls, Peter. "Bravura or Bravado?" In *Modernism and Masculinity*. Edited by Julian Murphet and Natalya Lusty, 233–54. Cambridge University Press, 2014.
Nicholls, Peter. *Ezra Pound: Politics, Economics, and Writing—A Study of the Cantos*. Macmillan, 1984.
Nicholls, Peter. *George Oppen and the Fate of Modernism*. Oxford: Oxford University Press, 2007.
Nicholls, Peter. "Lost Object(s): Ezra Pound and the Idea of Italy." In *Ezra Pound and Europe*. Edited by Claus Melchior and Richard Taylor, 165–76. Rodopi, 1993.
Nickels, Joel. *The Poetry of the Possible: Spontaneity, Modernism, and the Multitude*. University of Minnesota Press, 2012.
Niedecker, Lorine. *Collected Works*. Edited by Jenny Penberthy. University of California Press, 2002.

BIBLIOGRAPHY

Niedecker, Lorine. "A Cooking Book." University of Wisconsin Digital Collections. https://search.library.wisc.edu/digital/AGUYGSTZFBI4CV9C. Accessed February 2025.
Niemann, Michelle. "Towards an Ecopoetics of Food: Plants, Agricultural Politics, and Colonized Landscapes in Lorine Niedecker's Condensery." *Modernism/Modernity* 25, no. 1 (2018): 135–60.
North, Joseph. *Literary Criticism: A Concise Political History*. Harvard University Press, 2017.
North, Michael. "The Afterlife of Modernism." *New Literary History* 50, no. 1 (2019): 91–112.
Oakey, Christopher. "Prose Poetry and Purposiveness in Anne Boyer's *Garments Against Women*." *Contemporary Literature* 61, no. 2 (2020): 194–220.
"Observations and Comments." *Mother Earth* 3, no. 8 (1908): 310.
Oppen, George. *New Collected Poems*. New Directions, 2008.
Oppen, George. *Selected Letters*. Edited by Rachel Blau DuPlessis. Duke University Press, 1990.
Orage, A. R. "Journals Insurgent." *New Age* 13, no. 15 (1913): 415.
Orage, A. R. "Notes of the Week." *New Age* 10, no. 23 (1912): 529.
Orage, A. R. *Readers and Writers*. George Allen & Unwin, 1922.
Orage, A. R. [R. H. C., pseud.]. "Readers and Writers." *New Age* 23, no. 13 (1918): 201.
Oxford English Dictionary. "gay (*adj., adv., & n.*)." https://doi.org/10.1093/OED/9277815405. Accessed February 2025.
Palme Dutt, R. *Fascism and Social Revolution*. Martin Lawrence, 1934.
Parker, Richard, ed. *Readings in The Cantos*. Vol. 1. Clemson University Press, 2018.
Patterson, Anita. "Jazz, Realism, and the Modernist Lyric: The Poetry of Langston Hughes." *Modern Language Quarterly* 61, no. 4 (2000): 651–82.
Paul, Catherine E. "Italian Fascist Exhibitions and Ezra Pound's Move to the Imperial." *Twentieth Century Literature* 51, no. 1 (2005): 64–97.
Penberthy, Jenny, ed. *Niedecker and the Correspondence with Zukofsky*. Cambridge University Press, 1993.
Penty, A. J. "Art and Revolution." *New Age* 14, no. 20 (1914): 617.
Penty, A. J. "The Restoration of Beauty to Life." Part 1. *New Age* 1, no. 1 (1907): 5.
Penty, A. J. "The Restoration of Beauty to Life." Part 2. *New Age* 1, no. 2 (1907): 21.
Penty, A. J. *Tradition and Modernism in Politics*. Sheed & Ward, 1937.
Perelman, Bob. *The Trouble with Genius: Reading Pound, Joyce, Stein, and Zukofsky*. University of California Press, 1994.
"Peripatetic Philosophers of This Many-Sided Town." *New York Times*, May 29, 1910.
Perloff, Marjorie. *Wittgenstein's Ladder: Poetic Language and the Strangeness of the Ordinary*. University of Chicago Press, 1996.
Pesotta, Rose. *Bread Upon the Waters*. Dodd, Mead, 1944.
Peters, Anna. "Books of the Day." *Daily Worker*, April 30, 1938, 11.
Peters, Margot. *Lorine Niedecker: A Poet's Life*. University of Wisconsin Press, 2011.
Ponce, Martin Joseph. "Langston Hughes's Queer Blues." *Modern Language Quarterly* 66, no. 4 (2005): 505–37.
Por, Odon. *Fascism*. Translated by E. Townshend. Labour, 1923.
Por, Odon. "Towards National Guilds in Italy." *New Age* 14, no. 10 (1919): 153.

BIBLIOGRAPHY

Posmentier, Sonya. *Cultivation and Catastrophe: The Lyric Ecology of Modern Black Literature*. Johns Hopkins University Press, 2017.
Postone, Moishe. *Time, Labor, and Social Domination*. Cambridge University Press, 1993.
Pound, Ezra. *ABC of Economics*. Peter Russell, 1953.
Pound, Ezra. *ABC of Reading*. Faber and Faber, 1991.
Pound, Ezra. "Antheil, 1924–1926." *New Criterion* 4, no. 4 (1926): 695–99.
Pound, Ezra. "*Cambridge Left* (Review)." *Poetry* 42, no. 6 (1933): 353.
Pound, Ezra. *Cathay*. Elkins Mathews, 1915.
Pound, Ezra. *The Cantos*. New Directions, 1993.
Pound, Ezra. *Collected Early Poems of Ezra Pound*. Edited by Michael John King. New Directions, 1976.
Pound, Ezra. "Contemporania." *Poetry* 2, no. 1 (1913): 1–12.
Pound, Ezra. "Credit and the Fine Arts: A Practical Application." *New Age* 30, no. 22 (1922): 284–85.
Pound, Ezra. "The Damn Fool Bureaukrats." *New Masses* 4 (1928): 15.
Pound, Ezra. "Demarcations." *British Union Quarterly* 1, no. 1 (1937): 38.
Pound, Ezra. "The Depression Has Just Begun." *Contempo* 1, no. 16 (1932): 4.
Pound, Ezra. *Ezra Pound to His Parents*. Edited by Mary de Rachewiltz, A. David Moody, and Joanna Moody. Oxford University Press, 2010.
Pound, Ezra. *Ezra Pound Speaking: Radio Speeches of WWII*. Greenwood, 1978.
Pound, Ezra. *Ezra Pound's Chinese Friends: Stories in Letters*. Edited by Zhaoming Qian. Oxford University Press, 2008.
Pound, Ezra. "A Few Don'ts by an Imagiste." *Poetry* 1, no. 6 (1913): 200–206.
Pound, Ezra. *Gaudier-Brzeska: A Memoir*. New Directions, 1970.
Pound, Ezra. *Guide to Kulchur*. Peter Owen, 1972.
Pound, Ezra. "How to Save Business. Invoking Social Credit Plus Free Economy to Prove No Man Wants Ten Million Washtubs." *Esquire* 1 (1936): 195–96.
Pound, Ezra. "I Gather the Limbs of Osiris: A Rather Dull Introduction." Part 2. *New Age* 10, no. 6 (1911): 130–31.
Pound, Ezra. "I Gather the Limbs of Osiris: On Technique." Part 9. *New Age* 10, no. 13 (1912): 297–99.
Pound, Ezra. "The Individual and His Milieu: A Study of Relations and Gesell." *Criterion* 15, no. 58 (1935): 30–45.
Pound, Ezra. "Italian Charter of Labour." *Action* 135 (1938): 4.
Pound, Ezra. *Jefferson and/or Mussolini: L'Idea Statale: Fascism as I Have Seen It*. Stanley Nott, 1932.
Pound, Ezra. *Lustra*. Elkin Matthews, 1916.
Pound, Ezra. *Machine Art and Other Writings: The Lost Thought of the Italian Years*. Edited by Maria Luisa Ardizzone. Duke University Press, 1996.
Pound, Ezra. "Machines." *New Review* 1, no. 4 (1931–32): 291–92.
Pound, Ezra. "Mike and Other Phenomena." *Morada* 5 (1930): 43.
Pound, Ezra. "Mussolini Defines State as 'Spirit of the People': Fascism Analyzed by Ezra Pound, Noted American Writer." *Chicago Tribune*, April 9, 1934, 5.
Pound, Ezra. [Bastien von Helmholtz, pseud.]. "On the Imbecility of the Rich." *Egoist* 1, no. 20 (1915): 389.
Pound, Ezra. "Open Letter to Tretyakow, Kolchoznik." *Front* 1, no. 2 (1931): 124–26.
Pound, Ezra. "Orientation and News Sense." *New English Weekly* 2, no. 12 (1933): 353.

BIBLIOGRAPHY

Pound, Ezra. "A Pact." *Poetry* 2, no. 1 (1913): 11–12.
Pound, Ezra. "Patria Mia." Part 4. *New Age* 11, no. 22 (1912): 515–16.
Pound, Ezra. "Patria Mia." Part 6. *New Age* 11, no. 24 (1912): 564.
Pound, Ezra. "Patria Mia." Part 8. *New Age* 11, no. 26 (1912): 611–12.
Pound, Ezra. "Pax Saturni." *Poetry* 2, no. 1 (1913): 8–10.
Pound, Ezra. "Pound Joins the Revolution!" *New Masses* 2, no. 2 (1926): 3.
Pound, Ezra. *Pound/Lewis*. Edited by Timothy Materer. Faber and Faber, 1985.
Pound, Ezra. *Pound/Williams*. Edited by Hugh Witemeyer. New Directions, 1996.
Pound, Ezra. *Pound/Zukofsky*. Edited by Barry Ahearn. Faber and Faber, 1987.
Pound, Ezra, ed. *Profile: An Anthology Collected in MCMXXXI*. John Scheiwiller, 1932.
Pound, Ezra. "The Revolt of Intelligence." *New Age* 26, no. 18 (1920): 287–88.
Pound, Ezra. *Selected Letters of Ezra Pound 1907–1941*. Edited by D. D. Paige. Faber and Faber, 1982.
Pound, Ezra. *Selected Prose 1909–1965*. Edited by William Cookson. New Directions, 1973.
Pound, Ezra. "The Serious Artist." Parts 1–2. *New Freewoman* 1, no. 9 (1913): 161–63.
Pound, Ezra. "The Serious Artist." Part 4. *New Freewoman* 1, no. 11 (1913): 213–14.
Pound, Ezra. *Social Credit: An Impact*. Stanley Nott, 1935.
Pound, Ezra. [Bastien von Helmholtz, pseud.]. "Suffragettes." *Egoist* 1, no. 13 (1914): 254–56.
Pound, Ezra. "Through Alien Eyes." Part 1. *New Age* 12, no. 11 (1913): 252–54.
Pound, Ezra. "Through Alien Eyes." Part 3. *New Age* 12, no. 13 (1913): 300–301.
Pound, Ezra. "Translator's Postscript." In *The Natural Philosophy of Love*, by Remy de Gourmont, translated by Ezra Pound, 295–311. Boni and Liveright, 1922.
Pound, Ezra. "Where Is American Culture?" *Nation* 126, no. 3276 (1928): 443–44.
Pound, Ezra. "Workshop Orchestration." *New Masses* 2, no. 5 (1927): 21.
Presley, Sharon, and Crispin Sartwell, eds. *Exquisite Rebel: The Essays of Voltairine de Cleyre, Feminist, Anarchist, Genius*. State University of New York, 2005.
Price, Leah, and Pamela Thurschwell, eds. *Literary Secretaries/Secretarial Culture*. Ashgate, 2005.
Pryor, Sean. "Canto 17." In *Readings in the Cantos*. Vol. 1. Edited by Richard Parker. Clemson University Press, 2018.
Pryor, Sean. *Poetry, Modernism, and an Imperfect World*. Cambridge University Press, 2017.
Pryor, Sean. "So Slow: Canto CVI." In *Glossator: Practice and Theory of the Commentary*. Vol. 10, *Astern in the Dinghy: Commentaries on Ezra's Pound's* Thrones de los Cantares XCVI–CIX, ed. Alexander Howard. Glossator, 2018.
Pryor, Sean. *W. B. Yeats, Ezra Pound, and the Poetry of Paradise*. Ashgate, 2011.
Pryor, Sean, and David Trotter, eds. *Writing, Medium, Machine: Modern Technographies*. Open Humanities, 2016.
Purdon, James. *Modernist Informatics: Literature, Information, and the State*. Oxford University Press, 2016.
Qian, Zhaoming, ed. *Ezra Pound and China*. University of Michigan Press, 2003.
Qian, Zhaoming. *Orientalism and Modernism: The Legacy of China in Pound and Williams*. Duke University Press, 1995.
Rabinowitz, Paula. *Labor and Desire: Revolutionary Women's Fiction in Depression America*. University of North Carolina Press, 1991.

Rainey, Lawrence. *Ezra Pound and the Monument of Culture: Text, History, and the Malatesta Cantos*. University of Chicago Press, 1991.
Rainey, Lawrence. *Institutions of Modernism: Literary Elites and Popular Culture*. Yale University Press, 1998.
Raitt, Suzanne. "The Rhetoric of Efficiency in Early Modernism." *Modernism/Modernity* 13, no. 1 (2006): 835–51.
Rampersad, Arnold. *The Life of Langston Hughes*. 2 vols. Oxford University Press, 1986–88.
Rancière, Jacques. "A Few Remarks on the Methods of Jacques Rancière." *Parallax* 15, no. 3 (2009): 114–23.
Randall, Bryony. *Modernism, Daily Time and Everyday Life*. Cambridge University Press, 2007.
Redding, J. Saunders. "Langston Hughes in an Old Vein with New Rhythms." *New York Herald Tribune Book Review*, March 11, 1951, 5.
Redman, Tim. *Ezra Pound and Italian Fascism*. Cambridge University Press, 1991.
Reed, Anthony. *Freedom Time: The Poetics and Politics of Black Experimental Writing*. Johns Hopkins University Press, 2014.
Reed, John. "Sangar." *Poetry* 1, no. 3 (1912): 71–74.
Reed, John. "A Word to Mr. Pound." *Poetry* 2, no. 3 (1913): 112–13.
Regenstein, Milton. "Pictures of the Ghetto." *New York Times*, November 14, 1897.
Reich, Steven A. *A Working People: A History of African American Workers Since Emancipation*. Rowman & Littlefield, 2013.
Reid, B. L. *Art by Subtraction: A Dissenting Opinion of Gertrude Stein*. University of Oklahoma Press, 1958.
Reid, Margaret G. *Economics of Household Production*. John Wiley, 1934.
Reznikoff, Charles. *Family Chronicle*. Universe, 1971.
Richards, Juno Jill. *The Fury Archives: Female Citizenship, Human Rights, and the International Avant-Gardes*. Columbia University Press, 2020.
Richards, Juno Jill. "Oceans, Archives, Perverts: Sex Work in the Colonial Port City." *GLQ* 28, no. 4 (2022): 541–66.
Ridge, Lola. *The Ghetto, and Other Poems: An Annotated Edition*. Edited by Lawrence Kramer. Fordham University Press, 2023.
Ridge, Lola. *To the Many: Collected Early Works*. Edited by Daniel Tobin. Little Island, 2018.
Riis, Jacob. *How the Other Half Lives: Studies Among the Tenements of New York*. Dover, 1971.
Riley, Denise. *"Am I That Name?" Feminism and the Category of "Women" in History*. University of Minnesota Press, 1988.
Riley, Peter. *Whitman, Melville, Crane, and the Labors of American Poetry: Against Vocation*. Oxford University Press, 2019.
Roach, Rebecca. "'How Writers Work': Interviewing the Author in Everyman." *Textual Practice* 30, no. 4 (2016): 645–67.
Robbins, Bruce. "The Sweatshop Sublime." *PMLA* 117, no. 1 (2022): 84–97.
Roberts, John. *The Intangibilities of Form: Skill and Deskilling in Art After the Readymade*. Verso, 2007.
Robinson, Cedric J. *Black Marxism: The Making of the Black Radical Tradition*. University of North Carolina Press, 2000.

BIBLIOGRAPHY

Roche, Hannah. *The Outside Thing: Modernist Lesbian Romance*. Columbia University Press, 2019.
Rodgers, Daniel T. *The Work Ethic in Industrial America: 1850–1920*. University of Chicago Press, 2014.
Roediger, David. *Wages of Whiteness*. Verso, 1991.
Roediger, David R., and Elizabeth D. Esch, eds. *The Production of Difference: Race and the Management of Labor in U.S. History*. Oxford University Press, 2014.
Roessel, David. "'A Racial Act': The Letters of Ezra Pound and Langston Hughes." In *Ezra Pound and African American Modernism*. Edited by David Coyle, 207–42. University Press of New England, 2001.
Ronda, Margaret. "'Not Much Left': Wageless Life in Millennial Poetry." *Post45*, October 9, 2011. https://post45.org/2011/10/not-much-left-wageless-life-in-millenial-poetry/.
Ronda, Margaret. *Remainders: American Poetry at Nature's End*. Stanford University Press, 2018.
Ronda, Margaret. "'Work and Wait Unwearying': Dunbar's Georgics." *PMLA* 127, no. 4 (2012): 863–78.
Rosenfeld, Morris. "The Sweatshop." In *Sing, Stranger: A Century of American Yiddish Poetry: A Historical Anthology*. Translated by Benjamin Harshav and Barbara Harshav. Edited by Benjamin Harshav. Stanford University Press, 2006.
Rosenthal, M. L., and Sally M. Gall. *The Modern Poetic Sequence: The Genius of Modern Poetry*. Oxford University Press, 1983.
Rosner, Victoria. *Machines for Living*. Oxford University Press, 2020.
Ross, Kristin. *Communal Luxury: The Political Imaginary of the Paris Commune*. Verso, 2015.
Ruddick, Lisa. *Reading Gertrude Stein: Body, Text, Gnosis*. Cornell University Press, 1990.
Rutherford, Janice Williams. *Selling Mrs. Consumer: Christine Frederick and the Rise of Household Efficiency*. University of Georgia Press, 2003.
Sabin, Arthur J. *Red Scare in Court: New York Versus the International Workers Order*. University of Pennsylvania Press, 1993.
Saint-Amour, Paul. "Weak Modernism, Weak Theory." *Modernism/Modernity* 25, no. 3 (2018): 437–59.
Santayana, George. *The Letters of George Santayana*. Vol. 5. Edited by W. G. Holzberger. MIT Press, 2004.
Schneider, Caitlin. "Read a Publisher's Rejection Letter to Gertrude Stein." *Mental Floss*, June 30, 2015. https://www.mentalfloss.com/article/65717/read-publishers-rejection-letter-gertrude-stein.
Scott, Jonathan. "Advanced, Repressed, and Popular: Langston Hughes During the Cold War." *College Literature* 33, no. 2 (2006): 30–51.
Secombe, Wally. "The Housewife and Her Labour Under Capitalism." *New Left Review* 1, no. 83 (1984): 3–24.
Sedgwick, Eve Kosofsky. *Tendencies*. Duke University Press, 1993.
Shapiro, Herbert. "Lincoln Steffens and the McNamara Case: A Progressive Response to Class Conflict." *American Journal of Economics and Sociology* 39, no. 4 (1980): 397–412.
Sharpe, Christina. *In the Wake: On Blackness and Being*. Duke University Press, 2016.

BIBLIOGRAPHY

Shelley, Percy Bysshe. *Adonais and A Defence of Poetry*. James Brodie, 1955.
Sherry, Vincent B. *Ezra Pound, Wyndham Lewis, and Radical Modernism*. Oxford University Press, 1993.
Shiach, Morag. *Modernism, Labour and Selfhood in British Literature and Culture, 1890–1930*. Cambridge University Press, 2004.
Shudson, Michael. "Delectable Materialism." In *Consumer Society in American History*. Edited by Lawrence B. Glickman, 341–58. Cornell University Press, 1999.
Sieburth, Richard. "In Pound We Trust: The Economy of Poetry/The Poetry of Economy." *Critical Inquiry* 14, no. 1 (1987): 142–72.
Silliman, Ron. "Third-Phase Objectivism." *Paideuma* 10, no. 1 (1981): 85–91.
Singh, Julietta. *Unthinking Mastery: Dehumanism and Decolonial Entanglements*. Duke University Press, 2017.
Skinner, B. F. "Has Gertrude Stein a Secret?" *Atlantic Monthly* 153, no. 1 (1934): 50–57.
Smethurst, James Edward. *The New Red Negro: The Literary Left and African American Poetry, 1930–46*. Oxford University Press, 1999.
Sohn-Rethel, Alfred. *Intellectual and Manual Labour: A Critique of Epistemology*. Translated by Martin Sohn-Rethel. Macmillan, 1978.
Solomon, Jeff. "Gertrude Stein, Opium Queen: Notes on a Mistaken Embrace." *Journal of Lesbian Studies* 17, no. 1 (2013): 7–24.
Soyer, Daniel, ed. *A Coat of Many Colors: Immigration, Globalization, and Reform in New York City's Garment Industry*. Fordham University Press, 2004.
Spahr, Juliana. *Everybody's Autonomy: Connective Reading and Collective Identity*. University of Alabama Press, 2001.
Spahr, Juliana. *Well Then There Now*. Black Sparrow, 2011.
Stanford Friedman, Susan. *Planetary Modernisms: Provocations on Modernity Across Time*. Columbia University Press, 2015.
Steffens, Lincoln. *The Autobiography of Lincoln Steffens*. Harrap, 1931.
Stein, Gertrude. *The Autobiography of Alice B. Toklas*. Literary Guild, 1933.
Stein, Gertrude. *Everybody's Autobiography*. William Heinemann, 1938.
Stein, Gertrude. *Fernhurst, Q.E.D., and Other Early Writings*. Liveright, 1971.
Stein, Gertrude. *The Geographical History of America, or The Relation of Human Nature to the Human Mind*. Johns Hopkins University Press, 1995.
Stein, Gertrude. *Lectures in America*. Random House, 1935.
Stein, Gertrude. *The Making of Americans*. Dalkey, 1995.
Stein, Gertrude. *Money*. Black Sparrow, 1973.
Stein, Gertrude. *Narration: Four Lectures*. University of Chicago Press, 1935.
Stein, Gertrude. *Portraits and Prayers*. Random House, 1934.
Stein, Gertrude. *Stanzas in Meditation: The Corrected Edition*. Edited by Susannah Hollister and Emily Setina. Yale University Press, 2012.
Stein, Gertrude. *Tender Buttons*. Claire Marie, 1914.
Stein, Gertrude. *Wars I Have Seen*. B. T. Batsford, 1945.
Stein, Gertrude. *Writings 1903–32*. Library of America, 1998.
Stein, Gertrude. *Writings 1932–46*. Library of America, 1998.
Stein, Gertrude. *The Yale Edition of the Unpublished Writings of Gertrude Stein*. 7 vols. Yale University Press, 1951–58.
Steven, Mark. "Reading Capital, Writing History: Pound's Marx." *Modernism/Modernity* 24, no. 4 (2017): 771–90.

BIBLIOGRAPHY

Steven, Mark. *Red Modernism: American Poetry and the Spirit of Communism*. Johns Hopkins University Press, 2017.
Stevens, Wallace. *Collected Poetry and Prose*. Library of America, 1997.
Stewart, Susan. *The Poet's Freedom: A Notebook on Making*. University of Chicago Press, 2011.
Stimpson, Catharine R. "The Mind, the Body, and Gertrude Stein." *Critical Inquiry* 3, no. 3 (1977): 489–506.
Stimpson, Catharine R. "The Somagrams of Gertrude Stein." *Poetics Today* 6, nos. 1–2 (1985): 67–80.
Stone, Marla. "Staging Fascism: The Exhibition of the Fascist Revolution." *Journal of Contemporary History* 28, no. 2 (1993): 215–43.
Strasser, Susan. *Never Done: A History of American Housework*. Pantheon, 1982.
Strychacz, Thomas. *Modernism, Mass Culture, and Professionalism*. Cambridge University Press, 1993.
Sullivan, Hannah. *The Work of Revision*. Harvard University Press, 2013.
Surette, Leon. "A Dangerous Difference: Pound, Douglas, and Proudhon." In *Ezra Pound and Referentiality*. Edited by Hélène Aji, 249–66. Presses de l'Université Paris Sorbonne, 2003.
Svoboda, Terese. *Anything That Burns You: A Portrait of Lola Ridge, Radical Poet*. Schaffner, 2016.
Swan, Alessandra Anatola. "The Iconic Body: Mussolini Unclothed." *Modern Italy* 21, no. 4 (2016): 361–81.
Taylor, Julie. *Djuna Barnes and Affective Modernism*. Edinburgh University Press, 2012.
Taylor, Julie, ed. *Modernism and Affect*. Edinburgh University Press, 2015.
Taylor, Julie. "On Holding and Being Held: Hart Crane's Queer Intimacy." *Twentieth Century Literature* 60, no. 3 (2014): 305–35.
Terrell, Carroll F. *A Companion to the Cantos of Ezra Pound*. 2 vols. University of California Press, 1980.
Thompson, E. P. "Time, Work-Discipline, and Industrial Capitalism." *Past & Present* 38 (1967): 56–97.
Tiffany, Daniel. *Radio Corpse: Imagism and the Cryptaesthetic of Ezra Pound*. Harvard University Press, 1995.
Toklas, Alice B. *The Alice B. Toklas Cookbook*. Lyons, 1984.
Toklas, Alice B. *What Is Remembered*. Holt, Rinehart and Winston, 1963.
Toscano, Alberto. *Late Fascism: Race, Capitalism, and the Politics of Crisis*. Verso, 2023.
Trachtenberg, Alan. "The Politics of Labor and the Poet's Work: A Reading of 'A Song for Occupations.'" In *Walt Whitman: The Centennial Essays*. Edited by Ed Folsom. University of Iowa Press, 1994.
Tracy, Steven C. *Langston Hughes and the Blues*. University of Illinois Press, 1988.
Trotsky, Leon. *Leon Trotsky on Literature and Art*. Edited by Paul N. Siegel. Pathfinder, 1970.
Trotter, David. *The Literature of Connection: Signal, Medium, Interface, 1850–1950*. Oxford University Press, 2020.
Turner, Jack. *Awakening to Race: Individualism and Social Consciousness in America*. University of Chicago Press, 2012.
Turner, Kay, ed. *Baby Precious Always Shines: Selected Love Notes Between Gertrude Stein and Alice Toklas*. St. Martin's, 2000.

Turner, Lindsay. "Lullaby & Labor: Alice Notley and the Work of Poetry." *Contemporary Women's Writing* 12, no. 3 (2018): 289–305.
Turner, Lindsay. "Writing/Not Writing: Anne Boyer, Paralipsis, and Literary Work." *ASAP/Journal* 3, no. 1 (2018): 121–42.
Tyler, Gus. *Look for the Union Label: A History of the International Ladies' Garment Workers' Union*. Routledge, 2016.
"Under the Lash of the Whip: A Column of Constructive Criticism of Men and Measures in the Hope of Correcting Errors and Evils." *Chicago Whip*, February 25, 1927.
Vaingurt, Julia. "Poetry of Labor and Labor of Poetry: The Universal Language of Alexei Gastev's Biomechanics." *Russian Review* 67, no. 2 (2008): 209–29.
Vaingurt, Julia. *Wonderlands of the Avant-Garde: Technology and the Arts in Russia of the 1920s*. Northwestern University Press, 2013.
van Gyseghem, André. *Theater in Soviet Russia*. Faber and Faber, 1943.
Verdad, S. "S. Verdad and Foreign Politics." *New Age* 9, no. 26 (1911): 619–20.
Virno, Paolo. *A Grammar of the Multitude*. Translated by Isabella Bertoletti, James Cascaito, and Andrea Casson. Semiotext(e), 2004.
Vogel, Lise. *Marxism and the Oppression of Women: Toward a Unitary Theory*. Brill, 2013.
von Geldern, James. "Culture, 1900–1945." In *The Cambridge History of Russia*. Vol. 3, *The Twentieth Century*. Edited by Ronald Grigor Suny, 579–604. Cambridge University Press, 2006.
Wain, John. "The Shadow of an Epic." *Spectator* (1960): 360.
Waithe, Marcus, and Claire White, eds. *The Labor of Literature in Britain and France, 1830–1910*. Palgrave, 2018.
Wald, Alan. *American Night: The Literary Left in the Era of the Cold War*. University of North Carolina Press, 2012.
Wald, Alan. *Exiles from a Future Time: The Forging of the Mid-Twentieth-Century Literary Left*. University of North Carolina Press, 2002.
Wald, Alan. *Writing from the Left: New Essays on Radical Culture and Politics*. Verso, 1994.
Wald, Priscilla. *Constituting Americans: Cultural Anxiety and Narrative Form*. Duke University Press, 1995.
Wall, Joshua Logan. "Family Business: Charles Reznikoff in Text and Textile." *Studies in American Jewish Literature* 37, no. 1 (2018): 37–55.
Wall, Joshua Logan. *Situating Poetry: Covenant and Genre in American Modernism*. Johns Hopkins University Press, 2022.
Walton, Jean. "Female Peristalsis." *differences* 13, no. 2 (2002): 57–89.
Warren, Lansing. "Gertrude Stein Views Life and Politics." *New York Times*, May 6, 1934.
Warwick Research Collective. *Combined and Uneven Development: Towards a New Theory of World-Literature*. Liverpool University Press, 2015.
Washington, Mary Helen. *The Other Blacklist: The African American Literary and Cultural Left of the 1950s*. Columbia University Press, 2014.
Watten, Barrett. *The Constructivist Moment: From Material Text to Cultural Poetics*. Wesleyan University Press, 2003.
Weber, Max. *The Protestant Ethic and the Spirit of Capitalism*. Translated by Stephen Kalberg. Oxford University Press, 2011.

BIBLIOGRAPHY

Weeks, Kathi. *The Problem with Work: Feminism, Marxism, Antiwork Politics, and Postwork Imaginaries*. Duke University Press, 2011.
Welch, Lew. *How I Read Gertrude Stein*. Grey Fox, 1996.
Whitman, Walt. *Complete Poetry and Collected Prose*. Library of America, 1982.
Wild, Jonathan. *The Rise of the Office Clerk in Literary Culture, 1880–1939*. Palgrave Macmillan, 2006.
Wilhelm, James J. *Ezra Pound in London and Paris*. Pennsylvania State University Press, 1990.
Wilkinson, John. "Jim the Jerk: Bathos and Loveliness in the Poetry of James Schuyler." In *On Bathos: Literature, Art, Music*. Edited by Sara Crangle and Peter Nicholls, 71–89. Continuum, 2010.
Will, Barbara. *Gertrude Stein, Bernard Faÿ, and the Vichy Dilemma*. Columbia University Press, 2015.
Will, Barbara. *Gertrude Stein, Modernism, and the Problem of "Genius"*. Edinburgh University Press, 2000.
Williams, R. John. *The Buddha in the Machine: Art, Technology, and the Meeting of East and West*. Yale University Press, 2014.
Williams, Raymond. *Culture and Materialism: Selected Essays*. Verso, 2005.
Williams, Raymond. *Marxism and Literature*. Oxford University Press, 1977.
Williams, Raymond. *The Politics of Modernism: Against the New Conformists*. Verso, 1989.
Williams, William Carlos. *Spring and All*. New Directions, 2011.
Willis, Elizabeth. "The Poetics of Affinity: Lorine Niedecker, William Morris, and the Art of Work." *Contemporary Literature* 46, no. 4 (2005): 579–603.
Wilson, Peter. *A Preface to Ezra Pound*. Longman, 1997.
Winant, Gabriel. *The Next Shift: The Fall of Industry and the Rise of Health Care in Rust Belt America*. Harvard University Press, 2021.
Winnicott, D. W. *Playing and Reality*. Routledge, 2002.
Winterson, Jeanette. "All I Know About Gertrude Stein." *Granta* 115, May 19, 2011.
Wisconsin: A Guide to the Badger State, Compiled by Workers of the Writers' Program of the Works Projects Administration in the State of Wisconsin. Duell, Sloan and Pearce, 1941.
Witemeyer, Hugh. "Clothing the American Adam: Pound's Tailoring of Walt Whitman." In *Ezra Pound Among the Poets*. Edited by George Bornstein, 81–105. University of Chicago Press, 1985.
Wordsworth, William, and Samuel Taylor Coleridge. *Lyrical Ballads*. Edited by R. L. Brett and A. R. Jones. Routledge, 1988.
Worrall, Nick. *Modernism to Realism on the Soviet Stage: Tairov, Vakhtangov, Okhlopkov*. Cambridge University Press, 1989.
Wright, Richard. *12 Million Black Voices: A Folk History of the Negro in the United States*. Viking, 1941.
Yeats, W. B. *Collected Poems*. Macmillan, 1951.
Yeats, W. B. Introduction to *The Oxford Book of Modern Verse, 1892–1935*. Clarendon, 1936.
You, Mia. "Buttons and Holes: Picasso and Stein at the Bon Maché." *ELH* 87, no. 3 (2020): 791–828.
Zamagni, Vera. *The Economic History of Italy 1860–1990: Recovery After Decline*. Oxford University Press, 1993.

Zieger, Robert H., Timothy J. Minchin, and Gilbert J. Gall. *American Workers, American Unions*. Johns Hopkins University Press, 2014.
Zimmer, Kenyon. *Immigrants Against the State: Yiddish and Italian Anarchism in America*. University of Illinois Press, 2015.
Zukofsky, Louis. *Prepositions +*. University Press of New England, 2000.
Zukofsky, Louis. "Sincerity and Objectification: With Special Reference to the Work of Charles Reznikoff." *Poetry* 37, no. 5 (1931): 272–85.

INDEX

A-A'-B structure, 112
ABC of Economics (Pound, E.), 55
ABC of Reading (Pound, E.), 2
"Accidentals" (Ridge), 94
administrative labor, 140
agrarian societies, 61, 64
Ahmed, Sara, 155–56, 202
Aldington, Richard, 45
Alice B. Toklas Cookbook, The (Toklas), 167
amateur crafted objects, 32, 206–7
American Guide (Federal Writers Project), 191
American Negro Labor Congress, 108–9
anarchism, 74, 86, 233n13, 233n23
"Anarchism" (de Cleyre), 84
Anarchist Federation of America, 74
anarchist feminism scene, 83–85
anarchist social ideal, 78
Anew (Zukofsky), 190
Antheil, George, 53
Arendt, Hannah, 14–15
Armantrout, Rae, 199
art, 5–6, 22, 119, 120
artisans, 11, 31–32
artists, 34–43, 228n59
Art of Worldly Wisdom, The (Rexroth), 190
Arts and Crafts movement, 37, 175, 225n6
Ashbery, John, 157, 167
Ashton, Howard, 75
Ashton, Jennifer, 146

Ashton, Julian, 75
Attridge, John, 24
Audubon, John James, 191
Autobiography of Alice B. Toklas, The (Stein), 140, 148, 157–58, 164
avant-garde, 143, 169

Bacigalupo, Massimo, 63
Bajorek, Jennifer, 7
ballad, 69, 127
"Ballad for Ozie Powell" (Hughes), 127
"Ballads for Lenin" (Hughes), 127
Ballet Mécanique (film), 53
Baraitser, Lisa, 142
Barry, Kevin, 100
bathos mode, 188–89, 198
Battle for Grain propaganda, 58
Beasley, Rebecca, 67
Beauvoir, Simone de, 207
Bel Esprit scheme, 44–45, 227n52
Bell, Ian F. A., 58
Berke, Nancy, 232n11
Berkman, Alexander, 74, 235n57
Berlant, Lauren, 164–65
Berman, Jessica, 43
Bernes, Jasper, 22, 188
Bevis, Matthew, 69
"Big-Timer, The" (Hughes), 121
Binyon, Laurence, 60
biomechanics, 123–24

Black and White (Chernye i belye), 114–15, 239nn42–43
Blackhawk Island, *178*, 182–84, *183*
Black Marxism (Robinson, C.), 105
Blackness: aesthetic experiment, 105–6; capitalism denying freedom to, 116; folklore of, 134; labor movement of, 108–9, 222n32; radical literature of, 237n6; school lectures to, 242n96; struggle for freedom of, 134; women, 221n32
Bloch, Ernst, 36
blue-collar labor, 187
"Blueprint for Negro Writing" (Wright), 136
blues poems, 30–31, 110–11, 113
Bodenheim, Maxwell, 78
bodily emissions, 149–50
Bogdanov, Aleksandr, 119, 123
Bookstaver, May, 158
"Bound No'th Blues" (Hughes), 111–12
Boyer, Anne, 68, 98, 100, 236n74
Brady, Andrea, 70
Braverman, Harry, 229n78
Brenner, Robert, 22
Brik, Osip, 119
"Broke" (Hughes), 121
Brooker, Peter, 46
Brotherhood of Sleeping Car Porters (BSCP), 109
Brown, Sterling, 30, 110–11
Bryan-Wilson, Julia, 176, 207
BSCP. *See* Brotherhood of Sleeping Car Porters
Bunting, Basil, 2, 218
Burckhardt, Jacob, 38
Burstein, Jessica, 150

Cahier d'un retour au pays natal (Césaire), 14, 96
calendar, of Niedecker, *179*
Cantos, The (Pound, E.), 3; Canto I, 43–44; Canto CII, 64; Canto CVI, 62–63, 65; Canto CVIII, 58; Canto LIII, 60; Canto LIV, 64; Canto LXIX, 58–60; Canto LXVI, 61; Canto VIII, 46; Canto XCIX, 64, 66; Canto XCVII, 33; Canto XVII, 47–50; Canto XXII, 56; Canto XXVI, 51; Canto XXVII, 51; Canto XXXIII, 55; "Malatesta Cantos," 45–46
Capital (Marx), 7–8, 56, 126

capitalism, 25–26; accumulation in, 12; Black freedom under, 116; daily life fragmentation under, 10; de Cleyre on, 84–85; labor alienation in, 35–36, 67; labor power in, 7–8, 11, 16–17; the working day in, 97; poems valuing, 29; pre-capitalist history in, 222n62; production in, 21, 126–27; racial, 12, 105; radical anticapitalism in, 57; as system of domination, 105; unequal development in, 14; violence of, 129; workers suffering under, 202
capitalist labor market, 19–20
Carter, Huntly, 118
Cecire, Natalia, 38, 141
Césaire, Aimé, 14, 96–97
"Chant for May Day" (Hughes), 121–26, 129, 132, 135–36
"Chant for Tom Mooney" (Hughes), 121–22, 241n74
chant poems, of Hughes, 121
Chao, Tze-chiang, 63
Chernye i belye (Black and White) (film), 114–15, 239nn42–43
Chi, Tsui, 60
child labor, 55
China, 60–61, 230n107
Chinese agrarian practices, 29, 60–61, 65–67
Chow, Juliana, 246n55
chronocatachresis, 169
civilization, poetry creating, 45
Civilization of the Renaissance in Italy, The (Burckhardt), 38
Clark, T. J., 10, 127
Cleyre, Voltairine de, 84–85
Coal Mines (Minimum Wage) Act, 37
Coke, Edward, 58
Collected Works (Niedecker), 177–78, 180
collective life, 70–71, 85–86, 101, 119, 126–27
"Colored Soldier, The" (Hughes), 121
"Command Poem, A" (Stein), 164
common language, 90
communism, 26, 116
Communist Party USA, 52, 116
"Composition as Explanation" (Stein), 245n39
condensery, 1–3, 5, 197
Conrad, Joseph, 10
Constructivism, Russian, 30, 104, 106, 122
Constructivist theater, 104, 115–16, 131–32
"Contemporania" (Pound, E.), 29, 39–40, 67
Cooke, Jennifer, 165

INDEX

cooking, poems concerning, 181
"Cooking Book, A" (Niedecker), *184*, 185
Corman, Cid, 176–79
Cornell, Andrew, 233n13
Cory, Daniel, 186, 250n34
craft essays, 225n6
craft labor, 29, 37, 43, 47, 52, 65–67, 175, 190, 199
craft model, 32, 35–36
craft of prosody, 46
craftsman, 3, 36–43, 50, 229n78
Crane, Stephen, 76
Credit Power and Democracy (Douglas, C.), 44
Creekmore, Hubert, 190
Cruz-Fernández, Paula A. de la, 235n65
cultural past, 9, 54
custodial labor, 176

Dalla Costa, Mariarosa, 16–17, 139
"Dark Youth of the U.S.A." (Hughes), 121
Davidson, Michael, 245n49
Davie, Donald, 48–50, 62
Davies, Kevin, 172
da Vinci, Leonardo, 136
Dawahare, Anthony, 104
De'Ath, Amy, 19
Decker, James A., 190, 251n43
Denenberg, Gussie, 235n47
Denning, Michael, 5, 12, 111, 237n6
Depestre, René, 96
Derleth, August, 190
Desires of Mothers to Please Others in Letters, The (Mayer), 210
Deutsch, Babette, 78–79
Divus, Andreas, 43
Dollar Diplomacy (Nearing), 52
domestic labor, 19, 152–54, 175, 182, 185, 194
Don't You Want to Be Free? (Hughes), 134, 136
Douglas, Ann, 151
Douglas, C. H., 44, 54, 227n47
Douglass, Frederick, 240n56
"Draft 6" (DuPlessis), 216
Drafts (DuPlessis), 23, 32, 213–14, 217
Drafts & Fragments (Pound, E.), 57
Dunbar, Paul Laurence, 112
DuPlessis, Rachel Blau, 15, 175, 211–12; "Draft 6" by, 216; *Drafts* by, 23, 32, 213–14, 217; feminist practices and, 215; *Interstices* by, 213; "Midrush" by, 215–16;

on Niedecker, 173; Noah and floods from, 214–15; poetics of gift exchange from, 180; *Surge* by, 213
Dydo, Ulla E., 140, 142n79, 157–58

Economic Democracy (Douglas, C.), 44
ecstasy, 203–6
education, higher, 223n67
Edwards, Brent Hayes, 111
efficiency gospel, 11–12
Ehlers, Sarah, 27, 71, 129
"Elevator Boy" (Hughes), 107, 110–12
Eliot, T. S., 20–21, 43–45, 227nn52–53, 228n57
Elkins, Amy, 27
engineers, 229n78
environmental devastation, 208
E.P.I.C. *See* Ezra Pound International Conference
epic, 26, 43, 214, 217
"Epilogue" (Pound, E.), 42–43
epistemic virtue, 226n23
epyllion, 214
equality, 14, 101–2
études (physical exercises), 124, *125*
Everybody's Autobiography (Stein), 143
E. W. Bliss Company, 53
Exhibition of the Fascist Revolution, 61
eyesight, Niedecker's deteriorating, 194
Ezra Pound International Conference (E.P.I.C.), 33

factory labor, 52–54
Family Chronicle (Reznikoff), 86
Farm Security Administration, 133
fascism, 36, 57, 61, 64, 114, 225n7
"Favorite Sunlit Road Calendar, The" (Niedecker), *179*, 179
FBI report, on Hughes, 103, 242n95
Fearing, Kenneth, 113
Federici, Silvia, 17, 19, 70, 99, 139, 222n62
Feldman, Matthew, 225n7
Felski, Rita, 24
female citizenship, 87
femininity, 15–16, 20, 63–64
feminism: anarchist feminism scene and, 83–85; craft techniques embraced by, 32, 175–76; DuPlessis on practices of, 215; Marxist-Feminist perspective in, 15–20; modernism's revision of, 23–24; movement in, 176

INDEX

feminist labor theory, 196
Fenollosa, Ernest, 91
Fifield, Alfred C., 244n22
Fifth Decad of Cantos, The (Pound, E.), 36, 58
55 Poems (Zukofsky), 190
Fine Clothes to the Jew (Hughes), 30, 104, 106–8; Fearing's review of, 113; Rampersad's praise for, 236n4; as stanzaic blues poem, 110
First All-Union Congress of Soviet Writers, 116
Fitts, Dudley, 65
Foley, Barbara, 9, 237n6
"For Best Work" (Niedecker), 199, 201, 206
forced labor, 8
Ford, Henry, 53, 54
"Foreclosure" (Niedecker), 182–83
For Paul (Niedecker), 180
Fourth Congress of the Communist International, 116, 129
Frank, Leo, 100, 236n77
"Frank Little at Calvary" (Ridge), 94
Fraser, Nancy, 8, 105, 139
Frederick, Christine, 31, 152–53
freedom, 6, 134, 206
Freedom, Elizabeth, 169
Freedom Time (Reed, A.), 106
Freeman, Elizabeth, 142
Friedman, Susan Stanford, 25
Fury Archives, The (Richards, J.), 87

Gall, Sally, 78
Gallup, Donald, 145
Gan, Aleksei, 129
Ganz, Marie, 73
gardening, 167–69
garment industry, 69, 71–74, 99; immigrants in, 233n14; textiles in, 94–95; women in, 78–87
Garments Against Women (Boyer), 98
garment workers, 86–87
Gastev, Alexei, 124
Gaudier-Brzeska (Pound, E.), 38
Gaudier-Brzeska, Henri, 34, 91
gayness, 156–57, 222n46, 246n73
gendered labor, 14, 19, 152, 190, 213
gendered social roles, 18–19, 23, 246n62
genderless subjects, 19

generative process, 171
genetic engineering, of seeds, 209–10
Georgics (Virgil), 220n28
German Ideology, The (Marx), 8
Gesell, Silvio, 58
"Ghetto, The" (Ridge), 69–75, 77–81, 101–2; city seen through textiles by, 94–95; fifth section of, 88–89; religious observance in, 93–94; review praising vision of, 90–92; working women in, 80–82, 234n39; Yiddish language in, 30
Ghetto and Other Poems, The (Ridge), 69, 73–79, 94
gift-giving, 179–80
Gilman, Charlotte Perkins, 151–52
Ginsberg, Allen, 57
Glaser, Amelia, 71
glassblowing, 51–52
Glazer, Nona Y., 196
Glazhdinsky, 86
global assembly line, 97–98
Global Modernists on Modernism (Moody and Ross), 25
Godley, Andrew, 235n65
Gold, Mike, 52, 120, 140
Goldman, Emma, 75, 84, 86, 99, 235n64
Goodman, Bergdorf, 143
Gotby, Alva, 222n62
Gough, Maria, 106
Grebner, Georgii Eduardovich, 114
Guide to Kulchur (Pound, E.), 60
Guild system, 230n98
Gypsy Theater, 120

Haas, Robert, 148
Hardt, Michael, 8
Harootunian, Harry, 14, 61
Harrison, Austin, 143
Hartel, Maude, 185
Hartman, Saidiya, 86
Harvey, David, 12
health care industry, 195–97
Heap, Jane, 145
Hejinian, Lyn, 31, 139, 168, 170–71
Hemingway, Ernest, 145–46
Hepworth, Barbara, 34
heteronormative relationship, 159
Hieratic Head of Ezra Pound (Gaudier-Brzeska), 34

INDEX

higher education, 223n67
historicism, 13
Hoard's Dairyman, 173, 194
Hochschild, Arlie Russell, 196
Hog Butchers, Beggars, and Busboys (Marsh), 22
Hollingworth, Mary, 228n59
Hollister, Susannah, 158
Home, The (Gilman), 151
home economics courses, 246n57
home life, of Niedecker, 182–83
Homemade/Handmade Poems (Niedecker), 190, 197–98, *198*, 200, 202–3; amateur crafted objects embraced in, 206; cover for, *177–78*; disappointments in, 181–82; poetic self-seriousness and, 185–86
"Homemade Poems" (Niedecker), 176, 178
home ownership, 183
"Hospital Kitchen" (Niedecker), 197–98, 201, 205–6
hospital labor, 197
Houghton, Norris, 117
housework, unwaged, 17
How the Other Half Lives (Riis), 76
Hughes, Langston, 25, 70, 103, 138, 211; "Ballad for Ozie Powell" by, 127; "Ballads for Lenin" by, 127; "The Big-Timer" by, 121; in Black radical literature, 237n6; "Bound No'th Blues" by, 111–12; "Broke" by, 121; "Chant for May Day" by, 121–26, 129, 132, 135–36; "Chant for Tom Mooney" by, 121–22, 241n74; chant poems of, 121; "The Colored Soldier" by, 121; "Dark Youth of the U.S.A." by, 121; "Elevator Boy" by, 107, 110–12; FBI report on, 242n95; *Fine Clothes to the Jew* by, 30, 104, 106–8, 110, 113, 236n4; on freedoms, 6; *I Wonder as I Wander* by, 131; Lee on inconsistencies from, 239n42; Negro school lectures by, 242n96; *A New Song* by, 30–31, 120–23; *Not Without Laughter* by, 107; papers by, 114; political imagination of, 105; on politics and poetry, 106, 132–33; porter's labor described by, 109–10; E. Pound friendship with, 38n40; purges addressed by, 240n56; race relations film by, 114; revolutionary verse by, 30; *Scottsboro Limited* by, 134; in Soviet Union, 116–17; "Wait" by, 128–29, 131–32; *The Weary Blues* by, 106, 135

Huiswoud, Otto, 116
human characteristics, 7
humanist ideas, 8
human labor, 199

idealism, 9
ideograms, 66, 231n128
"I Gather the Limbs of Osiris" (Pound, E.), 38
ILGWU. *See* International Ladies' Garment Workers' Union
immigrants, 74, 232n1, 233n14
"In a Station of the Metro" (Pound, E.), 36, 42–43, 47
"The Incinerator" (Spahr), 98
indigenous dwelling structures, 191
individuals, in collective life, 126–27
industrialization, 11–12, 155–56
industrial laundries, 252n66
Industrial Workers of the World (1905), 12
inefficiency, of domestic labor, 152–54
institutional cleaning, 195
International Ladies' Garment Workers' Union (ILGWU), 74, 82–84
International Workers Order (IWO), 120, 241n67, 241n69
Interstices (DuPlessis), 213
intimate relationships, 165
I vitrei, 51
IWO. *See* International Workers Order
I Wonder as I Wander (Hughes), 131
Izenberg, Oren, 71

Jackson, Virginia, 69
James, Selma, 16–17, 139
Jameson, Fredric, 7, 9–11, 14, 26
Jarrell, Randall, 65
Jefferson and/or Mussolini (Pound, E.), 54
Jennison, Ruth, 11, 26, 193
Jewish community, 69, 71
Jim Crow America, 108, 116
Jones, Gail, 236n77
Jones, Howard Mumford, 35
Jones, Louise, 99
Jones, Milo, II, 172
Julian Ashton Art School, 79
Julius, Henry George, 75
Junghans, Karl, 115

INDEX

Kadlec, David, 39
Karamu Theater, 134
Kelley, Robin, 116
Kempf, Christopher, 225n6
Kennedy, John F., 143, 244n19
Kenner, Hugh, 46, 50, 65
Kettle's Yard, 34
Kimball, Dexter S., 61
KKK. *See* Ku Klux Klan
Kleberg, Lars, 118
Knopf, Blanche, 144–45
Kreymborg, Alfred, 91
Kuan-Tzu, 63–64
Ku Klux Klan (KKK), 100, 239n42

La Berge, Leigh Clare, 5
labor, 3–8, 13–14, 21–22, 212–13; administrative, 140; artistic, 34–35; blue-collar, 187; capitalism's alienation of, 35–36, 67; capitalist market for, 19–20; child, 55; craft, 43; custodial, 176; daily reproduction of, 147; dehumanization of modern, 81; domestic, 19, 152–54; exploitation of, 97; factory, 52–54; feminist theory on, 16–19, 196; global transformation of, 25; hospital, 197; human, 199; industrial, 154–56; literary, 220n28; movement, 108–9, 221n32; Niedecker's hospital, 195; of porters, 109–10; power, 11, 16–17; queer, 169; racial divisions in, 251n54; reproductive, 16–18, 20, 23, 31–32, 182, 196; retirement from, 182; saving devices, 153, 154; unfreedom of, 4, 5, 8; violent transformations of, 194; by women, 222n47
"Labor" (Ridge), 94
landsleit, 82, 234n45
language, 125, 155
Laughlin, James, 148
"Laundromat" (Niedecker), 32, 203–4
Leaves of Grass (Whitman), 187, 190
Lee, Steven S., 239n42
Left of Poetry (Ehlers), 71
Léger, Fernand, 53
Leick, Karen, 140
Lemlich, Claire, 82, 234n42
Lenin, Vladimir, 116, 225n17
lesbian domesticity, 153, 158
Lesjak, Carolyn, 10

Letatlin (flying machines), 31, 136–38, *137*
Lewis, Sophie, 156
Lewis, Wyndham, 45, 150
life, rhythms of, 170
Literary Essays of Ezra Pound (Pound, E.), 34
literary modernism, 9–10, 212
literary production, 3, 7, 220n28
literary-professional model, 3–4
little barely audible poems, 175, 207
living labor, 8
Lloyds Bank, 44, 227n52
Long Gay Book, The (Stein), 245n39
Lorange, Astrid, 140
"Low Down" (Brown, S.), 110
Lower East Side, NY, 69, 72, 74–76, 211
Lucy Church Amiably (Stein), 144
luminous detail, 38, 43, 65, 91
Lynch, David, 24
lyricization, 69
lyric, 47, 70–72, 103, 126–27, 132–33, 189, 234n35
Lyrics of Lowly Life (Dunbar), 112

"Machine Art" (Pound, E.), 53
machine press, 53
Macleod, Joseph, 118, 230n98
Making of Americans, The (Stein), 31, 144–49
Malatesta, Sigismondo, 45–47, 51–52
"Malatesta Cantos (Cantos IX to XII of a Long Poem)" (Pound, E.), 45–46
Malcolm, Janet, 140
"Manhattan Lights" (Ridge), 94–95
Mao, Douglas, 24
"Market Street Woman" (Brown, S.), 110
Marsden, Dora, 39
Marsh, John, 22, 108
Marx, Karl, 54, 229n89; *Capital* by, 126; *The German Ideology* by, 8; on workers, 16–17, 21
Marxism, 7–9, 15–20, 54
Marxism and Literature (Williams, R.), 127
Marxist-Feminist perspective, 15–20
masculinity, femininity and, 63–64
materialism, 7–15, 27
Materials, The (Oppen), 199
maternity, 142, 200–202, 210, 216
Maun, Caroline, 232n11
Mayakovsky, Vladimir, 114, 120, 131

INDEX

Mayer, Bernadette, 208–10
McAlmon, Robert, 146
McCarthy, Joseph, 133
McKay, Claude, 116, 122–23
McNamara, J. B., 41
McNamara, J. J., 41
mechanical reproduction, 245n49, 246n55
Melamed, Jodi, 12, 105
Meyerhold, Vsevolod, 31, 123, *125*
Michels, Tony, 74
Micir, Melanie, 158
"Midrush" (DuPlessis), 215–16
Midwinter Day (Mayer), 210
Mies, Maria, 98
migration, mass, 97
Milkweed Smithereens (Mayer), 209
Millen, Al, 173, 183, 207–8, 250n28
Miller, Cristanne, 91
Miller, Tyrus, 24
miners' strike, 225n17
Minna and Myself (Bodenheim), 78
Minor, Robert, 109
"Miss Furr and Miss Skeene" (Stein), 156–57, 246n73
"Moby Dick" (Wilson, A.), *189*, 189–90
modernism, 2–3, 24–25; conservativism of, 24; gender and, 19; intermediality of, 27, 212; intimate archives in, 158–59; labor and technology transformations in, 13–14; literary, 9–10, 212; long poems in, 218; Marxist criticism and, 9–10; poetry of, 1–4, 7, 22–23, 232n11; prescience of, 24; professional model and, 3–4; social relations in, 212–13; utopian impulses within, 10–11; world system and, 14
Monroe, Harriet, 41–42, 55
Moody, Alys, 25
Mooney, Tom, 241n74
Moore, Marianne, 146, 245n39
"Morning Ride" (Ridge), 100, 236n77
Morris, William, 37
Moscow Art Theater, 115, 117, 239n46
Moscow Rehearsals (Houghton), 117
Mostra (Fascist exhibitions), 29, 61, 66
motion-picture theaters, 239n46
Mulatto (play), 134
Mullin, Katherine, 18
multitude, of voices, 241n78
Murano glass, 50

Mussolini, Benito, 54, 57, 58, 60, 63
"My Life" (Hejinian), 170–71

Nakano Glenn, Evelyn, 251nn53–54
National Council of American-Soviet Friendship, 133
National Household Economic Association, 151
Natural Economic Order, The (Gesell), 58
Nealon, Christopher, 26–27
Nearing, Scott, 52
Nersessian, Anahid, 101, 200–201
New Age, The (socialist weekly), 36–38, 40, 44, 225n10
"new Factory Act, The" (1847), 229n89
New Freewoman, The, 39
New Goose (Niedecker), 190–91, 193
New Housekeeping, The (Frederick), 31, 152–54
New Masses, 52, 113, 140
New Song, A (Hughes), 30–31, 104, 120–23, 127
New Spirit in Russian Theater, The (Carter), 118
"New St. Louis Blues" (Brown, S.), 110–11
New York, Lower East Side, 30, 69, 72, 74–76
Nicholls, Peter, 55, 64–66
Niedecker, Lorine: amateur crafted objects embraced by, 206–7; bathos mode of, 188–89, 198; Blackhawk Island home of, 178, 182–84, *183*; on blue-collar labor, 187; calendar of, *179*; *Collected Works* by, 177–78, 180; "A Cooking Book" by, *184*, 185; Corman receiving autograph book from, 177–79; Corman receiving letters from, 178–79; critical renaissance for, 26; on custodial labor, 176; DuPlessis on, 173; eyesight deteriorating of, 194; "The Favorite Sunlit Road Calendar" by, 179, *179*; feminist movement and, 176; "For Best Work" by, 199, 201, 206; "Foreclosure" by, 182–83; Hartel receiving autograph book from, 185; health care industry job of, 195–97; *Hoard's Dairyman* work by, 173, 194; home life disarray of, 182–83; homemade book gift-giving by, 179–80; "Homemade Poems" by, 176, 178; "Hospital Kitchen" by, 197–98, 201, 205–6; hospital labor

Niedecker, Lorine (*continued*)
described by, 195; "Laundromat" by, 32, 203–4; little barely audible poems by, 175, 207; Millen and, 173, 207–8, 250n28; *New Goose* by, 190–91, 193; nursery rhymes repurposed by, 191; "Old Remedies" by, 185; Oppen describing life of, 206; *For Paul* by, 180; "Pioneers" by, 193; poem as act of translation, 2–3; on poetic work, 27–28, 174; poetry of, 27–28, 173–74; "Poet's Work" by, 2, 5, 6; resolute unproductivity from, 212–13; "Santayana's" by, 186–87; self-publishing by, 178; "Switchboard Girl" by, 194; "Who was Mary Shelley?" by, 200–202; "Wintergreen Ridge" by, 208, 210; from Wisconsin, 2, 25; working life of, 172–73; writing life of, 173; Zukofsky receiving letter from, 172, 180, 183–84, 187, 196–97, 203, 248n7, 249n17, 250n29, 251n48; Zukofsky receiving gift from, 179, 208. *See also* Homemade/Handmade Poems
North, Joseph, 13, 24
North, Michael, 24
Not Without Laughter (Hughes), 107
nursery rhymes, 160, 191–93

Oakey, Christopher, 99
objectivism, 26, 175, 249n10
Odyssey, The, 43
Okhlopkov, Nikolai, 31, 131
"Old Remedies" (Niedecker), 185
Olympiad of Autonomous Art, 118–19
Oppen, George, 175, 199, 206–7
Orage, A. R., 3, 36–37
ordinary folk, 3, 173
Otis, Harrison Gray, 41
Our Agenda manifesto, 119
Oxford Book of Modern Verse, The (Yeats), 47, 61

"A Pact" (Pound, E.), 40
Parsons, Albert, 100
Pasternak, Boris, 120
"Patria Mia" (Pound, E.), 56
"Patriotism" (Goldman), 75
Paul, Mick, 75
"Pax Saturni" ("Saturn's Peace") (Pound, E.), 40–42

Penberthy, Jenny, 177
Penty, A. J., 36, 57
peristalsis, 149–50
Perloff, Marjorie, 140
Pesotta, Rose, 82–84
Peters, Anna, 123
"Petrograd" (McKay), 122–23
photograph, of Ridge, *80*
physical training, 124
"Picasso" (Stein), 149–50, 155
Piekut, Benjamin, 176
"Pioneers" (Niedecker), 193
Plato, 46
poems, 121; A-A'-B structure of, 112; blue-collar labor, 187; blues, 30–31, 110–11, 113; capitalist values in, 29; cooking truths in, 181; disappointment in, 192; ecstasy and, 203–6; IWO publishing, 120; like nursery rhymes, 191–93; little barely audible, 175, 207; lyric, 47, 234n35; modernism with long, 218; Niedecker's act of translation in, 2–3; E. Pound later, 66–67; repetition in, 170; revolutionary, 30, 103; scriptures and rituals in, 214–15; Sedgwick critical of Stein, 143–44; sensory confusion in, 167; solidarity, 100; about or by women, 28; word's grammatical functions in, 161–62; working-class, 26
poetic vocation, 21
poetry: civilization created through, 45; about community and folk, 173; defining, 2; femininity of, 15–16; gendered abstractions in, 19; Hughes and, 106, 132–33; modernist, 1–4, 7, 22–23, 232n11; as natural act, 3–4; Niedecker on, 27–28, 173–74; phases of, 119–20; of E. Pound, 29; pronoun-driven, 160; Ridge publishing, 68–69; social relations in, 42; of social reproduction, 139–40; on and by women, 28
Poetry, 40–41
poets, 174–75
"Poet's Work" (Niedecker), 2, 5–6
"Political Equality of Women, The" (de Cleyre), 84
Political Unconscious, The (Jameson), 9–11
politics, 35–36, 101–2, 105, 132–33, 141–42
porter's labor, 109–10
Posmentier, Sonya, 113

INDEX

Postone, Moishe, 18
Pound, Ezra: *ABC of Economics* by, 55; *ABC of Reading* by, 2; artistic labor from, 34–35, 39; on China, 230n107; Chinese agrarian practices interest of, 29, 60–61, 65–67; "Contemporania" by, 29, 39–40, 67; craft of prosody of, 46; Davie commenting on, 49; *Drafts & Fragments* by, 57; Eliot and Bel Esprit scheme by, 44–45, 227n52, 228n57; "Epilogue" by, 42–43; fascism development of, 36, 225n7; *The Fifth Decad of Cantos* by, 36; *Gaudier-Brzeska* by, 38; *Guide to Kulchur* by, 60; Hughes's friendship with, 38n40; "I Gather the Limbs of Osiris" by, 38; "In a Station of the Metro" by, 36, 42–43, 47; *Jefferson and/or Mussolini* by, 54; later poems of, 66–67; *Literary Essays of Ezra Pound* by, 34; luminous detail theory of, 91; "Machine Art" by, 53; Macleod letter from, 230n98; "Malatesta Cantos" by, 45–46; on Marxist economics, 54; Mussolini and, 54, 57; "A Pact" by, 40; "Patria Mia" by, 56; "Pax Saturni" by, 40–42; politics of craft model from, 35–36; radical anticapitalism of, 57; Santayana joking about, 186; *Selected Poems 1908–1969* by, 47; "The Serious Artist" by, 55; "The Serious Artist" by, 39; as syndicalist, 225n15; technique discussed by, 38; *Thrones* by, 62–63, 65–67; "Through Alien Eyes" by, 37; "Translator's Postscript" by, 224n3; unalienated labors and, 212; Whitman's ideological difference with, 42; "Workshop Orchestration" by, 52–53. *See also The Cantos*
Pound, Homer, 56
Pound, Thaddeus Coleman, 56
Power of Women and the Subversion of the Community, The (Dalla Costa and James), 16, 139
pre-capitalist history, 222n62
Preface to Ezra Pound, A (Wilson, P.), 47
Princeton Encyclopedia of Poetry and Poetics, The, 69
Printworks Act (1845), 229n89
"Product" (Oppen), 199
production: in capitalism, 21, 126–27; global assembly line for, 97–98; labor's value in, 4; of language, 155; literary, 3, 7, 220n28; Marx on worker, 16–17, 21; material conditions determining, 9; resolute unproductivity and, 212–13
Professional Theater Festival, 115
"Promenade" (Ridge), 95
protofascism, 224n5
Pryor, Sean, 47, 50
Pullman Company, 109

Q.E.D. (Stein), 158
Quartermain, Peter, 175
queerness, 142, 155, 157, 159, 169

race relations, 114
racial capitalism, 12, 105
racial divisions, 251n54
racial hierarchies, 110
racism, 73, 108, 113, 135
radical anticapitalism, 57
Rainey, Lawrence, 45
Raitt, Suzanne, 246n62
Rampersad, Arnold, 104, 236n4
Rancière, Jacques, 101
Rankine, Claudia, 24
Red Flag (Ridge), 100
Redman, Tim, 36, 57
Reed, Anthony, 105–6, 113
Reed, John, 40–41, 52
religious observance, 93
repetition, in poems, 170
reproduction: daily labor of, 147; as generative process, 156, 171; of labor power, 16–18, 20, 23, 31–32, 182, 196; mechanical, 245n49, 246n55; middle class, 142; refusal of, 88, 201, 209; as restriction, 176, 200, 202; social, 31, 139–42, 146, 148, 149, 169, 210
resolute unproductivity, 212–13
Retallack, Joan, 157–58
revolutionary poems, 30, 103
Revolution at Point Zero (Federici), 19
Rexroth, Kenneth, 190
Reznikoff, Charles, 86, 175
Richards, Bernard G., 76
Richards, Juno, 18, 72, 87
Ridge, Lola, 6, 14, 25, 211; "Accidentals" by, 94; in anarchist feminism scene, 83–85; anarchist social ideal and, 78; collective life

INDEX

Ridge (*continued*)
  exploration of, 70–71, 101; critical renaissance for, 26; Denenberg describing, 235n47; Deutsch complaints about, 78–79; ecstatic consideration of life from, 87; eyes with motive and emotion from, 92; "Frank Little at Calvary" by, 94; garment workers commonality with, 86–87; *The Ghetto and Other Poems* by, 69, 73–78, 94; at Julian Ashton Art School, 79; "Labor" by, 94; life subject of, 94; "Manhattan Lights" by, 94–95; as modernist poet, 232n11; "Morning Ride" by, 100, 236n77; names before becoming, 68; in New York, 75; photograph of, 80; poetry published by, 68–69; "Promenade" by, 95; *Red Flag* by, 100; review praising vision of, 90–91; Singer Manufacturing in sight of, 95–96; social structure of tenement living from, 77–78; solidarity poems of, 100; triple intersection of, 71–72; uncertainty valued by, 102; "Women and the Creative Will" by, 77; Yiddish-speaking Jewish inhabitants and, 30. See also "The Ghetto"
Riis, Jacob, 76
Riley, Denise, 18
Riley, Peter, 21, 188
"Riverbank Blues" (Brown, S.), 111
Robbins, Bruce, 98
Robeson, Paul, 118, 120
Robinson, Cedric, 12, 105
Roche, Hannah, 162, 247n84
Rodchenko, Alexander, 31, 129–31, *130*
Ronda, Margaret, 112, 194
Roosevelt, Eleanor, 143
Rosenfeld, Morris, 81
Rosenthal, M. L., 78
Ross, Stephen, 25
Rosskam, Edwin, 133
Roumain, Jacques, 71
ruling class, 192
rural life, 14, 175, 193
Ruskin, John, 37
Russian Constructivism, 30, 104, 106, 122

"Sacred Edict" (*Sheng Yu*), 62
Saint-Amour, Paul, 25
San Francisco Preparedness Day bombing (1916), 121–22
"Sangar" (Reed, J.), 40

Sanger, Margaret, 84
Santayana, George, 186
"Santayana's" (Niedecker), 186–87
"Saturn's Peace" (Pax Saturni) (Pound, E.), 40–42
Schuyler, James, 189
Schwundgeld (stamp scrip), 58
scientific management, 52, 54, 124, 149, 152, 155
Scott, Evelyn, 79
Scottsboro Limited (Hughes), 134
scriptures, 214–15
Sedgwick, Ellery, 143–44
seeds, genetic engineering of, 209–10
Selected Poems 1908–1969 (Pound, E.), 47
self-becoming, 85
self-publishing, 178
self-seriousness, 185–86
sensory confusion, 167
sequence, 70, 77–78, 234n35
"Serious Artist, The" (Pound, E.), 39, 55
Setina, Emily, 158
"Seven Lakes Canto." See Canto LXIX
sewing machines, 99
Shelley, Mary, 200
Sheng Yu ("Sacred Edict"), 62
Shiach, Morag, 18
"Shooting from the Bow" (étude), 125
A Short History of Chinese Civilisation (Chi), 60
Sieburth, Richard, 61
Signs of Change (Morris), 37
Silliman, Ron, 175, 249n10
Singer Manufacturing Company, 95–97, 235n65
Singer sewing machines, 14
Singh, Julietta, 207
slavery, 135
Smethurst, James, 104, 237n6
Snow, Carmel, 244n19
socialism, 124
socialist literary theory, 104
socialization, of women, 152
social relations, 42, 212–13
social reproduction, 31, 139–42, 146, 148, 149, 169, 210
social values, 212
solidarity, 10, 70, 100, 102
"A Song for Occupations," 188
Soviet Union, 114, 116–19, 240n61

INDEX

Spahr, Juliana, 98
speed-up system, 73–74
"Spring Journal" (Mayer), 209
stamp scrip (*Schwundgeld*), 58
Stanzas in Meditation (Stein), 31, 142, 157, 160–70, 247n76
Steffens, Lincoln, 40–42
Stein, Gertrude, 4; *Autobiography* by, 148, 157–58, 164; bodily emissions and, 149–50; book publishing struggles for, 144–45; "A Command Poem" by, 164; "Composition as Explanation" by, 245n39; desultory and circular actions of, 141; economic value of, 143; *Everybody's Autobiography* by, 143; Hemingway taking up cause of, 145–46; intimate relationships uncertainties and, 165; Kennedy's note to, 244n19; *A Long Gay Book* by, 245n39; *Lucy Church Amiably* by, 144; *The Making of Americans* by, 31, 144–49; middle class reproduction by, 142; minor labor of, 147–48; "Miss Furr and Miss Skeene" by, 156–57, 246n73; "Picasso" by, 149–50, 155; *Q.E.D.* by, 158; queer labor from, 169; Sedgwick critical of poems by, 143–44; social reproduction concern of, 31, 143, 169; *Stanzas in Meditation* by, 31, 142, 157, 160–70, 247n76; subject interrogations by, 153–54; *Tender Buttons* by, 31, 142, 145, 148, 153–56, 166–67; Toklas getting love notes from, 162–64, *163*; Toklas with, 158–59; *Wars I Have Seen* by, 141
Steven, Mark, 26
Stimpson, Catherine, 141
Stokes, Adrian, 50
Stones of Rimini, The (Stokes), 50
Strange Birds of Africa (film), 115
subject interrogations, 153–54
Sullivan, Noël, 115
Surge (DuPlessis), 213
"Sweatshop, The" (Rosenfeld), 81
sweatshops, 72–73, 76, 98
"Switchboard Girl" (Niedecker), 194
syndicalist, Pound, E., as, 225n15
System of Cutting for Dressmakers and Tailors (Glazhdinsky), 86

Tang Dynasty, 25
Tatlin, Vladimir, 31, 136–38

Taylorism, 11, 27, 30, 124, 151
Teatr Krasnoi Presni, 131
technique, Pound, E., discussing, 38
technological determinism, 13
technology, 13–14, 24–25, 73
Ten Days That Shook the World (Reed, J.), 40, 52
Tender Buttons (Stein), 31, 142, 145, 148, 153–56, 166–67
tenement living, 77–78
Terrell, Carroll, 64
textiles, 94–95
Thompson, E. P., 21, 58
Thompson, Louise, 134
Three Lives (Stein), 169, 245n29
Thrones (Pound, E.), 62–63, 65–67
"Through Alien Eyes" (Pound, E.), 37
Tiffany, Daniel, 43
Time, Labor, and Social Domination (Postone), 18
Time and Western Man (Lewis, W.), 150
Toklas, Alice B., 143, 158–59; administrative labor of, 140; *The Alice B. Toklas Cookbook* by, 167; Stein giving love notes to, 162–64, *163*
"Tornado Blues" (Brown, S.), 110
Toscano, Alberto, 36
trade union poster, *130*
"Translator's Postscript" (Pound, E.), 224n3
Triangle Shirtwaist Factory fire, 82–83
12 Million Black Voices (Wright), 133–34

unalienated labors, 212
unemployment, 44, 227n47
unequal development, 14
United States, 121; Depression-era capitalism in, 26; economic ambitions in, 93; immigrants arriving to, 74, 232n1; industrialization in, 11–12; Pesotta's first job in, 82–83; Ridge publishing poetry in, 68–69; sewing machine purchased outside of, 96
Unthinking Mastery (Singh), 207
unwaged condition, of housework, 17
urban social life, 204
Utopia, 10–11, 138

Vakhtangov Theater, 115
value-producing activity, 17–18
values, of labor, 4

van Gyseghem, André, 118
Van Vechten, Carl, 103, 113, 144
Venetian glass, 50–51
violence, of capitalism, 129
violent transformations, of labor, 194
Virgil, 220n28
Virno, Paolo, 123
visual information, 92
vita activa, 14–15
vocations, labors and, 21–22
voices, multitude of, 241n78
Vorwärts (German socialist newspaper), 89–90

Wages for Housework campaign, 16–20, 151
Wain, John, 65
"Wait" (Hughes), 128–29, 131–32
Wald, Alan, 126, 237n6
Walkowitz, Rebecca, 24
Walls, Joshua Logan, 79, 86
Walsh, Phyllis, 194
Walton, Jean, 149–50
Wanamaker, John, 42
Wars I Have Seen (Stein), 141
washing machines, 252n66
Waste Land, The (Eliot), 20–21
watercolors, 177–78, *178*
Watson, Dana Cairns, 140
Watten, Barrett, 104
Wayward Lives, Beautiful Experiments (Hartman), 86
Weary Blues, The (Hughes), 106, 135
Weeks, Kathi, 9, 18, 141, 222n44
Well Then There Now (Spahr), 98
white-collar bureaucracy, 14
white jade, 59
white supremacy, 110
Whitman, Walt, 40, 42, 188
"Who was Mary Shelley?" (Niedecker), 200–202
Wilkinson, John, 189
Will, Barbara, 140
Williams, Jonathan, 176
Williams, Raymond, 90, 127
Williams, William Carlos, 45
Willis, Elizabeth, 175, 180

Wilson, Ann, 189–90
Wilson, Peter, 47
"Wintergreen Ridge" (Niedecker), 208, 210
Wisconsin (Works Progress Administration), 173, 191
women: of color, 196; female citizenship of, 87; in garment industry, 78–87; in health care industry, 195; labor by, 222n47; in labor movement, 221n32; poetry on and by, 28; socialization of, 152; sweatshop and health of, 76; washing machines targeting, 252n66; working, 234n39
"Women and the Creative Will" (Ridge), 77
Woolworth Building, 95
words, grammatical functions of, 161–62
work: as abstract mode of domination, 18; art's relationship with, 22; conditions for, 4, 83; gendered social roles in, 18–19, 23; housework as unwaged, 17; life with, 172–73; materialist approach to, 7–15; by Niedecker, 173, 194; poetry as, 27–28, 174; poetry as women's, 28; poor with, 227n47; society, 18; women with, 234n39
workers: Marx on, 16–17, 21; suffering, 202
Workers' Theater Olympiad, 115
working-class masculinity, 187
working-class poets, 26
"Working Day, The" act (1825), 229n89
Work of Art in the Age of Deindustrialization, The (Bernes), 22
Works and Days (Mayer), 209
"Workshop Orchestration" (Pound, E.), 52–53
Works Progress Administration, 173
Wright, Richard, 133–34, 136

Yeats, W. B., 15–16, 61
Yetta, Sarah, 86
Yiddish speakers, 30, 72, 74–75, 88–92, 94, 235n57
You, Mia, 154

Zukofsky, Louis, 52, 176; *Anew* by, 190; *55 Poems* by, 190; letters of Niedecker to, 172, 180, 183–84, 187, 196–97, 203, 248n7, 249n17, 250n29, 251n48; Niedecker sending gift to, 179, 208

GPSR Authorized Representative: Easy Access System Europe, Mustamäe tee 50, 10621 Tallinn, Estonia, gpsr.requests@easproject.com

www.ingramcontent.com/pod-product-compliance
Lightning Source LLC
Chambersburg PA
CBHW022038290426
44109CB00014B/897